The Torch

A Guide to S.E.L.F.

By

Bro. Mishaal Talib
Mahfuz El Bey

Califa Media Publishing

The Torch: A Guide to Self

Califa Media Publishing™

Lafayette, Indiana

Written by

Mishaal Talib Mahfuz El Bey

ISBN-13: 978-1952828041

ISBN-10: 1-952828-04-X

Cover Design by Sis. T. Najee-Ullah El

Califa Media Publishing

Other Works by Bro. Mahfuz El Bey

- Isonomi: The Great Masonic Secret: Master Keys
- Holistic Philosophy

Moorish Americans - Northwest Amexum

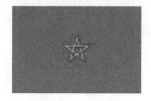

The Torch: A Guide to S.E.L.F.

Table of Contents

Work Cited:

- Holy Koran Circle 7 - Sheik Shariff Abdul Ali
- Clock of Destiny Volume 1 & 2 - C.M. Bey
- The Symbolist: A Simplified Guide to Tarot Symbols and Terms - Corrine Kenner
- Claritydaily.org
- RVBeyPublications.com
- Wikipedia.com
- Rules for Radicals - Saul Alinsky
- King Alfred Plan Rex 84
- Mastering the Uniform Commercial Codes
- Joanne Sacred Scribes.com
- Mysteries of the Silent Brotherhood of the East
- Breaking the Chains of Slavery: Who are the Moorish Americans? - Moors Order of the Roundtable
- Dr.AlimElBey.com
- Maurians.org
- MoorishCivilletter.net
- YaffaBey.com
- KemetianAdept.com
- Exhuming of a Nation - Elihu Pleasant-Bey
- AlMuoriMoorish.wordpress.com
- Zodiacal View on youVol.1 & 2;Why Astrology - R.V. Bey
- The Message of The Stars - Max Heindel
- Journal Of the Moorish Paradigm #8 - Hakim Bey

SUPPORT YOUR OWN!!!

- CalifaMedia.com (literature and publishing)
- RVBeyPublications.com (literature)
- Dr. AlimElBey.com (herbs, crystals, literature, and more)
- MoorsandMasonry.org (etymology, history, jurisprudence and more)
- MoreignaHeir.com (Moorish American apparel)
- WillofAllah.com (music)
- RiseoftheMoors.com
- 13krystalign.com (detoxes and cleanses)
- UprisingTea.com
- ObashangoEl.com
- LedHealthy.com
- MoorsinFullLife.com
- Matrix-Five.com

Honors

Marcus "Messiah" Garvey

Peace and Blissings be upon him.

Peace and Blissings be upon the Womb that carried and brought forth this Son and to The Man who helped spark the Idea.

"A people without the knowledge of their past history, origin and culture is like a tree without roots."

"Liberate the minds of men and ultimately you will liberate the bodies of men."

Sheik Sharif Abdul Ali

Peace and Blissings Be Upon Him.

Peace and Blissings be upon the Womb that carried and brought forth this Son and to The Man who helped spark the Idea.

"If I could just get you to thinking, you would save yourselves."

"Study, study, study; and when you have studied well and would ask me what to study next, I would reply study yourselves."

Peace and Blissings Be Upon Him.

Peace and Blissings be upon the Womb that carried and brought forth this Son and to The Man who helped spark the Idea.

"Freedom is everybody's job."

"Appreciation is a wonderful law. The things we greatly appreciate and those we greatly fear we attract to ourselves."

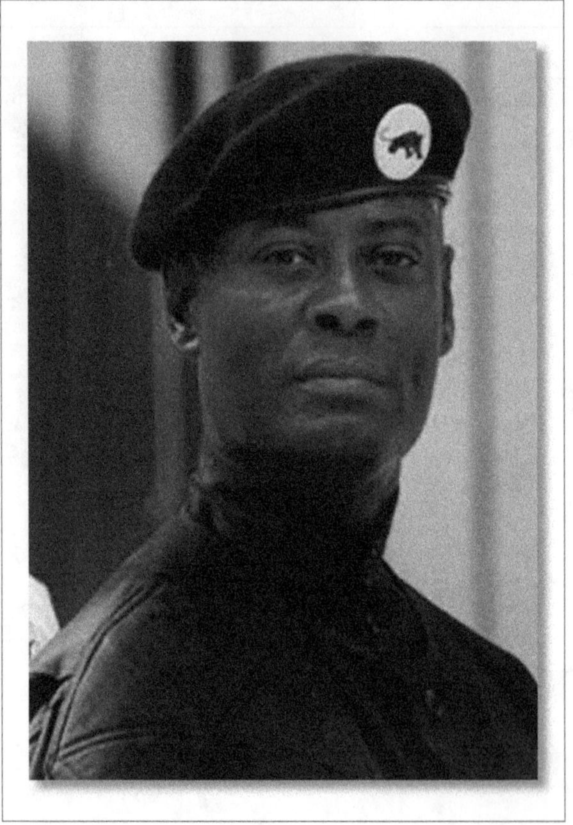

Khalid Abdul Muhammad

Peace and Blissings be upon him.

Peace and Blissings be upon the Womb that carried and brought forth this Son and to The Man who helped spark the Idea.

"I'm a Moor and got sense enough to know I'm A Moor..."

"The best way to fight an oppressive and alien culture is to live your own."

C. Freeman El

Peace and Blissings be upon him.

Peace and Blissings be upon the Womb that carried and brought forth this Son and to The Man who helped spark the Idea.

"The illusion of inferiority is an abomination to the lord."

"The failure to succeed is a misconception of one's own nature."

The Torch:
A Guide to S.E.L.F.

Foreword:

To initiate means to begin; organize; to admit (a person) by special forms or ceremonies (into secret knowledge, mysteries, or a society). From the moment, we are thought of by our creator we become initiates of the boundless infinitude of creation. The first initiation comes by way of the womb, where we learn to navigate the waters of the unseen. Once we pass through the ankh/gates of life (mother), canal of the "gods" we then gain initiative which is defined as the active parts in taking the first steps in any undertaking; lead; readiness and ability to be the one to start a course of action. As soon as we traverse the walls of our source toward the light of the unknown, we begin our rite of passage which leads to the fulfillment of our purpose and destiny, both as a collective and as individuals given and commanded of us by way of Th Supreme Higher Force. There are 5 steps of initiation: to know thyself, to heal thyself, to build thyself, to trust thyself, and to will thyself. The first is last and the last is first, so knowledge or knowing is our natural gift but also our objective is to know our higher/true selves which get clouded by external and internal turbulence/turmoil. Thus, our lives are a journey of rediscovery and self-realization which leads to greater depths of wisdom, knowledge and innerstanding because the road in some ways is actually more valuable than the destination itself; the steps taken spawning humility, the daughter of grace, which then transforms into salvation i.e. man becoming the savior they were always meant to be. Flow with me and always remember to add on; trust, know and be.

Part 1: Know ThySelf

"Whoever does not know self, does not know anything, but whoever knows self, already has acquired knowledge of the depth of the universe."-Secret teachings of Yahshuah, "Book of Thomas"

Intro: Man know thyself! This is the ancient axiom by which we are called to the remembrance of who and what we really are. In it is both the question and the answer; the death and life of man; "the snake eating its own tail"; coming full circle beginning and ending from/at zero point. Through social engineering we have been reduced to a one- dimensional status which puts us at a severe disadvantage for the world is multidimensional and is an ever-flowing paradigm always growing, changing, and creating hence we must be on the same wavelength in order to maximize and realize both the depths and heights of ourselves. Stagnation leads to infestation which ultimately breeds self-destruction. Simplicity is naturalness, naturalness is wisdom, and wisdom in its purest form is common sense which we've grown accustomed to ignoring in modern days and times. Getting back to common sense is synonymous with obeying divine law for in doing so we submit to the will of love that is innately in us and all around us leading to the restoration and healing of our estates (consciousness)

Chapter 1: Heritage

A. Moors:

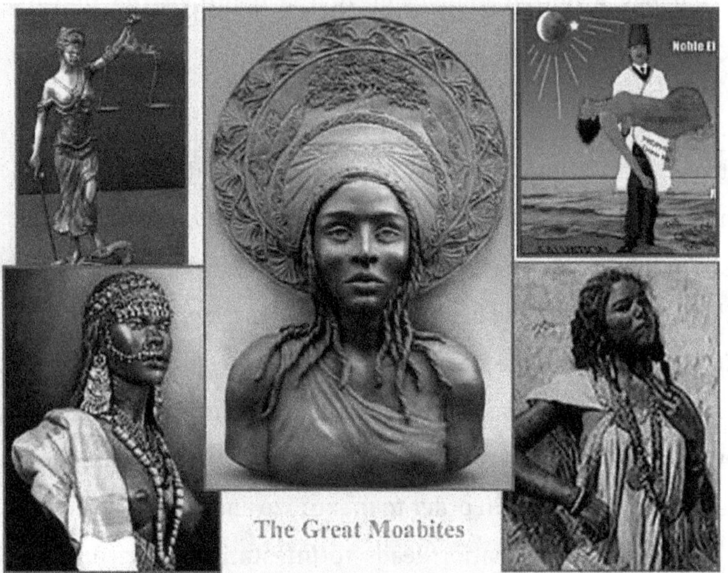

I. Who and What We are

* First Peoples PRINCIPLES OF LEARNING

- Learning ultimately supports the well-being of the self, the family, the community, the land, the spirits, and the ancestors.
- Learning is holistic, reflexive, reflective, experiential, and relational (focused on connectedness, on reciprocal relationships, and a sense of place).
- Learning involves recognizing the consequences of one's actions.
- Learning involves generational roles and responsibilities.
- Learning recognizes the role of indigenous knowledge.
- Learning is embedded in memory, history, and story.
- Learning involves patience and time.
- Learning requires exploration of one's identity.
- Learning involves recognizing that some knowledge is sacred and only shared with permission and/or in certain situations.

Holy Circle 7 Koran

CHAPTER XLVII

EGYPT, THE CAPITAL EMPIRE OF THE DOMINION OF AFRICA-Holy Koran Circle 7

2. The inhabitants of Africa are the descendants of the ancient Canaanites from the land of Canaan.

3. Old man Cush and his family are the first inhabitants of Africa who came from the land of Canaan.

4. His father Ham and his family were second. Then came the word Ethiopia, which means the demarcation line of the dominion of Amexem, the first true and divine name of Africa. The dividing of the land between the father and the son.

5. The dominion of Cush, North-East and South-East Africa and North-West and South-West was his father's dominion of Africa.

6. In later years many of their brethren from Asia and the Holy Lands joined them.

7. The Moabites from the land of Moab who received permission from the Pharaohs of Egypt to settle and inhabit North-West Africa; they were the founders and are the true possessors of the present Moroccan Empire. With their Canaanite, Hittite, and Amorite brethren who sojourned from the land of Canaan seeking new homes.

8. Their dominion and inhabitation extended from North-East and South-West Africa, across great Atlantis even unto the present North, South, and Central America and also Mexico and the Atlantis Islands; before the great earthquake, which caused the great Atlantic Ocean.

9. The River Nile was dredged and made by the ancient Pharaohs of Egypt, in order to trade with the surrounding kingdoms. Also, the Niger river was dredged by the great Pharaoh of Egypt in those ancient days for trade, and it extends eastward from the River Nile, westward across the great Atlantic. It was used for trade and transportation.

10. According to all true and divine records of the human race there is no negro, black, or colored race attached to the human family, because all the inhabitants of Africa were and are of the human race, descendants of the ancient Canaanite nation from the holy land of Canaan.

11. What your ancient forefathers were, you are today without doubt or contradiction.

12. There is no one who is able to change man from the descendant nature of his forefathers; unless his power extends beyond the great universal Creator Allah Himself.

13. These holy and divine laws are from the Prophet, Noble Drew Ali, the founder of the uniting of the Moorish Science Temple of America.

14. These laws are to be strictly preserved by the members of all the Temples, of the Moorish Science Temple of America. That they will learn to open their meeting and guide it according to the principles of Love, Truth, Peace, Freedom and Justice.

15. Every subordinate Temple of the Grand-Major Temple is to form under the covenant of Love, Truth, Peace, Freedom and Justice; and to create their own laws and customs, in conjunction with the laws of the Holy Prophet and the Grand Temple. I, the Prophet, Noble Drew Ali, was sent by the great God, Allah, to warn all Asiatics of America to repent from their sinful ways; before that great and awful day that is sure to come.

16. The time has come when every nation must worship under its own vine and fig tree, and every tongue must confess his own.

17. Through sin and disobedience every nation has suffered slavery, due to the fact that they honored not the creed and principles of their forefathers.

18. That is why the nationality of the Moors was taken away from them in 1774 and the word negro, black and colored, was given to the Asiatics of America who were of Moorish descent, because they honored not the principles of their mother and father and strayed after the gods of Europe of whom they knew nothing.

Chunk of Africa found hidden under Alabama

Jacqui Goddard

Thursday April 24 2014, 1.01am BST, The Times

Geologists believe Florida and parts of the south-eastern US states comprise ancient rock from what is now Africa
GETTY IMAGES

Geologists have found what they believe is a slab of Africa still stuck under America, 250 million years after the two were squeezed together by a giant tectonic collision to form a single 'super-continent'.

Unusual magnetic readings from deep below the earth's surface suggest that Florida and parts of the south-eastern US states comprise ancient rock from what is now Africa, which broke away from the land mass that is now North America 250 million years ago to form a separate continent.

A quarter of a billion years ago Africa slammed into North America and left a scar that can be seen today with special instruments.

Continental breakups are proving to be just as destructive as some human separations. Geologists say they have found a fragment of Africa embedded in the southeastern U.S., a remnant of the rift that occurred between the two continents some 250 million years ago.

Scientists have known for some time of the presence of a strange band of magnetic rock that stretches from Alabama through Georgia and offshore to the North Carolina coast, but its origin has been debated. The ribbon of rock is buried about 9 to 12 miles below the surface.

According to a new study published in the journal Geological Society of

America, the fissure, known as the Brunswick Magnetic Anomaly, was created hundreds of millions of years ago when the crusts of Africa and North America were yanked apart like stitches in a piece of cloth.

"There was an attempt to rip away Florida and southern Georgia," geologist Robert Hatcher, of the University of Tennessee in Knoxville, told Discovery. "So you have a failed rift there...Ther are pieces of crust that started in Africa."

Florida Peninsula Was Once African Territory

By Boyce Rensberger

June 30, 1985

Florida is a long-lost piece of Africa.

When North America split apart from Africa around 200 million years ago to form the Atlantic Ocean, a little bit of Africa stuck to North America -- the Florida peninsula and an adjacent region of southern Georgia.

Before the two continents began drifting apart, they had collided about 50 million years earlier in an impact that buckled the eastern edge of North America to form the Appalachian Mountains. The southeastern corner of North America then had no peninsula, but when the continents were pushed apart by a rift, part of Africa stuck to North America.

When North America split apart from Africa around 200 million years ago to form the Atlantic Ocean, a little bit of Africa stuck to North America -- the Florida peninsula and an adjacent region of southern Georgia.

Before the two continents began drifting apart, they had collided about 50 million years earlier in an impact that buckled the eastern edge of North America to form the Appalachian Mountains. The southeastern corner of North America then had no peninsula, but when the continents were pushed apart by a rift, part of Africa stuck to North America.

The discovery that Florida was originally part of Africa, by geologists at Cornell University, emerged from a new method of sending shock waves into the ground and measuring their reflection back to seismographs at the surface. The shocks are generated by special trucks that drive to various locations and, in effect, thump the ground.

Although the induced vibrations are much weaker than those of an earthquake, they travel deep into the ground, bounce off the surface of the crust's "deep basement" layer 30 miles below, and return to the surface. A profile of the deep layer revealed a suture line, or joint between two continental plates. The suture line corresponds to a long-known line of unusually low magnetism that runs roughly east and west from the southern coast of Georgia to southern Alabama.

It had been known that if North America were fitted back against Africa, the magnetic anomaly line would match a similar line in west Africa. Discovery of the suture confirms that the crustal plate to the south originated as part of the African plate.

Article 8

1. Indigenous peoples and individuals have the right not to be subjected to forced assimilation or destruction of their culture.

2. States shall provide effective mechanisms for prevention of, and redress for:

   (a) Any action which has the aim or effect of depriving them of their integrity as distinct peoples, or of their cultural values or ethnic identities;

   (b) Any action which has the aim or effect of dispossessing them of their lands, territories or resources;

   (c) Any form of forced population transfer which has the aim or effect of violating or undermining any of their rights;

   (d) Any form of forced assimilation or integration;

   (e) Any form of propaganda designed to promote or incite racial or ethnic discrimination directed against them.

MOORS IN SOUTH CAROLINA.—It may not be generally known that some of the best families in South Carolina are Moors by descent. The blood of the African son washes out, but that of the Indian and the Moor, after half a score of generations, shows itself almost as strongly as ever. The crisp, curling black hair, dark sad eyes, long silken lashes, and swarthy complexion, come up generation after generation. Many of our old Huguenot families, down to the present day, show strong traces of the Moorish descent. When the Moors were driven out from Spain, u on the conquest of Granada, thousands of them took refuge in the south of France, carrying with them the art of cultivating the vine and of growing silk. Remembering their bitter persecutions in Spain, they never could become Catholics, though forced by their position to renounce Mohamedanism and become Christians. They became eventually Protestants, and when the revocation of the Edict of Nantes took place, withdrawing toleration from the Protestant religion, they were again driven to seek new homes, and in large numbers emigrated to South Carolina. *Clarendon (S. C.) Banner.*

Sacramento Daily Union, Volume 17, Number 2564, 15 June 1859

* * *

Notes and Queries: The following names, in addition to those that have already appeared, are given subject to correction: Blackamoor, a negro, in contradistinction to a "tawny" or "tanny" Moor. The two divisions of Africa, north and south of Senegal; were known of old respectively as Mauritia, or the country of the Moors, and Nigritia, the country of the blacks; but all Mahometans, whether black or "tanny," were formerly designated "Moors"—e. g., Othello.

Blue Caps or Blue Bonnets, the Scotch: "He is there, too * * * and a thousand blue caps more." — Shakespeare, "I. Henry IV.," II., iv.

England shall many a day
Tell of the bloody fray
When the blue bonnets came over the border. —Scott.

Blue Nose (quoted ante, p. 90, in an editorial note), a native of Nova Scotia or of Newfoundland, the climate of the latter being very cold, and the island covered with snow for five months in the year.

Bogtrotter, an Irishman.

Bonnet Rouge, a French Red Republican, in allusion to the red cap of liberty.

Cabbage eater, Kapustaik, a Russian.

Canuck, a Canadian. See "N. & Q., 8th S. ii., 38.

* * *

Sacramento Daily Union, Volume 98, Number 83, 12 November 1899

A Mexican Relic.

Among the many articles of interest in the new Natural History Museum at Vienna perhaps nothing has been more discussed than an old Mexican relic which is preserved with great care under glass.

This relic, which is now known as the field badge of King Montezuma, had lain for 300 years in the Ambrase collection, where it was at first catalogued as a Moorish hat of long, heavy, glistening green and gold feathers.

One investigator held that it was an Indian hat, another an Indian apron; but in 1820 it was at last known to be a Mexican badge of high rank, and through Ferdinand Hochstetter it was proved to be the genuine field decoration of King Montezuma, captured by Cortez in 1520, after the battle of Otumba.

This battle was followed by the wild flight of the Mexicans, and the robbing of the land by Cortez, who sent the standard and wardrobe of the King, with much gold, to the Emperor Charles V. of Spain. The latter gave the standard to Pope Clement VII., who sent it to Grand Duke Ferdinand of Tyrol, for the Ambrase collection.

It is shaped like a fan, and is made from tail-feathers of the bird of paradise, which have a glitter like gold over their red, green and blue colors. The moths had partly destroyed it, but of the 500 original feathers only forty-one were much injured, and those have been replaced by new ones, and the former beauty is fully restored.

French Physicians Favor a Device for

Sacramento Daily Union, Volume 80, Number 63, 3 November 1890

NATIONAL NICKNAMES.

Terms That Have Come to Be Commonly Applied.

(Notes and Queries.)

Blackamoor, a negro, in contradistinction to a "tawny" or "tanny" Moor. The two divisions of Africa, north and south of Senegal, were known of old respectively as Mauritia, or the country of the Moors, and Nigritia, the country of the blacks; but all Mahometans, whether black or "tanny," were formerly designated "Moors."—e. g., Othello.

Blue Caps and Blue Bonnets, the Scotch

"He is there, too . . . and a thousand blue caps more."—(Shakespeare, 'I Henry IV,' ii, iv.

England shall many a day
Tell of the bloody fray
When the blue bonnets came over the
border.—(Scott.

San Bernardino Sun, Volume 44, Number 79, 31 May 1916

Moorish America.

What kind of people do live in South America? The Spanish, the Portuguese, but chiefly the descendants of these European races who have intermarried with the Indians. Other nations have made lesser contributions. Brazil, which is only a few days by steamer from West Africa, is one-third negro, the crudest type of negro on the American hemisphere. There is a strong mark of the Moor upon the Spaniard. The Arabic Moor wrought his customs very deeply into the life of Spain. The people of Mexico and Cuba might be called Moorish Americans rather than Latin Americans. The customs, manners and heart experiences in these people of Latin America are more Moorish than Christian, more Moslem, more Arabic than Spanish.—World Outlook.

San Bernardino Sun, Volume 44, Number 79, 31 May 1916 (Same Article)

MOORS ENDORSE VILLAGE IDEA

The following letter is one of the many received by the Guide relative to the establishment of a town owned and completely operated by those persons belonging to the Moorish Science Temple of America:

January 29, 1929

Islam:

In response to the question asked concerning the Moors having a town, homes, etc., we will say all honor to the prophet, who is going to give us something of our own. And we all are going to do all in our power to help build the Moorish Science Temple of America so that we can have something of our own.

Peace,

(Signed:)

Bros. E. & D. Jackson Bey

Sister J. Jackson Bey.

Chicago, Illinois.

SPECIAL NOTICE

Please address all matter that is to be published in the Moorish Guide to the Editor or Assistant Editor, 3140 Indiana Ave., Chicago, Illinois.

Page 4

Convention Blasts Use of "Colored"

PHILADELPHIA, 1848—A Negro convention in Philadelphia has urged Negroes to abandon the word "colored" and especially the words "Afric-" and "African." Philadelphia leaders recommend use of the phrase "'Oppressed Americans."

Article 26

1. Indigenous peoples have the right to the lands, territories and resources which they have traditionally owned, occupied or otherwise used or acquired.

2. Indigenous peoples have the right to own, use, develop and control the lands, territories and resources that they possess by reason of traditional ownership or other traditional occupation or use, as well as those which they have otherwise acquired.

3. States shall give legal recognition and protection to these lands, territories and resources. Such recognition shall be conducted with due respect to the customs, traditions and land tenure systems of the indigenous peoples concerned.

From Congressional Globe: House of Representatives, Friday, January 3, 1845: in regards to the "Annexation of Texas" The stupendous deserts between the Nueces and the Bravo rivers are **the natural boundaries between the anglo-saxon and the Mauritanian races** there ends the valley of the West. There Mexico begins. **Thence, beyond the Bravo, begin the Moorish people and their Indian associates***, to whom Mexico properly belongs;** who should not cross that vast desert if they could, as on our side we to, ought t stop there, because internal conflicts must ensue either our going south or their coming north of that gigantic boundary. While peace is cherished, that boundary will be sacred. Not till the spirit of conquest rages will the people on either side molest or mix with each other and whenever they do, one or the other race must be conquered, if not extinguished.

In these same congressional recordings it mentions the common law of private rights: "Where he who hath the true property, to "jus proprietatis", in lands but is out of possession thereof and hath no right to enter without recovering possession in an action, hath afterwards the free hold cast upon him by some subsequent and of course **defective title;** in this case he is remitted or sent back, by operation of law **to his ancient and more certain title**. The right of entry which he had gained by a bad title, shall be, ipso facto, annexed to his own inherent good one; and his defeasible estate shall be utterly defeated and annulled by the instantaneous act of law, without his participation or consent. 9 Blackstone's Com.19.

Amar, Amor, Amore, Amir, Ameer, Emir, Omar, Mur, Mar, Amaru, Mr; these titles and words are all variations of the word Moor. Here is the meaning of each:

Amar:

- Sanskrit: everlasting, eternal, immortal, deathless, imperishable
- Spanish/Portuguese: love
- Hebrew: to utter, say, answer, appoint, avouch, bid, certify, declare, demand, etc.
- Sumerian: faithful, warrior, hero, calf, young bull
- Akkadian: chosen
- Armenian: summer

Amara:

- Arabic: taken, from the root A-M-R meaning "to command"
- Ethiopic: show, know

Amor:

- Latin/Portuguese/Spanish: Love Amore/Amare:
- Italian: Love

Amir:

- Arabic: taken from the root A-M-R= to live a long time, command, enliven, to give orders, commander, prince, instruction, ordinance, decree, power, authority
- Hebrew: the top, summit, treetop
- Persian: King
- Turkish: Chief

Emir:

- Arabic: from the root A-M-R= emperor, commander-in-chief, general, prince

Ameer:

- Variation of Amir/Emir

Omar:

- Hebrew: he that speaks, eloquent
- Arabic: Long living; (as a verb) to live long, to be long lived, to thrive, to prosper, to flourish, to flower, to bloom, to be inhabited, to be peopled, to be populated, to be civilized, to be cultivated, to be full, to be filled, to fill with life, to make prosperous, to inhabit, live, dwell, to pervade, to reign, to build, to construct, to restore, to recondition, to populate, to overhaul, to rebuild, to refurbish, to grant long life, to prolong life, to erect, to repair
- Persian: life

Mar/Mor:

- Syriac: "my lord", given title to all saints, with the variant moran/maran meaning "our lord"
- Aramaic: "lord" from Mari
- Old High German: "mari" meaning "famous, great"
- Hungarian: "Moorish" (of or relating to the Moors or their Moorish culture)
- Old Irish: big, great, large, important, powerful, extravagant, grand (Maar, mar)
- Old Norse: famous, glorious, illustrious
- Proto-Germanic: shining, renowned, famous, great
- Ancient Greek: mighty
- Latin: from "merus" meaning "undiluted, sheer, pure
- English: "morian" meaning "A Moor"
- Proto-Slavic: "mir" meaning "Peace, world"
- Welsh: maur/mawr "big, great, and large'
- Turkish: mor "purple as a blackberry"

Amaru:

- Akkadian: to see, pile of bricks, pyramid; "maru" meaning "son, young bull calf"

- Ancient Germanic: "maru" meaning "famous"
- Japanese: "maru" meaning "circle, completeness, perfection" and also a name attached to merchant ships to secure celestial protection; the Japanese flag is also known as "Hinomaru" meaning "circle of the sun"

Mr:

- Arabic: to live, to be wholesome, healthy, manly
- Hebrew: to speak
- Egyptian: love, Mry meaning "pyramid, beloved"

(The references for these definitions can be found at Claritydaily.org/ Etymology)

Mor:

- Breton/Cornish: sea
- Czech: plague, pestilence
- Danish: mother
- Dalmatian: wall
- Kurdish: violet
- Irish: big, large, great Murshid: Arabic for "teacher"

Ma-ur [hieroglyphs], Palermo Stele, the title of the high-priest of Anu.

*The Hebrew word for teacher is moreh, which is the charge and obligation of all sons of the light. Also, Strong's concordance Hebrew- Strong's exhaustive concordance (Hebrew & Chaldea dictionary pg. 60- 3974) Ma'owr; Ma'or; M'owrah; M'orah- luminous body or luminary, light; brightness.

Black's law 4th Ed.: Moor: An officer in the Isle of Man, who summons the courts for the several sheadings. The officer is similar to the English bailiff of a hundred.

Black's Law 4th Ed.: Mooring: In maritime law, anchoring or making fast to the shore or dock; the securing or confining a vessel in a particular station, as by cables and anchors or by a line or chain run to the wharf. A vessel is "moored in safety", within the meaning of a policy of maritime insurance, when she is thus moored to a wharf or dock, free from any immediate danger from any of the perils insured against. 1 Phil. Ins. 968; Bramhall v. Sun Mut. Ins. Co., 104 Mass. 516, 6 Am. Rep. 261.

Moors are the spiritual embodiment of what has been deemed /coined the "light" i.e., knowledge whereas, they are those who are the guardians and progenitors of the essential principles of civilization that evokes or rather propels the wheels of evolution toward the higher planes of consciousness. Thus, they are luminaries that withstand/ stand within and under the umbrella of Love, truth, peace, freedom and justice and reflect that in every aspect of creation.

In just about every language, dialect, culture, etc., you will find an aspect of the term Moor in it whether positive or negative some credence will be paid to the ancient founders of civilization, the culmination of their ancestor's wisdom combined with their own knowledge which has brought forth the understanding that is the fountainhead from which the waters of eternal life spring and from which all peoples have taken a sip and whom some have even attempted to poison or destroy.

My [a **possessive-determiner** - ([Ownership: the act, state, or right of possessing something: *as in the ownership of land |and* birth right]

Original [**adjective** - Ab-original (of human races, animals, and plants) inhabiting or existing in a land from the earliest times or from before the arrival of colonists; Those who are indigenous.]

Orthodox [**adjective** - (of a person or their views, esp. spiritual or political, or other divine understandings or practices - conforming to what is generally or traditionally acceptable, right and proper as being true to their established practices]

Religion [**noun** - (a pursuit of primary importance which scribes supreme spiritual importance of a Devine Nature = Re [*legion*]-ing - - Re-alining or re-legion-ing with that which one was previously connected to and with e.g. as a vast host, multitude, or number of people, any of the national associations of servicemen and servicewomen instituted as a group working together with a singular United Cause.

II. Who/What is a Mason and what is Masonry?

EL
MIND
SPIRIT
RA
IS
IS RA EL
IS (Spirit) + RA (Mind)
BALANCED =
A manifest of consciousness
represented as EL which is the God within

Moor and mason are synonymous, and the universe reminds us of that fact by the marks on our palms (m on each hand).

The formal definition of a mason is one who builds with natural and artificial materials; a bricklayer; carpenter; a maker. These are symbolic to the potential and duties of man as we are charged to be "fruitful and multiply."

Every child is a Mason at birth as it means a mother's son (ma-son) and represents the natural order and divine balance of creation. Therefore, a true Moor/Mason is one who not only acknowledges the laws of nature but adheres to them always mindful to respect and give back to the sustainer and giver of breath.

Masonry is a system of disciplined learning. It deals with all manners of divine architecture/science: Gnosticism, cosmology, alchemy, geometry, algebra, numerology, astrology, and philosophies which when mastered and combined are called "magic". It is the high culture, refined by the original ancient ones, simplified and given to the people so as to harness the cosmic energies of existence to better connect with the unseen but nonetheless substantial reality which we owe our being to.

Though every being on this planet, excluding djins, clones, robots and androids, are Moors/Masons physically not all are Masons spiritually. As I mentioned a true mason adds on and only destroys what is necessary for goodness to spread and prevail. However, there are those who abuse knowledge and in turn abuse the grand title of Mason/Moor, those who only seek to destroy and want of selfish gain and unsubstantial materials. These are the freemasons who were not evil in origin but like all other institutions were infiltrated and polluted by Satanists. These were, originally, keepers of the Moorish shrines and the preservers of the ancient science which was/is vital to the maintaining of nations. Once freed our sons and daughters were given the keys while we Moors went into darkness so as to pay off our karmic debts for, we were not wholly innocent as the condition of the heirs shows the proof of that fact.

There are two spirits of man that exists: Moors, which represent morals and expansion, and Caucasian which symbolizes coldness, bitterness and to quote Elijah Mohammed, "Is an evil not confined to one 's self that affects others." These two things have nothing to do with dogma but everything to do with the intentions of the heart thus a pale man could be more of a Moor than one who has a darker hue in spirit but not genetically per se.

There is an arrogance that exists on both sides of the so-called "color line" both manifesting as levels of superiority and inferiority that essentially takes both out of the human family and strips them of their birthright, and freedom.

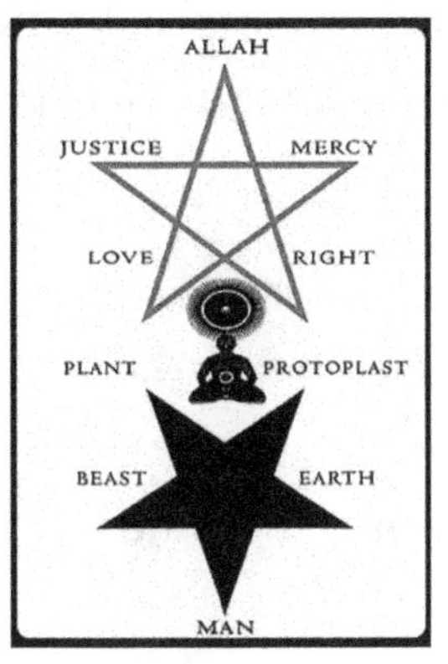

There are 3 levels of attachment that go along with the 3 phases/levels of existence. They are oath, obligation and covenant. Now the first isoath which is what binds a lot of would be soldiers and warriors to the denizens of this world whereby they forsake their obligation to their own children and blaspheme their covenant with Th Creator. An oath need not be made to any man or organization; only to Th divine self which thus is to know the truth, accept the truth, be the truth and speak the truth. If any so-called Eastern star or Mason/Freemason or would be adepts should come across this manuscript, then remember these scriptures:

Ezekiel 3:18-.... thou givest him not warning, nor speaketh to warn the wicked from his wicked way, to save his life; the same wicked man shall die in his iniquity; but his blood shall I require at thine hand.

Luke 12:47-And that servant, who knew his lord's will, and prepared not himself, neither did according to his will, shall be beaten with many stripes.

Matthew 5: 14-16: (14) ye are the light of the world. A city that is set on a hill cannot be hid. (15) Neither do men light a candle, and put it under a bushel, but on a candlestick; and it giveth light unto all that are in the house. (16) Let your light shine before men, that they may see your good works, and glorify your father which is in heaven.

Colossians 2:8-See to it that no one takes you captive through hollow and deceptive philosophy...

Chapter 3 Matthew 23:23-34 New International Version (NIV)

23"Woe to you, teachers of the law and Pharisees, you hypocrites! You give a tenth of your spices—mint, dill and cumin. But you have neglected the more important matters of the law—justice, mercy and faithfulness. You should have practiced the latter, without neglecting the former. 24You blind guides! You strain out a gnat but swallow a camel.

25"Woe to you, teachers of the law and Pharisees, you hypocrites! You clean the outside of the cup and dish, but inside they are full of greed and self-indulgence. 26Blind Pharisee! First clean the inside of the cup and dish, and then the outside also will be clean.

27"Woe to you, teachers of the law and Pharisees, you hypocrites! You are like whitewashed tombs, which look beautiful on the outside but on the inside are full of the bones of the dead and everything unclean. 28In the same way, on the outside you appear to people as righteous but on the inside you are full of hypocrisy and wickedness.

29“Woe to you, teachers of the law and Pharisees, you hypocrites! You build
tombs for the prophets and decorate the graves of the righteous. 30And you say,
‘If we had lived in the days of our ancestors, we would not have taken part with
them in shedding the blood of the prophets.’ 31So you testify against yourselves
that you are the descendants of those who murdered the prophets. 32Go ahead,
then, and complete what your ancestors started!

33“You snakes! You brood of vipers! How will you escape being condemned
to hell? 34 Therefore I am sending you prophets and sages and teachers. Some
of them you will kill and crucify; others you will flog in your synagogues and
pursue from town to town.

A Moorish Master must maintain and demonstrate:

- An Instructive tongue (courage/freedom/compassion)
- A faithful heart (good intent/loyalty/sincerity)
- A knowledgeable mind (confidence/competence/awareness)

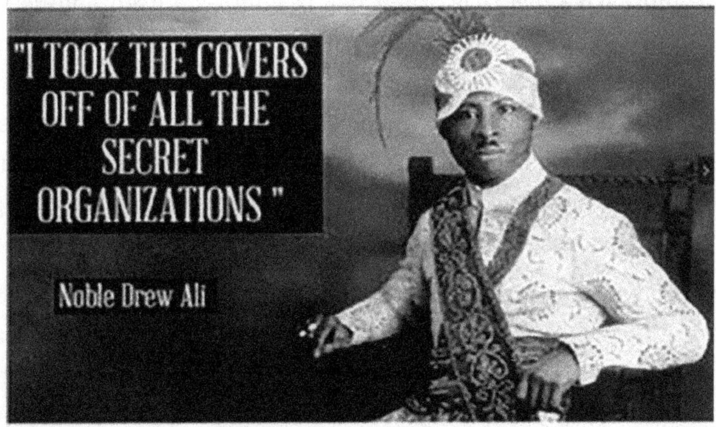

The prior requirements translates and manifest as 3 levels of Man (Mind):

- The Knower (Faith) (Wisdom)
- The Thinker (Belief) (Strength)
- The Doer (Fruition) (Beauty)

3 Aspects of S.E.L.F:

- Intuition
- Imagination
- Intellect

Tools of The Moorish Master: The Compass:

- A V-shaped tool with two legs hinged together at one end. One leg is the pivot or another leg, which draws its stability from the center. The marker leg reaches out to a prescribed area and, moving from right to left, encircles everything from the center to the outer bounds. Passion, desires, and other emotional disorders are the results of attractions of external manifests and are housed within. Each will respond to the callings of these manifests that quickly become pseudo-gods of which the patient knows little or nothing.
- The compass is the first tool used when geometry is in action. Whether the idea is a day, a creation or temple, if it is made it must have its possibilities encircled to its purpose and no further. Like so, the lower self of desires, with its carnal nature that sprang from fleshly things (known sometimes as the devil) must have their day. Their day is limited to itself and no other. The Elohim made the devil and gave the soul and flesh to man (spirit man). Still, all these are thing...and "The Elohim made everything that is, was or will be made." All things must pass when their day meets their encompassed time. Thus, "there is no failure for the human soul and man will be fully saved, redeemed and perfected" by the things he suffers through his great gifts from the Elohim. Indeed, the only way out of the fire is through the fire.
- As the Compass was used in the divine designing of things, upon each plane, likewise as man perfects himself, he must use the compass to draw circles around his passions and desires to keep them in the bounds of righteousness. The above is known as "the fixed" (MHK17:37) which was encompassed by Allah, the husbandman (MHK-1). That which is fixed by Allah is known by Allah and is for man to solve.

The Square:

- The Egyptian Adept Noble Drew Ali teaches us about the celestial tools used to build the temples of perfected man. The compass, square, hammer and ax are among the many tools possessed by all men albeit only a few have the knowledge of how to use them. "We use the square to measure all our lines, to straighten out the crooked places of the way and to make the corners of our conduct square." The square is formed by the perpendicular intersection of two straight lines, at ninety degrees. Further symbolic study reveals the L-shape of the square serves a dual purpose to stand upright and level. The square, as a symbol of virtue, is used to certify the character at a right angle. When a man's conduct is not stable or constant with his knowledge of truth, then the instrument is not being used.

- Next to the compass, the square is the most universal of tools. One is considered "out of square" if not in agreement with laws (principles) as laid down or not at right angles. Usually, to be square signifies honesty, fairness, consciousness or straightforwardness. Today there is an array of meanings for the square. However, all of them whether aught or naught, are hinged upon original Lamuria (Mu) Atlantean design and purpose of "as above, so below"...basically meaning "as a man thinketh, so is he."
- It should be remembered that man was first formed as God-in- Divine flesh before falling into the human state of Adam. Adam became the living square because of the way man is made: the spirit of Allah stands in the perpendicular image and level in his likeness with the earth he also made. Master-minds of old describe this, the greatest of all creations: 'as above so below'.
- The man, made by the great God, was made on the square. Noble Drew Ali speaks of the square of divinity as, "the rule of life; so that obedience to his precepts is happiness to thyself" (MHK 35:21). Although the word "man" means "thinker", it does not take a psychologist to resolve when anyone is out of character; it is simply because they are out of their rightful mind! Not squared with 'as above so below'. No man can be himself without being squared at a right angle. His natural habitat is to be in the kingdom of God. This is why the square is one of the preeminent tools of the Gods (Ancient Men). The man who knows how to pray is on the square.
- The square is the staple tool among declarations of Maat used to civilize the nations of the Earth. Often refereed to as "The Golden Rule", the square was given to the earliest Chinese (Manchurian) In their books of great learning, "A man should not do unto others what he would not have them do unto him."Yehoshua (Issa; Jesus), also an Egyptian (Tamerian; Kemetian) adept, taught, "You shall love Allah with all your heart, with all your soul, and with all your minds. Love your neighbor as yourself. On these two commandments hang all the law and the prophets."(Matt. 22:37-40)

- Noble Drew Ali of the same Kemetian Adept Lineage calls the square, "principles of actions, and see to it that thou ever act according to them."(Mhk41:9-10). Among many tools used in the workshop of the mind, where conscious people build up character, are the hammer, level, compass, plum and plane. The Moorish construct their character in the form of an upright open five-pointed pentagram (star). It is impossible to construct the omnipotent five-pointed symbol, within the heart of man, without a clear conception of the tools. The mere awareness of the work, which is required to build a conscious Moor, immediately transforms a mortal of human knowledge into an architecture of the S.E.L.F (Sacred Eternal Life Force). This inward journey of attainment, in its simplicity, is the most economical and natural way for man to think. Only then does his every act on the physical level become perpendicular to the harmony of his Creator. This is how the Moorish today become their forefathers of yesterday.

The Hammer:

- The prophet Ali's education of the hammer is to "use the hammer to drive home the truth, and pound it in until it is a part of every part."(MHK 5:17). The true name of the hammer is "resolution". Nothing drives the truth like "reason". When reason is used before the intent of each action, it establishes firmness, stability, contentment and happiness to one's thinking, understanding, reasoning and will (these are the "actions of the soul" or mind). The hammer is a tool used repetitiously because each stroke represents pounding, buffetings and remembrance to the character. Each sphere is an unfolding consciousness into infinite wisdom. Resolution purifies the heart and mind. This purification is one of the "must" required in the constitution to be Moorish Americans (Act 7-divine Constitution and By-Laws).
- Slaves are men subjugated by other men. Those subjugated rely primarily upon their nature and what they have been furnished with by those who gave them a body of flesh. The problem is a nature, formed from a body of desires, sprang forth from those fleshly things and rendered the Moorish of America into the realms of "inconstancy".

The Level:

- The level is used to balance the character's "attitude". The level is truth and is used to seek the harmoniousness of life. The level extends from justice and mercy to the divinity of love and right (MHK 3:9). The level is man, in his higher self and proper attitude. A man's attitude is strictly based upon his own perceptions. It is how he sees karma or "just what is happening", "the events occurring and reoccurring , yet are all governed according to law."

- His use of the level determines if he sees the play or becomes a part of the mad human drama, which he witnesses on the stage of maya. His level, when in proper balance, glides him above the ego's clouds of duality. He is love. Therefore, he does not suffer pains of hate because only the ego suffers pain.
- The level shows counterpoise and equilibrium in a well- balanced character. It has no curves, bends nor irregularities and keeps the soul undisturbed by passion. Passions and desires (uncontrolled and misdirected) affect the attitude and interfere with the harmony of truths that are taught by the level. The differences among men, which they readily use to classify their hatred and other weaknesses, lose its meaning when the level is used. The level is an instrument, which is balanced upon love and therefore teaches the equalities in what appear as differences among men.
- Discrimination is the ability to discern truth from falsehood, infinite from the finite and the immutable from the concerns of time. When the level is mastered, it alone gives one the power to discriminate. The level also makes a man reliable.

The Plum:

- The complete plummet consists of three (3) parts: known as the plumb rule, the plumb line and the plumb bob. The plumb rule is a strip of wood from which the plumb line is vertically suspended from the center. At the other end, attached to the same plumb line is the plumb bob. Together, their duty is to determine verticality and/or depths. When these parts are functioning on all points, the plummet is in fact the spirit, soul and flesh of man. This function is also regarded as a body being drawn through human nature by the earth's center of gravity. Meanwhile his soul, pending use of the will, is a gifted thin-line uniting divinity and matter. When the wall of a man's character for his temple has been plummeted, then it is straight and true; otherwise, it is out of the plumb.
- Symbolically, the plummet marks the true growth of man through matter to his lofty estate. In building the temple of perfected man, the character must be plumbed straight and true in order for the resurrection to be fact. He

must grow through flesh and the soul to be himself; this is how Noble Drew Ali began to uplift the Moorish Americans. When a Moor is conscious of the plummet, he is aware of his present station topside earth. He is knowledgeable of lead-like weight (body of flesh) that has him bound down to carnal life. Yet, like the caged bird, he knows not to tear himself apart by it, for it has been appointed. This instrument acts as and is the all of love (MHK 7:22-23).

- The plum is the line of a conscious Moor's character. It is used to keep the temple of his pentagram erect, accurate and firm, his temple, or star of perfected man, is always plum-lined to the will of his Creator; lest he go astray.

The Plane:

- The plane, usually with an adjustable blade, is a character's tool used to smooth or level wood. "We use the plane to smooth the rough, uneven surface of joint and block and board that go to build the temple for the truth"(MHK5:18). And when the character becomes rough and uneven, the plane enables the initiate to resist the tempting winds that are certain to blow. Rough and uneven surfaces in the building of one's character are basically past decisions based upon irresolution and/or a sluggish will. These are errors, sins or ill thoughts that can be corrected. This is the purpose for the plane. The plane (and often the ax) is a tool used when one recognizes weaknesses, flaws or discords between the god-Self and his Creator. Since the nearest place to meet Allah is in the heart, it also stands to reason the plane must be used along this straight path. As a Moor builds his(her)self, he becomes more aware of such frailties of the ego and even those which lay dormant in the clearest of human knowledge, e.g. attachment, addictions, envy, anger, hatred, vanity, intemperance, etc., etc. Those who desire to be themselves, upright. Independent and fearless, use the plane.

Ancient Mystic Oriental Masonry by Dr. R. Swinburne Clymer:

Initiation is not what it is generally supposed to be. All Masons know what Ceremonial Initiation is, but this is simply the outward symbol of the inner work. A Mason who has the three degrees may think that he has all that can be had, but little does he know of that inner work, that

Grand and Supreme Initiation which is possible for those who truly desire it. -Pp. 6

All real Initiation is an internal, not an external process. The outer ceremony is dead and useful only so far as it symbolizes and illustrates, and thereby makes clear the inward change. To transform means to regenerate, and this comes by trial, by effort, by self- conquest, by sorrow, disappointment, failure, and a daily renewal of the conflict. It is thus man must 'work out his own salvation.' The consummation of initiation is the finding of the Christos."-Pp. 14

"No civilization known to man has ever risen to any great heights, or long maintained its supremacy, that debased woman. Indeed, the Secret Doctrine demonstrates with unmistakable clearness that sexual debasement in any form is the highway to degeneracy and destruction of both man and woman; and of Nations quite as certainly as of individuals."-Pp. 16

The cradle of the Symbolism used in all Masonry is placed by many of the best authorities in that country which they believe was first inhabited, i.e., the plateau of Tartary, and from there transmitted to this generation by the sages of India, Persia, Ethiopia, and Egypt. We are not indebted to either ancient Egypt for either Religion or Masonry, but to America. -Pp. 25

It is a fact that at Memphis, Egypt, in the Pyramids, under the guidance of the Kings, the Mystic Rites of Masonry were worked many thousands of years ago, but at that time Egypt and the continent of America were one and the same. -Pp. 25

"When, following the course of the constellations, those immovably and perpetually fastened upon America are reached, it will appear that, while all that is sublime in the historic past centers upon Egypt, all that is sublime in the prehistoric past centers upon America (Atlantis) ; and as the curtain which has hitherto concealed the prehistoric connection between the peoples of ancient Egypt and of America, is lifted, it will be seen that, the people of the Eagle on the Nile being descended from the original people of the Eagle on this Continent, the twain are one, and that prehistoric America was the Original Egypt....-Pp. 27

Says Agassiz: "First born among continents, America has been falsely denominated the New World. Hers was the first dry land lifted out of the "Waters, hers was the first shore washed by the ocean that enveloped all the earth besides; and while Europe was represented only by islands rising here and there above the sea, America (Atlantis) already stretched in an unbroken line of land from Nova Scotia to the far West."-Pp. 27

Chapter 4 Luke 17:20-21 1599 Geneva Bible (GNV)

20 [a]And when he was demanded of the Pharisees, when the kingdom of God should come, he answered them, and said, The kingdom of God cometh not with [b]observation.

21 Neither shall men say, Lo here, or lo there: for behold, the kingdom of God is [c]within you.

Chapter 5 Matthew 24:23-26 New International Version (NIV)

[23]At that time if anyone says to you, 'Look, here is the Messiah!' or, 'There he is!' do not believe it. [24]For false messiahs and false prophets will appear and perform great signs and wonders to deceive, if possible, even the elect. [25] See, I have told you ahead of time.

[26]"So if anyone tells you, 'There he is, out in the wilderness,' do not go out; or, 'Here he is, in the inner rooms,' do not believe it. [27]For as lightning that comes from the east is visible even in the west, so will be the coming of the Son of Man. [28]Wherever there is a carcass, there the vultures will gather.

James 5:12 - But above all things, my brethren, swear not, neither by heaven, neither by the earth, neither by any other oath: but let your yea be yea; and [your] nay, nay; lest ye fall into condemnation.

[19]My little children, of whom I travail in birth again, until **Christ be formed in you.**-Galatians 4:19

Psalms 82:6- "I said, 'You are gods'; you are all sons of the Most High."

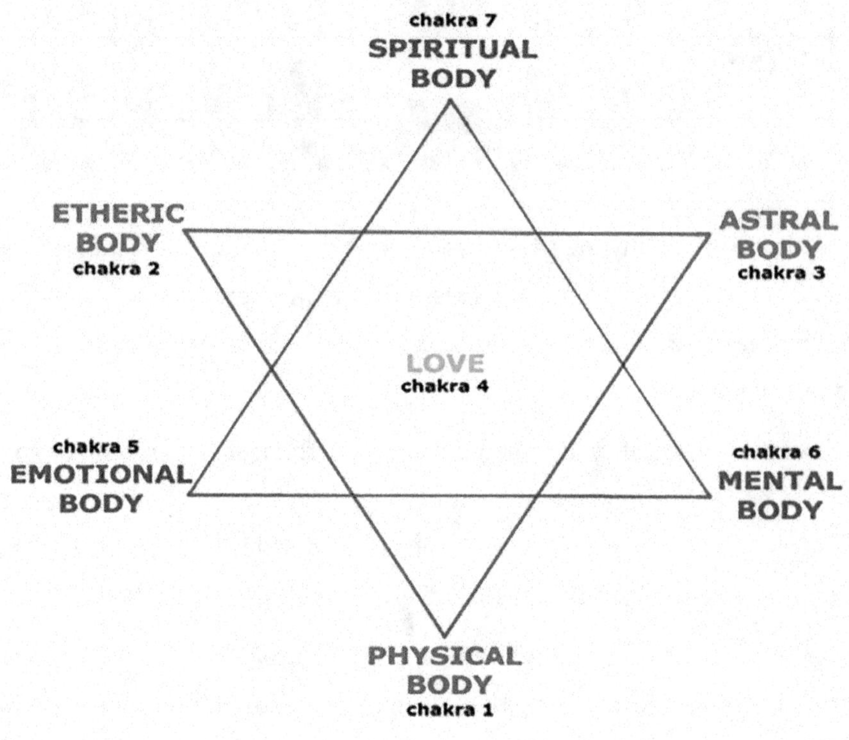
chakra 7
SPIRITUAL
BODY
ETHERIC
BODY
chakra 2
ASTRAL
BODY
chakra 3
LOVE
chakra 4
chakra 5
EMOTIONAL
BODY
chakra 6
MENTAL
BODY
PHYSICAL
BODY
chakra 1

ISLAMISM
THE FIRST RELIGIOUS CREED

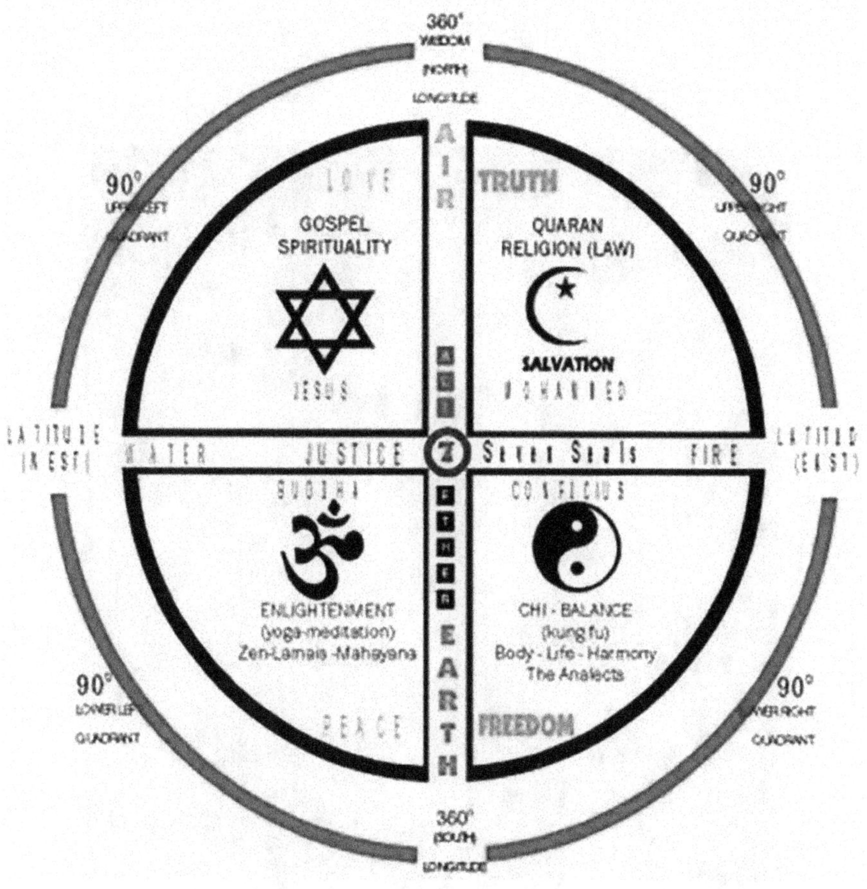

7

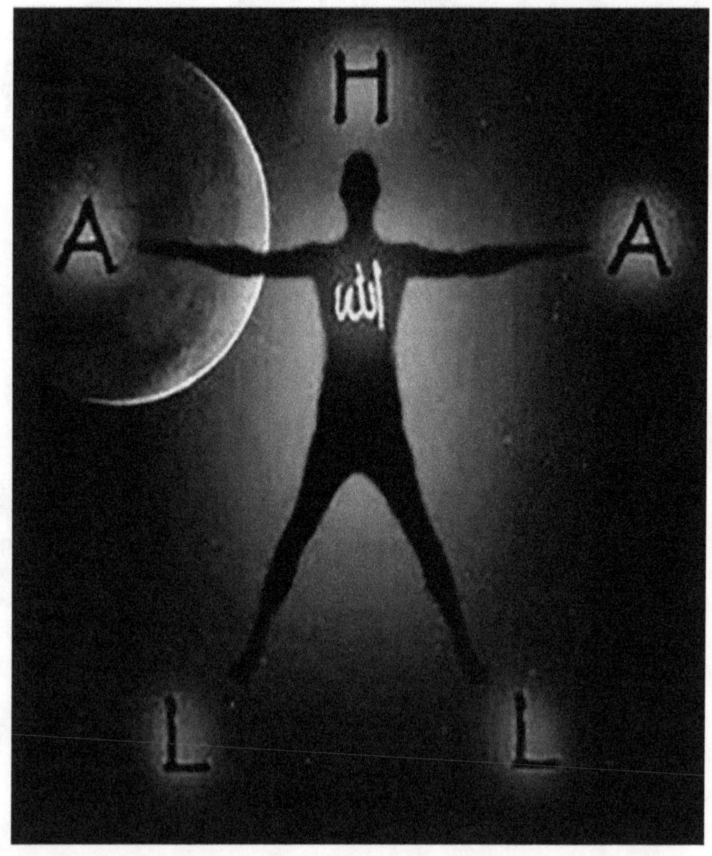
H
A
A
الله
L
L

THE MOORISH DIVINE AND NATIONAL MOVEMENT OF THE WORLD
ISLAM
OBVERSE

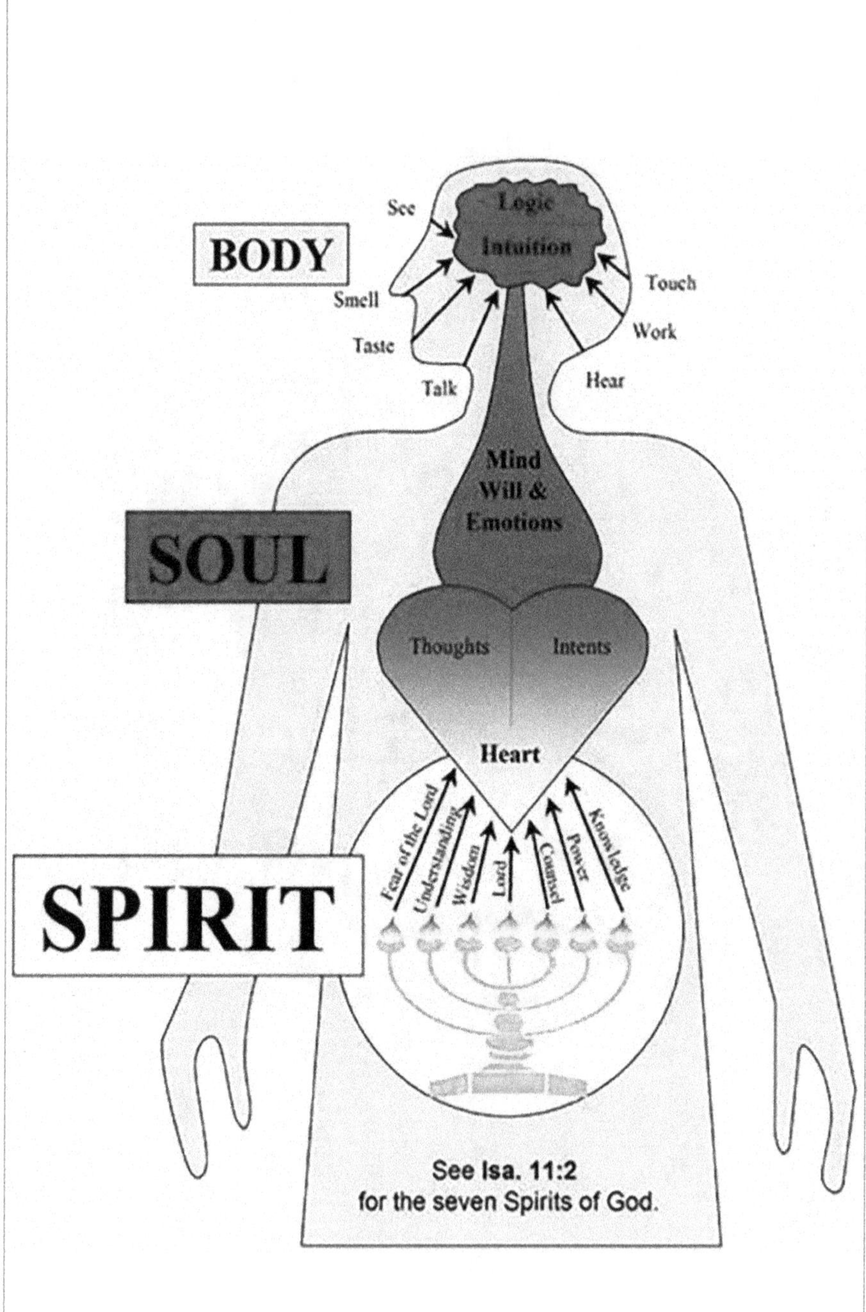
BODY
See
Logic
Intuition
Smell
Touch
Taste
Work
Talk
Hear
Mind
Will &
Emotions
SOUL
Thoughts
Intents
Heart
SPIRIT
Fear of the Lord
Understanding
Wisdom
Lord
Counsel
Power
Knowledge
See Isa. 11:2
for the seven Spirits of God.

K-(Knowledge) Applies to all that one knows and understands of facts and general truths and principles, by personal experience and observation

O-(Order) The condition in which every part or piece is in its right place; a regular, methodical, or harmonious arrangement; the state or condition of things in which the law is obeyed; to instruct or command.

R-(Rhythm) To flow; the proper relation of parts producing a harmonious whole.

A-(Astrology) Practical astronomy, as the prediction of tides and eclipse and the fixing of Easter.

N-(Nature) The personification of all-natural facts and forces; quality; character; vital powers; reality.

K=2 (Higher and Lower Self) O=6 (Harmony; balance; equality)

R=9 (Form; completion; manifestation) A=1 (Self; The Star)

N=5 (Principles; purpose; power)

2+6+9+1+5=14=5

5 represents the responsibilities of The Divine/Supreme being: Elevate, Protect, Inform, Uplift and Inspire by way of the five principles (Love, Truth, Peace, Freedom and Justice).

B. Pedigree

I. The first 5 Tribes

- El: Law makers and givers of North Gate; Elohim of the cosmos; likened to executives; legislative branch; means "god, force, or power."
- Bey: Governors of land in Moorish civilization; law enforcers of the Elohim; O-Bey the law; Mufti (Mohammedan Judge); executive branch; means "ruler, landlord."
- Dey: of the degrees of the eternal Zodiac (South Gate); masters/scientists of astrology and cosmology as well as other disciplines; means "knowledgeable."
- Al: of the law; earned degrees in mathematics, geometry, psychology, etc; means the same as El but Al (goddess) is feminine.
- Ali: Law bringers (ethereal); title of those who have mastered their craft/gifts completely; means "The exalted or Most High; Most Noble".

These 5 civilized tribes came together to form a union called the Iroquois confederation and establishing The Law of the Great Peace (Gayanerekowa). This confederation formed the first of the 4 constitutions, "The Articles of Confederation" which later spawned the Articles of Association, the Declaration of independence and the Original Organic Constitution of America.

II. Americans

American= Am + Eric (A) + An; Am= be = to exist, live, ess (e), essence, essential; a spiritual entity; Erica (A) [can be with or without the final "A"] = Is the root word of the Latin word Ericaceous= heath, forest; Eric (a) is a name meaning, "ruler, always ruler, and ruler forever"; An is a suffix meaning, "belonging to; adhering to; attached to; part of; connected to or connecting with." Putting it all together, this means that we Moors were meant to rule with the forest that we are the essence of, being that we are divinely connected with and are reflections of. This is why we were removed from the forests and placed in concrete jungles so as to cut us off from that vital essence of who and what we are hence the forest are dying and so are we.

According to both the 1828 Unabridged Webster's Dictionary and the 1936 Webster's Unabridged 20th century Dictionary on the English language an American is Defined as follows: (n) "An aboriginal or one of the various copper-colored natives found on the American continent by the Europeans; the original application of the name."

So clearly there has been a case of identity theft on this continent. The fraud known as the U.S. has committed atrocities in the name of America when in actuality, they are neither Americans nor their pale contemporaries. They have perpetrated fraud upon the natives and through social engineering have caused a mental separation of the original and primitive peoples of this continent, specifically the Asiatics of North-West Amexem/America.

They act as sovereigns when they are at best citizens and/or aliens. Some Europeans would argue, "I was born here so that makes me an American", which is a false statement. Your geography doesn't determine your nationality it is your bloodline, consanguinity and ancestral lineage that does so. For example, if two Scottish people live in China for 20 years and have 3 children are those children Chinese or citizens of China? The answer is obvious to any one with a logical mind thus the same goes over here in the west. Just because someone steals something from you doesn't make it theirs even though they may possess it still doesn't truly belong to them. However, the true heirs refuse to correct their status and live by the standards of their lineage, so they unwittingly give up their birthright every time they call people American who aren't and call themselves "black, colored, negro, citizens" of which they aren't either.

It has been said the truth would set you free and the time has come for all to worship under their own vine and fig tree; every tongue must confess their own and live and stand on the foundation of their ancient fore bearers.

TITLE 29

State Government

General Provisions

CHAPTER 1. Jurisdiction and Sovereignty

§ 106 Lenape Indian Tribe of Delaware; recognition.

(a) Legislative findings. — The General Assembly finds all of the following:

1. The Lenape Indian Tribe of
2. Delaware, referred to as "the Tribe" in this section, has an unbroken history of hundreds of years of settlement and continued residency in the vicinity of the Town of Cheswold in Kent County.
3. Members of the Tribe preserved, displayed, and manifested close cultural ties with one another by conducting themselves in such a social and economic manner so as to identify themselves as being culturally and ethnically distinct.
4. **The Tribe can date their ancestral ties as far back as the early 1700s. The Tribe was formerly known as "the Moors" and, for many decades of the twentieth century, state documents such as driver's licenses designated the Tribe's race with an "M".**
5. The Delaware School Code of 1921 provided that the State Board of Education could establish a school "**for the children of people called Moors.**" As a result, 2 schools were built, 1 in the Town of Cheswold and 1 at Fork Branch on Denney's Road in Kent County.
6. There has been unofficial statewide acceptance and recognition of the Tribe for at least 125 years. Through a formal process of reviewing applicable state laws, historical and anthropological references, and previous actions of the General Assembly and State agencies, the Department of State concluded by 2009 that this State has historically acknowledged the Tribe.
7. The Smithsonian Institute issued an annual report in 1948, in which the Tribe was referred to as the "Moors of Kent County, Delaware," and identified as a surviving Indian group of the eastern United States.

8. The United States Census Bureau approved a defined "state designated tribal statistical area" for the Tribe for the 2010 Census.

9. The Tribe has a constitutional tribal government, and the preamble of its constitution states that its purpose is to:

a. Preserve the legacy of its ancestors.
b. Promote the interests of its people.
c. Affirm its tribal identity.
d. Establish justice.
e. Ensure domestic tranquility.
f. Defend the general welfare.
g. Exercise its governmental jurisdiction.
h. Protect its environmental, cultural, and human resources.
i. Secure its national sovereignty for future generations of its people.

AN EMBLEM OF AMERICA.

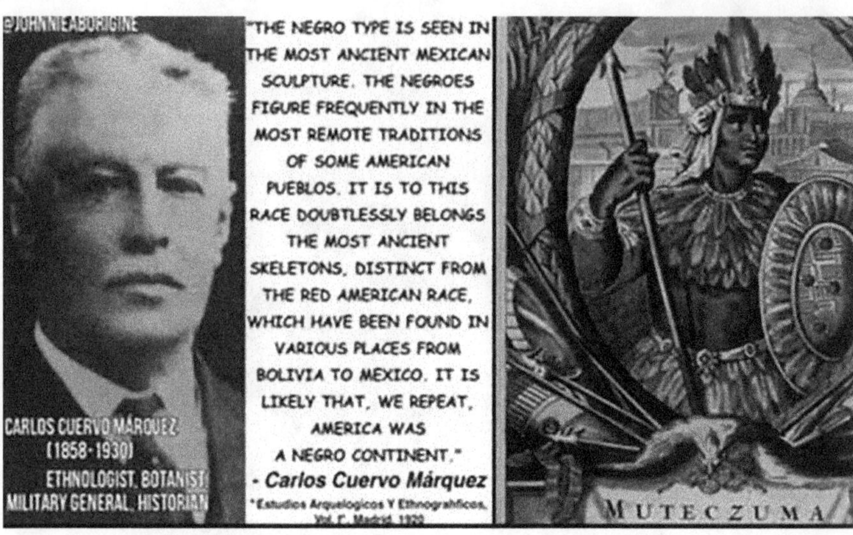

@JOHNNIEABORIGINE
CARLOS CUERVO MÁRQUEZ
(1858-1930)
ETHNOLOGIST, BOTANIST,
MILITARY GENERAL, HISTORIAN
"THE NEGRO TYPE IS SEEN IN THE MOST ANCIENT MEXICAN SCULPTURE. THE NEGROES FIGURE FREQUENTLY IN THE MOST REMOTE TRADITIONS OF SOME AMERICAN PUEBLOS. IT IS TO THIS RACE DOUBTLESSLY BELONGS THE MOST ANCIENT SKELETONS, DISTINCT FROM THE RED AMERICAN RACE, WHICH HAVE BEEN FOUND IN VARIOUS PLACES FROM BOLIVIA TO MEXICO. IT IS LIKELY THAT, WE REPEAT, AMERICA WAS A NEGRO CONTINENT."
- Carlos Cuervo Márquez
*Estudios Arquelogicos Y Ethnograhficos,
MUTECZUMA

H.J.R 331 (excerpts):

Resolved by the House of Representatives (the Senate concurring), That— **(1) the Congress, on the occasion of the two hundredth anniversary of the signing of the United States Constitution, acknowledges the contribution made by the Iroquois Confederacy and other Indian Nations to the formation and development of the United States; (2) the Congress also hereby reaffirms the constitutionally recognized government-to-government relationship with Indian tribes which has been the cornerstone of this Nation's official Indian policy; (3) the Congress specifically acknowledges and reaffirms the trust responsibility and obligation of the United States Government to Indian tribes, including Alaska Natives, for their preservation, protection, and enhancement, including the provision of health, education, social, and economic assistance programs as necessary, and including the duty to assist tribes in their performance of governmental responsibility to provide for the social and economic well-being of their members and to preserve tribal cultural identity and heritage; and (4) the Congress also acknowledges the need to exercise the utmost good faith in upholding its treaties with the various tribes, as the tribes understood them to be, and the duty of a great Nation to uphold its legal and moral obligations for the benefit of all of its**

citizens so that they and their posterity may also continue to enjoy the rights they have enshrined in the United States Constitution for time immemorial.

Agreed to October 21, 1988

Our ancestors built this continent, this planet even, and here are some Moor facts to substantiate and support that claim; here is a list of American inventors that the schoolbooks conveniently leave out:

- Aero plane Propelling: James S. Adams
- Biscuit Cutter: A.P. Ashbourne
- Folding Bed: L.C. Bailey
- Coin Changer: James A. Bauer
- Rotary Engine, Car coupler: Andrew J. Beard
- Letter Box: C.E. Becket
- Stainless Steel pads: Alfred Benjamin
- Torpedo Discharger: H. Bradberry
- Disposable Syringe: Phil Brooks
- Home security system: Marie Brown
- Corn planter, cotton planter: Henry Blair
- Ironing Board: Sarah Boone
- Street Sweeper: C.B. Brooks
- Horse Bridle Bit: L.F. Brown
- Typewriter: Burridge and Marshman
- Train alarm: R.A. Butler
- Image converter, radiation detector: George Curruthers
- Peanut butter, paints and stains, lotions and soaps: George W. Carver
- Automatic fishing reel: George Cook
- Ice cream mold: A.L. Cralle
- Printing press: W.A. Lavallette
- Envelope Seal: F.W. Leslie
- Laser Fuels: Lester Lee
- Pressure Cooker: Maurice W. Lee
- Window Cleaner: A.L. Lewis
- Pencil Sharpener: John L. Love
- Fire Extinguisher: Terri J. Marshall
- Lock: W.A. Martin
- Shoe Lasting Machine: Jan Matzelger
- Lubrications: Elijah McCoy
- Rocket catapult: Hugh Macdonald
- Elevator: Alexander Miles
- Gas mask, traffic signal: Garrett Morgan
- Hair Brush: Lyda Newman
- Heating furnace: Alice H. Parker
- Air ship (bump): J.F. Pickering
- Folding Chair: Purdy and Sadgwar
- Hand Stamp, fountain pen: W.B. Purvis

- Dust Pan: L.P. Ray
- Insect destroyer Gun: A.C. Richardson
- Baby Buggy: W.H. Richardson
- Sugar Refinement: N. Rillieux
- Clothes dryer: C.T. Sampson
- Cellular Phone: Henry Sampson
- Pressing comb: Walter Sammons
- Curtain Rod: S.R. Scottron
- Lawn Sprinkler: J.W. Smith
- Automatic Gear Shift: R.U. Spikes
- Urine Analysis Machine: Dewey

It is clear that so-called "black" and "African-American" history is quite simply American history as well as world history for the things aforementioned run this world and provide safety and convenience to billions excluding the few weapons on the list. They hide these truths and when revealed they taint it with misnomers which is partly why these inventors were so well hidden as there is no statue of limitations on fraud thus anything done in such is liable to be confiscated and can legally be claimed by the heir of that title. You cannot transact business in another man's name. The only thing colonizers have truly invented was the patent which was the way they were able to steal the ideas and hard work of the true geniuses which is why they stripped us of our titles/ appellations in the first place. It is not racism; it is birthright theft. However, this list is just a point of reference so as to provide clarity and inspiration.

III. Nationals

There are 4 classifications of status:

- National: The highest-ranking member of a society; these are natural, primitive inhabitants of the land. Is this you? If so, then declare your nationality!
- Naturalized Citizen: These are those who came here and became citizens, through the naturalization process (not to be confused with nationalization).
- Subject: This is where subject citizens and corporations (U.S.A, U.S. [Union States], THE STATE OF, etc.) rest, and corporate people rest there as well (blacks, coloreds, Negroes, Spaniards).
- Aliens: These are foreigners who remain loyal and as foreigners with their mother country while residing here.

All of these are clothed with certain rights of citizenship, however they can be unclothed, with the exception of the national. Their unalienable/inalienable substantive birthrights cannot be abridged and are preserved in the constitution.

Only nationals can claim the resources (natural and political), of their own land, their natural people, territories, and jurisdictions. The naturalized citizens (subjects and aliens), have abused the natural resources of the Natural and Primitive peoples, to the point where the nation's economy is destroyed and collapsed. The Universal remedy is Nationalization.

Being a national comes by way of a nationality which is the quality or character which arises from the act of a being belonging to a nation or state. Nationality determines the political status with reference to allegiance; while domicile determines civil status. (Black's Law Dictionary, 4th Ed.)

Status is the legal standing of a man in accordance with their national allegiance and creed. It is the first rule in law, and it sets the stage for jurisdiction which is the basis for either prosecution or dismissal (adjudication).

The Asiatics of North-West Amexem/America who have been classified and branded as "negro, black, colored, African-American, etc.," have essentially been stripped of their nationality which has removed them from the mound of nations i.e. the human family hence they are subject to abuse and mistreatment.

All nations have a standard which was established by the foremothers and fathers of the land by which they operate and maintain. The so- called black man has been conditioned, both by other Asiatics as well as Europeans, to exist in a perpetual cycle of inactivity masked as progress yet the manifest of such a dead culture which is false and fictitious in origin is all around them and a proverbial laughing stock to all who know the true meaning of civics and how it functions.

A lot of marching, praying, organizations and tons of finance later the condition has worsened yet they refuse to acknowledge due to pride, selfishness and voluntary ignorance the truth of who they really are and what we as a people represent to the world.

Every man is bound to honor their mothers and fathers so that thy days may be long on the earth plane which Th Creator hath given. But if a man honors not thy mother and thy father then he has marked/cursed himself and his offspring and whatever he does will fail. Black Wall Street, NAACP, Black Panthers, NOI, etc, are all examples of treadmill movements that provided no remedy to the ills of the people who built them for that purpose. Some were utterly destroyed, others are fronts to keep you in bondage, but they both essentially were/are wolves in sheep's clothing that devour the energy of the sheep that flock to them.

We are nationals and free by birthright for this is the land of our ancestors that pre-date the so-called slave trade which in all honesty was an extreme fabrication and one of the most powerful acts of sorcery known to man. To quote an Elder, "To turn people into slaves, ye must first teach them they were slaves, came from slaves over and over until their offspring become volunteer slaves", Da 13th Sun. We are home and our rights are unalienable and secured by the supreme law of the land which are the Constitutions mentioned earlier that place "We Th People" under the umbrella of divine isonomic law.

Our status was unearthed and restored by Th Holy and illustrious Prophet El Sharif Abdul Ali A.K.A Noble Drew Ali whose great and diligent missionary work, as well as those faithful Moors of Th Divine and National movement who stood and stand beside him, have revived the creed of our people and sparked the path that leads out of darkness (ignorance; death) into marvelous light (knowledge; awareness; life).

10:46 74%

bringing or aiding such male slaves to come into this state, on indictment for misdemeanor, and on conviction thereof, shall be fined and imprisoned, or either, at the discretion of the court.

46. *Jurisdiction of inferior court.*—The inferior courts of the several counties of this state, shall have jurisdiction of the several offences created or mentioned by this act, in all cases in which, by the constitution of the state, jurisdiction may be entertained by them.

47. *Exceptions in favor of aborigines, Moors, and Hindoos.*—The provisions, prohibitions, and penalties of this act shall not extend to any American Indian, free Moor, or Lascar; but the burthen of proof, in all cases of arrest of any person of color, shall be on such person of color, to show him or herself exempt from the operations of this act.

43. Dec. 23, 1833, sec. 8, *Prince* 808.
44. Dec. 26, 1835, sec. 4, ib. 811.
45. Ib. sec. 5, ib.
46. Dec. 26, 1835, sec. 6, *Prince* 811.
47. Ib. sec. 7, ib.

Excerpt from The Codification of Georgia Statues Pg.833

IV. Reclamation of Birthright

"If you don't do anything else declare your nationality," were the instructions of the Prophet Noble Drew Ali. There are 5 points of substance, 5 essential qualities of real man: spirit, flesh, soul, nationality and creed.

This is why persons branded as blacks or any other racial/ethnic misnomer are considered 3/5 a man according to the constitution because in the taking of one's nationality you also strip them of their creed which sets the standards by which men conduct themselves.

Surah 13(Ar-Ra'ad):11-For each one are successive [Angels] before and behind him who protect him by the decree of Allah. Indeed, Allah will not change the condition of a people until they change what is in themselves. And when Allah intends for a people ill, there is no repelling it. And there is not for them besides him any patron.

"Nobody can give you freedom. Nobody can give you equality or justice or anything. You're a man, you take it."-El Hajj Shabazz Malik El (Malcolm X)

"Dogs and slaves were named by their master and only free men name themselves."-Dr. John Henrik Clarke

Asian Interviewer: "Can you address their concerns Mr.Chang?"

MR. CHANG: "The concerns of Black people? Yes I can. The fact is, that we all live under a system of White Supremacy. We Asian people look back at our long history of conflict with the European. We observe their strategies and develop our own, in response and in kind. There is no need for loud mass movements on our part, because we intend to overtake them in time, through action and personal sacrifice".

Asian INTERVIEWER: "And the Black man?"

MR. CHANG: "He does not count into our situation. He is simply here. We do not hate the Black man. We just love the Asian man most. Real love--not cliche. We want to see Asian man happy, so we employ him. We eat together. We spend time with each other. We want his kids to be educated, so we invest in our own schools that offer our children the technical abilities to change the world's power structure in our favor.

We want to see the Asian man safe, so we purchase and organize our own communities. We want him to remain Asian, so we reduce the outside influence of others ideologies and cultures. While he fought to sniff behind the White man, the Black man has had the opportunity and every right in the world to do the same, but he chooses to indict people like me for not hiring him over my own brothers. For me to do this would be foolish and that would not be Asian love.

In contrast, the Black man will fight for the right to be up under everyone else other than other Black people who he should feel the most love for. If our indifference to their situation make us racist, then what would you call the Black man's indifference to his own situation?"

WAKE UP

- Nortey-Ra -
PhotoGrid

It must be innerstood and overstood that being a national, like every other state/status, begins mentally. In other words, you must know and feel that you are free. You must carry yourself as sovereign in all aspects of your life which ultimately means you are by, for, and of law; the common and natural law of creation but that you also navigate the laws of man accordingly. Paperwork cannot and will not set you free, fiat (so-called money) won't set you free, and nor will arrogance or self pity. The only key to freedom is knowledge and application of law divine i.e. obedience to naturalness and simplicity, courage and compassion abounding. Continue to learn and grow as to become active Moors participating in the upliftment of the world and enriched posterity of the Moorish nation.

Many active and conscious Moorish-Americans across our Northwest continent (America) have been consistent and dedicated in their duties and responsibilities to answer up to their constitution principles. In exercising their (our) Unalienable Rights and their (our) Divine Birthrights, Moors have been working to take their places in the affairs of men.

On December 22, 2011, Rahm Emanuel, Mayor of Chicago (Mecca) published a Proclamation that affirmed that Moors are the aboriginal and indigenous people of North America, South America, Central America and the adjoining Islands. To date '7' other City Officials have proclaimed the very same proclamation.

A Proclamation is the act of 'Proclaiming' or 'Publishing', which is an 'Avowal' (open Declaration) or a formal 'Declaration'. This act causes some 'State' matters to be 'Published' or to be made generally known; and by virtue of the said 'matter' being placed in 'written form' and issued by proper authority.

Article IV (American Constitution)

> *Section 1. Full faith and credit shall be given in each state to the public acts, records, and judicial proceedings of every other state. And the Congress may by general laws prescribe the manner in which such acts, records, and proceedings shall be proved, and the effect thereof.*

This is a list of state proclamations showing and proving that the true identity of the Asiatics of North-West Amexem is documented, known and respected:

- Chicago, Illinois Rahm Emanuel, Mayor December 22, 2011
- Omaha, Nebraska Jim Smith, Mayor January 5, 2012
- Tacoma, Washington Marilyn Strickland, Mayor January 4, 2012
- Charlotte, North Carolina Anthony R. Foxx, Mayor January 2012
- Baltimore, Maryland Stephanie Rawlings, Mayor January 8, 2012
- Fayetteville, North Carolina Anthony G. Chavonne January 2012
- Lynchburg, Virginia Joan F. Foster, Mayor January 2012
- Little Rock, Arkansas Mark Stodola, Mayor January 8, 2012
- Trenton, New Jersey Tony Mack, Mayor January 2012
- Tyler, Texas Barbara Bas, Mayor January 2012
- Atlanta, Georgia C.T. Martin, Council Member January 2
- "Noble Drew Ali Day" Washington, D.C. Mayor, September 2011
- "Noble Drew Ali Day" Philadelphia, Pennsylvania John Street, Mayor January 2001
- Philadelphia, Pennsylvania David Cohen, Pres. City Council September 1991
- Philadelphia, Pennsylvania Senate Resolution #75 April 1933, "Use of 'names' - Beys and Els"
- Sundry Free Moors State Records of South Carolina January 1790; South Carolina Journal of the House of Representatives
- H.R. 1203

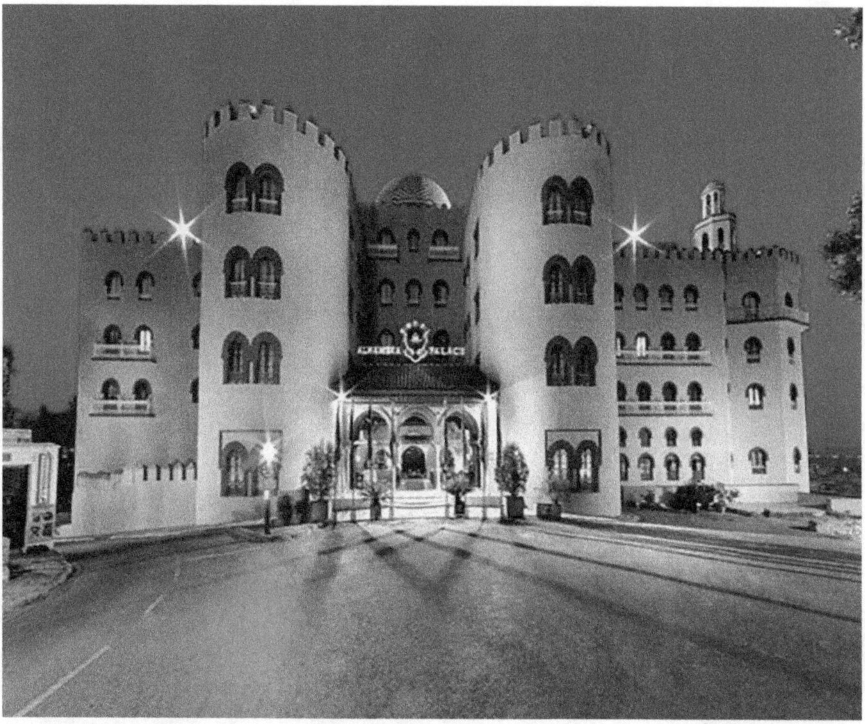

Alhambra Palace Restaurant Chicago, Illinois

Khalifa Territory

MARISCOS FABULOSOS
773-252-3840
DELIVERY
OPEN

Opa Locka, Florida

Miami Heat Moroccan Party

Noble Drew Ali Plaza Brownsville, New York

"The Moors were enslaved by reducing their mentality to that of Negroes, blacks, and colored people. As a man thinketh, so is he. Moors you sleep too much. Wake up and see the seven bridges crossing in the sky. Can you see you are a people?" EL Sharif Abdul Ali (A.K.A Noble Drew Ali)

"Only by fixing a perpetual brand [can]... a distinction be made between [free-negroes] offspring and the descendants of an Englishman."-William Gooch, 1723

Everybody Knows what's up!

Everybody Knows What's Up!

St. Benedict the Moor Church (Pittsburgh)

Cozumel, Mexico

BROTHERS & SISTER!!
BETTER PAY ATTENTION!!

Yes my Mexican brethren you too are a Moor.. Moreno. Moro.

Salvation *Allah* *Unity*

The Moorish Science Temple of America

The Divine Constitution and By-Laws

Act 1: The Grand Sheik and the chairman of the Moorish Science Temple of America is in power to make law and enforce laws with the assistance of the Prophet and the Grand Body of the Moorish Science Temple of America. The Assistant Grand Sheik is to assist the Grand Sheik in all affairs if he lives according to Love, Truth, Peace, Freedom, and Justice, and it is known before the members of the Moorish Science Temple of America.

Act 2: All meetings are to be opened and closed promptly according to the circle seven and Love, Truth, Peace, Freedom, and Justice. Friday is our Holy Day of rest, because on a Friday the first man was formed in flesh and on a Friday the first man departed out of flesh and ascended unto his father God Allah, for that cause Friday is the Holy Day for all Moslems all over the world.

Act 3: Love, Truth, Peace, Freedom, and Justice must be proclaimed and practiced by all members of the Moorish Science Temple of America. No member is to put in danger or accuse falsely his brother or sister on any occasion at all that may harm his brother or sister, because Allah is Love.

Act 4: All members must preserve these Holy and Divine laws, and all members must obey the laws of the government, because by being a Moorish American, you are a part and parcel of the government, and must live the life accordingly.

Act 5: This organization of the Moorish Science Temple of America is not to cause any confusion or to overthrow the laws and constitution of the said government but to obey hereby.

Noble Drew Ali

Noble Drew Ali
Founder

Act 6: With us all members must proclaim their nationality and we are teaching our people their nationality and their divine creed that they may know that they are a part and a parcel of this said government, and know that they are not Negroes, Colored Folks, Black People, or Ethiopians, because these names were given to slaves by slave holders in 1779 and lasted until 1865 during the time of slavery, but this is a new era of time now, and all men now must proclaim their free national name to be recognized by the government in which they live and the nations of the earth, this is the reason why Allah the Great God of the universe ordained Noble Drew Ali, the Prophet to redeem his people from their sinful ways. The Moorish Americans are the descendants of the ancient Moabites whom inhabited the North Western and South Western shores of Africa.

Act 7: All members must promptly attend their meetings and become a part and a parcel of all uplifting acts of the Moorish Science Temple of America. Members must pay their dues and keep in line with all necessities of the Moorish Science Temple of America, then you are entitled to the name of "Faithful." Husband, you must support your wife and children; wife, you must obey your husband and take care of your children and look after the duties of your household. Sons and daughters must obey father and mother and be industrious and become part of the uplifting of humanity. All Moorish Americans must keep their hearts and minds pure with love, and their bodies clean with water. This Divine Covenant is from your Holy Prophet Noble Drew Ali, through the guidance of his Father God Allah.

MOORISH AMERICAN PRAYER

Allah The Father of the universe, the Father of Love, Truth, Peace, Freedom, and Justice. Allah is my protector, my guide, and my salvation by night and by day, through his Holy Prophet Drew Ali. "Amen."

THE MOORISH SCIENCE TEMPLE OF AMERICA

Home Office: 37th & Federal St. Chicago, IL, U.S.A.

THE NEGRO LAW of SOUTH CAROLINA, 1848 CHAPTER I.

The Status of the Negro, his Rights and Disabilities.

Section 1. The Act of 1740, sec. **I, declares all negroes and Indians, (free Indians in amity with this Government, negroes, mulattoes and mestizoes, who now are free, excepted) to be slaves: —the offspring to follow the condition of the mother: and that such slaves are chattels personal.**

Sec. 4. The term negro is confined to slave Africans, (the ancient Berbers) and their descendants. It does not embrace the free in habitants of Africa, such as the Egyptians, Moors, or the negro Asiatics, such as the Lascars.

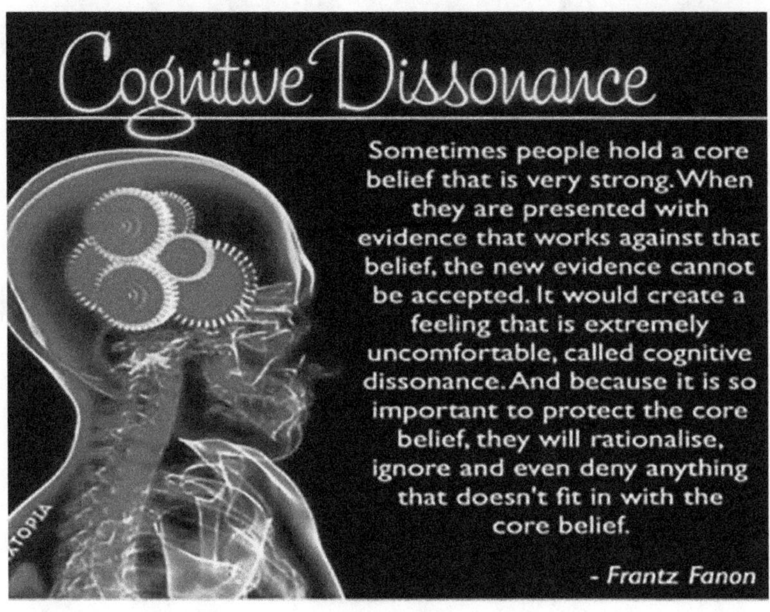

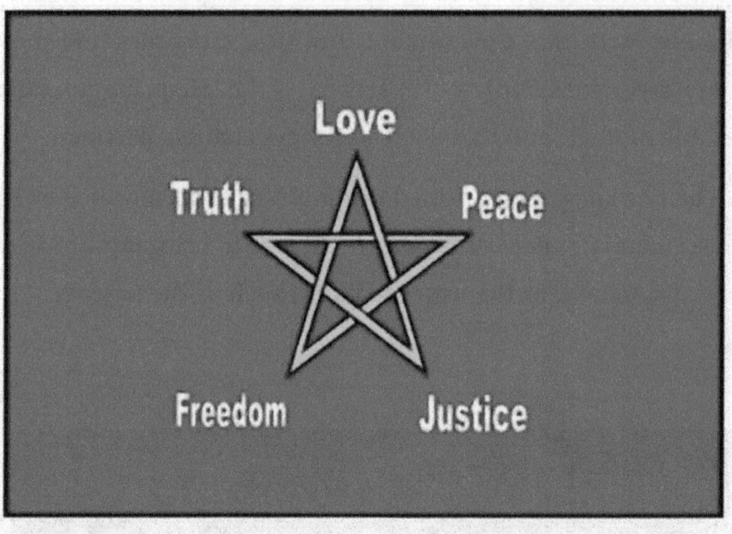

"Any group of people must answer up to the constitutional standards of law by name and principles, because to be a citizen of any government you must claim your national descent name, because they place their trust upon issue and names formed by their forefathers."

--Noble Drew Ali

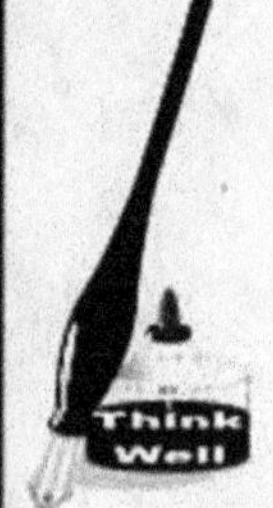

C. Moorish Geography: Moroccan Empyreal Culture

I. Landmass

"The name of a people must connect them instantaneously to land, history, and culture."-Dr. John Henrik Clarke

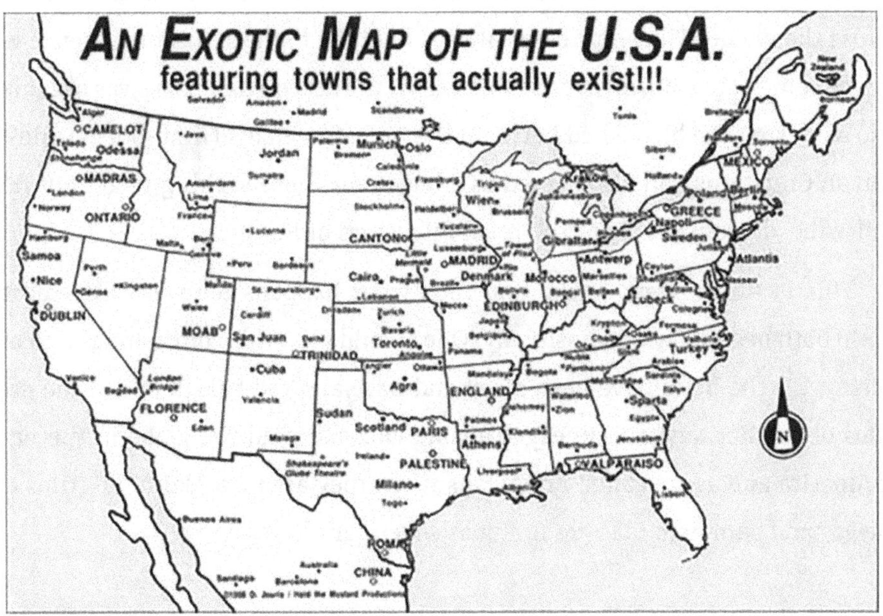

This continent upon which we stand has, such as the primitive peoples who inhabit the many territories, have and had many names. Amexem; Maghrib Al Aqsa meaning, "the most extreme west"; Turtle Island; Ameru; Morocco; Th Garden of Eden; The promised Land; Th Holy Lands, Yirushalayim, Yisrael, etc.

The word America, if you removed all the vowels, you'd be left with "Mrcn", an abbreviation for Moroccan, Murican, Maurican, Morican, Marican, and Merican.

As was stated earlier in this manuscript the whole world was fitted together as pieces of puzzle before the great cataclysms that eventually split the world into sections whereby nations were continued.

Some of the ancient names for this uniform landmass were Mu (mother's unity), El Khem Muria, Mauretania, Atlantis, Kamat, and Atlantis. The modern term this ancient landmass came to be known as was Pangaea which was first proposed in 1912 by German meteorologist Alfred Wegener. The name is derived from the Greek pangaia, meaning "all the earth."

Now it must be innerstood that there were/are two types of jurisdiction when it comes to Morocco: The Empire (Americas) and the Kingdom (Africa/ Kush) which we used as a beachhead to barter and trade with other nations across the divide. The empire has always held the highest authority hence why people come here from all over as this was/is the beacon light that was organized a so as to stop the bloodshed between the Mohammedans (first-borns) and the Roman Christians and also served as a haven for those seeking to get out from under the draconian rule of the royal impostors of Europe.

This is North-West Afrika and thus what happens here has infected the world both negatively and positively. One should view this continent as a cosmic mirror. We the heirs have been sleep and have allowed beasts to soil the great titles of our heritage and lineage causing chaos around the globe in the name of America and as so-called Americans when they are in actuality pilgrims and thieves and vampires masquerading as sovereigns.

PANGEA

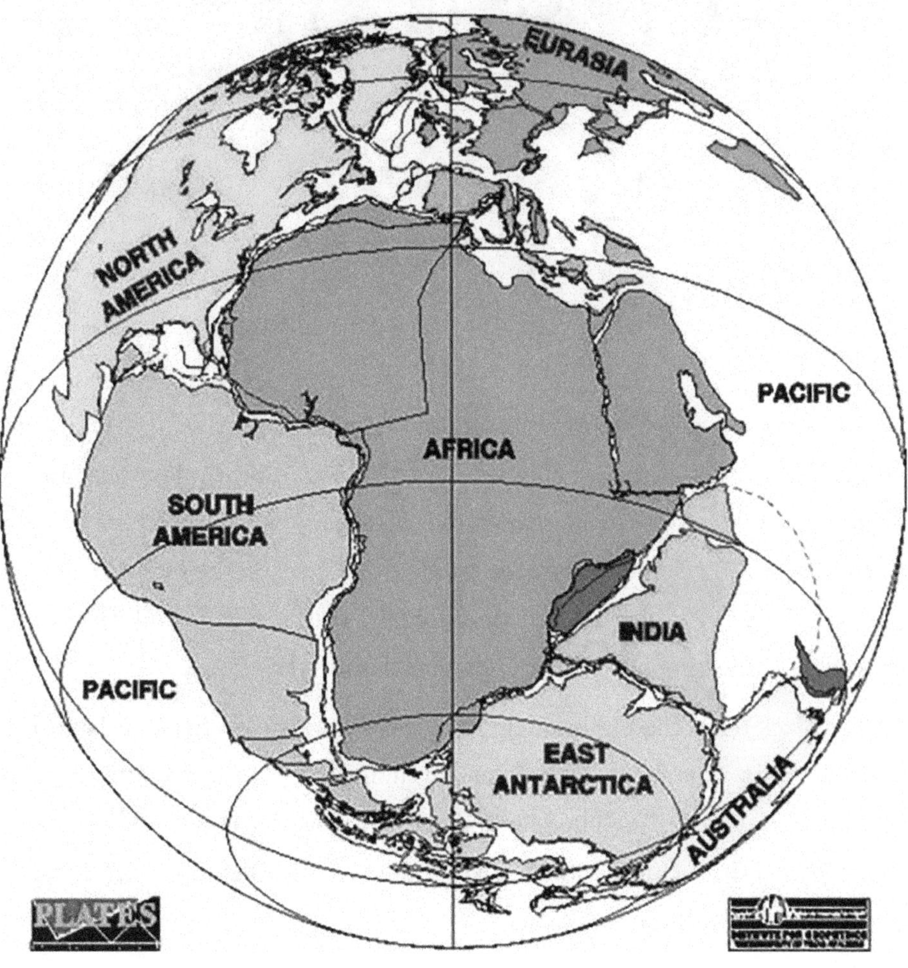
EURASIA
NORTH AMERICA
PACIFIC
AFRICA
SOUTH AMERICA
INDIA
PACIFIC
EAST ANTARCTICA
AUSTRALIA
PLATES

II. Costumes

(RVBeyPublications.com)

Receiving a degree regarding "The Fez": The fez is the ancient and modern national headdress of the Moabites/Moors. The Fez is a brimless headdress – most commonly produced in scarlet red usually of felt with an ebony/black tassel. The red Fez is matched by the red field displayed in the Moorish National Standard [flag]. The fez is also produced in black, white, and other color variations- indicating other meanings, social order, positions, etc.

The black fez is the highest degree. It is worn by the mufti (Moorish United Front towards Islam) or Mohammedan judge- enforcement and security. The one who wears it symbolizes that he/she knows the law in full, and is able to defend it, including knowledge of martial arts (defense physically and spiritually), likened to a black belt.

The Fez is worn as a symbol of the womb. The top of it has a nipple shape that symbolizes the navel. The strands of the tassel are 360 degrees, as in 360 degrees of knowledge. The tassel is not tied down as it is in the secret societies. Properly, the free-flowing tassel indicative of one who is born of the womb, endowed with and aspiring to and beyond 360 degrees of knowledge. They navigate upon the earth and their potential is not limited, not pinned down, or kept secret; however, it is sacred. The 4 sets of air holes are equal to the number of wombman- 9, and add to 13, the number of times a woman cycles in a year, which is harmonious with the moon.

It (fez) is geometrically formed to represent the eternal zodiac. The body at the fez symbolizes the womb of the cosmos and the womb of woman- mother. The 1-inch final which extends out of the center of the fez is the number one and the 9th letter in the Phonetic Moorish Alphabet- I. This also symbolizes the navel (eye).

Last King Of Hawaii Kalākaua

The cord extending from the I (eye) symbolizes the universal umbilical cord of universal life and represents oneness of all life. It also represents the tie to the source of humanity- Zudiacus- the first woman.

The circular (round) ball of the tassel represents the mundane circle of earth. The cord wrapped about the tassel strands, hold the form of the circle and represent the unity of life through the zodiac constitution of humanity. It also represents the cyclical and reciprocal nature of life; the highest law and authority of civilization. The zodiac crown of light is the national headdress of the masters of the cosmos science, 3rd, 33rd, and 360-degree Moorish Master masons and Eastern Stars. This is the part of the hidden truth which has been buried in the dark corner of the North Gate.

The fez is also called a tiara, corona Del sol (crown of the sun), a tarbush and other names which describe its royal status.

Tarbush is derived from the Persian word sarpus, sar-head + pus- cover. It is a long-standing Moorish tradition for one to be covered, particularly the head (crown). In doing research you'll find that the ancestors always, for the most part, kept themselves covered from head to toe especially the Queens as was mandated by divine Law (see 1Corinthians 11:5-6; Surah 24:31; Eph. 6:17; Lev. 21:10; Ex. 20:16; Isaiah 59:17) (See Tignon laws).

Moors wore/wear turbans, kufis, and beautiful head wraps made of fine linen which we also dawned as standard overall attire. We believed in the covering of the crown for 2 distinct reasons: we believed in cleanliness and the covering of our hair kept from contamination especially as newer people who were not so well versed in the art of cleanliness began to cohabitate with us. The other reason being that we knew well the evil and mischievous spirits that roam the earth and that can possess the temple of man by way of the 7 holes of Allah (eyes, nostrils, ears, and mouth) and the antennae (hair), our major energy centers. By covering the crown, we protect our wisdom and knowledge (our mental energies), keeping a firm connection with Th Higher Vibrational frequencies of the cosmos thus strengthening and defending our 360s aiding in our aura enhancement and refinement. (See Judges 16:19)

One of the most important things we must realize about our hair is that it is our antennae. We literally "tune out" when we remove, artificially alter, or just flat out don't take care of our hair. Forced conditions were created during our "enslavement" whereas we were socially engineered to hate the beauty of our natural hair thus came the conking and straightening which severed our connection with the ethers. This is why in modern times they encourage the cutting of our hair because those in power know how vital it is to our maturation. A beard for a man symbolizes dignity, sovereignty, virility, and wisdom; sign of a king. The cutting of our hair is forbidden by divine law. (Leviticus 21:5) There is an innate desire for this generation to wear their hair naturally which will only aid in their advancement as the outpouring of melanin from the heavens continue to shower the earth with Th frequency/vibrations of the Infinite/Akashic records unlocking the codes lying dormant within the dna of man.

Regarding "White Fez": It has already been established that the fez represents the womb. Th 4 sets of breather holes spell out numerically the sacred number of 13 which is the combining of the two sacred numbers/ vibrations 9 + 4. The white of the fez represents the moon and the gold tassel the sun; white symbolizing purity which is the energy of the womb and the sun symbolizing light (knowledge) and beauty. The Moabite Nation flag, the Matriarch, is white with a gold crescent and star. The crescent (mother) cradles the child (star). More specifically the mother and son, as she can easily duplicate herself, but to transform a female egg into a male specimen is the miracle, thus she has created the "miracle son"; the prodigal son from her womb.

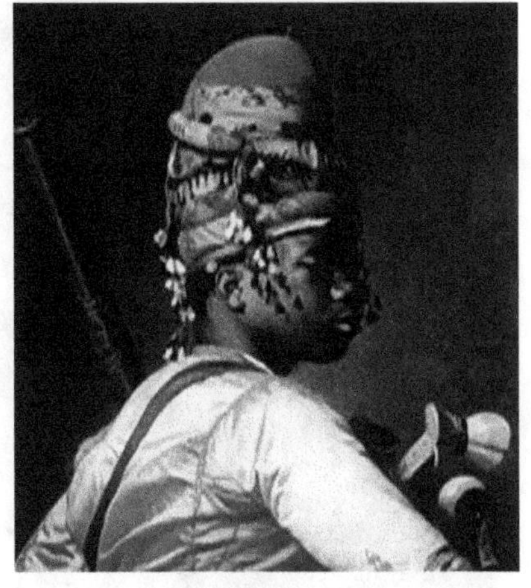

The Moorish Nation flag is the flag of her sons. It is red with a five-pointed green star (Venus- the Mother) in the center . When she became unconscious, the flag of her sons was flown. It represents the great blood shed ensued upon the land which was a result both of war and the broken chastity of Th womb resulting in the forming of the different nations, many divisions and tongues, false prophets, mass destruction and the like. The scepter of power was passed to her sons while she lay unconscious. It is not the sons' fault, as it was she who caused the great destruction, and it will be she who repairs it. Her awakening is or will be "Th Great Wrath of Allah."

HOLY QURAN

The 5-pointed green star centered red flag is the fag of the people, not to be confused with the continental flag, which is the flag of the continents and has the pine tree or the evergreen  , representing everlasting life, as man is mind and there never was a time when man was not- thus everlasting life. The stars and stripes banner commonly and erroneously referred to as the American flag is not but rather is a banner of amity and commerce which symbolizes the peace between Christians and Moslems and the right to do commerce with one another.

All men do the bidding of the woman. This is a fact and an innate characteristic of the male specie. It is our duty, and an honest man will admit that truth and if he doesn't, in all reality he is affected by her from the time he is born and while he is in the womb being made. If he is arrogant, possessive and insecure, she taught him to be that way. Much of these things were learned in the first university/classroom of physical existence- Th womb. Thus, he did not stand a chance to be otherwise. Submitting to the will of Allah is done in the womb during the time of biological manifestation. Allah is all law manifested in the flesh as Arm-Leg-Leg-Arm-Head. Everyone is a Moslem, as a Moslem is a fetus, muscles, bones and tissues, or Muslim (same) muscles and limbs. This is why they (Europeans) wear fezzes with Moslem, Islam, El Bey, and Morocco, amongst other ancient writings upon them. This is their way of paying homage albeit secretly to their mothers and fathers for they truly have no ancient history and owe all their supposed power and success to Th Moors.

Many wear Th womb as a royal crown except for the Moorish woman, and she is the original man (being), primitive and Th Creators finest creation, mother of all civilization. It is time for her to awake so that the "Great Meeting" can take place. For those Seastars who are in the secret societies, the Eastern Stars, etc., the secret is about you because it is you. You are aware of Esther (Easter, Ishtar, Isis, Astarte, and Venus). An indication and proof that that the universal language is cosmology. This is why you are called Eastern Star (Venus is the Eastern Star). To my Seastars who are not in the secret societies, there is no need for you to be because you are innately "A Star from the East"- Venus is the cosmic mother, which rules Libra with her scales (Maat) and preserves the "balance" of nature with her scales of justice and a sword of truth and retribution. It is time my mothers, my queens, my seastars to rise from ignorance and see you for who you are so that you may fulfill your obligation and responsibility to humanity.

Duse Mohamed Ali

If you, woman, do not plan (plant) to bring any more royal crowns here, please teach your daughters, who are the direct descendants of the founders and builders of civilization. Teach them ancient culture, mathematics, cosmology, cosmogony, naturopathy, agriculture, philosophy and the science of the womb, as everyone else is drawing wealth and knowledge from it and wearing it symbolically atop their heads as their royal crown except for Th first of all nations; Th Asiatic Female.

Fez is also the name of the old Moorish capitollium and city which, is located in Northwest Morocco (Kushite territory/Africa). Morocco, Moroccan and Moors are one in the same pedigree and peoples. Remember, American is a dialectical corruption of the name Al Moroccan, which means descendant or descendants of Moroccan. The lack of consciousness on the part of any so-called negro/black freemason, concerning the ancient history of the Americas, has stagnated and retarded their ability to see through the veil of their own "hoodwinking."

Is fez a city in Europe? Is the fez the national headdress of the Europeans or is it the national headdress of the Moors? Who is wearing the fez only by ritual, and who should be wearing the fez by right of natural dress and culture? Who is who in the great controversy of who is worthy to wear the fez and who is not? Who is honoring their ancient mothers and fathers, and who is not? Who is denying connection to Ruth Th Moabitess and who is not, by way of recognizing or not the origins of the great philosophies and wisdom found in the halls of learning called masonry?

If you see a fez with pinned down tassels, writings, reverse symbols, etc., these are cues that you are in the midst of lodge member, essentially a traitor of The Moorish nation especially if they be Asiatic; Klansmen and/or knights of Rome they are. The main signs of a freemasonic converso are fez with the symbol of the sword over the head of the Moabitess and the sword over the top of the 5-point star. The former indicates subjugation of the Moabite woman and the latter represents the subjugation of her children as 5 is the number of humanity which all spawned from Th Great Moabite Moorish woman. You may also see the crescent moon (mother), and the star (her posterity generationally; child) turned downward, or upside down. The correct position is crescent moon to the left and star underneath it at the tip as if hanging as fruit from the womb of mother, which is the tree of life from whence we come.

Many have been mistaken to think that the Europeans who wear the fez in secret are the originators of the fez. They (Europeans) are aware of the meaning and purpose of the fez, as it is a crown worn by those of the Moorish Nation, which represents Th Matriarch. The Europeans have usurped and stolen the crown as well as the birthrights, and they have utilized the science and high culture embodied and represented in the wearing of the fez, which is the science of the universe, the workings of nature and natural order. This is one of the reasons Th Prophet Noble Ali said that they live off of our virtues hence why some may describe them as "vampires" who feed and live off the royal blood of the original heirs and who cannot come out into the light of the sun, or the light of truth.

Our mis-education has lead us into mis-givings and into an age of darkness (ignorance), thus we suffer from a lack of knowledge and are easily led astray resulting in, among other things, arguments about this and that as far as the origin of many things, including the fez.

Another misconception that comes from the mouths of many is that the fez belongs to the Turks, without knowing that the original Turks are Moors of the Ottoman Empire. The Ottoman Empire being active into the world wars, which coincides with the 40's wherein cointelpro changed Moors of Th Moorish Science Temple, claiming they were in co-hoots with Japan against the UNITED STATES (an abstract). Others think the fez was originated and belongs to the pale Arabs of today, without knowing that original Arabs are Moors, and that some sold each other into slavery even while wearing turbans and fezzes, as they still do till this day. This is why TH Prophet Noble Ali said: "Be careful Moors, some of your own will put you back in slavery", because Th spirit is eternal whether that of a converso (traitor) or Nobleman.

The freemasons both European and Asiatic wear the fez behind closed doors, in secret societies wherein they perform rituals, take oaths to demi-gods and work hard to keep the light of truth regarding Th North Gate (North-West Amexem/Africa/Kush) closed to the masses, even unto the mothers and fathers of civilization, who in fact taught them (Albion/Europeans) and brought them out of the dark ages during the European renaissance. They taught a chosen few through Masonic orders, the science of the universe, the sacred lessons of life and nature; how it correlates with physical and the utilization of such energies, in an effort to civilize them and bring them into cultured society. They were infiltrated and splintered thus clandestine orders came about with their sole purpose being to dumb down the masses with science while simultaneously keeping the true knowledge to themselves.

Don't ever be fooled into thinking that those in power don't know your lineage upon which they owe an obligation to, because of their feigned ignorance and abuse of power i.e. reconstruction and the tampering and altering of her-story which became his-story. They are fully aware, albeit of different degrees, of Morocco, they are aware of Islam (Th science) and know the true meaning of Moslem, and they are aware of Th 5 noble titles: El, Bey, Dey, Al and Ali. These titles were transferred and renamed as the 5 civilized tribes of acceptance during the so-called "Indian" agreements. However, many are aware that this is not India. Th people were/are aboriginal and primitive to not only this continent/ landmass but Th whole planet as well.

III. Language

In ancient times passed Moors spoke at minimum 5 different languages or dialects as we were travelers and merchants so inter tribal communication was vitally important. Moors brought the gift of language and English itself is truly a combination of all languages stemming from the ancient roots of Sanskrit, Ibri (Hebrew), etc., so even today we are multilingual though we are unaware of that fact plus this is why when asked most of the Moors from around the world will say that English is the hardest or one of the most difficult to learn due to the aforementioned reason and all the grammatical technicalities that come along with it.

We used different languages for different functions in civilization, for example Ibri (Hebrew) we used to invoke the metaphysical/spiritual essence of nature and the ancestral spirits, Arabic was more so used for the science of mathematics i.e. architecture; angles and such, and Latin we used to codify jurisprudence. Other dialects such as French and Italian we used as romance or courtship tongues hence why both are considered languages of love and in both languages amor means love.

In all actuality, these dialects were just that as opposed to what later became brands signifying culture to classify different sects of Moors. For example, Ibri means "crossing; those who came from the other side" which describes the migration of Moors from the east to west which we did regularly before the great divide/separation of the lands between father and son, "Ham and Kush". It is not in itself an identity or an actual belief system rather it was something we did whereas those who crossed the river before it became an ocean were called Ibri which in modern times was anglicized into Hebrew but there is no h in that original dialectical lexicon. Another example, Arab can be translated into "wanderers of the desert" which describes the nomads of the region, the Bedouins, and again points to a doing not an actual classification which was later used to divide the peoples of the earth. In studying both dialects you'll find that a lot of the words intertwine this being because they are sister tongues and are both rooted in the ancient science of agriculture and mathematics.

Keep in mind that no country conquers/civilizes another and then adopts their cultures and customs. Therefore, the notion that we were named and given any language by the very same people (Albions) that we (Moors) civilized and refined, who were living in barns and were illiterate by the way, is a total fabrication and disregard for the greatest science known to man: common sense.

There has been a systemic dumbing down of the masses especially the Asiatics of the North-Western Hemisphere because as we go so goes the world though the planet as whole has and is continuing to shift its consciousness and vibration.

I'll end this chapter with two quotes:

George Washington, 9th president of the U.S.A:

"If we would agree to take the fezzes and turbans off the Moors' heads and remove the sandals from their feet and enforce severe punishments, and to also swear a death oath between ourselves to religiously and faithfully not allow anyone to teach the Moorish children who their forefathers were, and only allow the Moorish children to be taught that they were truly negroes, black people, and colored folks, 200 years from today the Moorish people would not know their nationality nor the national name of their forefathers. They would not know from which land or ancestors that they are descended from."

Lord Macaulay's address to the British Parliament on 2 February,1835:

"I have traveled across the length and breadth of India and I have not seen one person who is a beggar, who is a thief. Such wealth I have seen in this country, such high moral values, people of such caliber, that I do not think we would ever conquer this country, unless we break the very backbone of this

*nation, which is her spiritual and cultural heritage, and, therefore, I propose that we replace her old and ancient education system, her culture, **for if the Indians think that all that is foreign and English is good and greater than their own, they will lose their self-esteem, their native self-culture and they will become what we want them, a truly dominated nation."***

D. Repairing a Nation

I. Reparation

A repairing or keeping in repair; repairs; the act of making amends, offering expiration, or giving satisfaction for a wrong or injury; something done or given as amends or satisfaction; the payment of damages: indemnification; specifically, compensation in money or materials payable to a defeated nation for damages to or expenditures sustained by another nation as a result of hostilities with the defeated nation.

- USA: 2001: 56 million to Seminoles of Oklahoma
- USA: 1990: 1.2 billion or $120,000 each to Japanese American citizens
- Austria: 1990: 25 million to holocaust survivors; Jewish claims on Austria
- Canada: 1988: 250,000 square miles of land to "Indians" and Eskimos
- Canada: 1988: 230 million to Japanese Canadian citizens
- USA: 1986: 32 million to Ottawa of Michigan
- USA: 1985: 31 million to Chippewa of Wisconsin
- USA: 1985: 12.3 million to Seminoles of Florida
- USA: 1985: 105 million to Sioux of South Dakota
- USA: 1980: 81 million to Klamath of Oregon
- USA: 1971: 1 billion and 44 acres of land to Alaska native settlement
- German: 1952: 822 million to holocaust survivors; German Jewish settlement
- Iraq: 2002: apology and an unspecified amount of finance

As you can see despite what people preach the beast doesn't do what it wants it does what the people allows and even then, if those people stand up it must pay dues for such is Th Law of dynamic exchange. If you read closely, you'll notice that all these people that received reparations have one thing in common; a nationality. They suffered the same atrocities as we Asiatics of Northwest Amexem have yet they had remedy because they honor their mothers and fathers (Ancestors). We haven't got any because we continue to put beliefs in the place of nationality. Muslim, Buddhist, Hebrew Israelites, etc., are all faith/belief systems not nationalities therefore to identify yourself as such only places you outside the human family and makes you incompetent. Believe what you want in your own home and in the privacy of your conscience but when navigating the waters of the physical practicality/facts are the tools that must be applied along with the metaphysical, but you cannot have one without the other as they are reflections of each other so to exclude one for the other is foolish and juvenile.

Cosmic Divine Order (stages of birthright and inheritance)

5. Domestic
6. International
7. Intergalactic
8. Intercosmic
9. Omnicosmic

3 levels of Ascension

- Initiation-attained knowledge of S.E.L.F.(Sacred Eternal Life Force; You).
- Illumination-attained wisdom of the unity of Man and The Creator.
- Perfection-attainment of supreme consciousness (confidence/competence/courage) which manifest the will to live purposefully, guided by principles and integrity.

DEMANDING OURS

The idea inculcated in the purposes of the Moorish Science Temple of America is to have everything that belongs to us as a nation that has become a part of another nation, just the same as all other European groups are demanding.

We must have the history of our fore-fathers taught to our children. We have ceased to calculate our history from the landing of the "First Twenty" or the close of the Civil War. While all records of the tombs in the old world are proclaiming our glory to the nations, we have come now demanding that we be given credit for the great work done in the past by our ancestors. We are not asking others to give these records to the world for us but we demand that such records be broadcasted to the four winds by us and for us.

A pride that goes with the knowledge of great deeds will serve to cause our posterity to take heart and look into the vast future with a hope eternal. Such can never be done except they be taught who they are and where they are from. Yes, we are demanding that these things be done and we know that it will require some time before we have created that consciousness in others of our group to assert themselves likewise but that day is coming when such will be the case.

Moorish Guide Newspaper

NEGRO
BLACK
AFRO AMERICAN
AFRICAN AMERICAN
Moor
@PrincessOhayaIsrael

CHAPTER 2: THE ZODIAC

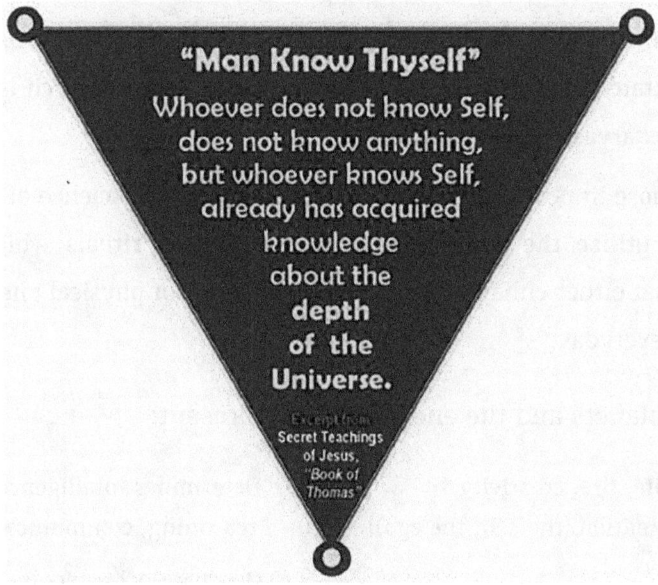

"Man Know Thyself"
Whoever does not know Self,
does not know anything,
but whoever knows Self,
already has acquired
knowledge
about the
depth
of the
Universe.
Secret Teachings
of Jesus,
"Book of
Thomas"

A. Cosmic Energies

I. Ancient and modern significance

Our ancestors ran the whole world by the science of geometry and by the science of astrology and astronomy which they used to plot the stars, in which they told time, and identified the beginning and ending of the seasons i.e. predicting the cycles of rhythm and vibration/frequency which is Th mother of change.

The word zodiac is derived from Old French zodiaque, < Latin zodiacus "zodiac" < Greek zodiakos (kyklos) "zodiac (circle)", literally "circle of little animals", from zodian, diminutive of zion- "animal." The word horoscope is < Middle French horoscope, learned borrowing from Latin horoscopes < Greek horoscpous < hora-time + skopos-watcher < scopein- watch.

The zodiac is, in its simplest form, a compass used to plot and calculate the angels/angles of the heavenly constellations whereas different energies are channeled unto the earth plane that correlates with the biological make-up of man as we are reflections of the galaxy and the zodiacal wheel represents the anatomy of the human body both inward and outward.

This ancient technology is used to plot events as well as its basic yet most important function which is that of agriculture whereas the seasons or ethereal energies dictate the time to plant and the time to harvest which is vital, for a nation that starves is no nation at all.

All of those in power use advisers well versed in the science of astrological charts and utilize the energies of the universe via rituals which serve as mediums that either enhance or diminish the power of physical phenomena we experience everyday.

II. The planets and the energies they represent:

1. Sun: life, fire, creativity (illumination, the self, the ego); Sunday

- Giver of life, vitality and individuality, appearance. Rules human spirit.
- Occupation: government employments.

2. Moon: Soul (1st quarter: New Moon: inspiration and beginnings; 2nd quarter: Waxing Moon: growth, development; 3rd quarter: Full Moon: maturity, completion; 4th quarter: Waning Moon: reflections, planning); Monday

- Determines your emotional nature, impregnations. Rules your desires and instincts.
- Occupation: Common Employments.

3. Mercury: intellect, intuition (speed, communications); Wednesday

- Determines intelligence, reasoning, communication
- Occupation: schools, intellectual affairs and publishing.

4. Venus: love nature of the all (attraction, spiritual treasure, fertility); Friday

- Determines your Love nature, pleasures, coalitions and physical expression.
- Occupation: entertainment, art, social functions.

5. Mars: outward actions based on passions (energy, aggression, self-defense, action); Tuesday

- Determines your assertiveness, actions, and dynamic outward energy.
- Occupation: manufacturing, building, munitions.

6. Jupiter: receiving of your gifts, happiness (luck, growth, expansion, enthusiasm); Thursday

- Determines your idealism, bestower of your gifts, luck and expansion.
- Occupation: religious, legal, financial affairs.

7. Saturn: discipline, sharpen tools (limits, boundaries, tradition); Saturday

- Rules your discipline and retribution, limitations and obstructions.
- Occupation: mining, farming, cement work.

8. Uranus: impulse of change (independence, rebellion, freedom)

- Rules change, unpredictability, originality, altruism
- Occupation: railroads, aerial, electric industries.

9. Neptune: imagination and aspiration (glamour, illusions, sensitivity)

- Rules your inspiration, new ideas, divinity
- Occupation: oil and fishing industries.

10. Pluto: transformation (death, regeneration, unavoidable change)

- Transformation, spirituality, secrets, illusions, underworld, subconscious, inward energy and activity.
- Occupation: waste recycling and research work.

Planets have their home location where they rule and are most comfortable. They influence our physical, emotional, mental and intuitional selves and rule certain inclinations of occupations. They travel (transit) through other houses bringing their energies, sensitivities, influences, spectrums and essences, individually and collectively molding natal charts. Just as people who visit your house bring their energies. The signs have their home location as well, we might want to think of them as the guard of their house, but they don't stay home very long. They transit through other houses channeling or filtering energies of the house with their traits and characteristics. If there are other planets in that house, they usually have a stronger ruling energy. Their affects depends on their nature. This is why planetary aspects are important in a chart. They can place enhancements to what may otherwise be a detriment, or a detriment to what may otherwise be enhanced.

The planets travel on a separate course at their pace, and the signs on a separate course at their pace, all of them are visiting the houses in the neighborhood. The transit of the signs are based on 300 (days). Most planets, however, stay in a sign longer than assign stays in a house. Uranus, Neptune and Pluto stay for 7, 13, 20years, respectfully, affecting generations of natal charts. Jupiter and Saturn are next in line for long visits, but none as short as the Moon. She (the Moon) moves every 2 ½ days.

Planet	Time it takes to transit all 12 signs	Stays in place for:
Moon	27 days, 7 hours and 43 minutes	2 ½ days
Sun	1 year	30 days
Mercury	1 year	30 days
Venus	1 year	30 days
Mars	22 months	55 days
Jupiter	12 years	1 year
Saturn	29 ½ years	2.4 years
Uranus	84 years	7 years
Neptune	165 years	13.75 years
Pluto	248 years	20.6 years

Planets—Malefic, Benefic and Neutral:

It is important to note that all signs and all planets are "good". No planet is evil in nature. It is our reaction to their action that may be judged by us, as good or bad. This depends on what stage we are in, in our lives. For every action there is an opposite and equal reaction. Negative and positive exist at the same time. It is a matter of what side of the "pole" you are on. "Do you see the glass as half full or half empty?" When something 'bad' happens in our lives we must grasp that it is meant to happen and is designed as a lesson for us in some way. There is a silver lining behind each cloud. I have always said if we cannot count our fortune/providence today, we will receive none tomorrow. When planets lay something "heavy" on you, it is yours to deal with and there is nothing that can stop the process. However, they will come around and reward you as soon as you come around.

A neutral planet's influence (Mercury, Neptune, Pluto) is good or stable when well aspected with other planets, but malefic when adversely aspected. A malefic planet describes the inherit nature of the planet force, i.e. Mars has dynamic outward energy, Saturn is obstructive by nature as it obstructs as needed for discipline and Uranus has an unwillingness to bend or bow down, it's electrifying impulses will tear down from within. Jupiter is considered benefic as its nature is to bestow deserving gifts and bring growth and expansion. Venus is also benefic as it is harmonious by nature. The Sun and Moon are also considered benefic.

Terms used when a planet has poor aspects are malefic, adverse, bad, unfavorable, detrimented, debilitated, opposed, afflicted. Terms used when a planet has good aspects are benefic, favorable, harmonious, exalted, dignified.

Planets—Dignified/Debilitated:

Each planet has a location in respect to another planet or sign, that is home (extremely comfortable), a location that exalts them (enjoys their company), a location that places them in detriment (doesn't like them much) and a location that causes a complete fall of its influences or rays (total disharmony). Another planet or signs' rays or energy may deflect or weaken, reflect or strengthen a planet depending on it's relationship or proximity. In short they may "get in the way".

In regard to their logistics, if a planets' proximity to another planet causes a square it is an all-out fight for who will be the ultimate influence. No matter who wins out for the day or the moment, the conflict inherently exist, causing a constant struggle. Again, these outcome of the effects depend on what house the planet(s) are in, and what sign(s) are in the house. For example, Aries, ruled by dynamic Mars, loves a good fight and will probably instigate disharmony, but actually he is so dynamic that he steps up the energies that are around.

You also must consider who rules the house. If the ruler of the house is in harmony with one of the planets that are in conflict, naturally it will strengthen or exalt them. It's like people taking sides or making favor, yet the conflict is constant.

When reading your chart, you must take into consideration the areas of your life in which you will have a constant struggle. However, unlike most people, the planets work with precise exacting energies that co- exist and figure it all out in the end, based on mathematical and geometric relationships. Planets are also known to weaken when they are in retrograde. During retrogrades the rays of the planet are somewhat withdrawn or weakened. Planets are usually in retrograde for a limited amount of days at different times in their course of a transit.

If surrounding planets are in good angle to each other, then they can create very harmonious influences in the houses they are in and bring a dignified influence to the forefront.

When a planet is in a house that is neither its home, exalted, detriment or fall it follows the type of the house it is in:

- If transiting an Angular house, the planet is equal to being at home or exalted.
- If transiting a Succedent house, the planet is equal to being at detriment.
- If transiting a Cadent house, the planet is equal to being in fall or total debilitation.

Summation of Planets

1. **Sun:**

- Type-Benefic
- Home (strongest)-Leo
- Detriment (weakened)-Aquarius
- Exalted (strengthened)-190 Aries
- Fall (weakest)-190 Libra

- Dignified/Exalted: Ambitious, honorable, lofty, dignified, loyal, faithful, distinguished, gallant.
- Detriment/ Debilitated: disdainful, proud, domineering, despotic, arrogant, authoritative, haughty.

2. Moon:

- Type-Benefic
- Home (strongest)-Cancer
- Detriment (weakened)-Capricorn
- Exalted (strengthened)-3o Taurus
- Fall (weakest)-3o Scorpio

- Dignified/Exalted: reflective, receptive, pliable, variable, refined, domestic, public, maternal, productive, adaptable.
- Detriment/Debilitated: frivolous, passive, weak, conceited, common, nonsensical, personal, childish, changeable, luny.

3. Mercury:

- Type-Neutral
- Home (strongest)-Gemini/Virgo
- Detriment (weakened)-Sagittarius/ Pisces
- Exalted (strengthened)-15o Virgo
- Fall (weakest)-15o Pisces

- Dignified/Exalted: perceptive, observant, intellectual, accomplished, skillful, vigilant, adroit, fluent, lucid, expeditious, studious, concentrative, possessed of good mental ability and memory.
- Detriment/Debilitated: careless, indecisive, profuse, imitative, shiftless, desultory, embarrassed, nervous, rambling, unpoised, uninformed, forgetful, diffusive, shrewd, crafty, artful, untruthful.

4. Venus:

- Type-Benefic
- Home (strongest)-Taurus/Libra
- Detriment (weakened)-Scorpio/ Aries
- Exalted (strengthened)-27o Pisces
- Fall (weakest)-27o Virgo

- Dignified/Exalted: affectionate, harmonious, chaste, sympathetic, contented, cheerful, graceful, humane, compassionate, refined, companionable, artistic.
- Detriment/Debilitated: immodest, disorderly, lewd, emotional, indolent, loud, untidy, thoughtless, gaudy, extravagant, excessive love of pleasure and ease.

5. **Mars:**

- Type–Malefic
- Home (strongest)–Aries
- Detriment (weakened)–Libra
- Exalted (strengthened)–28o Capricorn
- Fall (weakest)–28o Cancer
- Dignified/Exalted: courageous, venturesome, strong, daring, aggressive, energetic, active, fearless, constructive, passionate.
- Detriment/Debilitated: bold, contemptuous, violent, irritable, coarse, audacious, forceful, impulsive, impatient, combative, destructive, sensual.

6. **Jupiter:**

- Type–Benefic
- Home (strongest)–Sagittarius
- Detriment (weakened)–Gemini
- Exalted (strengthened)–15o Cancer
- Fall (weakest)–15o Capricorn
- Dignified/Exalted: benevolent, philanthropic, generous, truthful, honest, moral, sincere, charitable, reasonable, compassionate, impartial.
- Detriment/Debilitated: prodigal, wasteful, extravagant, pretentious, improvident, dissipated, hypocritical, thriftless, unjust, dishonest, artificial, despotic.

7. **Saturn:**

- Type–Malefic
- Home (strongest)–Capricorn
- Detriment (weakened)–Cancer
- Exalted (strengthened)–21o Libra
- Fall (weakest)–21o Aries
- Dignified/Exalted: prudent, contemplative, cautious, responsible, precise, persistent, persevering, industrious, provident, patient, economical, reserved, serious, resolute, considerate, mathematical, temperate, chaste, executive.
- Detriment/Debilitated: skeptical, melancholic, deceitful, incompetent, exacting, avaricious, perverse, indifferent, laborious, impotent, repining, acquisitive, secretive, suspicious, fearful, slow, callous, lewd, pessimistic, unreliable.

8. Uranus (higher of Mercury):

- Type–Malefic
- Home (strongest)–Aquarius
- Detriment (weakened)–Leo
- Exalted (strengthened)–Aquarius/ Scorpio
- Fall (weakest)–Leo/Taurus

- Dignified/Exalted: original, inventive, ingenious, progressive, reformative, intuitive, socially talented, metaphysical, unique, unconventional, clairvoyant, magnetic, premonitory, constructive.
- Detriment/Debilitated: abnormal, fantastic, extreme, roving, eccentric, abrupt, repellant, erratic, grotesque, precipitate, premature, destructive, radical.

9. Neptune (higher of Venus):

- Type–Neutral
- Home (strongest)–Pisces
- Detriment (weakened)–Virgo
- Exalted (strengthened)–Leo
- Fall (weakest)–Aquarius

- Dignified/Exalted: psychic, inspirational, idealistic, psychometric, impressionable, mystical, spirit-perceptive, poetical, musical.
- Detriment/Debilitated: vague, emotional, indulgent, superstitious, deceptive, dreamy, vacillating, scheming, obsessed.

10. Pluto (higher of Mars):

- Type–Neutral
- Home (strongest)–Scorpio
- Detriment (weakened)–Taurus
- Exalted (strengthened)–Pisces
- Fall (weakest)–Virgo

- Dignified/Exalted: conscientious, purifying, regenerative, liberating, just, incorruptible.
- Detriment/Debilitating: suspicious, destructive, decaying, vicious, sorrowful, suffering, deadly, violent.

III. 3 traits of the signs/seasonal cosmic energy

- Cardinal(Angular): beginnings of seasons; pioneers, initiation; spring equinox, summer solstice, autumn equinox, and winter solstice. Open to change. Emphasis on action. Tries to change environment. Projects self onto surroundings.
- Fixed: middle of season; stabilizers; sustaining force. Resistant to change. Single-minded in pursuits. Not easily swayed. Tries to mold environment to the will.
- Mutable: end of season; modifier; beautifier; beginning of a new. Changeable and flexible. Mentally explorative. Emphasis on intellectual activity. Adaptable to environment.

I think of these three energy signatures in the form of 3 archetypes: the (1) General, the (2)Emperor/Empress and the (3)Advisor.

(1.) The word general means *(adjective)* affecting or concerning all or most people, places, or things; widespread. "books of general interest"; considering or including the main features or elements of something, and disregarding exceptions; overall. "a general introduction to the subject", chief or principal ; *(noun)* a commander of an army, or an army officer of very high rank; (ARCHAIC) the general public.

These people or this type of energy is one that projects effectively and thus has a greater impact on society in terms of influence. Coupled with this archetype is the characteristic of the "workhorse". They are always at the forefront of whatever it is they are apart of and are thus leaders quite naturally though that leadership manifests in different ways depending on the element and the aspects/angles within one's chart.

The Aries (ram)is the first go and do, The Cancer (crab) is the first to feel and know, the Libra (scales) is the first to balance and see, and the Capricorn (goat) is the first to strive and manifest.

(2). An Emperor/Empress is a sovereign ruler of great power and rank, especially one ruling an empire; from Latin imperator 'military commander', from imperare 'to command', from in- 'towards'

+ parare ‘prepare, contrive’.

Coupled with this archetype is the designation of ‘supervisor’ which is basically what any head of a vast company or kingdom is essentially. One who oversees the interest of the whole and checks the balances. These energy signatures are those that have an eye for detail and a talent for management of assets whether it be people or ideas. They are firm energies and are the manifest of the cardinal energy in that they take the information gathered from the first and make it concrete and workable. They maintain the ‘kingdom/Empire’.

The Bull (Taurus) has such a presence of strength and beauty that they draw to themselves whatever they require and are diligent and patient enough not to waste resources and thus they are the treasury of their Empire. The Lionheart (Leo) inspires others with charisma and confidence and are dynamic in dealing with their subjects and peers. They make excellent representations of their Kingdom and overall Empire; the Mariner (Scorpion) dives deep within the oceans of themselves due to their ‘desire’ and others marvel at the pearls that they bring to the surface and the intensity with which they do it, thus adding to the riches of the Kingdom of their own estate as well as others; and the Scientist (Aquarius) has such a keen mind and insight that they see far ahead and are able to connect dots, being a bridge between dimensions and thus adding to the erudition of a society.

(3). An advisor is a person who gives advice in a particular field; *NORTH AMERICAN* (in a school, college, or university) a teacher or staff counselor who helps a student plan a course of study.

Coupled with this signature is the designation of ‘counselor’. These are the travelers who you’ll always find at a crossroad. They are the ones who ‘expand’ the Empire. They are the invisible power behind the General and are the manifestation of the Empiric energy of the Empress who gain wisdom due to there willingness to ‘test the waters’ and are those who can elevate the trajectory of a society or be the apex of its decline depending how open they were on their journey and the perspective that accompanied them. They clarify the general perspective and they aid in the transformation/transmutation of the divine ruler who must adapt to the evolution of the cycles.

The Twins (Gemini) are master communicators and can see and walk the veil of existence meaning they have an instinctive knowledge or are at least aware of the greater knowing making them excellent at gathering information from multiple sources because they are not afraid to go where others won't and are thus more relatable overall. The Analyst (Virgo) observes the path they walk and have a keen vision for what is useful and what is not and doesn't deem anything worthy unless it has been refined internally and externally, thus what they bring and give is pure. The Man-beast (Sagittarius) learns and absorbs things quite naturally and what they absorb is of the highest highs and lowest lows and they will give you both perspectives almost interchangeably. The Mermaid/Merman (Pisces) exists and travels in another dimension and is quite attuned with the deeper physic/emotional aspect of existence and has keys, that if they are willing to come out of their preferred 'otherworldliness',

IV. 5 major aspects (special angles) of astrology Each house/sign is 30 degrees

- Conjunction: (Union; 300) Planets and points that form a conjunction are energies that are united. They are blended; therefore, they act together. The closer they are in conjunction, the more subjective these combined energies are. They don't stand alone, and they have a difficult time truly acknowledging each other as distant or separate. In effect, conjunctions can be a blind spot. When the sun is in close conjunction to Neptune, for example, others may note the distinction, but it can be hard for the native to distinguish between their sense of individuality and their spirituality, evasive, or roundabout nature. The native may just assume, naturally that others are much the same way.
- Sextile: (Cordial; 600) the sextile is often read like a trine, although there is a distinction between the two aspects. Sextiles, like trines, point to some talent and ease. However, sextiles have a little more "oomph" to them. While trines come so naturally to people that they might have to be reminded of their own talents or tendencies, sextiles are a little more overt to the native. These are talents that people appreciate in themselves. They may be more inclined to notice and work on these talents. Sextiles are communicative and relationship- friendly aspects. They point to energies that are capable of being directed. Sextiles reveal the potential for intelligent use of the energies.

- Square: (Friction; 90o) this aspect creates tension between the planets and points involved. Tension is necessary in order to stimulate action, but too much tension translates to stress. The planets involved in a square are acting at cross purposes. With squares, we may overdo and run into countless obstacles before we "get it right." However, squares force us out of complacency and get the ball rolling. Squares are often more difficult when we are young, as these aspects force us to grow and learn our lessons.
- Trine: (Compatible; 120o) Planets in trine support each other. Trines, by nature, are accepting. They allow us to accept others, ourselves, and situations. The talents that trine offer a native is so natural that they are almost unconscious. Often enough, natives don't truly appreciate the talents these trines offer them, and they may not develop them. However, these talents are second nature and completely natural. So, for example, if a man has a Venus trine Neptune, he may be poetic, romantic, or artistic, and he/she may easily accept their romantic partner for who he/she is. Another man with Venus square Neptune may have similar qualities and may possess a strong desire to accept their partner blindly but doing so is not as natural as the first man. They have to work on it and might come up against difficult situations in which he/she feels duped or abused by their partners as a result of that acceptance.
- Opposition: (Reflection; 180o) "it takes two" is the expression, and the opposition is created by dividing the circle in 2. Therein lies the key to the meaning of this aspect; relationship.

People with oppositions seek out others, as if to mirror their own internal struggles. They learn about themselves through interactions with others. Very often, oppositions cause us to swing from one side to the other and we feel torn. Oppositions represent a state of divided loyalties. Inner discontent, uncertainty, and insecurity can be a result. While a square is urgent and courageous, an opposition is unsure and wavering. When we use our oppositions correctly, we are more willing to consider the other side and we can be adept negotiators.

V. The 4 gates

- East- Independent (motivated by personal satisfaction)
- West- Dependent (motivated by public approval)
- North- Subjective (molded and influenced by circumstances)
- South- Objective (molds and creates circumstances)

VI. 4 categories of houses

- House of life: 1, 5, 9 (Fire signs)
- House of Wealth: 2, 6, 10 (Earth signs)
- House of relationships: 3, 7, 11 (Air signs)
- House of endings: 4, 8, 12 (Water signs)

The house types are Angular, Succedent and Cadent.

Angular houses: (1st, 4th, 7th, 10th) These houses are on angles at the cardinal points where the seasons change. Aries, Cancer, Libra and Capricorn reside here because they are cardinal signs. In your chart, the influences of the planets and signs that end up in these houses, will be prominent, depending on the energies of the other signs and planets that may be in the house with them. (much like other people being in the same room, how they vibrate with each other determines the outcome of the meeting.)

Succedent houses: (2nd, 5th, 8th, & 11th) are in the middle of the angle or in the middle of the season. Taurus, Leo, Scorpio, and Aquarius reside here because they are fixed signs. In your chart any planets and signs in these houses will neither be weakened or strengthened, they sort of stand fixed on their own merit, depending on the energies of the other planets or signs that may be in the house with them.

Cadent houses: (3rd, 6th, 9th, 12th) these are the houses that are at the end of the angle or end of the season. They are ready to mutate out of the season. Signs and planets that end up here can easily be influenced or weakened because of too much flexibility, depending on the energies of the other planets or signs that may be in the house with them.

VII. 12 mansions

1. House of Self: Rules personality, nature of expression, body and appearance. Body Parts: head, face, eyes. Ruled by Mars.
2. House of Possessions: Rules financial affairs. Gains and Losses. Body parts: throat and ears. Ruled by Venus.
3. House of Communications: Rules mentality, studies, writings,

siblings, short journeys. Body Parts: shoulders, arms, hands, lungs, collar bones, nervous system. Ruled by Mercury.

4. House of Home: Rules parent who is nurturer, domestic life, conditions in latter part of life, property. Body Parts: breast, stomach, digestive organs. Ruled by Moon.
5. House of Creativity: Rules children, pleasures, speculation, love affairs. Body Parts: heart and upper back. Ruled by Sun.
6. House of Service and Sickness: Rules employees, service, sickness, food, hygiene, clothing. Body Parts: Solar Plexus, bowels. Ruled by Mercury.
7. House of Partnerships: Rules coalitions, partnerships, marriage, contracts, lawsuits, enemies, general public. Body Parts: Kidneys, ovaries, lower back. Ruled by Venus.
8. House of Death and Regeneration: Rules partner's money, legacies, manner in which one exits this world. Body Parts: Muscular system, bladder, sex organs. Ruled by Pluto.
9. House of Aspirations/Mental Explorations: Rules long journeys away from place of birth. Philosophy, spirituality, visions, education, intuition, higher development. Body Parts: liver, thighs. Ruled by Jupiter.
10. House of Social Status: Rules career, occupation, honor, fame, promotion, public prestige, parent who is provider. Body Parts: knees, skeletal system. Ruled by Saturn.
11. House of Friends, hopes, wishes: Rules group associations, social institutions, financial condition of employer. Body Parts: Ankles. Ruled by Uranus.
12. House of Secrets; sorrows; self-undoing: Rules unseen circumstances, restraints, limitations, secret enemies. Body Parts: Feet. Ruled by Neptune.

VIII. 4 elements

The houses identify with 4 categories, Life, Wealth, Relationships, and Endings. The Sun signs identify with four categories or elements respectively, Fire, Earth, Air and Water. Each element is assigned to 3 of the Sun signs these are called triplicities. Fire and Air are complimentary, Earth and Water are complimentary. There is a balance necessary in all things. Fire needs a certain amount of air to burn, yet too much air will burn a fire out of control. Earth is the best when putting out a fire. Earth needs water to nourish her body, yet too much water can cause a muddy solution or quicksand where nothing grows. If you are around someone of a conflicting element to you, disharmony may be created. This same concept is how "bad aspects" are created, especially if there are conflicting planets in the same houses in your natal chart.

Fire (Life) people, (Aries, Leo, Sagittarius) possess dynamic energy, they are an outgoing, forthright, assertive and aggressive energy that either gets things started, keeps things going or destroys the moment. Aries is one who would go through a wall instead of around it in their relentless push to whatever goal is in front of their objective. They represent the spark of life as they govern the coming forth of life in the first house of self. Leo's carry so much pride and can give off an air that they are the only ones in the room, this lends to their authoritativeness and ability to be great supervisors. They are also kind, considerate and creative people. They possess the spark of life as they govern the house of pro-creation. Sagittarius people can be very restless with their fire. They have an optimistic view of life and are always jovial and upbeat and adapt to circumstances, they seek to learn something from everything. They possess the spark of life through the fire of higher learning. Fire signs usually associate with or work in fields involving metals or fire, machinist, engineers, chauffeurs, barbers, surgeons, soldiers, anything hazardous or dangerous. If you have a majority of signs in the fire element, this applies to you as well.

Earth (Wealth) people, (Taurus, Virgo, Capricorn) are concerned with all things that have to do with the Earth. They are bound to the material world by way of possessions(Taurus), employment (Virgo), and social status (Capricorn). Earth people are usually practical, possessive and seek a sense of security on this earthly plane. They feel very much tied too the earth. They usually associate or work in fields involving agriculture, building materials, food, clothes, gardening, land mines, real estate, anything that has to do with the earth and the necessary items to nourish, cloth and shelter their bodies. If you have a majority of signs in the earth element, this applies to you as well.

Air (Relationships) people, (Gemini, Libra, Aquarius) are usually intellectual, talkative, communicate well and have a genuine concern for other people be it neighbors, partners, or friends. Some say the airy Gemini is known to think faster than they speak and will change their direction quickly. They represent close relationships of brothers, sisters and neighbors where early communication skills are developed. Libras, although make sound decisions, can sometimes take a moment to balance all issues, thereby leading others to think they are indecisive. They are very much concerned with relations of partnerships, especially about who they mix their blood with. Aquarians thinking is so far into the future, they can seem to be unpredictable, yet they are always concerned about the relationship of society and associations thereof. Air people usually associate or work in fields involving, accounting, bookkeeping, messengers, lecturers, publishers, writers, architects, civil engineers, designers, scientist, electricians, aviators, inventors, anything where a quick-witted mind is necessary. If you have a majority of planets in the Air element, this applies to you.

Water (Endings) people, (Cancer, Scorpio, Pisces) are deeply oriented Into the endings and beginnings of life. Home, death, and spiritual growth. These are "still waters that run deep". Water people are sensitive, emotional, empathetic, and have good imaginations. Cancers are natural nurturers; their concerns are about the home life. Scorpio actually worries about what may happen. They can dictatorial yet are in deep need of reassurances. Their concerns lay in the manner in which they will exit this Earth. Pisces feels deep sorrow for they know the unimportance of the physical world. Their concerns lay in spiritual growth, the secrets of the universe are translated to peoples secrets that may lead to their own undoing and confinement. Water people usually associate or work in fields as sailors, fishermen, ship builders and owners, marine engineers, liquid refreshments, anything involving liquids. They also are attached to hospitals, jails, and places of confinements. If you have a majority of planets in the Water element, this applies to you.

The elements –dignified/debilitated:

Element	Dignified	Debilitated
Fire Aries, Leo, Sagittarius	Energy, active, enthusiastic, passionate, outgoing, extroverted, expressive.	Lacks initiative, difficulty putting ideas into action, does not promote self aggressively, waits to be motivated by others.
Earth Taurus, Virgo, Capricorn	Practical, stable, emphasis on security, patient, industrious, strong-willed, withstands long-range objectives.	Impractical, can't hold onto money, lacks ability to work hard, grows impatient.
Air Gemini, Libra, Aquarius	Communicative, intelligent, likes to deal on the mental plane, quickly grasps ideas, can speak or write effectively, takes rational viewpoints.	Difficulty in communicating, not interested in abstract ideas or intellectual pursuits
Water Cancer, Scorpio, Pisces	Emotional, intuitive, sensitive to surroundings and to others, creative, good imagination, empathetic, hidden depths.	Not sensitive to others feelings, self- oriented or selfish, difficulty expressing emotion, keeps feelings bottled up.

IX. 12 tribes

1. Aries: March 21- April 19

- Emblem: Ram
- Organ: head
- Element: fire
- Polarity: positive (masculine; gives energy)
- Modality: cardinal (spring equinox)
- Aspects: conjunctions/unions= Pisces, Taurus; sextile/cordials= Aquarius, Gemini; Squares/ frictions= Capricorn, cancer; Trines/Compatibility= Sagittarius, Leo; Opposition/ reflection/ideal mate= Libra
- Character: Most energetic
- Personality: The initiator
- Moniker: "I Seek myself (I am)"
- Mansion: House of life
- Ruling Planet: Mars
- Gate: East
- Likes: comfortable clothes, taking on leadership roles, physical challenges, sports.
- Dislikes: inactivity, delays, work that isn't conducive to their talents and abilities.
- Higher self: leaders, energetic, persistent and steadfast, enterprising, courageous, ardor, industrial, generous, pioneering, practical, constructive.
- Lower self: belligerent, headstrong, excitable, audacious, impatient, irresolution, imprudent, insubordinate, quarrelsome, foolhardy, selfish, disregarding, jealous.
- Whole: Inspirational, creators, productive, decisive.
- How to harmonize with: "Play chess" (use strategy); be logical and direct.

Summary: as the first zodiac sign, the presence of Aries almost always marks the beginning of something energetic and turbulent. They are continuously looking for dynamic, speed and competition. They are always first in everything from work to social gatherings. Thanks to its ruling planet Mars, Aries is one of the most active zodiac signs. People born under this sign are meant to emphasize the search for answers to personal and metaphysical questions. This is the biggest feature of this incarnation. It is in their nature to act, sometimes before they think about it well. Their fiery ruler affects their excellent organizational skills, so you'll rarely meet an Aries who doesn't like to finish more things at once, often even before the lunch break! Their challenges are increased when they are impatient, aggressive and vent angers on others. Aries rules the head leads with the head, often literally walking headfirst, leaning forward for speed and focus. They are naturally brave and rarely afraid of trial and risk. They possess a youthful strength and energy, regardless of age and they perform tasks in record time. By aligning with themselves they could get the best results.

Associates and relatives: Aries is constantly on the move, so activity is the keyword for this zodiac sign. When it comes to associates, the more varied the better. They need a range of different personalities in order to close their circle of associations. Due to the fact that people born under this sign can easily enter into communication, in the course of their lives they make a massive amount of connections and acquaintances. Yet the long term and real associates are something completely different. Only those who are just as energetic and who are inclined to go in the long run may accompany them. Independent and ambitious, they can early determine the required direction they want to go. Although, they are not often in touch with their relatives, they are always in their hearts. You can always expect a direct and honest approach from them, even when they are expressing their feelings.

2. Taurus: April 20- May 20

- Emblem: bull
- Organ: throat
- Element: earth
- Polarity: Negative (feminine; receives energy)
- Modality: fixed
- Aspects: conjunctions/unions= Aries, Gemini; sextiles/cordials= Pisces, Cancer; squares/ Frictions= Aquarius, Leo; trines/ compatibility= Capricorn, Virgo; opposition/reflection/ideal mate= Scorpio
- Character: Most dependable
- Personality: The maintainer
- Moniker: "I Have"
- Mansion: House of wealth
- Ruling planet: Venus (ancient/day ruler); earth (modern/night ruler)
- Gate: East
- Likes: gardening, cooking, music, romance, high quality clothes, working with hands
- Dislikes: sudden changes, complications, insecurity of any

Summary: powerful and reliable, Taurus is the first when it comes to harvesting the fruits of their labor. They love everything that is good and beautiful, and they are often surrounded by material pleasures. People born under this sign are very sensual and tactile. Touch is extremely important for them, both in business and in romance. Stable and conservative, they are the most reliable sign. Stubbornness is a trait that forces them to excel things to the end, in order to comply with the standards. As an earth sign, Taurus can be overprotective of their loved ones. They are great in making money and they will stick to their projects until it is successfully completed. Bulls are often noted for their stubbornness, but it can also be interpreted as a complete commitment to execution of tasks. This makes them excellent cooks, entertainers and artists. They are loyal and don't like sudden and unwanted changes. Some may have very conservative views of the world or can be too fond of money and wealth; they have the ability to bring a practical voice of reason in any chaotic situation.

Associates and relatives: Loved ones and home are very important to Taurus. They are very intelligent and have a good sense of humor, which makes them an excellent person to socialize with; very loyal and always willing to lend aid and assistance. A lot of their close relationships/associations begin in childhood. They love children and appreciate the time spent with relatives, so they will always be present at gatherings and events. They enjoy hosting house parties and get-togethers.

3. Gemini: May 20-June 20

- Emblem: twins
- Organ: shoulders, hands, arms, and lungs
- Element: air
- Polarity: positive (masculine)
- Modality: mutable
- Aspects: conjunctions/unions= Taurus, Cancer; sextiles/cordials= Aries, Leo; squares/frictions= Pisces, Virgo; trines/compatibility= Aquarius, Libra; opposition/reflection/ideal mates= Sagittarius
- Character: Most communicative and social
- Personality: The questioner
- Moniker: "I think"
- Mansion: house of relationships
- Ruling planet: Mercury
- Gate: East

- Likes: music, books, magazines, chats with nearly anyone, short trips around the town.
- Dislikes: being alone, being confined, repetition and routine.
- Higher self: inquisitive, inventive, entertaining, versatile, open-minded, students of the zodiacs, intelligent, expressive, ambitious, dexterity, courageous, tolerant, responsive, generous, temperance, breadth, liberal.
- Lower self: gossip, split personality, restless, easily bored, can be very emotional, effusive, tricky, shifty, diffusion, diffidence, waywardness, improvidence, impulsive, exaggeration, theory, lack of concentration, verbose.
- Whole: charming and persuasive, versatile, adept.
- How harmonize with: be mindful of what you don't see and what is not said; expect the turn round. Don't be boring or overly judgmental. Don't follow.

Summary: expressive and quick witted, Gemini represents two different sides of personality and you will never be sure with whom you will face. Can be sociable, communicative and ready for fun, while on the other hand can be very serious, thoughtful, restless and even indecisive. As an air sign, they are concerned with all aspects of mind. This sign is ruled by Mercury which is a planet that represents communication, writing and teaching others. They get fascinated by almost everything in the world and they have a feeling as if there is not enough time to experience everything they want to see. This makes them excellent artists, writers and journalists. People born under this sign tend to feel as if their other half is missing, so they are forever seeking for new associates, mentors and colleagues. At their best they are versatile, inquisitive, and fun loving and want to experience everything, so their company is never boring.

Associates and relatives: those born under Gemini are very social people and love to spend time with loved ones. They have friends in abundance and love to chat and be innerstood, so they seek those who are also good communicators. Relatives are important to them, especially those who are similar to them. Camaraderie with siblings is very common, and the time spent with them is precious. Tribal responsibilities often present a challenge for Gemini, but they always know how to cope with it.

4. Cancer: June 21–July 22

- Emblem: crab
- Organ: chest and stomach
- Element: water
- Polarity: negative (feminine)
- Modality: cardinal (summer solstice)
- Aspects: conjunctions/unions= Gemini, Leo; sextiles/cordials= Taurus, Virgo; squares/frictions= Aries, Libra; trines/compatibility= Pisces, Scorpio; Opposition/ reflection/ideal mates= Capricorn
- Character: Most sensitive
- Personality: The nurturer
- Moniker: "I feel"
- Ruling planet: Moon
- Gate: North
- Mansion: house of endings
- Likes: art, home-based hobbies, relaxing in or near water, helping loved ones, a good meal with associates.
- Dislikes: strangers, any criticism of mom, revealing secrets of personal life.
- Higher self: compassionate, helpful and caring, protective, intuitive, quick learners, devoted to loved ones and tenacious, conscientious, maternal, kind, social, adaptable, patriotic, economical, patient, domestic, sympathetic.
- Lower self: possessive, easily hurt, moody, stuck in their ways, selfish, moody, guarded, vane, fancy, dreamy, untruthful, changeable, sentimental, resentful, prideful, disorderly, indolent, timid.
- How to harmonize with: don't play with them as in taking their kindness for weakness or mistaking their emotionalism as a lack of intelligence; they are sharp and must be dealt with in the same manner, with keenness and intuitiveness; respectful compassion.

Summary: deeply intuitive and sentimental, cancer can be one of the most challenging signs to get to know. They are very emotional and sensitive, and they care about loved ones and home. They are sympathetic and are very attached to the people who surround them. People born under this sign are very loyal and empathetic beings, able to feel the pain of others and their suffering. Because of their ruling planet the Moon, the many phases of its lunar cycle can deepen cancer's internal mysteries and create fleeting emotional patterns that they cannot control, especially when a child. This can show itself as mood swings, selfishness, manipulation and fits of rage. They are quick to help others and avoid conflicts. One of their greatest strengths is persistent determination. They don't have great ambitions, for the most part, because they are content to have a loving home structure surrounded by those they care most about; tranquil and harmonious. They often take good care of their co-workers and treat them as relatives.

Associates and relatives: cancers are great parents. They care about relatives and home and value home comforts more than anything else. They are deeply sentimental and prone to diligently preserving tribal memories. They love sharing their life experiences with their loved ones. When it comes to associations, so long as they don't interfere with home life, they are always willing to lend a hand. They respect their comrades a lot. People who enjoy socializing in the home will be at the top of their list of associates. Their intuitive nature makes them very compassionate, but sometimes it's impossible to innerstand them.

5. Leo: July 23-August 22

- Emblem: lion
- Organ: heart and spinal cord
- Element: fire
- Polarity: positive (masculine)
- Modality: fixed
- Aspects: conjunctions/unions= Cancer, Virgo; sextiles/cordials= Gemini, Libra; squares/frictions= Taurus, Scorpio; trines/ compatibility= Aries, Sagittarius; Opposition/reflection/ideal mate= Aquarius
- Character: Most Generous
- Personality: The loyalist
- Moniker: "I will/create", "I Love"
- Mansion: house of life
- Ruling planet: Sun
- Gate: North
- Likes: theater, taking holy-days, fun with associates, being admired, expensive things.
- Dislikes: facing difficult reality, not being treated royally.
- Higher self: loyal, dignified, kind, generous, courageous, noble, leaders, creative, outspoken, arduous, philanthropic, inspiring, magnetic, hopeful, industrious, chivalrous, fearless, magnanimous, idealist, sincere, hospitable, intuitive, comprehensive.
- Lower self: stubborn, smug, arrogant, conceited, prone to bragging, gloomy, disagreeable, ill and dark sense of humor, lazy, liars, dictatorial manner,

overbearing, condescending, impetuous, pompous, dominating, sensitive, promiscuous, gullible, fussy, striking, hot-head.
Whole: Great supervisor, inspirational, prodigious productivity.

- How to harmonize with: Be encouraging and stand your ground with patient understanding.

Summary: people born under this sign are natural born leaders. They are dramatic, creative, self-confident, dominant and extremely hard to resist. They can achieve anything they want, whether it's about work or time spent with loved ones. They love life and expect to have a good time. They are able, like the other fire signs; to use their mind to solve even the most difficult problems and take the initiative in solving various complicated situations. Ruled by the sun, they embody the brightness of the sun metaphorically by way of their radiance and charisma, their ego. The good of this is that they can easily search and find what they need. But, on the other hand it can be problematic when they ignore the problems of others in order to fulfill their desires. They often have too many friends due to their loyalty and generosity. Self- confident and attractive, they can unite many groups of people at every opportunity. Problems can arise, when Leos become too fond of their achievements. They can also be arrogant, lazy and inflexible, because they assume that someone else will clean up after them. A healthy sense of humor can make the collaboration with other people easier.

Associates and relatives: the most generous sign, Leo is faithful and loyal. They will try hard to help others, even if it takes a lot of time and energy. Strong and reliable, they have the ability to appeal to almost anyone. Humble and gracious, they enjoy hosting celebrations and events. They are rarely alone; because interac nd nature, they choose their closest associates by their ability to keep pace with their high energy, dignity and commitment to individual values. When it comes to relatives, they will do whatever it takes to protect them.

6. Virgo: August 23-September 22

- Emblem: virgin maiden
- Organ: intestines
- Element: earth
- Polarity: negative (feminine)
- Modality: mutable
- Aspects: conjunctions/unions= Leo, Libra; sextiles/cordials= Cancer, Scorpio; squares/frictions= Gemini, Sagittarius; trines/compatibility= Taurus, Capricorn; opposite/reflection/ideal mate= Pisces
- Character: Most cautious
- Personality: The modifier
- Moniker: "I analyze"
- Mansion: house of wealth
- Ruling planet: Mercury (ancient/day ruler); earth (modern/night ruler)
- Gate: north
- Likes: animals, healthy food and living, books, nature, cleanliness.
- Dislikes: rudeness, asking for help, taking center stage.
- Higher self: gentle, helpful, organized, dedicated, loyal, hardworking, analytical, flexible, good conversationalists, witty, serious, thoughtful, active, efficient, cautious, intelligent, perceptive, contemplative, concise, intuitive, discrete, provident, methodical, thrift, industry.
- Lower self: prone to worry, prudish, goody-goody, fussy, undemonstrative, short tempered, over-thinking, secretive, overly critical of self and others, demanding, mercenary, selfish, apprehensive, discontenting, cold, inconsistent, sloppy, indecisive, timid, lack of self-confidence.
- Whole: honest, healthy, modest, reliable and prudent.
- How to harmonize with: Be stimulating; appreciation and gratitude; be respectful.

Summary: they are always paying attention to the smallest details and their deep sense of humanity makes them one of the most careful signs. Their methodical approach to life ensures that nothing is left to chance. They are often tender but very careful. Virgo is an earth sign, which prefers conservative and organized things, and those dependent on them. People born under this sign have very organized lives, and even if they are messy, their goals and dreams are put on strictly defined terms and points in their mind. Since Mercury is their ruling planet, this sign has a well-developed sense of speech and writing, as well as other forms of communication. Many Virgos may choose a career as a writer or journalist. They are often misunderstood, because of the symbolism of the name of its emblem. Virgo experiences everything for the first time. They always want to serve and please others, so they often work as caregivers. On the other hand, this sign can be very critical and overly concerned. They need to learn the difference between constructive criticism and being just plain judgmental.

Associates and relatives: Virgos as associates are extremely useful to have. They are excellent advisers and they really know how to solve a problem. They are always there to remind you to take more care of yourself, because they focus on health and wellness. They are very dedicated to their relatives and associates, and very attentive to the elderly and sick people. They make awesome parents. However, they are not the type that will directly show their feelings; they would rather do it through concrete acts.

7. Libra: September 23–October 22

- Emblem: scales of justice
- Organ: kidneys
- Element: air
- Polarity: positive (masculine)
- Modality: cardinal (autumn equinox)
- Aspects: conjunctions/unions= Virgo, Scorpio; sextiles/cordials= Leo, Sagittarius; squares/frictions= Cancer, Capricorn; trines/ compatibility= Gemini, Aquarius; opposition/reflection/ideal mate= Aries
- Character: Most fair and flexible
- Personality: The judge
- Moniker: "I unite"
- Mansion: house of relationships
- Ruling planet: Venus
- Gate: west
- Likes: harmony, gentleness, sharing, the outdoors.
- Dislikes: violence, injustice, loudmouths, conformity.
- Higher self: thoughtful, impartial, conciliatory, foresight, grace, modest, decorum, adaptable, artistic, persuasive, affectionate, peaceful, cheerful, sympathetic, forgiving, generous, idealist, tactful.
- Lower self: sulky, fed up, indecisive and unclear, cunning and manipulative, liars, fearful and flirtatious, extremist, reckless, hesitance, susceptible, impressionable, illusionary, punctilious, pedantic, vane, aloof, shirking, careless, vacillating.

- Whole: diplomatic, balanced, and refined.
- How to harmonize with: shine truth; be straightforward yet open-minded.

Summary: peaceful, fair and they hate being alone. Partnership is important to them, and with their victorious mentality and cooperation, they rarely are without one. Libra being an air sign has an expressed intellect and keen mind. They can be stimulated by a good book, insurmountable discussions, and interesting people. Their ruling planet is Venus who is a lover of beautiful things, so the quality is always more important than the quantity with them. They are often surrounded by art, music and beautiful places. They are cooperative by nature, so they often work in teams. They are fascinated by the balance and symmetry of life. Libra-born prefers justice and equality, and they can't tolerate injustice. They avoid indulging in all types of conflicts and prefer to keep the pace, where this is possible. The problem for Libra-born is when they are forced to choose sides, because they are very indecisive and sometimes forget that they have their own opinion.

Associates and relatives: Libra-born is fun and always willing to help, which makes them excellent associates. They may be inclined to delays due to their indecisiveness, but they are truly amazing companions and others desire to be in their company. This flexible zodiac sign loves spending time with loved ones and will not hesitate when it's time to organize some gathering. They are social, lovable, and know how to create harmonious atmospheres making any get together a joyous occasion. When it comes to challenges, they know how to see the solution to disagreements which makes them excellent for problem solving.

8. Scorpio: October 23- November 21

- Emblem: Eagle (Phoenix), serpent and scorpion
- Organ: genitals
- Element: water
- Polarity: negative (feminine)
- Modality: fixed
- Aspects: conjunctions/unions= Libra, Sagittarius; sextiles/ cordials= Virgo, Capricorn; squares/frictions= Leo, Aquarius; trines/compatibility= Cancer,

Pisces; Opposition/reflection/ideal mate= Taurus

- Character: Most passionate
- Personality: The catalyst
- Moniker: "I desire"
- Mansion: house of endings
- Ruling planet: Mars (ancient/day ruler); Pluto (modern/night ruler)
- Gate: west
- Likes: truth, facts, being right, longtime camaraderie, teasing, a grand passion and purpose.
- Dislikes: Dishonesty, revealing secrets, passive people.
- Higher self: intense, great personal magnetism, great powers of persuasion, strong willed, great depths of perception (not easily fooled), protective and concerned, investigative, energetic, positive, fearless, penetrating, eloquent, devoted, patient, thoughtful, ambitious.
- Lower self: possessive, jealous and temperamental, insulting, manipulative, severing, callous, caustic, sarcastic, suspicious, destructive, vindictive, dogmatic, shrewd, parsimonious, tyrant, passion.
- Whole: transformation and regeneration, discovery, defensive, and secrets.
- How to harmonize with: be mindful and sincere.

Summary: passionate and assertive people, they are determined and decisive, and will research until they find the truth. Scorpios are great leaders, always aware of the situation and always features prominently in resourcefulness. Being a water sign they live to express their emotions, although as Scorpios they manifest them differently than the other water signs. In any case you be sure that they will keep your secrets whatever they may be. Pluto is their adopted ruling planet, which represents transformation and regeneration. They are known by their cool and calm behavior and by their mysterious persona. People often say that Scorpio-born are fierce, probably because they innerstand very well the rules of the universe. Some tend to look older than they actually are. They make good leaders because they dedicate themselves to whatever it is they do. They hate dishonesty and they can be very jealous and suspicious, so they need to learn how to adapt more easily to different human behaviors. Scorpios are brave hence they tend to attract a lot of associations.

Associates and relatives: honesty and fairness are the two qualities that make Scorpio a great Associate. When it comes to work, they are very dedicated and loyal. They are quick-witted and fun-loving people. They are full of surprises and will give you everything you need, but if you let them down once there is no return. They are very emotional, when they are in pain, it is quite simply impossible to make them feel better. They take good care of their family.

9. Sagittarius: November 22-Deccember 21

- Emblem: archer; half-man, half-beast
- Organ: hips and thighs
- Element: fire
- Polarity: positive (masculine)
- Modality: mutable
- Aspects: conjunctions/unions= Scorpio, Capricorn; sextiles/cordials= Libra, Aquarius; squares/frictions= Virgo, Pisces; trines/compatibility= Aries, Leo; opposition/reflection/ideal mate= Gemini
- Character: Most traveling
- Personality: The adventurer
- Moniker: "I aspire/I see"
- Mansion: house of life
- Ruling planet: Jupiter
- Gate: West
- Likes: freedom, travel, philosophy, being outdoors
- Dislikes: clingy people, being constrained, off-the-wall theories, details
- Higher self: optimistic, honest, enthusiastic, inspiring, open-minded, great sense of humor, Don Juans of the zodiac, sincere, frank, just, foresight, prophetic, persevering, frank, dependable, buoyant, genial, jovial, hopeful, logical, charitable.
- Lower self: exaggerates, argumentative (loves drama), impatient, take unnecessary risks, prone to not lending a hand, boisterous, over-confident, changeable, prodigal, brusque, sportive, uncompromising, speculative, blunt.
- Whole: idealistic, ingenuity, intellectual and just, soul controllers of the zodiac (can get along with most signs at one point or another).
- How to combat and/or deal with: Mirror (reflect and deflect); be upright and secure; don't be intimidated.

Summary: curious and energetic, they are one of the biggest travelers of the zodiac. Their open-mindedness and philosophical view motivates them to wander around the world in search of the meaning of life/truth. They are extroverts, and optimistic, enthusiastic and appreciate change. They are able to transform their thoughts into concrete and complete actions. Like other fire signs, they need to be constantly in touch with the world to experience as much as possible. Jupiter, their ruling planet, is the largest planet of the zodiac. Their enthusiasm knows no bounds therefore Sagittarius-born possesses a great sense of humor. Freedom is their greatest treasure, because then they can travel freely and explore different doctrines and views/interpretations of divine truth. Because of their honesty, they are often impatient and tactless in what they say and do, so it's important for them to learn to express themselves in a tolerable and diplomatic manner.

Associates and relatives: they are fun and always surrounded by associates. They love to laugh and enjoy the diversity of life and culture, so they will easily acquire many associates around the world. They are generous and not a person who will lecture others about personal things. When it comes to tribal matters they are dedicated and will do almost anything.

10. Capricorn: December 22–January 19

- Emblem: sea goat
- Organ: knees
- Element: earth
- Polarity: negative (feminine)
- Modality: cardinal (winter solstice)
- Aspects: conjunctions/unions= Sagittarius, Aquarius; sextiles/ cordials= Scorpio, Pisces; squares/ frictions= Aries, Libra; trines/ compatibility= Taurus, Virgo; opposition/reflection/ideal mate= Cancer
- Character: Most serious
- Personality: The pragmatist
- Moniker: "I use"
- Mansion: house of wealth
- Ruling planet: Saturn
- Gate: south
- Likes: relatives, tradition, music, understated status, quality craftsmanship.
- Dislikes: just about everything at some point.
- Higher self: organized, hardworking, ambitious, considerate, dignified, prudent, cautious, reverence, practical, thoughtful, diplomatic, profound, magnetic, concentrative service.
- Lower self: critical, controlling, overly detail oriented, insecure, nervous, limited, conceited, jealous, selfish, discontented, capricious,

suspicious, authoritative, gloomy, depressive, avarice, impatient.

- Whole: determined and disciplined, accomplished and successful; great managerial capacity, benevolent.
- How to harmonize with: respect them; watch and learn, be warm.

Summary: when it comes to professionalism and traditional values, Capricorn is the first. They are practical and considered the most serious sign of the zodiac, which possess an independence that enables them to advance significantly both in business and on a personal level. There is nothing more important to them than loved ones. They are masters of self-control and have the potential to be great leaders or managers as long as it is in the sphere of business. Saturn is their ruling planet which represents restrictions of all kinds. The influence of Saturn makes them responsible, so they know how to save for the future. They excel when challenged to show and prove due to the fact of their stubbornness. Problems occur when they are forced to be close to people. They have a hard time accepting the differences of others and in these situations, tend to resort to manipulation or outright controlling based on the need to have order and be the one who enforces and keeps it. They tend to impose their traditionalist values on others. They tend to think that they are the only ones who can solve the problem, whatever it may be, and they must learn how to be more forgiving and to appreciate what others bring to the table.

Associates and relatives: they are very intelligent and humorous, so they can be great comrades. They want their associates to be honest and consistent/loyal. They go all out for those who they deem worthy. They respect and uphold tribal traditions. They don't have a large circle of close associations so those who are must be as committed to values as they are. Outbursts of emotion are a common thing for them, being that they express their emotions through actions.

11. Aquarius: January 20- February 19

- Emblem: water bearer
- Organ: ankles
- Element: air
- Polarity: positive: (masculine)
- Modality: fixed
- Aspects: conjunctions/unions= Capricorn, Pisces sextiles/cordials= Sagittarius, Aries; squares/ frictions= Taurus, Scorpio; trines/ compatibility= Gemini, Libra; opposition/reflection/ideal mate: Leo
- Character: Most innovative
- Personality: The reformer
- Moniker: "I know"
- Mansion: house of relationships
- Ruling planet: Saturn (ancient); Uranus (modern)
- Gate: south
- Likes: fun with associates, helping others, fighting for causes, intellectual conversations, good listeners.
- Dislikes: limitations, broken promises, being alone, dull or boring situations, disagreeable people.
- Higher self: witty, clever, humanitarian, inventive, original, truthful, co-operative, sociable, earnest, humane, service, unbiased, patient, steady, philosophical, intuitive, pleasant, progressive, cosmopolitan.
- Lower self: stubborn, sarcastic, unemotional, rebellious, aloof, mental fanaticism, non-rational, political extremism, derive enjoyment from shocking people, gullible where social injustice is involved.
- Whole: visionary, creative, independent, wise and supportive, leadership.
- How to harmonize with: don't try to outthink them; be interested and interesting; care about something.

Summary: shy and quiet, but also eccentric and energetic. However, in both cases, they are deep thinkers and highly intellectual people who love helping others. They are able to see without prejudice on both sides, which makes them people who can solve multiple problems. Although they can easily adapt to the energies that surround them, Aquarius-born have a deep need to be alone at times so as to regain and recharge their own energies. They see the world as a place of endless possibilities. As an air sign, they use their minds at every opportunity. If there is no mental stimulation, they are bored and lack motivation to achieve the best result. The ruling planet of Aquarius, Uranus, has a timid, abrupt and sometimes aggressive nature, but it also gives them visionary capabilities. They can perceive the future and they know exactly what they want to be doing ten years from now. Uranus also gave them the power of quick transformation, so they are known as progressives and humanists. They feel good in a group or a community, so they constantly strive to be surrounded by other people. The biggest problem for them is the feeling of limitation and confinement. Because of their desire for freedom and equality for all, they will always strive to ensure freedom of speech and movement. Aquarius-born has a reputation for being cold and insensitive due to their brutal honesty, but this is just a defense mechanism against premature intimacy. They need to learn to trust others and express their emotions in a healthy way.

Associates and relatives: although they are communicative, they need time to get to know and get close to people. Considering that they are highly sensitive people, closeness to them means vulnerability. Their inclination for immediacy combined with their strong views; make them a challenge to meet. They will do anything for a loved one to the point of self-sacrifice if necessary. Their associates should possess these three qualities: creativity, intellect, and integrity. When it comes to relatives they expect the same qualities and will not maintain ties if these traits aren't manifested.

12. Pisces: February 19- March 20

- Emblem: Fish
- Organ: Feet
- Element: water
- Polarity: negative (feminine)
- Type: mutable
- Aspects: conjunctions/unions= Aquarius, Aries; sextiles/cordials= Capricorn, Taurus; squares/frictions= Gemini, Sagittarius; trines/compatibility= Cancer, Scorpio; opposition/reflection/ideal mate= Virgo
- Character: Most tolerant and patient
- Personality: The visionary
- Moniker: "I believe"
- Mansion: house of endings
- Ruling planet: Jupiter (ancient/day ruler); Neptune (modern/night ruler)
- Gate: south
- Likes: being alone, sleeping, music, romance, visual media, swimming, spiritual themes.

- Dislikes: know-it-alls, being criticized, past revelations, cruelty of any kind.
- Higher self: trusting, helpful, creative, gentle, innerstanding and intuitive, concentrative, peaceful, refinement, purity, perceptive, psychometric, methodical, orderly, idealist, hospitable.
- Lower self: self-pitying, dependant, insecure, own worse critic, fearful, too trusting, a desire to escape reality, lethargic, careless, indolent, indecisive, easy-going, improvident, apologetic, submissive, self-deprication, variable, timid, inferior complex, loyal to wrong circumstances.
- Whole: faithful, psychic, inspiring.
- How to harmonize with: be open, grounded and empty; watch for deception; don't believe the hype; be indifferent; don't let them drown you (in emotion). Be gentle.

Summary: they are very easy going, so they often find themselves in the company of many very different types of people. They are selfless and always willing to help others, without expecting anything in return. Being a water sign, Pisces are characterized by empathy and expressed emotional capacity. Their ruling planet is Neptune, so they are exceptionally intuitive and have artistic talents. Neptune is connected to music, so they may reveal music preferences in the earliest stages of life. They are generous, compassionate and extremely faithful and caring. People born under this sign have an innate innerstanding of the life cycle and thus achieve the best emotional relationships with people. They are known by their wisdom, but under the influence of Uranus, they can sometimes take on the role of a martyr, in order to catch the attention. They are never judgmental and always forgiving. They are also known as the most tolerant of all the zodiac signs.

Associates and relatives: gentle and caring, they can be the best acquaintances that exist. In fact, they often put the needs of others ahead of their own. They are loyal, devoted, compassionate, and wherever there's a problem with those they care for, they will do their best to resolve it. Deeply intuitive, they can sense when there's a problem even before it happens. They are expressive, and they will not hesitate to let their feelings be known to those in their circle and expect the same upfront and blunt communication from their loved ones.

XIII. Th 13th tribe

- The serpent-bearer
- Represents activated cranial triune (pineal, pituitary, and thalamus)
- Interpreter of dreams, vivid premonitions; attracts good luck and fruitful blissings; lofty ideals; seeker of harmony and peace; doctor of medicine and science; naturopathic; adds, increases, joins and gathers together-poetical, inventive nature, expanding qualities; seeks higher education and wisdom-overseer; supervisor of work-fame, either grand or misunderstood completely-longevity, aspirations of healing the ills of man; architect, builder; reaches for the stars figuratively and literally; tax assessor, or levies taxes; astrological talents; intuitive; large immediate tribe but apt to be separated from them when young; the number 12 holds great significance; foresight and good fortune to benefit from hard times; has secret enemies in tribe and/or close circle; many are jealous of this one; notable father, apple of his father's eye when young; high position in life expected (depending on aspects); highest legend achieved after death; wise, genius mentality; receives favor from those in authority

It must be understood, innerstood and overstood that we are Yisrael meaning that the 12 tribes are in fact the celestial energies of the cosmos housed within these vessels of flesh. The objective of life is to master the wheel, the life compass of self as we are truly the embodiment of all these cosmic powers and phenomena. While it is true that some of these attributes, both negative and positive, describe us, in terms of personality, that does not mean we should narrow our potentiality due to a few cross ups or whatever we may discover about our astrological triune. The initial 12 are the journey or "stairway to heaven" and the 13 is the culmination of that journey, the model of our finest qualities most of which we possess already though not as conscious control. We are Th 13 and the time is now to reclaim the power of our divine wisdom which is embedded in our cellular memory. The key to activate the triune is the triune: study, create and give.

XIV. As above so below; heavenly correspondence To Man

1. Aries: brain, cerebral hemispheres, cranium, eyes, face, upper jaw, internal carotid arteries.
2. Taurus: neck, throat, palate, larynx, tonsils, lower jaw, ears, occipital region, cerebellum, atlas, axis, external carotid arteries, jugular veins, pharynx, thyroid gland, cervical vertebrae.
3. Gemini: shoulders, arms, hands, upper ribs, lungs, trachea, bronchi, capillaries, breath, oxygenation of blood.
4. Cancer: stomach, esophagus, diaphragm, the mammae, lacteals, upper lobes of liver, thoratic duct, pancreas, serum of blood, peristalsis of the stomach, chymification.
5. Leo: heart, dorsal region of spine, spinal cord, aorta, superior and inferior vena cava.
6. Virgo: abdominal region, large and small intestines, lower lobe of liver, spleen, duodenum, chylification, peristalsis of the bowels.
7. Libra: kidneys, adrenals, lumbar region, skin, uterus, vasomotor system.
8. Scorpio: bladder, urethra, genitals, descending colon, prostate gland, sigmoid flexure, nasal bone, pubic bone, red hue of matter in the blood.
9. Sagittarius: hips, thighs, femur, ileum, coccygeal vertebrae, sacral region, sciatic nerves, ischium.
10. Capricorn: skin, knees, joints, hair.
11. Aquarius: lower limbs, ankles.
12. Pisces: feet, toes, fibrin of the blood.

*Physiological afflictions of the signs:

- Aries: neuralgia, insomnia, cerebral congestion, brain fever, baldness, headache, dizziness, eye afflictions, toothache, gumboils.
- Taurus: goiter, diptheria, laryngitis, tonsillitis, croup, polyp, quinsy, glandular swelling of the throat, apoplexy.
- Gemini: bronchitis, asthma, pneumonia, consumption, pleurisy, corrupted blood, nervous trouble, anemia.
- Cancer: indigestion, dipsomania, gastric catarrh, hiccough, flatulency, dropsy, sclerosis.

- Leo: heart disease, angina pectoris, locomotor ataxia, hyperemia, spinal disease, spinal meningitis, fevers.
- Virgo: peritonitis, malnutrition, dysentery, colic, constipation, diarrhea, cholera, typhoid, appendicitis, tapeworm.
- Libra: Bright's disease, lumbago, suppression of urine, nephritis, diabetes, renal calculi, uremia.
- Scorpio: syphilis, rupture, gravel, scurvy, fistula, piles, diseases of the womb or uterus, urethral structure, prostatic stincture, nasal catarrh, disease of nasal mucous membrane and nasal cartilage.
- Sagittarius: locomotor ataxia, sciatica, lumbago, rheumatism, hip disease, accidents to thighs.
- Capricorn: eczema, erysipelas, leprosy, disassociation of bones, weak knees.
- Aquarius: varicose veins, swollen ankles, leg ache, nervous diseases, sensitive skin.
- Pisces: bunions, gout, deformed feet and toes, tumors, dropsy

*Anatomy and physiology correlated to the planets:

- Sun: vital fluid, spleen, distribution of heat, pons varolii, oxygen, heart.
- Venus: throat, kidneys, thymus gland, venous circulation.
- Mercury: nerves, bronchial tubes, pulmonary circulation, thyroid gland, right cerebral hemisphere, cerebro-spinal system, sensory nerves, vital fluid in nerves, vocal cords, ears, sight, tongue, all sense perception, breath.
- Moon: esophagus, uterus, ovaries, lymphatics, sympathetic nervous system, synovial fluid, alimentary canal, lymph, chyle, nerve sheaths.
- Saturn: gallbladder, pneumogastric or vagus nerve, teeth, skin, joints, ligaments, sigmoid flexure.
- Jupiter: liver, glycogen, suparenal, arterial circulation, fibrin of blood, disposition of fats.
- Mars: iron in blood, red spectrum matter in blood, genitals, motor nerves, left cerebral hemisphere, muscular movements, desire body, rectum.
- Uranus: ethers, eyes, pituitary glands/body, gases.
- Neptune: pineal gland, spinal canal, nerve fiber.

ZODIAC MINERAL SALT – BIOCHEMICAL MAPPING

Based on Astrological Composite – Supplemental balance should be included with in daily nutritional intake

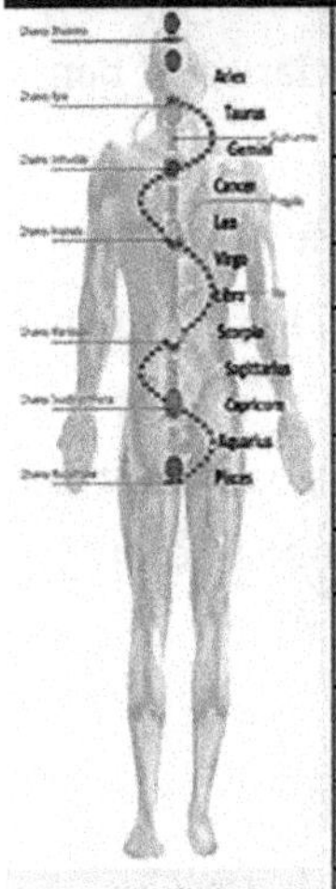

Birth Mineral Salt	Supplemental Bal Salt 1	Supplemental Bal Salt 2	Supplemental Bal Salt 3	IMAPCTED AREAS
ARIES Potassium Phosphate(Kali Phos)	Taurus Sodium Sulphate	Gemini Potassium Chloride	Cancer Calcium Fluoride	Exhaustion, Impulse Weakness, Sleeplessness CEREBRUM, SPINAL CHORD, SENSORY NERVES, FACE TO LOWER JAW
TAURUS Sodium Sulphate(Nat Sulph)	Gemini Potassium Chloride	Cancer Calcium Fluoride	Leo Magnesium Phosphate	Cold, Digestive Weakness, Headache CEREBELLUM, LIVER GALL BLADDER< NECK, THROAD
GEMINI Potassium Chloride(Kali Mur)	Cancer Calcium Fluoride	Leo Magnesium Phosphate	Virgo Potassium Sulphate	Overweight, Pharyngitis, Rhinitis BRONCHIAL TUBES, PLEURA GLANDS, SHOULDERS, HANDS, LUNGS, all fibers & Tissues
CANCER Calcium Fluoride(Cal Flour)	Leo Magnesium Phosphate	Virgo Potassium Sulphate	Libra Sodium Phosphate	Joint Pains, Skin Illnesses, Varicose Veins ELASTIC TISSUE, BREAST, STOMACH, SPLEEN
LEO Magnesium Phosphate(Mag Phos)	Virgo Potassium Sulphate	Libra Sodium Phosphate	Scorpio Calcium Sulphate	Cramps, Migraines, Pain HEART, MOTOR NERVES back and sides of heart
VIRGO Potassium Sulphate(Kali Sulph)	Libra Sodium Phosphate	Scorpio Calcium Sulphate	Sagittarius Silica	Asthma, Eczemas, Sinusitis SOLAR PLEXUS OIL, BOWELS
LIBRA Sodium Phosphate(Nat Phos)	Scorpio Calcium Sulphate	Sagittarius Silica	Capricorn Calcium Phosphate	Raised Blood Lipid Concentration, Furnace Mouth, Overweight BLADDER, KIDNEYS, ACID NEUTRALIZER
SCORPIO Calcium Sulphate(Cal Sulph)	Sagittarius Silica	Capricorn Calcium Phosphate	Aquarius Sodium Chloride	Artois, Puss, Rheumatism PRO CREATIVE ORGANS, VASCULAR COATINGS AND CASTS
SAGITTARIUS Silica	Capricorn Calcium Phosphate	Aquarius Sodium Chloride	PISCES Iron Phosphate	Connective Tissue Weakness, Arteriosclerosis, Defensive, Weakness HIPS, THIGHS, SURGEON SPADE INSULATOR
CAPRICORN Calcium Phosphate(Cal Phos)	Aquarius Sodium Chloride	PISCES Iron Phosphate	Aries Potassium Phosphate	Back Pains, Blood Circulation, Disturbances, Regulation DIGESTION, BONES, KNEES, SACRUM, ALBUMIN
AQUARIUS Sodium Chloride(Nat Mur)	PISCES Iron Phosphate	Aries Potassium Phosphate	Taurus Sodium Sulphate	Diabetes, Dry Skin, Rheumatism ANKLES, SALINE, SOLUTION OF THE BLOOD, WHITE CORPUSCLES
PISCES Iron Phosphate(Fer Phos)	Aries Potassium Phosphate	Taurus Sodium Sulphate	Gemini Potassium Chloride	Fever, Colds, Inflammations FEET ARTERIAL BOOD< RED CORPUSCLES

Illustration/Graph
Dr. D E Lowry-Charles, PhD, ND, CNHP, CHS

*Dandelion Root and leaves contain all 12 mineral tissue salts.

	Fire	Earth	Air	Water
CARDINAL (Renewal System) MAGNETIC FORCE Creating /Rebuilding	♈ ARIES MARS #6 KALI PHOS Male/ Hot Outgoing	♑ CAPRICORN SATURN #2 CALC PHOS Masculine/ Cold Receptive	♎ LIBRA VENUS #10 NAT PHOS Male/ Medium Out-going	♋ CANCER MOON #1 CALC FLUR Feminine/Cold Receptive
FIXED (Energetic System) VITAL FORCE	♌ LEO SUN #8 MAG PHOS Male/ Hot Out-going	♉ TAURUS VENUS #11 NAT SULPH Female/ Medium Receptive	♒ AQUARIUS SATURN/ URANUS #9 NAT MUR Neutral/ Medium Out-going	♏ SCORPIO PLUTO/ MARS #3 CALC SULP Feminine/ Coldest Receptive
MUTABLE (Cleaning System) ELECTRIC FORCE Purification	♐ SAGITTARIUS JUPITER #12 SILICA Male/ Hot Outgoing & Neutral	♍ VIRGO MERCURY/ CHIRON #7 KALI SULPH Neutral/ Cold Receptive & Neutral	♊ GEMINI MERCURY #5 KALI MUR Neutral/ Cold Out-going & Neutral	♓ PISCES NEPTUNE/ JUPITER #4 FERR PHOS Neutral/ Cold Receptive & Neutral

Tissue and Salts Chart

XII. The Decans

Most people see themselves as their sun sign (Zodiac Sign) character and they associate themselves with the planet that rules their sun sign. But there are actually 3 ruling planets for each sun sign. They change every 10 days or 10o because degrees are days. Each sign encompasses 30o (days) of the 360o wheel. Each 30o is broken up into 3 sections of 10o (days). These are called decanates or decans, wherein the changing of the ruling of the ruling planet takes place. They help bring in, maintain and usher out the initiatives or purpose of the sun sign. The changing ruling planet(s) will always be the ruler of the signs in the same element (i.e. if you are a fire sign, the new rulers will be the rulers of the other two fire signs, etc.). The ruling planet then gives a different attribute to the sun sign, thereby causing different influences to those who have the same sun sign. Another reason two people of the same sign are not the same.

The attributes of 3 ruling planets (decanates or decants) follow the same pattern found in the "Qualities"- initiating/cardinal, fixed/stabilizing, flexible/mutating. This being natural order within the signs and seasons.

- First Decant 0o-10o (days)= Cardinal qualities or initiative of Sun sign.
- Second Decant 11o-20o (days)= Fixed qualities of the Sun sign.
- Third Decant 21o-30o (days)= Mutable qualities of the Sun sign.

Sun Sign	Ruler by Degree 0o-10o	Ruler by degree 11o-20o	Ruler by degree 21o-30o
Aries	Mars	Sun (Leo)	Jupiter (Sagittarius)
Taurus	Venus	Mercury (Virgo)	Saturn (Capricorn)
Gemini	Mercury	Venus (Libra)	Uranus (Aquarius)
Cancer	Moon	Pluto (Scorpio)	Neptune (Pisces)

Leo	Sun	Jupiter (Sagittarius)	Mars (Aries)
Virgo	Mercury	Saturn (Capricorn)	Venus (Taurus)
Libra	Venus	Uranus (Aquarius)	Mercury (Gemini)
Scorpio	Pluto	Neptune (Pisces)	Moon (Cancer)
Sagittarius	Jupiter	Mars (Aries)	Sun (Leo)
Capricorn	Saturn	Venus (Taurus)	Mercury (Virgo)
Aquarius	Uranus	Mercury (Gemini)	Venus (Libra)
Pisces	Neptune	Moon (Cancer)	Pluto (Scorpio)

XIII. Birthday Number

Birthday Number is one of the most important information about a person. It tells us about personal characteristics, lessons learned, as well as about weaknesses which should be avoided.

1. Independence

Character, possibilities:

These people are independent and capable of deep love. They are able to make their own decisions. They are forgiving, respectable, accurate and honest. They are straightforward and can express themselves clearly. They like modern things and they introduce them with flexibility. They can think creatively and they use creativity to promote their objectives and to search for new possibilities. They are positive and smart. These people are self-confident, goal-directed, dynamic and inventive. They like to rely on themselves. They are hardworking and full of energy. They usually climb up the career ladder quickly. They are kind and they are good colleagues. They like to help others. They like travelling. They love life. They are able to appreciate beauty. They are aware of themselves. They have a strong spirit and great leadership skills. They have the ability to predict the future. They cling to their opinions. They do not like untidiness, laziness, negligence, false pride, empty promises and flattery. They like freedom and it is hard for them to tolerate the dominance of others. Sometimes they like being alone for short or longer periods of time.

Weaknesses, what should be learned:

These people are stubborn. They are hard to get along with because they think they are the center of the universe. They can be very dependent on other people; low self-confidence. They can get angry easily, be short-tempered and have difficulty communicating with others - these characteristics can get them into unpleasant situations. They are selfish and lonely. They only see themselves and talk about themselves. They are jealous and bossy. It is hard for them to accept when a friendship has ended. When they fail to achieve what they want, they become sad, pessimistic, angry and depressed. They cannot take criticism but they like to criticize others. They are easily influenced and they influence others. They rush into decisions and they take risks. They are too proud. They buy things they cannot afford.

2. Sociability

Character, possibilities:

These people are very considerate and they are a good listener. They are loyal and emotional. They like to do things for other people and they are able to understand how others feel. They are gregarious and keep close to their family. They are diplomatic.

They are romantic and they have an artistic talent. They have a delicate nature. They are intuitive; harmony is important. They like giving and receiving; important decisions should only be made after careful consideration. They want to have a partner because without one they feel lonely. When dealing with a problem it is necessary to seek mutual agreement even if compromises will have to be made. They can be silenced easily.

Weaknesses, what should be learned:

These people are hypersensitive and vulnerable. They often blame others.

They may manipulate others or be dependent on them, especially on their partners. Beware of trivial arguments. They should avoid distrust, fear and disharmony. They lack courage and ambition. They are indecisive. They may emotionally blackmail others. They are bitter and quarrelsome. They tend to accumulate wealth. They often do not finish their work. They should be careful about what they eat. Watch out for anger.

3. Friendship

Character, possibilities:

These people are social and friendly. They like people and have many friends. They are honest. They are creative and have many ideas. They are not afraid of other people. In a romantic relationship they want to be independent. It is very important that they find a partner who is social. These people are bold, active, reliable, and initiative. They want to make an impact. They like success. They are lucky in love.

They like to travel. They usually think thoroughly before they act. They like dressing up. It is important to be cheerful and to take life as it is. They should not waste energy. They should spend enough time with their partner and children. They should try to be more flexible and be interested in all opportunities, not immediately rejecting them.

Weaknesses, what should be learned:

These people should avoid mocking others. They should avoid shallowness. They are eccentric and too ambitious. They are jealous and hot-tempered. They are arrogant. They blame and criticize others. They play with other people´s emotions. They are hypersensitive and easily distracted. They are nervous. Beware of unnecessary discussions and dictatorial tendencies, especially at home.

4. Mental balance

Character, possibilities:

These people are practical and balanced. They like routine. They are decisive.

They have good organizational skills. They are reliable and compassionate. They are warm, generous and loyal to people they like. They are systematic and patient.

They work very hard to achieve security and stability in everything. Stable romantic relationship plays an important role. Inborn insecurity is the reason for accumulation of property. Their innate instinct forces them to always fight against something. They do not like spending money.

Weaknesses, what should be learned:

These people may lose their personality or they may lose hope. They are often aggressive and rude. They criticize everything and they are selfish. They should not make hasty decisions and they should avoid melancholy.

5. Perception

Character, possibilities:

These people are open, daring, energetic and principled. They like to be their own boss. They are perceptive. They like progress and need space for their activities. They like changes and nothing is fixed for them. They have almost magnetic influence on people, they are charming. They are warm, cheerful and quick-witted. They are willing to take risks. They think logically and they are articulate. They like communicating with others. They are always in a hurry and they like to travel. They look after their appearance and health. They like success. They like being appreciated. They are interested in novel things and about how they work. They are curious. They know what they want. They do not like if somebody tells them what to do. They often move from one thing to another. They are shallow. They need to be more patient. They should avoid boredom.

Weaknesses, what should be learned:

These people are neurotic and withdrawn, moody and irritable. They are quarrelsome. Some of them become cheaters and liars. They become vulgar and irritable when they get angry. They force their opinions on others. They are tense and easily stressed. They are unstable. Beware of deceitful relationships.

6. Harmony

Character, possibilities:

These people need love and warmth of home. They do everything to achieve harmony. They seek a partner for the whole life. They are kind, sensitive, considerate, and ingenuous. They love their family and other people. They live ordinary married life. These people need to make time for themselves and for others. They have good relationships with their parents, children and friends. They have many friends. They like to feel that they belong somewhere and that they have their place somewhere. They are fair and perceptive. They are gentle and they have a pleasant and warm voice. They are romantic and devoted. They consider sex as a natural part of relationship that makes the relationship complete. They like luxury and beauty, and they have an artistic talent. Team work is important to them. They like to be in a company of beautiful people. They are the so called home type.

They are secretive. They may have a problem to find a partner or they look for reasons for breaking up with their partner. They are naive. They have a lack of self-confidence. In order to maintain harmony in their romantic relationship they may lose their dignity.

Weaknesses, what should be learned:

These people tend to be lazy. They are always unnecessarily in a rush. They are full of emotions. They seek revenge. They have a tendency for drug and alcohol addiction. Extramarital affairs are stressful and dangerous for them. They are only interested in satisfying their own needs. They demand gifts in return for a favour, for example at work. They are selfish and may harass others. Beware of obsession.

7. Experience

Character, possibilities:

These people have the ability to listen to their inner voice. They are sensitive and perceptive. They need a partner in their life. They often have opinions of spiritual nature; they have interest in the environment and medicine. They often becomes an activist. They like helping others. They believe in themselves, in nature, in others, and in life. They face challenges very often and these challenges are the driving force of their personal growth. They are able to analyze situations very well. They choose their wording carefully. They are kind, social, romantic, artistic and sentimental. They are good speakers. They are friendly, nice and attractive for the opposite sex.

They want to try everything themselves and they do not take advice or warning from those who have already experienced the situation. They cannot stand fools, hypocrites and dishonesty. They like secrets. They do not follow advice blindly and avoid "what would happen if" thoughts. They need to let things take their natural course and stop slowing them down.

Weaknesses, what should be learned:

These people are reckless, anxious, and too extravagant. They are often naive when it comes to their relationships because they do not see their partner realistically. They have a tendency for drug and alcohol addiction. They like to use intrigues that may lead to the destruction of other people. They are restless and distraught. They like to use other people. They do not forgive. They change their opinions very often. They unnecessarily waste their energy and time. They realize their plans without thinking about them thoroughly. They have no respect for the work of others. They have agonizing feelings. They are oblivious of other people´s feelings.

8. Balance

Character, possibilities:

These people are full of energy. They have leadership inclinations. They are intelligent, quick-witted and enterprising. They have good imagination. They are hardworking and determined. They are patient, quick, honest, and serious. They have a strong will. They are willing to overcome a number of obstacles if they want to achieve their goal and they take every job seriously. Success, rewards, money, and social status play important roles in their lives. They are confident and efficient. They strive for material wealth. They will always have to balance their strength, energy and power with wealth and sentiment, glory, love and intelligence. They are adaptable. They do not forget unfair treatment.

Weaknesses, what should be learned:

These people are obstinate and stubborn in dealing with difficult situations and fighting enemies. Beware of greed, power, abuse of position and money. They are selfish and they have no understanding for others. They like to criticize and deceive others. They engage in various affairs and they are revengeful. They are boastful. They want to get privileges for themselves at the expense of others. They are manipulative and they do not play "fair". They are gloomy and they lack a sense of humor. They are intolerant. They may destroy everything around them when they get angry. Beware of passivity, alcohol and drugs. They are troubled by bad memories and sad past. They engage in various love adventures and love affairs. They spread rumors. They are aggressive, bossy, stubborn, strong-willed and they tend to terrorize others. It's a strong karmic number, so these people will get exactly what they deserve – multiple times.

9. Deliberation

Character, possibilities:

These people are very sensitive and reliable. They will tell the truth only after they think about it carefully. They have the ability to accept themselves for who they are. They want to be a rescuer. They are friendly and serious. They search for the deeper meaning of life. They are ambitious, creative, powerful, open, honest, independent and fearless. They are able to face very difficult situations. They work very hard. They are responsible and they like honor and glory. They use a lot of energy in order to gain admiration and sympathy. They have organizational abilities. They are always very active in order to achieve their goal. They are spiritual and forgiving. They like learning and experiencing new things. In a way, they are perfectionists. They search for a partner with similar interests. They are humble or shy. They do not procrastinate and they deal with problems immediately, because they believe that fast and radical solutions are the best. They are picky and they have a tendency to be extravagant. They take everything too seriously and they worry too much.

Weaknesses, what should be learned:

These people are afraid of everything. It is difficult to get along with them because they are irritable and easy to provoke. They find it difficult to control themselves. They are impulsive, aggressive and sometimes even cruel. They take unnecessary risks. They create conflicts in their marriage. They have a negative attitude towards their co-workers, friends and partners. They are arrogant and they get angry easily. Beware of inner anxiety, drugs, false pride and hypocrisy. They are intolerant and narrow-minded. They condemn others and they look for their flaws. They may be snobs and they may have hurtful comments.

10. Strength

Character, possibilities:

These people are emotionally very strong. They are independent, self-sufficient and proud. They are hardworking, honest and confident. They safeguard their privacy. They only achieve success if they work hard. They have leadership tendency. They are good at pushing through their interests and goals. They are creative, full of energy and dedicated to their work. They are compassionate. They only have a few good friends. They do not have mood swings. They like to think that they are unique. They should be careful not to cling to one big goal and lose track of other, sometimes even more important goals. They are sometimes afraid to push through their objectives. They avoid routine.

Weaknesses, what should be learned:

These people are reserved and withdrawn. They may temporarily leave their family. They are hard to understand. They are often dependent on sedatives. They can be very dependent on another people. They are stubborn and it causes tension in their relationships. They may feel superior. Beware of quarrels and alcohol.

11. Sensitivity

Character, possibilities:

These people are sensitive and intuitive. They are interested in the spiritual path. They are a charismatic person. They like other people. They are a daydreamer. They are diplomatic. They have revolutionary thinking and authoritative behavior. They have healing abilities. They are perfectionists. They like making collective decisions. They don't like sharing their feelings. They do not hurt others knowingly. It is important to maintain a balance between giving and receiving. Harmony is needed primarily at home. They need to rest every day. They rub their hands or bite their nails.

Weaknesses, what should be learned:

These people are stubborn, nasty, vulnerable and irritable. Misunderstandings may occur. They often get into a state of uncertainty. Sometimes they are dependent on others. Beware of anger and emotional outbursts. They are stubborn and selfish. They may be shallow and they may try to manipulate or confront others.

12. Versatility

Character, possibilities:

These people are creative and insightful. They are versatile and professionally capable. They are smart, popular and attractive. They excel in a number of areas. They are family-oriented. They are open, friendly, social, inquisitive, cheerful, independent and bright. They are goal oriented, flexible and creative. They like traveling and exploring new places. They love life. They like to cook. They love festivals and celebrations. They need a partner who does not have problems. They protect their privacy. They are too demanding. They do not like when others tell them that they will not be able to accomplish something. There may be confusion and chaos in their lives.

Weaknesses, what should be learned:

These people are impulsive, anxious and tense. Their decision-making is chaotic and they make decisions at the last moment. They may be indifferent, close and stubborn. They are arrogant, jealous and possessive. Watch out for anger, vindictiveness and violent emotions. They look for faults in other people.

13. Vulnerability

Character, possibilities:

These people are independent and ambitious. They are loyal, open and responsible. They are faithful to their partner. They works hard to get material security. They are practical and reliable. They always look for new opportunities and goals. They are good leaders. They like to have a responsibility. They are flexible, creative and active. Their work becomes their hobby. They are able to inspire others and create a home atmosphere. They are vulnerable. The influence of a dominant person (a parent, a partner or a relative) becomes evident. They lack self- confidence. They should avoid routine and monotone activities.

Weaknesses, what should be learned:

These people are quick-tempered. Sometimes they feel useless. They get offended easily and they are irritable. Sometimes they may say very hurtful things. Beware of explosions of anger and conflicts. Beware of confusion in life and extreme attitudes - e.g. they either love or hate someone. They try to get their own way without trying to find a compromise. They take unnecessary risks. Beware of dependence on e.g. food, alcohol, drugs, sex, medicines, etc. They may start arguments and make scenes.

14. Determination

Character, possibilities:

These people live their life the way they like. They need a safe home environment and a good job. They work hard and can make money. They are good at doing business and at trading. They are considerate, attentive and reliable. They are very active and they start big projects. They are good-natured, wise and they react quickly. An important change is the change that brings new ideas into action. They may have a musical talent and sometimes they are spiritual and religious. They are ambitious, persistent and full of ideas. They are independent, responsible, attractive and adaptable. They think quickly and often they also speak quickly. They want to make the most out of opportunities. Sometimes they like communicating with symbols or numbers. They do not like when other people give them advice. They like to keep their old habits even if they are not useful anymore. They should avoid laziness. Sometimes they try to avoid problems. They are dreaming of material wealth.

Weaknesses, what should be learned:

These people are quick-tempered and impulsive. It is hard for them to forget wrongdoings. When problems occur, they want to make changes immediately. Sometimes they may become dictators. Sometimes they underestimate situations, plan incorrectly and make wrong assumptions. They should select their friends carefully. They are nervous. They discard good opportunities. They make up stories and create problems for themselves as well as for others. Beware of alcohol and drugs. They are hot-headed.

15. Courage

Character, possibilities:

These people are perceptive, sensitive and independent. They are ambitious, active and energetic. They have courage. They are proud and hardworking. They are creative. They are caring and kind. Family is everything for them. These people sometimes express their opinions directly without inhibitions. They like money, popularity and luxury. They want to get richer. They also like freedom and life without restrictions. They are communicative and funny and they appreciate beauty. They want to try everything. They guard their privacy. They are obsessed with work, making money or with nutrition. They should learn to accept realistic commitments.

Weaknesses, what should be learned:

These people are rebellious. They do not tolerate stress well. It is difficult to get to know them. They spend a lot of money and they lead an extravagant life. They are sentimental. Sometimes they explode and become rude. Beware of emotional imbalances. Sometimes they like to create extreme life situations. They may like drinking etc. They are unbending and revengeful. They are stubborn in the pursuit of their intentions. Beware of anger, malice, and accusations of others.

16. Directness

Character, possibilities:

These people have a clear opinion on what is right and wrong in life. They fight intolerance. They are very observant. They have a sense of harmony. They are tender and sweet. They try to get along with others and understand their needs. They are able to do everything for a long time. They like to have an independent partner. They have a healing ability and they are inclined to have a spiritual life. They are even able to heal themselves. They see purpose of life in helping others. They may have a tendency to have so-called prophetic dreams. They are compassionate and they are good listeners. They are ambitious, social and responsible. They have a strong personality and they use intuition to achieve their goals. They have a good analytical thinking. They hate dogmatists. They want to try everything. Sometimes they are too fixed on their family or relatives. They have exhibitionist tendencies. They need to appreciate what they have. They should spend more time with their partner. Sometimes they live in illusions.

Weaknesses, what should be learned:

These people do not like rules and restrictions. They suffer from uncertainty and mental tension. Beware of intrigues. They are cautious and worried about losing their status. It is hard for them to accept failure. Their life can be full of ups and downs. They are full of themselves and as a consequence they lose a notion of reality. They are not assertive. They are hypersensitive and they may be lazy. Beware of anger, emotional imbalance, and attempts to interfere in other people´s lives. They are cold and calculating. They tend to provoke others. They are not willing to consider other people´s opinions.

17. Capability

Character, possibilities:

These people are strong and courageous. They are sensitive and ambitious.

They are very observant. They are efficient, quick-witted and hardworking. They have leadership skills. Romantic relationship is very important for them. They are social. They may have an ability to heal others. They are able to think correctly and for long periods of time. They will reach success later in life. They will get rich. They have the ability to implement their plans. They are materialistic. They have good logical thinking. They deeply believe in life and they do not panic. They are ambitious and determined. They seek unconventional ways to resolve problems. They like to take on responsibilities. When selecting friends they should only turn to family members or very good friends. They are determined. They should avoid manipulating others. They are either controlling or controlled. They have a lack of self-confidence.

Weaknesses, what should be learned:

These people are prone to dramatic emotional expressions and scenes. They are moody and irritable. Sometimes they are full of themselves. It is difficult to coexist with them. Sometimes their attitude brings inner conflicts. They are aggressive, egoistic, intrusive, stubborn and bossy. They only think of themselves. They cannot stand opposition. Beware of obsession with success and wealth; rapid way up and then collapse; they are terrified of failures.

18. Responsibility

Character, possibilities:

These people are strong and capable. They are ruminative and intelligent. They are caring and protective. They can get inspiration from higher sources. They may have a tendency to be philosophical. They are sincere and principled. They are able to overcome difficult situations. They are materialists and they do everything to make money. They long for recognition. They are smart and ambitious. They have organizational skills and strong will. They like to experiment. They have clear opinions and they always want to be right. They do not like to boast about their property, wealth, power, success and social status. They care about what others say about them. They want to know everything about their partner. They should avoid criticizing others; they should try to understand them instead.

Weaknesses, what should be learned:

These people are hasty, nutty, irritable and touchy. They suffer from inner conflicts and tension. They have a restless mind and a tendency to be melodramatic. Imbalance of energy leads to health problems. They are jealous. Their life is full of dramatic changes. Unbalanced energy interferes with every relationship and marriage. Sometimes they are spiteful and vicious. They may be rude and cruel. Watch out for Karma, mainly in the field of recognition. Beware of prejudice, authoritarianism and aggression. They are cynical and they have a skeptical approach towards life.

19. Participation

Character, possibilities:

These people are very strong and energetic. They are wise, understanding and empathetic. They are intellectual. They are patient and ready to please others. In romantic relationships they are devoted. They want to understand their partner and are generous. They passionately protect their family. They are appreciated, honoured, successful and rich. They usually have a well-paid job. In a way, they are pioneers in their field. They are inventive, creative, straightforward and vital in achieving their goals. They like to have a high social status, so they work hard to achieve it. They believe in themselves. They are pleasant and confident. They are independent, sometimes even loners. It is not good when someone ignores them, abuses them or disappoints them. They cling to their opinions and high demands.

Weaknesses, what should be learned:

These people are unbalanced and moody. It's hard to understand them. They may feel superior and they like to feel exceptional. They are stubborn, explosive, bossy, nervous, neurotic, jealous and unreasonable. They may be fawning, especially when they try to impress somebody important. Watch out for hatred and self-pity. They are determined to reach their goals. They like to criticize others. They lack self-confidence.

20. Intuition

Character, possibilities:

These people are sensitive, loyal and kind. their partner is very important to them. Love relationship plays an important role. They are patient. They need love and tenderness. They seek harmony. They are careful, open and caring. They are compassionate and they like to work with other people. They are good at resolving disputes because they are trying to reach an agreement. They are tolerant, reflexive and modest. They find it hard to be alone. They have strongly defined attitude toward others. They are moody.

Weaknesses, what should be learned:

These people may lose their self-control. They are irritable and bad-tempered. Beware of stress because it causes health problems. They are impatient and nervous. They change their mind often. Beware of emotional confrontations and emotional manifestations. They are indecisive and they often experience profound sadness. They are fearful, manipulative and vulnerable.

21. Sympathy

Character, possibilities:

These people have a great potential. They are sensitive, kind and tolerant. They try to understand others. They are creative and able to do a wide range of activities. They are social and diplomatic. They are considerate and gentle in their romantic relationships. Communication is very important for them. They are assertive so they have a good job. They are governed by instinct. They are optimists with a positive attitude to life. They like success and new challenges. They like cooperating with others. Sometimes they cling to their family. They lack self-confidence. They try to help others meet their needs so much that they forget about their own needs.

Weaknesses, what should be learned:

These people can hurt others with words. They are hot-tempered, impatient, anxious and irritable. Beware of superiority, confrontation, changing moods and emotions. They may be greedy and confrontational.

22. Endurance

Character, possibilities:

These people are sensitive and kind. That is why they need their partner's support. They are practical and thorough. They have methodological and organisational abilities. They easily make practical decisions. At work they are efficient and accurate. They are particularly successful in politics. They long for the realisation of their dreams. Their home and financial security of their family play an important role. They are responsible and reliable. They like responsibility and harmony. Routine activities suit them. They are caring and generous. They tend to accumulate material wealth that prevail over feelings. They need security. Sometimes they are not able to accept gifts. They may become workaholics. They hate emotional confrontation.

Weaknesses, what should be learned:

These people are tough and stubborn. Beware of marriage problems. Sometimes they have a sense of injustice. Watch out for emotional outbursts. They worry about their ability to secure the basic needs. They have a lack of self-confidence. They are manipulative. They are unfair, irritable and cruel. They do not care about the needs of other people. They are vulnerable.

23. Autonomy

Character, possibilities:

These people make decisions without help and cannot be influenced. They live their own life. Sometimes they seem to want freedom, but in reality they need a partner. They are sensitive, gentle, loving and they want to be loved. They are understanding, quick-witted and social. They are hardworking and they usually do not have work related problems. They are good entrepreneurs. They are witty and intelligent. They are popular and sometimes even famous. Exceptional abilities may appear. They long for realising their ideas. They are sincere, open, practical and expressive. They are reflective and have a good memory. These people are self-sufficient and they want freedom. Sometimes they are childish. They tend to be messy. They do not reveal their true feelings.

They are daydreamers. They need to avoid exhaustion.

Weaknesses, what should be learned:

These people are sometimes hard to understand. They have a tricky personality. It's hard to deal with them when things do not go as they wish. If they fail to maintain balance, they will live without love, except the love for their property. They are cold, selfish, moody, insensitive and hot-tempered. They shy away from responsibilities. They are easily distracted and unstable. They like to exaggerate or even lie. They often move from one relationship to another.

24. Kindness

Character, possibilities:

These people are very friendly, helpful and caring. They are sensitive, gentle, generous and kind. They have a methodical approach and are practical. They like harmony and beauty. Family life is very important to them. They are persistent and they have good organizational skills. They are systematic, efficient, diligent and constructive. They have a good heart and they try helping others. They try to reach an agreement with others and they are good negotiators. They are romantics. They may have a musical talent. They are convinced that everything happens in its due time. They are inclined to delay finding a solution to a problem. They take time to make decisions and they think carefully about the problem before they decide. They take their duties too seriously. They rely on other people. Their welfare, prestigious job or similar things are very important to them.

Weaknesses, what should be learned:

These people are secretive, hasty, irritable, hypersensitive and insecure. They may experience failure and betrayal. Watch out for work under stress. Beware of depression and emotional outbursts. They are moody and cranky. Sometimes they are passive or lazy.

25. Modesty

Character, possibilities:

These people are modest and humble. They are sensitive and kind. They need a sensitive partner in their life. They are creative and entertaining. They are artistic. They have good imagination and talent. They may get wealthy through marriage. They like communicating, even through media, for example computer. They are good listeners. They are intuitive, social and attractive. They have a good logical and analytical thinking. They are practical and patient. They have a sense for detail. They can make good use of opportunities.

Weaknesses, what should be learned:

These people need peace and they should try to adapt. They should avoid confusion in life. Sometimes their reactions are unpredictable. They want to try everything. They like to postpone things that need to be addressed without delay. They are emotional and indecisive. They cannot deal with stressful situations related to their love life. They often have a difficult childhood. They are moody, distracted, unstable, unclear and ambiguous. Beware of anger. Sometimes they're afraid of change. They often worry. They can be very dependent on another person. They only think of themselves. They are hypersensitive, irritable and their feelings are often hurt.

26. Assertiveness

Character, possibilities:

These people are sensitive, kind and understanding. They have a great inner strength to overcome difficulties. They have organizational and leadership skills. They have a very good judgment and they will notice everything. They are quick-witted and they are able to do anything. They are bright and they are able to do anything. They are independent, ambitious and generous. They separate their personal life from their work. They are hardworking, tenacious and successful. They will achieve success and high social status later in life. They want emotional security. They are gentle and they have a good heart. They are generous and they support others. They like to solve other people´s problems. They are diplomatic and they are able to inspire others. They are responsive, open and accessible. They can work very hard to achieve success. Their relationships and career are important to them. They will reach recognition or even fame.

Weaknesses, what should be learned:

These people need others to show interest in them. They are insecure and sometimes dependent on others. They take everything very seriously; they are too eager and obsessed with their feelings. They have problems in their romantic relationships so it is very important to choose a partner very carefully. They are greedy, arrogant and they overestimate themselves. It is necessary to maintain a balance. They are cruel, revengeful, hypersensitive, moody and aggressive. They hate those who hurt them. They pester other people. They are especially intolerable in managerial positions. Beware of pride and emotional tension.

27. Dutifulness

Character, possibilities:

These people are sensitive, emotional and intuitive. They are honest, pragmatic and conservative. They are not subject to new trends. They avoid shallow relationships. Romantic relationship is very important for them. They are enterprising. They are able to enforce their plans and ideas. They are devoted to their family. They may get rich. They try to get information about life and they look for the meaning of life. They feel good when they are in the nature. They like helping other people. Their home plays an important role. They are clever and quick-witted. They make decisions after careful consideration.

Weaknesses, what should be learned:

These people deeply experience disappointment. They react sensitively to various situations. They often succumb to illusions. They take everything very seriously. They are naive. They punish themselves. They think that they are useless. They tend to be self-destructive. Beware of addiction to drugs and alcohol. Beware of nervous breakdowns, anxiety and suicide attempts. They are often bossy. They are indecisive, moody, vulnerable and closed. They tend to criticize others.

28. Divergence

Character, possibilities:

These people are independent and try to succeed. They are guided by their emotions and only then by reasoning. Romantic relationship and family ties are important. They have a sense of humour. They like to have everything under their control. They decide things for themselves. They defend their rights with vigour. They are gentle, loving, warm and caring. They rather do something themselves then ask others to do it. They have many friends and acquaintances. They are interested in everything progressive and modern. They have a talent for doing business. They are dynamic and ambitious people. They are bright and they make decisions quickly. They are straightforward, open and intelligent. They appreciate cooperation and encourage other people.

Weaknesses, what should be learned:

These people are passive, insensitive, stubborn and impulsive. Usually they cannot be restricted or forced to do anything. They have doubts about their abilities. They are irritable, argumentative, aggressive and dominant. They may be lonely. Sometimes they are angry and spiteful. They are vulnerable and closed. They negatively affect other people. They are explosive and unpleasant. Beware of dictatorial tendencies. They insult and boss other people around. They are hypersensitive and inflexible.

29. Chaos

Character, possibilities:

These people are sensitive and perceptive. They have a great potential for extra-sensory perception. They have the ability to find truth and wisdom. They have excellent thinking processes. Spiritual activity is very important.

These people become wealthy and financially secure. They are hardworking, persistent and inventive. They have lot of ideas and a strong intuition. They are open and they have good logical reasoning. They make friends easily and they are attractive. They are clever and communicative. They often inspire and encourage other people to be creative.

Weaknesses, what should be learned:

These people should avoid boredom. Their romantic relationships are unclear. They find it hard to talk about their feelings. They have high expectations of other people. They are vulnerable. Dangerous misunderstandings may occur. They rather try to dull their feelings with alcohol and drugs than look for solutions. They are closed and secretive. Sometimes they are eccentric. Instability causes marriage problems. They may be insecure and lonely. They are irritable, hot-tempered, cunning and meticulous. Beware of quarrels, emotional outbursts and disappointments. They may be hasty and deal with others in an uncaring way. They are afraid of losing their material values.

30. Vigor

Character, possibilities:

These people have great creative imagination and a brilliant mind. They first think about the problem and then makes a decision. They have radical views on life. They are inventive. They are charming. Communication is important in their romantic relationships. They can work hard in order to achieve comfortable lifestyle. They do several things at once. They have a special philosophical way of thinking. They tend to help those who suffer. They are warm, friendly and they have a sense of humour. They are social, lively, active, adaptable and creative. They often like to sleep.

Weaknesses, what should be learned:

These people usually do not accept failure. They cannot tolerate mediocrity. Everything is fun to them. They like to be the centre of attention and they are eccentric. They look for faults in other people. Sometimes they unnecessarily waste their energy and do not finish what they started. They lack self-confidence. They put others down with criticism. They can abuse their good qualities for achieving something they want from life. They have a complicated personality and it is difficult to understand them and get them to talk. In some ways they may be tyrants. They are calculating and they have a sharp tongue. They tend to manipulate others. They are insensitive, shallow and easily distracted. They gossip and blame others. Beware of jealousy, quarrels, conflicts, and confusion in life. They are messy and lazy; sexual imbalance.

31. Motivation

Character, possibilities:

These people are very bright. They are descreet and willing to do everything to achieve success. They like company and spending time with intelligent people. Communication is important. They are straightforward, honest, generous, gentle, faithful and considerate. They do a lot for their family. They are courageous and they have leadership abilities. They are friendly and social and they love social events. It is important for them to do different activities.

Weaknesses, what should be learned:

These people usually stay in the opposition. They need security. Sometimes they do not finish what they have started and they abandon their goals. Sometimes they think others must work the same way they do. They are shallow and irresponsible. They have the ability to lie and cheat. They may have fraudulent intentions. They are spiteful, bossy and they like to mock others. They are closed. They may use people who are not able to defend themselves. There may be sudden and unexpected changes. There may be misunderstandings and loneliness. They may become shy and antisocial. Beware of feeling superior or exceptional.

XIV. Chinese Astrology

WHAT IS CHINESE ASTROLOGY?

Like our own western astrology, Chinese astrology uses twelve different signs or symbols to define twelve basic categories of human being. Similarly to western astrology, the Chinese system uses a person's birth date as the basis for his sign, so in some ways the two systems are alike. Now, let's have a look at how they differ.

Our own astrological signs are monthly. Each of our signs has a different heaven-inspired mythological name and corresponds to a period equivalent to a single Sun cycle. If you were born in the Sun cycle period labeled Aquarius, then in western astrological terms you are an Aquarian. Chinese zodiacal signs are yearly. Each Chinese sign has a different animal name and corresponds to a period equivalent to an entire Chinese calendar year. If you were born in a yearlong period which the Chinese label the Dragon Year, then in Chinese astrological terms you are a Dragon. Simple? Yes.

Chinese astrology is so simple that you need only know the year of your birth to find out which of the twelve signs is yours. But there is one tricky aspect to consider. The Chinese New Year falls on a different date every year. This holiday can occur as early as mid- January or not until late February. If you were born in either January or February, that is, if you are either Capricorn or Aquarius in western astrology, you need to know whether you were born before or after the Chinese New Year. This interpretation has calculated that information for you.

The Chinese animal symbols are: Rat, Ox, Tiger, Cat, Dragon, Snake, Horse, Goat, Monkey, Rooster, Dog and Pig. These animals always appear in the same order. Since the beginning of recorded Chinese time, 2637 B.C., the animal sequence has recurred faithfully every twelve years. It always begins with the Rat and ends with the Pig. And to make things even more convenient for us Twentieth- Century Westerners, 1900 was a Rat year. That means that the next Rat year was 1912 and 1924, 1936, 1948, 1960, 1972, 1984 were all Rat years. Anybody born in any of these years is a Rat.

Chinese astrology, in one form or another, was widely used all over the Orient from the fortieth century B.C. It became especially popular between 2953 and 2838 B.C. under the Emperor Fu Hsi and again under Shen Nung, who was born in the twenty-eighth century

B.C. The zodiacal system and its philosophies as we know them today were codified by Ta Nao, an able minister of Emperor Huang Ti, born about 2704 B.C. It was made official in 2637 B.C. and was formally inaugurated, as were other historical events, at the sixtieth anniversary of the same popular Emperor Huang Ti's accession to the throne. For forty-six centuries thereafter, this system was used as the national standard and touched on all state affairs in China.

People born in Pig years are all somewhat naive and hate to say no; Rats are aggressive and talkative; Dogs loyal and ardent, Snakes altruistic and attractive; Dragons healthy and noisy; Horses independent and pragmatic; Goats dependent and creative and have no sense of time; Oxen slow and eloquent; Tigers rash and magnetic; Cats flee conflict and love tradition; Monkeys are entertaining and give lots of presents; Roosters are resourceful and bossy and adore clothes.

YIN AND YANG

Yin and Yang are the two main opposite but equal Chinese philosophical forces. The power of Yin is sometimes interpreted as passive, female, docile, receptive and society-oriented. Conversely, the Yang energy is said to be aggressive, male and socially indifferent. To the Chinese, everything in life is either Yin or Yang, and the trick to achieving harmony is knowing how to balance Yin and Yang so they operate in synergy rather than clash.

According to Chinese thought, any circumstance in the universe - a rainstorm, a night of love, a child taking its first steps, a wobbly bedstead, a frantic phone call, a dish of steaming pasta, a traffic accident, a dancing bride and groom or a washing-line in the sunlight - is the direct result of an energy balance or imbalance between Yin and Yang.

THE FIVE ELEMENTS - WOOD, FIRE, EARTH, METAL, AND WATER

To allow for movement to occur and bring about change, Chinese philosophy calls upon the five elements as agents of change and reaction. Change, the Chinese think, derives from the influence of the five main elements - Wood, Fire, Earth, Metal and Water - on the basic Yin or Yang energies. Like in the old rock, paper, scissors game, each of these five Chinese elements has the ability to control and/or destroy the previous element, and is capable of producing the element that directly follows it. In the regenerative cycle of the elements, Water engenders Wood. Wood begets Fire. Fire burns to Earth. Earth creates Metal and Metal gives way to Water.

Wood is characterized by the color green. Wood heralds the beginning of life, springtime and buds, sensuality and fecundity. Wood's influence affects the liver, the gallbladder and, by extension, the digestion. Wood needs moisture to thrive. Its two opposite yet equally emotional forces are rage and altruism. The Wood person will be expansive, outgoing and socially conscious.

Wood, in its turn, can create and nourish Fire. Fire's signatory color is red. Fire is hot weather, satisfaction of nature, aridity and dust. The tongue and the small intestine are the centers of attention in the Fire person's body. Fire makes heat, which either warms or burns. The Fire person must constantly seek to balance a tendency to explode and possibly destroy, against a desire to create coziness and warmth. Passionate by nature, this impatient, ebullient person must strive to keep his flame under control.

Earth is created from the ashes of the Fire. Now we are in the soothingly satisfying late summer cycle. Earth's favorite color is yellow, which represents the equanimity between beginnings and endings. The weather of Earth is mild or temperate. In the human body, Earth influences spleen, pancreas and mouth. Earth's two opposite but equal forces which need to be kept in constant balance are enhancing and smothering. On the one hand Earth gives care and allows for growth and improvement. On the other, Earth buries roots and snuffs out breath. Earth people are gifted for fairness and have the ability to commit themselves to protracted projects and complete Herculean tasks with ease. They must struggle against a penchant for worry.

The Earth grows Metal in her veins. Metal says white and autumn. Metal is cool, crisp weather. Metal's effect on the body centers in the lungs and respiratory system. It only secondarily rules the large intestine and the nose. Metal people like to communicate. They need to keep discord and harmony in constant balance. Metal signifies the onset of winter. Its influence can sometimes add sadness or gloom to an astrological chart. Two of Metal's emotional forces are melancholy and romance. I see Metal as Wagnerian. Metal people must guard against a tendency to wallow in nostalgia.

Lastly, Metal begets Water - groundwater trickling its way through layers of the Earth's core. Water's color is blue. Its season is full-blown winter. Water is always moving, fluid, and mutational. In our bodies, water's influence affects our plumbing systems, the kidneys and the bladder. The ear, too, comes under the spell of Water. Hence people born in Water-ruled years are frequently musical. They pick up on everything. Be it good or bad, they never miss a vibe. Water-ruled creatures are always very sensitive and sometimes even mentally fragile. The downside of Water's influence, then, is a stressful nervousness. To balance that fidgety, squeamish, overly sensitive side, Water endows its subjects with the noblest quality of all, kindness and sympathy. Sometimes too permeable, the Water-ruled must take precautions against drowning in the chagrin of those they see as less fortunate than themselves.

So, the five elements cause the commotion and are responsible for creating and maintaining both balance and imbalance - for moving things around and making life interesting. These purveyors of change can be controlled or not, depending on how one manages them.

Each animal year of the Chinese zodiac has been assigned one of the five elements. The elements each turn up twice in the cycle going away for another ten years. The five elements are always presented in the above order. Once we know this, we can understand how the elements directly affect us and pertain to individual characters.

The elements work by governing each animal sign once through the sixty-year "century" You will not come across a Water Horse more than once in sixty years. This fact alone accounts for sixty different basic character or destiny types. Further, when a learned Chinese astrologer draws up a chart for an individual person according to the Chinese astrological system, he takes into consideration the month and the season, the time of day and the type of weather on the day of birth as well as certain astral configurations at the moment of birth. In all, good Chinese astrologers deal with a base of no less than 512,640 different possible personality charts. This means that only two people in a million stand a chance of being born with identical destinies.

These are the characteristics of the twelve signs of the Chinese zodiac:

Rat: The rat is a charmer and not slow to make the most of any favorable opportunity. Rats do well in real estate, public relations, and advertising. Rats are sociable, dealing easily with people from all backgrounds, and they certainly enjoy the good life. They have sharp wits and even sharper tongues. The Rat's element is water and the color black.

黄牛

Ox (Buffalo in the Vietnamese zodiac): The strong, conservative Ox is born to lead. Oxen don't suffer fools gladly, are slow to change their opinions and do well in military careers or other careers where leadership is required. The Ox is loyal and patient and sooner or later, will make his or her mark in life. The Ox's element is earth, the color is golden yellow.

Tiger: The tiger is a courageous and noble soul, but also highly sensitive and quick to take offence. Tigers are likely to leap in where less hot-headed animals would fear to tread, and they can be very hard to control. They need a career where they can be boss or strike out on their own with no one to give them orders. The tiger's element is wood, and the color green.

Rabbit (Cat in the Vietnamese zodiac): The elegant, peace-loving rabbit is the soul of tact and would never dream of deliberately hurting anyone. The rabbit would prefer a simple white lie to an outright truth which could ruin a moment or damage a friendship. Rabbits are considered very lucky and do well in careers that bring out their people skills, such as law, acting, or diplomacy. The Rabbit's element is Wood, and the color green.

龍

Dragon: The talented, artistic Dragons are the real show-offs of the Chinese Zodiac. They are always popular, and they easily influence those around them. Dragons are determined, successful, and enthusiastic. Dragons usually find successful careers in the performing or creative arts, or in politics. Their element is earth, their color gold.

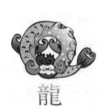

Snake: Snakes are the most enticing creatures in the Chinese Zodiac — they have much in common with the sign of Scorpio in western astrology. Snakes are alluring and highly intelligent and are often found in academic or scientific careers. But their great physical attraction also makes them renowned actors and entertainers. The Snake's element is fire, the color is red.

Horse: The hard working, confident horse puts its shoulder to even the most difficult task without complaint. Horses are justifiably proud of their elegance and strength, and while they may tend to parade their egos, they also love company and make stimulating friends. The horse does well in sports, the military and politics. The element of the horse is fire, the color red.

Goat: The goat is very agile and loves to climb but tends to worry a lot. They can be charming company, but at other times they will tend to bring their friends down by complaining and imagining the worst. Goats can find success in the caring professions, where they can worry for profit, or avoid the ulcers altogether by dropping out. The goat's element is earth, the color yellow.

Monkey: The clever, witty monkey is never short of friends. Always the life of the party, the monkey has a paw on the pulse of life and senses trends long before anyone else. So they find success in the media, advertising, and design. The monkey can also be very tricky and needs to guard against a tendency to take advantage of slower types. The Monkey's element is metal, and the color white.

Rooster: No one crows louder than the proud rooster, but few have more to crow about. The rooster is a shrewd, sharp, confident operator, who dreams big and looks to the stars. Roosters strut proudly and so choose careers where they can show off and reach impossible goals, such as the entertainment industry, or a business idea that breaks

barriers and travels worldwide. The element of the rooster is metal, and the color is white.

Dog: The faithful dog will always be there for family and friends. The dog takes setbacks philosophically, and find comfort in familiar, homely things. But there is a streak of adventure in the dog's soul that will see them running with the wind on occasion. The dog will also attack when it feels a loved one is threatened, so remember the wise advice and let sleeping dogs lie. Dogs do well in professions based on caring for others, such as teaching and nursing. The dog's element is earth, the color is yellow.

Pig: The honorable and scrupulous pig is one of the easiest signs of the Chinese Zodiac to get along with. But they are easily shocked, and also easily gulled into schemes cooked by some of the less scrupulous signs. The Pig has a creative side which should be nurtured, and will often find fulfillment, if not success, in the arts. The element of the pig is water, the color black.

The Chinese New Year begins on the second New moon after the Winter Solstice. Each new year comes under the influence of an animal in the Chinese zodiac. Here is a list of these animals and the years they rule:

Rat: 1912, 1924, 1936, 1948, 1960, 1972, 1984, 1996, 2008, 2020

Ox: 1913, 1925, 1937, 1949, 1961, 1973, 1985, 1997, 2009, 2021

Tiger: 1914, 1926, 1938, 1950, 1962, 1974, 1986, 1998, 2010, 2022

Rabbit: 1915, 1927, 1939, 1951, 1963, 1975, 1987, 1999, 2011, 2023

Dragon: 1916, 1928, 1940, 1952, 1964, 1976, 1988, 2000, 2012, 2024

Snake: 1917, 1929, 1941, 1953, 1965, 1977, 1989, 2001, 2013, 2025

Horse: 1918, 1930, 1942, 1954, 1966, 1978, 1990, 2002, 2014, 2026

Goat: 1919, 1931, 1943, 1955, 1967, 1979, 1991, 2003, 2015, 2027

Monkey: 1920, 1932, 1944, 1956, 1968, 1980, 1992, 2004, 2016, 2028

Rooster: 1921, 1933, 1945, 1957, 1969, 1981, 1993, 2005, 2017, 2029

Dog: 1922, 1934, 1946, 1958, 1970, 1982, 1994, 2006, 2018, 2030

Pig: 1923, 1935, 1947, 1959, 1971, 1983, 1995, 2007, 2019, 2031

The year of birth in which you were born corresponds to one of the five elements. An easy way for determining your element is to consider the last numeral in your year of birth and find your element below:

- 0 or 1: Metal
- 2 or 3: Water
- 4 or 5: Wood
- 6 or 7: Fire
- 8 or 9: Earth

Chinese Zodiac Compatibility:

There are twelve zodiacal animal signs in Chinese calendar and people born under each animal sign have different characteristics and personalities. It is possible to check details and compatibilities to gain guidance in life, for love or marriage. In fact, the zodiac compatibility can offer guidance for any relationship.

Which Chinese zodiac signs are compatible?

According to Chinese astrology compatibility, the animal signs that are four years apart from each other are believed to be compatible but are incompatible if they are six years apart. You can have a Chinese zodiac compatibility test between you and your partner through Chinese zodiac compatibility calculator; and the following Chinese zodiac compatibility chart is designed to help people find their Chinese horoscope compatibilities or love compatibilities before starting a relationship.

Chinese Zodiac Compatibility Chart

Animal Sign	Best Match	So-So	Worst Match
Rat	Ox, Dragon, Monkey	Rat, Tiger	Horse, Rooster
Ox	Rat, Snake, Rooster	Ox, Monkey	Tiger, Dragon, Horse, Sheep
Tiger	Dragon, Horse, Pig	Rat, Rabbit	Ox, Tiger, Snake, Monkey
Rabbit	Sheep, Monkey, Dog, Pig	Tiger, Rabbit, Dragon, Horse	Snake, Rooster
Dragon	Rooster, Rat, Monkey	Rabbit, Horse	Ox, Sheep, Dog
Snake	Dragon, Rooster	Dog	Tiger, Rabbit, Snake, Sheep, Pig
Horse	Tiger, Sheep, Rabbit	Rabbit, Dragon, Monkey, Dog	Rat, Ox, Rooster, Horse
Sheep	Horse, Rabbit, Pig	Rooster	Ox, Tiger, Dog
Monkey	Ox, Rabbit	Horse, Rooster	Tiger, Pig
Dog	Rabbit	Ox, Snake, Horse, Dog	Dragon, Sheep, Rooster
Pig	Tiger, Rabbit, Sheep	Rooster	Snake, Monkey

Compatibility Chart of 12 Zodiac Animals

	Rat	Ox	Tiger	Rabbit	Dragon	Snake	Horse	Sheep	Monkey	Rooster	Dog	Pig
Rat	Average	Perfect match	Average	Perfect match	Perfect match	Good friend	Worst couple	Good match or enemy	Complementary	Worst couple	Complementary	Complementary
Ox	Perfect match	Average	Worst couple	Complementary	Worst couple	Perfect match	Worst couple	Worst couple	Average	Perfect match	Complementary	Good match or enemy
Tiger	Average	Worst couple	Worst couple	Average	Complementary	Worst couple	Perfect match	Good friend	Worst couple	Complementary	Complementary	Perfect match
Rabbit	Complementary	Complementary	Average	Average	Average	Worst couple	Average	Perfect match	Perfect match	Worst couple	Perfect match	Perfect match
Dragon	Perfect match	Worst couple	Perfect match	Average	Good friend	Perfect match	Average	Worst couple	Complementary	Complementary	Worst couple	Good friend
Snake	Good friend	Complementary	Worst couple	Worst couple	Complementary	Worst couple	Good friend	Worst couple	Good friend	Perfect match	Average	Worst couple
Horse	Worst couple	Worst couple	Perfect match	Average	Average	Good friend	Worst couple	Perfect match	Average	Worst couple	Average	Complementary
Sheep	Good match or enemy	Worst couple	Good friend	Perfect match	Worst couple	Worst couple	Perfect match	Complementary	Complementary	Average	Worst couple	Perfect match
Monkey	Perfect match	Perfect match	Worst couple	Perfect match	Perfect match	Good friend	Average	Complementary	Good friend	Average	Complementary	Worst couple
Rooster	Worst couple	Perfect match	Complementary	Worst couple	Perfect match	Perfect match	Worst couple	Average	Average	Worst couple	Worst couple	Average
Dog	Complementary	Average	Complementary	Perfect match	Worst couple	Average	Average	Worst couple	Complementary	Worst couple	Average	Complementary
Pig	Complementary	Good match or enemy	Perfect match	Perfect match	Good friend	Worst couple	Complementary	Perfect match	Worst couple	Average	Complementary	Good friend

Perfect match · Complementary · Good match or enemy
Good friend · Average · Worst couple

Four Groups

The twelve animal signs can be divided into four groups of three. The groups are based on the surmise that each of the three animals concerned have similar ways of thinking or temperament, or at least the style of thinking and understanding.

- Group One: Rat, Dragon, Monkey.

  They are action oriented and show traits of intelligence. They can complement in intellect and are compatible with each other.

- Group Two: Ox, Snake, Rooster

  They are deep thinkers and always conscious about attaining their objectives. They are complementary to each other in intellect and habits.

- Group Three: Tiger, Horse, Dog

  They incline to freedom and have strong sense of personal ego. They can understand each other but sometimes are egoistical.

- Group Four: Rabbit, Sheep, Pig

  They love peace and believe in mutual co-operation. They can be sympathetic and usually make great pairs.

Zodiac and Ying Yang / Wu Xing

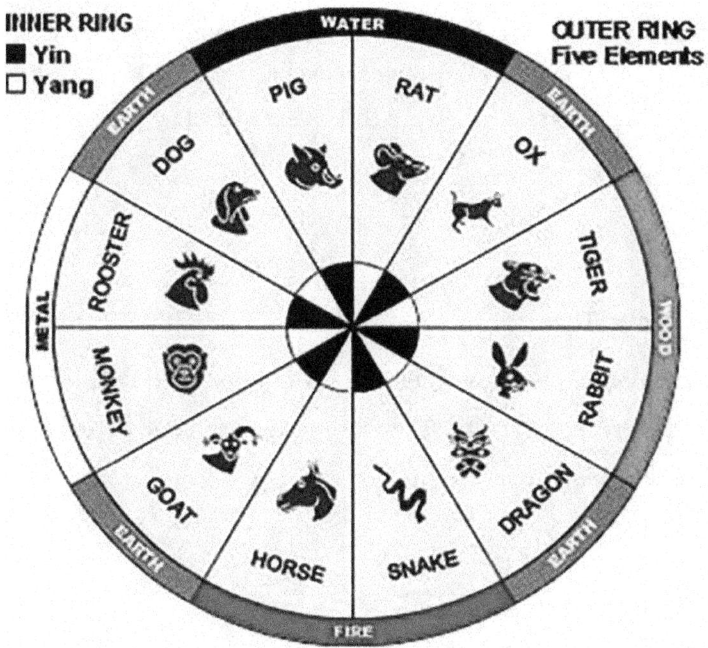

As part of Chinese astrology, Chinese zodiac animal signs are also related to the Ying Yang and Wu Xing (the Five Elements) theories. They are opposite but also supporting and generating to the other. One can realize personal shortcomings and learn from the positive attitudes of others as a complement.

Compatible Signs:

Starting from one's own sign as number one, the fifth signs either counted clockwise or anti-clockwise are the most compatible. If it is Ox sign, Rooster and Snake are the most compatible signs with Ox. This is the same as saying that the animal signs that are four years apart from each other are believed to be compatible.

- Either Compatible or Incompatible:

  The signs which are directly opposite to each other (i.e., 6 years apart) cannot see eye to eye with each other but their relationship can be fine if the older yields to the younger one.

  For example, Rat and Horse.

- Incompatible Combination:

  Starting from one's own sign as number one, the fourth signs either counted clockwise or anti-clockwise are very likely to be the non-compatible ones, i.e., they are three years apart.

  For example, Rat vs Rabbit and Rooster.

Chinese Zodiac Time

In ancient China, people divided a day and night into 12 time periods, each equaling to the present 2 hours. They also gave each time period a zodiac sign, named Chinese zodiac time.

Chinese Zodiac Hour Calculator

Present Time	Chinese Zodiac Hour	Zodiac Sign
23:00 - 01:00	Zi Shi	Rat
01:00 - 03:00	Chou Shi	Ox
03:00 - 05:00	Yin Shi	Tiger
05:00 - 07:00	Mao Shi	Rabbit
07:00 - 09:00	Chen Shi	Dragon
09:00 - 11:00	Si Shi	Snake
11:00 - 13:00	Wu Shi	Horse
13:00 - 15:00	Wei Shi	Goat
15:00 - 17:00	Shen Shi	Monkey
17:00 - 19:00	You Shi	Rooster
19:00 - 21:00	Xu Shi	Dog
21:00 - 23:00	Hai Shi	Pig

Chinese Zodiac Hour Meaning

Zi Shi – Rats are foraging. Zi Shi starts from 11 p.m. and ends at 1 a.m. It not only means the last moment of a day, but also refers to the beginning of a new day. Zi Shi is with Chinese zodiac Rat sign as rats are usually active for foraging at midnight.

Chou Shi – Oxes are chewing the cud. Chou Shi is from 1 to 3 a.m. It is the dark period before dawn, and the oxes begin to chew the cud at this time. Therefore, the Chou Shi belongs to zodiac Ox.

Yin Shi – Tigers are active to capture prey. Yin Shi refers 3 to 5 a.m. upon the dawn moment. Tigers wake up and capture prey at this point, so this time period is given the Tiger sign.

Mao Shi – Jade Rabbit is working with herbal medicines. The 2-hour period between 5 and 7 a.m. is Mao Shi. Although the sun is rising up, the moon can still be seen in the sky. In Chinese fairy tale, Jade Rabbit inside the Moon Palace is still working with herbal medicines. In this case, Mao Shi is related with zodiac Rabbit.

Chen Shi - Dragons are going to bring rainwater. During Chen Shi from 7 to 9 a.m., the sunlight is getting brighter and temperature is getting higher, the mythical creature dragons are about to bring rainwater to people, and this gives Chen Shi the zodiac Dragon.

Si Shi - Snakes are leaving their holes. Snake acquires Si Shi - 9 - 11 a.m., as they usually leave their holes for absorbing power from the warm sunshine in this comfortable time.

Wu Shi - Horses are energetic. 11 a.m. to 1 p.m. is Wu Shi. Horses is on behalf of Wu Shi as they are still sthenic while the others are tired and taking noon break.

Wei Shi - Sheep are pasturing. Sheep zodiac possesses 1 to 3 p.m. named Wei Shi. The heat is going to disappear in the early afternoon, and it is a good time for goats to pasture.

Shen Shi - Monkeys are crowing. Shen Shi is three to five o'clock in the afternoon. Monkeys are active and begin to crow by this time. Hence, the Chinese zodiac hour Shen Shi is with Monkey sign.

You Shi - Roosters are returning to dens. You Shi - 5 to 7 p.m. represents the moment of night falls. It belongs to Rooster among the twelve Chinese zodiac signs as roosters always go back to their homes from 17:00 to 19:00.

Xu Shi - Dogs are on guard. From 7 to 9 p.m. of Xu Shi in the evening, it's dark outside, and dogs start to do their job of gate guarding.

Hai Shi - Pigs are sleeping. Hai Shi is the ending hour from 9 to 11 p.m. in a day. All is quiet and pigs are in a deep sleep, so they have Hai Shi.

Chinese Zodiac Month

Ancient Chinese people also gave each of the 12 month a zodiac sign based on their relevance.

What are the Chinese zodiac signs for each month?

Lunar Month	Zodiac Sign	Chinese Zodiac Month Meaning
January	Tiger	Tigers are haunting through mountain forests for foraging.
February	Rabbit	Rabbits are active and kicking on the verdant grass.
March	Dragon	Dragons appear in the air along with thunder to bring people spring rain.
April	Snake	In warm April, Snakes are awake from hibernation.
May	Horse	Horses run and crow happily in the grassy lawn.
June	Sheep	Sheep are happily eating grass all over the mountains and plains.
July	Monkey	Monkeys roar constantly in the thick jungle.
August	Rooster	In the middle of autumn, people cook chicken and drink wine for reveling.
September	Dog	Dogs are required for guarding in the harvest time.
October	Pig	Pigs are getting plumper and plumper in October.
November	Rat	In snow season, Rats start to steal food at night.
December	Ox	Ox returns to cowsheds to avoid cold wind.

What's your solar eclipse identity?

Your Day of Birth:

1 - 5 Creator
6 - 10 Ruler
11 - 15 Guardian
16 - 20 Oracle
21 - 25 Angel
26 - 31 Seeker

The Last Number of Your Birth Year:

0 of Powerful
1 of Cosmic
2 of Divine
3 of Limitless
4 of Sacred
5 of Radiant
6 of Profound
7 of Spiritual
8 of Radical
9 of Magnificent

Your Zodiac Sign:

Aries - Passion
Taurus - Pleasure
Gemini - Ideas
Cancer - Compassion
Leo - Strength
Virgo - Excellence
Libra - Peace
Scorpio - Mysteries
Sagittarius - Truth
Capricorn - Wisdom
Aquarius - Revolution
Pisces - Visions

These Websites and books are the ones used to compile this section and they are highly reocommended to the reader for more enlightenement on their own 'detsiny'(birthchart):* **The Circle of Life by C.M. Bey; Why Astrology?, Zodiacal View on You Vol.1 & 2 By Rasmariah V. Bey; Asrology and Woman by Taj Tarik Bey; The Only Astrology book you'll ever Need by Joanne Woolfolk; The Message of The Stars by Max Heindel; Astromarix.com; Astroseek.com; CafeAstrology.com; Astrotheme.com; astrofix.com, grupovenus.com, and travelchinaguide.com.

Spiritual Affirmation

☽ Cultivate good seeds with divine manifestation.

☿ Bring positive changes quickly, and good health.

♀ Bring appreciation of all things in the spirit of Love.

☉ Shine golden rays on my creations.

♁ Make all my actions productive, positive, divine and rewarding.

♃ Expand my world, bring me fortune in all activities.

♄ Rule my world with justice and stability. Remove all obstacles, sheave all that is necessary to make me whole and stable.

♅ Bring positive thought impulses.

♆ Guide me to make the right intuitive decisions.

♇ Transform my world into one of fortune, eliminate that which is necessary to make way for transcendence of a fortunate life from this point forward.

Chapter 3: Fall of Th Nobles

A. Witchcraft

I. "The Spell that cursed my people" by Dr. Yaffa Bey:

There is a problem that is spreading all over the world. The problem is what you read, write and speak. In other words, our problem is English. English is the result of word expansion, contraction, and modification from every other dialect and language in this world. I call it a bunch of crap that was thrown against the wall and whatever stuck came to be known as English. Inspect and recognize what I'm about to show.

When you call someone "nice", is that a good thing? If a boy is called "bad" does that make him tough? Is "fun" equal to a wonderful time? Does being "fond" of a person mean you like them? If one is "sad" does that mean that they are depressed? To each of these I say absolutely not! I was never taught in any school that, if I wanted to know the real meaning of a word, I must find the brackets, or square parenthesis, like these [] and read every single thing inside.

Now that you know what to look for in the dictionary, the real definitions of the quoted words above are listed as follows: (1)" Nice"= stupid, foolish, ignorant, unwise, and not knowing; (2)" Bad" = an effeminate, or womanish man; (3)" Fun" = to befool, fond; (4)" Fond"= to be foolish, a fool; (5)" Sad" = satisfied, full, have enough.

So, when you open your mouth, what are you really saying? What frequency are you vibrating unto the swirling ethers? Our oppressor speaks with a forked tongue.

The Nazi German Jewish Christian European Alliance of Austria's Holy Roman Empire, also known as the German confederation, decided in Virginia whether the language to force on the conquered autochthonous people, of America, would be German or a new concoction called English. English was chosen. As a result, the opposition is still ruling the world today and English is probably one of the primary reasons why. This is due to the fact that since we currently speak their language, then we speak with a forked tongue too.

There is magic and power in speech. The darker one is, or the more melanin one has, the more magic and power in the speech! We get what we ask for. Ask and ye shall receive. It is said in the beginning was the word. Since English was not (and is not) our word, then it was the official beginning of our end. My people speak English, but do not English. We rarely know the real meaning of the words we utter. It is this lack of knowledge that destroys my people, because English is a "spell" that causes us to curse ourselves and empower our oppressor. English, which is Angloish, is their word, not ours.

To modify the spell, there are keys that must first be known about the term "spell." "Spell" is the root word of "spelian" and means "to substitute for." "Spell" also means a "tale" and a magic form of words. A "tale" is a fib, falsehood, and speech. These definitions all come from the Random House College Dictionary 1973 edition.

The 1956 edition of the Columbia Encyclopedia has very revealing data on the word "spell." It defines "spell" as "a word formula." It further states that once a spell has been cast, it remains in force until broken by a counter spell, or an "exorcism!" The term "exorcism" is the key that opens the door to the way out. It is a counter spell. Before I clarify the word exorcism, I must first show how deep the spell goes.

The spell begins immediately upon arrival to this planet. Depending on your perspective that might mean the moment you were conceived. Once a child is out the womb and walking, one of the first words the child learns is "no!" The word "no" is the name of one of the Gods called the forgotten ones. TSe Magician's Dictionary by E.E. Rehmus is a very revealing source for this type of data. It reveals that "no" is the name of quiet erasing and saying it erases the name of the utterer.

The spell continues in kindergarten when we learn the alphabet. Most are unaware that each letter is a complete word, color, number, frequency, tone, vibration, entity, and sound. The spell is complete by the time we master the vowels A.E.I.O.U. in the first grade. These vowels are arranged to form an acronym for a very powerful spell. That is the motto of Emperor Frederick III of the Hapsburg/Habsburg family (there strategy was to marry into power). This particular word formula is counterproductive to my people.

In Latin, it reads "Austriae Est Imperare Orbi Universo." It means, "It is Austria's destiny to rule the world." In German, it reads "Alles Erdreich Ist Oestereich Unterthan." It means, "The whole world is subjected to Austria." This can be verified in Ammo, Amas, Amat, and More by Eugene Ehrlich.

Remember again, that once a spell has been cast it remains in force until broken by a counter spell, or an exorcism! The exorcism is the most profound thing I have figured out, so get your dictionary and pay attention.

Look in the brackets, and flow with me. The Random House College Dictionary defines "exorcism" as the administration of an oath and directs the reader to see "exorcise." "Exorcise" is ex + horkizen. "Horkizen" means to cause (someone) to swear or bind from an oath. "Oath" is defined in the same dictionary as an irreverent, or blasphemous use of the name of God, or anything sacred.

"Blasphemous" means profane speech. "Profane" is pro + fane. "Fane" means church, or temple. So, to speak pro-church or pro-temple is blasphemous. Surprise! We have been had! WE must stop blabbing about (and glorifying) churches and temples. Now, with the other word in oath, we get to the real deal last key to get out of this mess we are in. "Irreverent" is "Ir +reverent" and it means not reverent.

"Reverent" is rever + ent and revere + ent. We need to rever, revere, reverse, reveret, and do a reversion. "Verse" means left and turn. This is another way of saying we must Sankofa or go back! To "revert" is to turn back, especially to former thought, habit, and practice, of those that were prime (first). This will revert things back to the former owners and their posterity, progeny, or heirs, which is us!

"Reversion" is defined as the reappearance of ancestral characters that have been absent in the intervening generations! It also means the returning of estate to the grantor, or her seeds after the interest granted expires. We must go left and turn back to our ancestor's characters!

"Character" is defined as traits, peculiarities, status, and being in accord with one's nature and disposition. More importantly, "character" is a significant visual mark, or symbol used in a letter of the alphabet; a symbol used in a writing system; a style of writing, or printing any symbol, number, or letter; a series of ones and zeros representing positive and negative impulses in a computer; to portray, engrave, or inscribe; also, a graving tool and its mark! This is the key, because we are currently using the mark of those who oppress us and oppose us. The definition for "Satan" means opponent, enemy, and adversary. Since the word Satan also means the beast, then we are using the mark of the beast!

Realize that the style of writing used by our ancestors is the reverse of today's English style. The enemy has us writing right-handed in scores of lines from top left corner of a page to the right and down. Our predecessors wrote in swirls from right to left and/or from bottom right corner of a page to the left and up. Prior to that they wrote in picture images and read it all as one view.

Returning to their style of writing and the symbols used in their writing system is a simple way to exorcise the brain and exorcise the spell to free your mind. This levitates (left-itates) the reprogramming of the computer inside your skull by creating (or closing) the bridge between the two hemispheres of the brain. Using your left hand (or non-dominant one) to write in reverse will wire and refire the electrical impulse currents in your brain.

The bridging of the gap opens the portals and doorways that we need so our ancestors can reconnect and get a swifter response to the perpetual flow or meaning and energy frequencies that radiate from them through the antakarana/antahkarana. They are always calling us, but too many of us are tuned into the oppressor's stupid God, church and temple, channels of irreverence, blasphemy, and distraction, or one's individual link to the ancient ones is outright severed.

Once you start exercising your brain, you will exorcise and counter the spell enough to let our ancestral progenitors blow your mind portal open, pour in data, and unify the forgotten pieces of your essence in motion. It is all still there inside of you and in the swirling ethers around you.

The opponent knows how brilliant and magnanimous your ancestors (ankh-ess-stors) were. After all, though many of our ancestor's records were burned, others were kept for the opposition to decode. Since you are a culmination of every single ancestor that preceded you and then some, then you are them. Even though my people do not seem to know how marvelous, magnificent, and magnanimous we are, one must understand, innerstand, and overstand, and comprehend, that your oppressing opponents (and those that work to empower them) most certainly do! We have been asleep and dormant too long! We must levitate and become quickened to modify everything now. We manufactured this mess and we must level it.

Be level and calm. Dr. Yaffa Bey

II. Symboleography

Symboleography according to Black's Law dictionary 4th Ed., is the art of cunning rightly to form and make written instruments. It is either judicial or extrajudicial; the latter being wholly occupied with instruments as concern matters not yet judicially in controversy, such as instruments of agreements or contracts, and testaments of wills. (Wharton)

According to the 1973 world book dictionary Symboleography or symbolaeography (n.) is the art of drawing up legal documents. < Greek symbolaiographia < symbolaiographos= notary < syn, together + ballein, to throw + graphia-graphy < Latin graphus < Greek graphos < graphein, draw, write.

A contract according to the 1973 world book dictionary is (n.) a mutual agreement, a written agreement that can be enforced by law, the branch of law that deals with such agreements, betrothal, and a formal agreement to marriage.; (v.t.) to draw together; make narrow; nit, to make smaller, to bring on oneself, enter upon, get, form. < Old French contract learned borrowing from Latin contractus, agreement < contrahere, draw together < Com, together + trahere, draw.

Contracts, bonds, binds are all synonymous terms. We live in a world of contracts for this is how the beast operates hence the terms "signing on the dotted line" and "selling your soul to the devil." A lot of the bonds/contracts we've entered into or that were forced upon us e.g. birth certificates, marriage licenses, social security, housing deeds, etc. were done so without the full knowledge of what these things imply.

The reason a lot of these institutions are failing and will eventually be destroyed is because they are based in fraud i.e. without the intelligent consent of the person upon whom it is encroached upon. However, the same reason will also be why a lot of people will also fall with them because they continue to empower the fiction by way of contracts which are bonds which in turn merges them with and thus transforms them into corporations/corpses. This is the source of the people's miseries especially those branded negroes, black, and colored because in accepting these terms you in turn accept the conditions that go along with them which being that no such people exist then you have basically agreed to be treated and counted as subhuman which opens the door for mistreatment both externally and internally.

There are a variety of different types of contracts, but the two main archetypes are: oral and written. The latter is the lock on the cage of the beast, however, the former is the key because satan cannot truly own your soul without your consent hence he must show you the mountain top first then ask for your signature which when one really thinks and sees with the proper perspective reveals the undeniable truth that the devil as it is called works for Th Most High as does all things and is allowed to separate the strong from the weak though there are casualties in the midst of this but all according to the divine plan. So long as you stand firm the beast has no real lasting power over you. But if you speak wrong or not at all then you make a pact with them for ignorance of the law is no excuse the reason being that you are the law for you are consciousness made manifest so if you ignore your conscience then you essentially ignore the law.

Whenever people classify you as anything other than what you are whether it be a socially engineered misnomer or just a regular case of mistaken identity and you do nothing to correct that assumption of status then you have accepted it whatever it may actually imply.

As with all things there are rules and protocols to contracting that must be followed and if they are not then any contract is void.

The unfortunate social and political reality is that the corrupt politicians have undermined the 'United States Republic' of North America. They have been robbing the Natural Aboriginals of the Land, who have been subverted by organized political Racketeers. The operative Demo governments of foreign-law have been violating and usurping the Constitution and trampling on the Unalienable Rights of the People. They are boldly functioning under a 'Color-of-Authority' through a foreign 'Body Politic' at all levels – Federal, State, City / Town, and Municipal governments, etc. The usurping 'Body Politic' (criminals / usurpers) blatantly refer to themselves as, 'The U.S. De- mocracy', yet they are bound by Official Oath to support and defend the Constitution for the United States of America, which is (by law) a Republican Form of Government. The Constitution (and their Official Oaths) are Contracts. As for the alleged [Democracy] form of government claimed by some of them— one body politic is Constitutional, and the other is not! By what 'Contractual validity' measurements are these facts or rulings determined?

A VALID AND LAWFUL CONTRACT MUST MEET THE FOLLOWING CRITERIA:

A. Contract must show, in its preliminary making and construction, the clear and '*Substantive Offer*' made by one party and demonstrates the '*Mutual Acceptance*' affirmed by the other party.

B. A Contract must be producible (and exist in evidence) upon demand made by either party to the Contract, which, in itself, may be in question, dispute, or controversy.

C. A Contract must be produced in manifest writing, (evidence) and contain the details of the agreements, debts, or promises, with all the terms, the obligations, and the conditions, which clearly show and serve as proof that a valid and enforceable obligation, promise, or debt, exists.

D. A Contract must be a deliberate and conscious agreement made between competent parties.

E. A 'party' to a contract cannot be a minor.

F. A Contract must be entered into by 'free-will'.

G. A Contract must not be created under threat, duress, or coercion, lest it be void in law.

H. A Contract must be substantive and germane to the subject matter.

I. A Contract must be of legal consideration. It cannot be based on an unlawful consideration.

J. A Contract must possess 'Mutuality of Agreement', and 'Mutuality of Obligation'.

K. A Contract must not be vague, unclear, uncertain, nor can it contain terms or conditions that are not ascertainable.

L. A Contract must show valid signatures of the parties to the Contract instrument, in order to verify its validity in law.

Note: If a Contract *fails to satisfy* the *laws that govern its making or construction*, then any such *Contract* is **void *Ab Initio***, and is considered "***dead in the view of the Law***".

Too often, the 'nature' and the required 'essence' of Contracts have not been properly taken into thoughtful consideration by many natural people. Furthermore, the lawful conditions that must exist for a contract to be deemed valid, (and the proper, legitimate construction of the same) have not been taught to the people by those corporate State agents or agencies (governments, schools, etc.). Many people (holding Seats of Authority) have 'colorably' abused the Natural People and have economically benefited from enforcing invalid and void contracts, at the peril of the misinformed. These opportunists prey upon contractual ignorance, groomed among the masses; an ignorance which they have perpetrated for reasons of affecting Constructive Fraud, Theft, Arbitrary, Racketeering, Legal Abuses, personal gain, and for other deviant forms of Deception, Malfeasance, Misrepresentation, and Misprision.

Remember to never accept legal instruments from the corporate States without cross—checking their presentments. Remember that (for the most part) they are operative Feudalists, feigning as legitimate Constitutional Governments. Their Color-of-Law activities have already proven them unworthy of trust or honor. Therefore, when dealing with the corporate State employees and quasi-government, pseudo-officers, always measure their actions by Constitutional Principles. Protect yourselves from their bureaucratic and institutionalized 'Fraud' whenever possible.

So, what is Fraud?

Fraud is an intentional perversion of truth for the purpose of inducing another, in reliance upon it, to part with some valuable thing belonging to him or to surrender a legal right. It is a false representation of a matter of fact, whether by words or by conduct, by false or misleading allegations, or by concealment of that which should have been disclosed, which deceives and is intended to deceive another so that he shall act upon it to his legal injury. ***Brainerd Dispatch Newspaper Co. v. Crow Wing County, 196 Minn. 194, 264 N.W. 779, 780.*** Fraud is any kind of artifice employed by one person to deceive another. ***Goldstein v. Equitable Life Assur. Soc. Of U.S., 160 Misc. 364, 289 N.Y.S. 1064, 1067.*** Fraud is a generic term, embracing all multifarious means which human ingenuity can devise, and which are resorted to by one individual to get advantage over another by false suggestions or by suppression of truth, and includes all surprise, trick, cunning, dissembling, and any unfair way by which another is cheated. ***Johnson McDonald, 170 Okl. 117, 39 P.2d 150.*** "Bad faith" and "fraud" are synonymous, and also synonyms of dishonesty, infidelity, faithlessness, perfidy, unfairness, etc. ***Joiner v. Joiner, Tex.Civ.App., 87 S.W. 2d 903, 914, 915.***

Also become familiar with the some of the varied forms of Contracts, so that we can Work towards being more aware and astute in our social and political affairs. Research these during your Culture, Law, and History Classes.

1. Certain and Hazardous Contracts.
2. Communicative and Independent Contracts.
3. Expressed and Implied Contracts.
4. Mutual Interest and Mixed Contracts.
5. Fair and Reasonable Contracts.
6. Constructive Contracts.
7. Consensual and Real Contracts.
8. Conditional Contracts.
9. Divisible and Indivisible Contracts.

10. Executed and Executory Contracts.
11. Gratuitous and Onerous Contracts.
12. Joint and Several Contracts.
13. A Pre-Contract.
14. A Parol Contract.
15. A Personal Contract.
16. A Principal and Accessory Contract.
17. A Sub-Contract.
18. A Special Contract.
19. Quasi Contracts.
20. Record, Simple, and Specialty Contracts
21. Unconscionable Contracts.
22. Unilateral and Bilateral Contracts.
23. Usurious Contracts.
24. Written Contracts.
25. A Contract of Sale.

Administrative Law and Administrative Law Judges

Administrative Law is that body of laws created by administrative agencies in the form of rules, regulations, orders and decisions. Administrative Law Judges are "Hearing Officers" or "Hearing Examiners", established by the Administrative Procedure Act 556. These are Officers who preside over administrative hearings, with power to administer Oaths, to take testimony, to rule on questions of evidence, and to make agency determinations of fact. Politically, and as used in Constitutional Law, Administrative Officers are of the Executive Department of Government, and generally one of inferior rank; and legally, a ministerial or executive officer, as distinguished from a Judicial Officer.

On the other hand, a Judicial Officer is a Judge or Magistrate. This fiduciary title and position applies generally to any officer of the court, but in a stricter legal sense, this position applies only to an officer who posses the authority to determine causes between parties, or who renders decisions in a legitimate judicial capacity, having the vested powers to decide causes or to exercise powers appropriate to the court. There is a clear distinction in law between Administrative Officers and true, and authorized judicial Officers (Judges).

• **"When acting to enforce a statute and its subsequent amendments to the present date**, the judge of the municipal court is acting as an administrative officer and not in a judicial capacity; courts in administering or enforcing statutes do not act judicially, but merely ministerially". *Thompson v. Smith*, 154 SE 583.

• "**A judge ceases to sit as a judicial officer** because the governing principle of administrative law provides that courts are prohibited from substituting their evidence, testimony, record, arguments, and rationale for that of the agency. Additionally, courts are prohibited from substituting their judgment for that of the agency. Courts in administrative issues are prohibited from even listening to or hearing arguments, presentation, or rational". *ASIS v. US, 568 F2d 284.*

• "**Ministerial officers are incompetent to receive grants of judicial power** from the legislature, their acts in attempting to exercise such powers are necessarily nullities". *Burns v. Sup., Ct., SF, 140 Cal. 1.*

• **The elementary doctrine that the constitutionality of a legislative act is open to attack** only by persons whose rights are affected thereby, applies to statute relating to administrative agencies, the validity of which may not be called into question in the absence of a showing of substantial harm, actual or impending, to a legally protected interest directly resulting from the enforcement of the statute." *Board of Trade v. Olson, 262 US 1; 29 ALR 2d 105.*

Jurisdiction is the power conferred by the Constitution or by Law. The courts charged with adjudicating matters stemming from violations of these administrative statutes, rules and regulations, lack 'Jurisdiction in Personam' over sovereign Moorish -American men and women. The federal and corporate state courts are aware of this "want of jurisdiction" However, they will not freely admit to their lack of authority, or to their lack of ethics and integrity. This goes to the pit and inner—most recesses of 'Judicial Corruption' and Racketeering in North America. It is essential that you have a clear understanding of the fact that *'Jurisdiction in Personam'* must be challenged, or the court will arbitrarily '*presume*' or '*assume*' jurisdiction over your *person* and may, thereafter, prosecute the 'matter' against you, to your legal, economic, and / or bodily injury or abridgement. Furthermore, there are many ways for you to '*waive jurisdiction'* and permit the court to proceed. Know that they are always seeking ways and methods of fooling you or intimidating you into allowing them to claim jurisdiction. You must be forever diligent and never waive any of your Unalienable Rights, or Constitutionally—secured Rights, regardless of the appearance of a convenience of doing so. You have no legal nor moral responsibility to waive your Rights merely for the 'colorable' convenience of the courts. Always remember that the court system is 'supposed' to be long and tedious; as '*due process*' is supposed to be difficult for the Judicators and the Courts to overcome. Do not ever (under any circumstances) make it easier for the Government, the Judicators, or the Courts to persecute you. Always take into consideration, the Constitution and the Ten (10) Amendments which comprise the 'Bills of Rights. Make challenging the Jurisdiction of the Courts one of the best and entrenched among the '*good habits*' that you never try or intend to break.

1. *Jurisdiction in Personum* refers to Jurisdiction over the 'Person' and involves the power to subject a person or parties in a particular case to decisions and rulings made in such a case. It is one (1) of 'three (3) kinds. Jurisdiction is the power of him who has the right of judging; and involves the authority, the capacity, and the power or the right to act. Jurisdiction also relates to the Judicators and the Courts (Judges, Magistrates, etc.) and exists when the Court has cognizance of the class of cases involved; when the proper parties are present; and when the point to be decided is within the issues. The *burden* of proving Jurisdiction '*for the record*' remains, at all times, upon the Judicators and the Court, upon a *challenge* made by the '*alleged*' Accused or Defendant.

2. *Jurisdiction of Subject Matter* refers to Jurisdiction of a particular class of cases in Law; and of the attending *subject matter* relative to the class to which the case belongs.

3. **Jurisdiction to render particular judgment which was given.** The capacity of the Judge to have the power to render decisions.

Consider and study the following types of Jurisdiction:

"Appellate Jurisdiction", "Concurrent Jurisdiction", "Contentious Jurisdiction", "Co-Ordinate Jurisdiction", "Criminal Jurisdiction" "Excess of Jurisdiction" "Exclusive Jurisdiction" "Foreign Jurisdiction", "General Jurisdiction", "Limited Jurisdiction", "Pendent Jurisdiction", "Probate Jurisdiction", "Special Jurisdiction" "Summery Jurisdiction" "Territorial Jurisdiction" and "Voluntary Jurisdiction".

A '*Contract*' founded on a base consideration, or against good morals is null. Base, in law, means that which is low, inferior, foul, servile, of a subordinate degree or nature; impure and adulterated or alloyed. Null is a term in Law which means," Naught" and being of no validity or effect in law. Null is usually conjoined with the word "void": as 'Null and Void'. In the law that governs 'Contracts' or 'Statutes', 'Null and Void' is used, applied, ruled, or recognized to establish, declare, or proclaim that such a low, inferior, foul, servile, or base Claim, Claimant, Judgment, Summons, Ticket, Bill of Exchange, or that any other Contractual Instrument, (befitting to the nature of the foresaid descriptions) are dead in law, colored, fraud, non-binding, unclean, and having no legal force or effect! Keep this concept of right—law civic knowledge in mind whenever someone says to you,

"You've got a lot of ***'Contracts'*** *out there! You are bound by them unless you make new contracts and file them with the State in order to dissolve or destroy these* ***'Contracts'*** *because they give* ***'Jurisdiction'*** *over you to the corporate States and / or to their quasigovernment agencies, employees, and contractors, who are seeking to cause you to be bound by some veiled 'straw-man' debt, and are thereby authorized by such assumed jurisdiction, to have lawful right to cause you a legal tort, imprisonment, or injury".*

Any Officers of the Courts, or Persons, or Employees, or Entities, exercising any Authority whatever, in the United States, or in any of the several States, or holds any office of public trust under them, or under any one of them, shall be bound by Oath or Affirmation to support the Constitution for The United States. All officers of the courts, and all Executive, Legislative, or Judicial officers, or any persons, personnel, employees, contractors, associates, agencies, or any others, who function or operate under their Authority or employ, shall be bound by that same Supreme Law of the Land (Constitution).

The *Constitution* for The United States is the '*Supreme Contract'* by which the ***Judges, and all other officers of the courts are bound.*** They must be ever cognizant of their '***Fiduciary Duties***', and never violate, supercede, or abridge their *limited, delegated Authorities*; and, with the '***Constitution Contract***' ever present in the exercising of their offices, always hold true, themselves, and their offices, to the high standards of *integrity* and *ethical behavior*, as sworn to or affirmed by them, by solemn Oath, and as befits the public trust vested in them.

Any *Authority* exercised by, or any *decisions* made by, any Judge, or any officers of any courts, under the *Authority* of the *United States Republic*, or claiming to be a party in any controversy to which the United States, or to which any of the several States, in union with the United States, is a party, *are bound by Official Oath*, as per ***Article VI*** of the ***Constitution***. Any Judge, or any other officers of the courts, who uses or exercises any Authority, not vested in them, or who uses or exercises any Authority not vested in the offices held by them, are acting under a ***Color-of-Law***; and are exercising a ***Color-of- Authority,*** which is a violation of the public trust. In such cases of violations of the public trust, that said Judge, or any of the said officers of the courts, or any employees or personnel functioning under them, are perpetrating a *supreme active and constructive fraud* upon the people of the United States and are in enmity to the Constitution. They shall be deemed ***void of Authority***, and are criminals, by being a party in such un-constitutional acts. They are then, acting upon their own personal or foreign interests, and with non-authoritative intent; and are guilty of acting under a ***Color-of-Office***. Any Judges or officers of the courts, who act upon ***decisions*** or ***orders*** issued by any such violating Judges, officers, persons, agencies, or entities, in association with them, are in ***conspiracy*** with them. And the ***principle*** of the said conspiracy is a guilty party, and the ***agents*** to the ***principle actors*** are also guilty and held as ***participants in collusion*** with them.

Contractual instruments and *Warrants*, or *Orders* issued from violators of the Constitution, and any ***Actions*** enforced, or entered into, or acted upon, by way of these unlawful instruments (contracts) shall never be valid or lawful. In the laws that govern contracts, ***there cannot exist base considerations.*** For if in any instance, the foresaid base considerations exists, or can be demonstrated, then that contract remains unlawful and non-binding from its inception and from its beginning. It is as if it never existed. The obligations implied by, or debts commanded by, any unclean or alloyed contract, or any '***Power of Authority***' or '***Power of Attorney***' assumed by anyone upon such an instrument, is a severe penal violation, and is unclean and foul.

Null. All claims of Jurisdiction, or Contracts issued under the assumed powers of Jurisdiction, are subject to the Laws governing Contracts; and are subject to the remedies put in place by law to punish such persons who engage in such '***colorable***' activities.

Research United States Codes of Law that relate to such colorable violations, such as:

Title 18, Part I, Chapter 13 §241 of United States Code of Law:

> *If two or more persons conspire to injure, oppress, threaten, or intimidate any person in any State, Territory, Commonwealth, Possession, or District in the free exercise or enjoyment of any right or privilege secured to him by the Constitution or laws of the United States, or because of his having so exercised the same;* **or** *If two or more persons go in disguise on the highway, or on the premises of another, with intent to prevent or hinder his free exercise or enjoyment of any right or privilege so secured— They shall be fined under this title or imprisoned not more than ten years, or both; and if death results from the acts committed in violation of this section or if such acts include kidnapping or an attempt to kidnap, aggravated sexual abuse or an attempt to commit aggravated sexual abuse, or an attempt to kill, they shall be fined under this title or imprisoned for any term of years of for life, or both, or may be sentenced to death.*

Title 18, Part I, Chapter 13 §242 of United States Code of Law:

> *Whoever, under color of any law, statute, ordinance, regulation, or custom, willfully subjects any person in any State, Territory, Commonwealth, Possession, or District to the deprivation of any rights, privileges, or immunities secured or protected by the Constitution or laws of the United States, or to different punishments, pains, or penalties, on account of such person being an alien, or by reason of his color, or race, then are prescribed for the punishment of citizens, shall be fined under this title or imprisoned not more than one year, or both; and if bodily injury results from the acts committed in violation of this section or if such acts include the use, attempted*

use, or threatened use of a dangerous weapon, explosives, or fire, shall be fined under this title or imprisoned not more than ten years or for life, or both, or may be sentenced to death.

Measure Judges, and all court officers by the limited authority vested in them. Measure and judge all Contracts by Constitutional principles and analyze them by the contract qualification laws that govern such instruments. Always hold the corporate State parties (court officers) to the high moral standards, as prescribed for them by the sworn or affirmed Oaths taken by them. And in accordance with the Constitutional obligations taken by the Oath Bound Officers of the Courts, consider that when any Administrative officer, (claiming to be a Judge) imposes himself into jurisdictional venues or matters wherein he possess no lawful judicial powers, and thus, lacks Jurisdiction, then Demand a Dismissal of the Case. There are no lawful ***pleas*** to be made before such a non-sanctioned and unlawful court, nor are there any ***lawful pleas*** to be made before the unlawful officers of that court! Such an act constitutes a waiver of Jurisdiction, which cannot be lawfully done or claimed by either party. This unwarranted condition presents, in law, a circumstance wherein a most *vile criminal* is presiding (as judge) over an 'alleged', accused or implied criminal, who has not yet been found guilty impartially, or (by a jury of his or her own peers). There are no greater crimes crafted against humanity, than that of inferior and non-judicial officers in government who have no honor or integrity, who lack Jurisdiction, and who willfully exercise such powers, vested in any of the offices of public trust, (not resting with them) and using such powers against the interests of, and to the injury of, the people.

The natural people possess, by Divine Law and by Nature's Laws, the Rights to life and to living. Living means, "Having life, and being active and functioning—exhibiting the life or motion of nature and having the means of subsistence; related to livelihood. This is a basic right and is protected and preserved in any civilized society. Constitutions are ancient in their character and existence. They are in place to secure the basic human rights of people from the evil and vile machinations of the uncivilized beings who tend to corrupt society.

Please remember to never place your signature upon an instrument that you were not personally involved in the drafting of without reserving your rights without prejudice, or for the fancier putting U.C.C1-103/1- 308/1-207, or if you are in a compromising position whereas you are being forced in any way then be sure to put before your nomen T.D.C (threat, duress, and coercion) which will null and void any assumed contractual liability.

Keep in mind that all deeds, and licenses are means by which the roman curia which is the administrative appendage/unit of the Holy See (Episcopal jurisdiction of the Vatican) that governs the property and/or affairs of the Popes of Rome. All negotiable instruments/contracts are used to hypothecate (to pledge [property, stock, etc.] to a creditor as security for a loan or debt without turning over; < Greek, hypo- down + tithenai-put) the heirs and their progeny as collateral for the accrued national debt. For example, marriage licenses are a means by which the church secures the "fruits of the womb" i.e. the children even before they are born. For clarification of this fact I encourage you to research and read an article entitled "Marriage Licenses: The real truth" by Virgil Cooper which will provide further enlightenment on the subject as it is based on an actual personal occurrence.

The Scholar or Neophyte is encouraged to do an expanded study and review of these conditions of Jurisdiction. You must also study the forms or types of Contracts in order to gain further clarification on the specific character, the nature, and the relative elements of Jurisdiction and of Contracts.

See James 5:12; Colossians 2:8; Proverbs 17:18; Numbers 30:2;

Proverbs 11:15; Proverbs 22: 26-27; Proverbs 6: 1-5

III. Status: Positive and Negative

Status according to the 1973 world book dictionary is the condition of being relative to others, social or professional standing, and legal position of a person as determined by his membership in some class of persons with certain rights or limitations. < Latin status < stare, to stand. Doublet of estate, state.

Negative Status:

1. Appearance:

- (Black's Law 4th Ed.) :" Appearance" is the act of appearing, coming, or being in sight, becoming visible or clear to apprehension of the mind, of being known as subject of observation or comprehension, or as a thing proved, of being obvious or manifest. Hallack& Howard Lumber Co. v. Bagly, 100 Colo. 402, 68 P.2d 442, 443.
- (Black's Law 4th Ed.) An appearance may also be either *compulsory* or *voluntary,* the former where it is compelled by process served on the party, the latter where it is entered by his own will or consent, without the service of process, though process may be outstanding. 1 Barb.Ch.Pr. 77. It is said to be *optional* when entered by a person who intervenes in the action to protect his own interests, though not joined as a party; it occurs in chancery practice, especially in England; *conditional,* when coupled with conditions as to its becoming or being taken as a general appearance; *gratis,* when made by a party to the action, but before the service of any process or legal notice to appear ; *de bene esse,* when made provisionally or to remain good only upon a future contingency ; or when designed to permit a party to a proceeding to refuse to submit his person to the jurisdiction of the court unless it is finally determined that he has forever waived that right. Farmers Trust Co. v. Alexander, 334 Pa. 434, 6 A.2d 262, 265; *subsequent,* when made by a defendant after an appearance has already been entered for him by the plaintiff; *corporal,* when the person is physically present in court.
- (Black's Law 4th ed.): An answer constitutes an "appearance." Wieser v. Richter, 247 Mich. 52, 225 N.W. 542, 543. A party who answers, consents to a continuance, goes to trial, takes an appeal, or does any other substantial act in a cause, although he has not been served with summons, is deemed to have entered his "appearance" unless he objects and preserves his protests to the jurisdiction of his person. Robinson v. Bossinger, 195 Ark. 445, 112 S.W.2d 637, 640. Acts of an attorney in prosecuting an action on behalf of his client constitute an "appearance." Pacilio v. Scarpati, 300 N.Y.S. 473, 165 Misc. 586.

This is why it is imperative for us to know law and how the legal process actually works. The fact is if you're responsible you shouldn't even be going to court unless you've been unjustly kidnapped, sued or harassed and if you do you must state your status for the record but of course you must first have one. Once you state that you are not a corpse then you really don't need to go back to that venue. This is also why one should not engage in verbal sparring with the criminals of color as to do so admits jurisdiction and drains energy; they are actors.

State the fact of your status and stand mute. Anything said that doesn't prove the jurisdiction of the court is merely a formality and a show that the actors put on for others who might be in attendance that don't know what's up. The fact is once you make your public declaration and demonstrate that you are a true sentient being then you really have no business going to court (see Leviticus 21:11). Corporations are corpses that were given presumed life via the 14th and 15th amendments. However, a corpse is dead entity so therefore those colorable courts are morgues/graveyards and only those whose profession is to cohabitate with the dead should be in these places, unless of course you are rescuing someone from the zombies.

2. Pro Se:

- (Black's Law 4th Ed.) For himself; in his own behalf; in person.

This definition is deceptive as it has gotten many of my people in deeper into the quagmire of fraudulent behavior by these supposed courts. To go pro se is really to keep the process going as it is the prime root of prosecutor which is one who charges another for a crime. However, in most cases a crime hasn't even been committed nor has the jurisdiction of the supposed court been either challenged or even proven accept when you go pro se which then gives the thieves mandate to go forth.

3. Civiliter Mortuus:

- (Black's Law 4th Ed.) Civilly dead; dead in the view of the law. The condition of one who has lost his civil rights and capacities and is accounted dead in law. Rasor v. Rasor, 173 S.C. 365, 175 S.E. 545.

This is the effect of identifying yourself as a socially engineered misnomer. You in turn get civil privileges called civil rights which can be taken from you at any time as it is an admission of no life or judicial standing thus you are at the mercy of those whom you serve, i.e. who have granted you the privileges you've begged for which are in actuality Creator endowed liberties and that should be reasonably demanded as it is the obligation of public servants to serve you, Th people but if you're dead then you don't fit into nature thus you are treated unnaturally.

4. Counsel:

- (Black's Law 4th Ed.): An advocate or barrister. A member of the legal profession whose special function is to give counsel or advice as to the legal aspects of judicial controversies, or their preparation and management, and to appear in court for the conduct of trials, or the argument of causes, or presentation of motions, or any other legal business that takes him into the presence of the court.
- (Black's Law 4th Ed.): In some of the states, the two words "counsellor" and "attorney" are used interchangeably to designate all lawyers. In others, the latter term alone is used, "counsellor" not being recognized as a technical name. In still others, the two are associated together in the courts; while in a few they denote different grades, it being prescribed that no one can become a counselor until he has been an attorney for a specified time and has passed a second examination.

This is another trick of these Romans who act in fraudulent capacities. These barristers/lawyers/attorneys are all officers of the court and their job is basically to deliver you to their fellow craftsmen and masters/magistrates so as to place you on the auction block to go to the highest bidder. This is why most times even though you hire a lawyer you still wind up losing whether it be time/energy or fiat/currency it is all designed so as the vamps can suck you dry of your resources.

5. Artificial (Corporate) Person:

- (Black's Law 4th Ed.): Persons created and devised by human laws for the purposes of society and government, as distinguished from natural persons. Corporations are examples of artificial persons. 1 Bl.Comm. 123. Chapman v. Brewer, 43 Neb. 890, 62 N.W. 320, 47 Am.St.Rep. 779.

This is why we were branded as misnomers and why they crafted all these constructs/contracts so as to transform men into machines i.e. switching places and morphing men into animals. So long as you accept and uphold the fraud of the nom de guerre (war name) then you basically admit to the universe that you are an abstract as opposed to substance. All these statues and ordinances are designed to ensnare and feed off of those who cling to falsehood by way of ignorance and the worse is yet to come.

6. Minor:

- (Black's Law 4th Ed.): An infant or person who is under the age of legal competence. One under twenty-one. A term derived from the civil law, which described a person under a certain age as less than so many years. Minor viginti quinque annis, one less than twenty-five years of age. Inst. 1, 14, 2; Audsley v. Hale, 303 Mo. 451, 261 S.W. 117, 123. Also, less; of less consideration; lower; a person of inferior condition. Fleta, 2, 47, 13, 15; Calvin.

We've been conditioned to think of ourselves as the minority when in actuality we are the majority. Truthfully, though this description is an accurate description of society at large as people are in stage of mental retardation and act in all manners of lawlessness. The heirs have adopted this brand and thus have been indoctrinated and possessed by the spirit of voluntary ignorance. This has, along with the acts of traitors/agents of Rome, have decimated the minds of Th descendants of the founders of civilization who set up provisions just for these very days and times, but the sons of man refuse to take heed.

7. Feudal:

- Pertaining to feuds or fees; relating to or growing out of the feudal system or feudal law; having the quality of a feud, as distinguished from "allodial."
- FEUDAL LAW: The body of jurisprudence relating to feuds; the real-property law of the feudal system; the law anciently regulating the property relations of lord and vassal, and the creation, incidents, and transmission of feudal estates.
- The body of laws and usages constituting the "feudal law" was originally customary and unwritten, but a compilation was made in the twelfth century, called "Feodarum Consuetudines," which has formed the basis of later digests. The feudal law prevailed over Europe from the twelfth to the fourteenth century, and was introduced into England at the Norman Conquest, where it formed the entire basis of the law of real property until comparatively modern times. Survivals of the feudal law, to the present day, so affect and color that branch of jurisprudence as to require a certain knowledge of the feudal law in order to the perfect comprehension of modern tenures and rules of real-property law.
- (1973 world book dictionary): n. the social, economic, and political system of the Middle Ages; feudal system. Under this system, vassals (servants/slaves) held land on condition of giving military and other services to the lord owning it, in return for protection and use of the land.

This is the model and blueprint for how the world is run especially North-West Amexem/America. The Roman colonizers operate off of contracts which require consent and/or acquiescence of the heirs who then become tenants in/on their own land.

8. Colored:

- An appearance, semblance, or *simulacrum*, as distinguished from that which is real. A *prima facie* or apparent right. Hence, a deceptive appearance; a plausible, assumed exterior, concealing a lack of reality; a disguise or pretext. Railroad Co. v. Allfree, 64 Iowa 500, 20 N.W. 779; Broughton v. Haywood, 61 N.C. 383; Wilt v. Bueter, 186 Ind. 98, 111 N.E. 926, 929.
- In pleading. Ground of action admitted subsisting in the opposite party by the pleading of one of the parties to an action, which is so set out as to be apparently valid, but which is in reality legally insufficient. A term of the ancient rhetoricians, and early adopted into the language of pleading. It was

an apparent or *prima facie* right; and the meaning of the rule that pleadings in confession and avoidance should *give* color was that they should confess the matter adversely alleged, to such an extent, at least, as to admit some apparent right in the opposite party, which required to be encountered and avoided by the allegation of new matter. Color was either express, *i.e.,* inserted in the pleading, or implied, which was naturally inherent in the structure of the pleading. Steph.P1. 233; Merten v. Bank, 5 Okl. 585, 49 P. 913. Wheeler v. Nickels, 168 Or. 604, 126 P.2d 32, 36.

- COLOR OF AUTHORITY: That semblance or presumption of authority sustaining the acts of a public officer which is derived from his apparent title to the office or from a writ or other process in his hands apparently valid and regular. State v. Oates, 86 Wis. 634, 57 N.W. 296, 39 Am.St.Rep. 912.
- COLOR OF LAW: The appearance or semblance, without the substance, of legal right. State v. Brechler, 185 Wis. 599, 202 N.W. 144, 148.
- COLOR OF OFFICE. An act unjustly done by the countenance of an office, being grounded upon corruption, to which the, office is as a shadow and color. Plow. 64. Day v. National Bond & Investment Co., Mo.App., 99 S.W.2d 117, 119. A claim or assumption of right to do an act by virtue of an office, made by a person who is legally destitute of any such right. Feller v. Gates, 40 Or. 543, 67 P. 416, 56 L.R.A. 630, 91 Am.St.Rep. 492; Citizens' Bank of Colquitt v. American Surety Co. of New York, 174 Ga. 852, 164 S.E. 817; Pontiac Trust Co. v. Newell, 266 Mich. 490, 254 N.W. 178, 181. Such person must be at least officer *de factor.* Burrall v. Acker, 23 Wend., N.Y., 606, 35 Am.Dec. 582; Day v. National Bond & Investment Co., Mo.App., 99 S.W.2d 117,119. See, also, Colore Officii.
- COLOR OF TITLE: The appearance, semblance, or *simulacrum* of title. Also termed "apparent title." Any fact, extraneous to the act or mere will of the claimant, which has the appearance, on its face, of supporting his claim of a present title to land, but which, for some defect, in reality falls short of establishing it. Howth v. Farrar, C.C.A. Tex., 94 F.2d 654, 658; Saltmarsh v. Crommelin, 24 Ala. 352.,
- Anything in writing purporting to convey title to the *land,* which defines the extent of the claim, it being immaterial how defective or imperfect the writing may be, so that it is a sign, semblance, or color of title. Theisen v. Qualley, 42 S.D. 367, 175 N.W. 556, 557. A title that is imperfect, but not so obviously so that it would be apparent to one not skilled in the law. Ipock v. Gaskins, 161 N.C. 673, 77 S.E. 843, 847.

- A writing upon its face professing to pass title but which does not, either through want of title in the grantor or a defective mode of conveyance. Philbin v. Carr, 75 Ind.App. 560, 129 N.E. 19, 24; Glass v. Lynchburg Shoe Co., 212 N.C.70, 192 S.E. 899.

- That which the law considers *prima facie* a good title, but which, by reason of some defect, not appearing on its face, does not in fact amount to title. An absolute nullity, as a void deed, judgment, etc., will not constitute color of title. Causey v. White, 143 Ga. 7, 84 S.E. 58; Stearns Coal & Lumber Co. v. Boyatt, 168 Ky. 111, 181 S. W. 962, 964. That which is title in appearance but not in reality. Fftschen Bros. Commercial Co. v. Noyes' Estate, 76 Mont. 175, 246 P. 773, 779; Boland v. Heck, 179 Okl. 403, 65 P.2d 1213, 1215.

- "Any instrument having a grantor and grantee and containing a description of the lands intended to be conveyed, and apt words for their conveyance, gives color of title to the lands described. Such an instrument purports to be a conveyance of the title, and because it does not, for some reason, have that effect, it passes only color or the semblance of a title." Brooks v. Bruyn, 35 Ill. 392.

- "Color of title" is not synonymous with "claim of title." To constitute "color of title" there must be a paper title to give color to the adverse possession, whereas a "claim of title" may be shown wholly by parol. Walton v. Sikes, 165 Ga. 422, 141 S.E. 188, 190.

- COLORABLE: That which has or gives color. That which is in appearance only, and not in reality, what it purports to be. Counterfeit, feigned, having the appearance of truth. Ellis v. Jones, 73 Colo. 516, 216 P. 257, 258.

- COLORED: By common usage in America, this term, in such phrases as "colored persons," "the colored race," "colored men," and the like, is used to designate negroes or persons of the African race, including all persons of mixed blood descended from negro ancestry. Collins v. Oklahoma State Hospital, 76 Okl. 229, 184 P. 946, 949, 7 A.L.R. 895; Theophanis v. Theophanis, 244 Ky. 689, 51S.W.2d 957.

- But where a state Constitution provided for separate schools for the white and colored races, the term "white race" was held to be limited to the Caucasian race, and the term "colored races" to embrace all other races. Rice v. Gong Lum, 139 Miss. 760, 104 So. 105, 107.

- It has also been held that there is no legal technical signification to the phrase "colored person" which the courts are bound judicially to know. Pauska v.

Daus, 31 Tex. 74. (All Black's Law 4th Ed.)

Everything that is legal is not necessarily lawful but everything that is lawful is legal. In other words, natural law takes precedent and anything outside of that is deemed "of color" meaning something fake whether it is persons who identify as such or institutions that don't adhere to the true essence of law, which is by, of, and for Th people. But if you actively engage in fraud combined with reckless abandon and disregard for the affairs of civil governance then you are thus invisible and outside Th law and its protections. "*Human beings aren't crayons.*"- Taj Tarik Bey

Positive Status:

1. Special Appearance:

- (Black's Law 4th Ed.): An appearance may be either general or special; the former is a simple and unqualified or unrestricted submission to the jurisdiction of the court, the latter a submission to the jurisdiction for some specific purpose only, not for all the purposes of the suit. Louisville & N. R. Co. v. Industrial Board of Illinois, 282 Ill. 136, 118 N.E. 483, 485. A special appearance is for the purpose of testing the sufficiency of service or the jurisdiction of the court; a general appearance is made where the defendant waives defects of service and submits to the jurisdiction. State v. Huller, 23 N.M. 306, 168 P. 528, 534, 1 A.L.R. 170.

This is the proper way to enter a colorable or any court/tribunal. You let it be known your status and you present yourself properly and without fear; speaking only what is necessary and factual, always respectful but nonetheless authoritative and cognizant.

2. In Propria Persona:

- (Black's Law 4th Ed.): In one's own proper person.
- It is a rule in pleading that pleas to the jurisdiction of the court must be plead *in propria persona*, because if pleaded by attorney they admit the jurisdiction, as an attorney is an officer of the court, and he is presumed to plead after having obtained leave, which admits the jurisdiction. Lawes, PI. 91.
- In some jurisdictions, however, this rule is no longer recognized. 1 C.J. 255.

All things whether done legally in terms of public or private business must be done in your Proper person i.e. within the context of substantive reality. In other words, you must be righteous but to be righteous you must be real in every aspect of your existence.

3. In Full Life

- (Black's Law 4th Ed.): Continuing in both physical and civil existence; that is, neither actually dead nor *civiliter mortuus.*

When you declare your nationality, this is what you are articulating to the universe seen and unseen that you are a sentient being and that you are prepared and willing to accept and fulfill the obligations that come with the gift of breathing and form.

4. Consul:

- (Black's Law 4th Ed.): International Law: An officer of a commercial character, appointed by the different states to watch over the mercantile interests of the appointing state and of its subjects in foreign countries. There are usually a number of consuls in every maritime country, and they are usually subject to a chief consul, who is called a "consul general." Schunior v. Russell, 18 S.W. 484, 83 Tex. 83.
- Old English Law: An ancient title of an earl.
- Roman Law: During the' republic, the name "consul" was given to the chief executive magistrate, two of whom were chosen annually. The office was continued under the empire, but its powers and prerogatives were greatly reduced. The name is supposed to have been derived from *consulo,* to consult, because these officers consulted with the senate on administrative measures.
- The word "consul" has two meanings: (1) It denotes an officer of a particular grade in the consular service; (2) it has a broader generic sense, embracing all consular officers. Dainese v. U. S., 15 Ct.C1. 64. See, also, Foreign Service Act of 1946, 22
- U.S.C.A. § 801 et seq.

The fact is you do not need an Attorney in most instances if you have diligently and properly studied but you can still seek the services of or be an actual consul whereas they or you do not represent or act for the client/ defendant but aid in his/her defense via cooperative consultation and synergy. There is no requirement of license to practice law as law is embedded in and stems from nature, so if you need not permission to breath, though it is a divine privilege, then in truth you need no permission from mammon to exercise and demonstrate self-defense in the form of competence which is your civic duty.

5. Natural Person:

- (Black's Law 4th Ed.): A man considered according to the rank he holds in society, with all the right to which the place he holds entitles him, and the duties which it imposes. People v. R. Co., 134 N.Y. 506, 31 N.E. 873.
- The word in its natural and usual signification includes women as well as men. Commonwealth v. Welosky, 276 Mass. 398, 177 N.E. 656.
- Term may include artificial beings, as corporations, 1 Bla.Com. 123; 4 Bingh. 669; People v. Comrs of Taxes, 23 N.Y. 242; quasi-corporations, Sedgw. Stat. & Const. L. 372; L. R. 5 App. Cas. 857; territorial corporations, Seymour v. School District, 53 Conn. 507, 3 A. 552; and foreign corporations, People v. McLean, 80 N.Y. 259; under statutes, forbidding the taking of property without due process of law and giving to all persons the equal protection of the laws, Smyth v. Ames, 18 S.Ct. 418, 169 U.S. 466, 42 L.Ed. 819; Gulf, C. & S. F. R. Co. v. Ellis, 17 S.Ct. 255, 165 U.S. 150, 41 L.Ed. 666; concerning claims arising from Indian depredations, U. S. v. Transp. Co., 17 S.Ct. 206, 164 U.S. 686, 41 L.Ed. 599; relating to taxation and the revenue laws, People v. McLean, 80 N.Y. 254; to attachments, Bray v. Wallingford, 20 Conn. 416; usurious contracts, Philadelphia Loan Co. v. Towner, 13 Conn. 249; applying to limitation of actions, Olcott v. R. Co., 20 N.Y. 210, 75 Am.Dec. 393; North Mo. R. Co. v. Akers, 4 Kan. 453, 96 Am.Dec. 183; and concerning the admissibility as a witness of a party in his own behalf when the opposite party is a living person, La Farge v. Ins. Co., 22 N.Y. 352.
- A. corporation is also a person under a penal statute; U. S. v. Amedy, 11 Wheat. 392, 6 L.Ed. 502. Corporations are "persons" as that word is used in the first clause of the XIVth Amendment; Covington & L. Turnp. Co. v. Sandford, 17 S.Ct. 198, 164 U.S. 578, 41 L.Ed. 560; Smyth v. Ames, 18 S.Ct. 418, 169 U.S. 466, 42 L.Ed. 819; People v. Fire Assn, 92 N.Y. 311, 44 Am.Rep. 380; U. S. v. Supply Co., 30 S.Ct. 15, 215 U.S. 50, 54 L.Ed. 87; *contra*, Central P. R. Co. v. Board, 60 Cal. 35. But a corporation of another state is not a "person" within the jurisdiction of the state until it has complied with the conditions of admission to do business in the state, Fire Assn of Phila. v. New York, 7 S.Ct. 108, 119 U.S. 110, 30 L.Ed. 342; and a statutory requirement of such conditions is not in conflict with the XIVth Amendment; Pembina Consol. S. M. & M. Co.

v. Pennsylvania, 8 S.Ct. 737, 125 U.S. 181, 189, 31 L.Ed. 650.

- It may include partnerships. In re Julian, D. C.Pa., 22 F.Supp. 97, 99. Also firms. State ex rel. Joseph R. Peebles Sons Co. v. State Board of Pharmacy, 127 Ohio St. 513, 189 N.E. 447, 448.
- "Persons" are of two kinds, natural and artificial. A natural person is a human being. Artificial persons include a collection or succession of natural persons forming a corporation; a collection of property to which the law attributes the capacity of having rights and duties. The latter class of artificial persons is recognized only to a limited extent in our law. Examples are the estate of a bankrupt or deceased person. Hogan v. Greenfield, 58 Wyo. 13, 122 P.2d 850, 853.
- It has been held that when the word person is used in a legislative act, natural persons will be intended unless something appear in the context to show that it applies to artificial persons, Blair v. Worley, 1 Scam., Ill., 178; Appeal of Fox, 112 Pa. 337; 4 A. 149; but as a rule, corporations will be considered persons within the statutes unless the intention of the legislature is manifestly to exclude them. Stribbling v. Bank, 5 Rand, Va., 132.
- A county is a person in a legal sense, Lancaster Co. v. Trimble, 34 Neb. 752, 52 N.W. 711; but a sovereign is not; In re Fox, 52 N.Y. 535, 11 Am.Rep. 751; U. S. v. Fox, 94 U.S. 315, 24 L.Ed. 192, but *contra* within the meaning of a statute, providing a penalty for 'the fraudulent alteration of a public record with intent that any "person" be defrauded, Martin v. State, 24 Tex. 61; and within the meaning of a covenant for quiet and peaceful possession against all and every person or persons; Giddings v. Holter, 19 Mont. 263, 48 P. 8. An Indian is a person, U. S. v. Crook, 5 Dill. 459, Fed.Cas.No.14,891; and a slave was so considered, in so far, as to be capable of committing a riot in conjunction with white men, State *v.* Thackam, 1 Bay, S.C., 358. The estate of a decedent is a person, Billings v. State, 107 Ind. 54, 6 N.E. 914, 7 N.E. 763, 57 Am. Rep. 77; and where the statute makes the owner of a dog liable for injuries to any person, it includes the property of such person, Brewer v. Crosby, 11 Gray, Mass., 29; but where the statute provided damages for the bite of a dog which had previously bitten a person, it was held insufficient to show that the dog had previously bitten a goat, [1896] 2 Q.B. 109; a dog will not be included in the word in an act which authorizes a *person* to kill dogs running at large, Heisrodt v. Hackett, 34 Mich. 283, 22 Am.Rep. 529.
- Where the statute prohibited any person from pursuing his usual vocation on the Lord's Day, it was held to apply to a judge holding court. Bass v. Irvin, 49

Ga. 436.

- A child *en ventre sa mere* is not a person. Dietrich *v.* Northampton, 138 Mass. 14, 52 Am.Rep. 242; but an infant is so considered; Madden v. Springfield, 131 Mass. 441.
- In the United States bankruptcy act of 1898, *it* is provided that the word "persons" shall include corporations, except where otherwise specified, and officers, partnerships, and women, and, when used with reference to the commission of acts which are therein forbidden, shall include persons who are participants in the forbidden acts, and the agents, officers, and members of the board of directors or trustees, or their controlling bodies, of corporations. 11 U.S.C.A. § 1.
- Persons are the subject of rights and duties; and, as a subject of a right, the person is the object of the correlative duty, and conversely. The subject of a right has been called by Professor Holland, the person of inherence; the subject of a duty, the person of incidence. "Entitled" and "bound" are the terms in common use in English and for most purposes they are adequate. Every full citizen is a person; other human beings, namely, subjects who are not citizens, may be persons. But not every human being is necessarily a person, for a person is capable of rights and duties, and there may well be human beings having no legal rights, as was the case with slaves in English law.
- A person is such, not because he *is* human, but because rights and duties are ascribed to him. The person is the legal subject or substance of which the rights and duties are attributes. An individual human being considered as having such attributes is what lawyers call a natural person. Pollock, First Book of Jurispr. 110. Gray, Nature and Sources of Law, ch. IL.

This is the difference between death and life. One who is natural is of and for life whereas one who is corporate is indeed the opposite, a fad or fleeting personality with no actual standing but that which uses society as a crutch e.g. entertainers, so-called organizational leaders particularly in impoverished communities, ministers, Monsanto, politicians, etc. All of these are examples of fictions/corpses that are given life/energy by the masses that uphold and empower them. "Birds of a feather flock together" and if you accept the pact to be a corporate entity then you are a corpse as well thus you are no better or different from the constructs that serve as poison to this planet and its resources and karma will have no mercy.

6. Sui Juris:

- (Black's Law 4th Ed.): Lat. Of his own right; possessing full social and civil rights; not under any legal disability, or the power of another, or guardianship.
- Having capacity to manage one's own affairs; not under legal disability to act for one's self. Story, Ag. § 2.

This is the mindset and character of a sovereign, a true national that is in accordance with ancestral lineage and creed and that responds to their ability thus they are deemed responsible. There is no such thing as without rules even within the framework of a lawless society there are still rules/laws that manage the savagery of disobedience this society of the present day North-West Amexem/America being a prime example of that. I say that to point out the fallacy of those who claim the title of Moor but who advocate and engage in lawlessness both of the extreme sense as in unjustifiable homicides, thievery and so forth and those who do it on a more clandestine and cunning way as those who mix falsehood with truth such as rights to travel, bear, arms and registering with corporations. These are all of the same spirit of the converso who have reincarnated in different forms but whose objective is the same; to keep as many as they can from freedom which is right knowledge. They distort the nobility of our ancestors to divide, corrupt and conquer those seeking refuge but who are infants in their mentality and slaves to their emotions thus they are easily controlled for one who cannot control their emotions is essentially a puppet. If you know better you should do better.

7. Allodial:

- (Black's Law 4th Ed.): Free; not holden of any lord or superior; owned without obligation of vassalage or fealty; the opposite of feudal. Barker v. Dayton, 28 Wis. 384; Wallace v. Harmstad, 44 Pa. 499.

To claim your ancestors land is the right and duty of the true heirs to this vast estate. However, it must be done so in honor and without fear of certain backlash and repercussions. You are not bound to the debt of your forefathers once you are off age for such equates to competence and has nothing really to do with age in terms of physical quantity of years you have spent in this particular incarnation. We are born free and the land we stand on is ours by consanguinity (bloodline). There are those who say we must reclaim our estates, but they do so with the mindset of actual corporeal things. The true estate is the state of mind for that is what we've lost. The land didn't go any where but our connection to it did thus severing the spirit of duties we owe to it. If you trust in and value something you take better care of it and such is why the state of man and her sons is in this current condition because we've basically stop caring about the land in which we inhabit failing to realize that she (the earth) is we and we are she so if we hurt she hurts and vice versa. The abnormal weather patterns, weird behaviors, and the mindset of the youth are all direct correlations to the fact of abandonment of principalities which is the foundation of a healthy existence.

8. Free White Person:

- (Black's Law 4th Ed.): "Free white persons" referred to in Naturalization Act, as amended by Act July 14, 1870, has meaning naturally given t& it when first used in 1 Stat. 103, c. 3, meaning all persons belonging to the European races then commonly counted as white, and their descendants, including such descendants in other countries to which they have emigrated.
- It includes all European Jews, more or less intermixed with peoples of Celtic, Scandinavian, Teutonic, Iberian, Latin, Greek, and Slavic descent. It includes Magyars, Lapps, and Finns, and the Basques and Albanians. It includes the mixed Latin, Celtic-Iberian, and Moorish inhabitants of Spain and Portugal, the mixed Greek, Latin, Phoenician, and North African inhabitants of Sicily, and the mixed Slav and Tarter inhabitants of South Russia. It does not mean Caucasian race, Aryan race, or Indo-European races, nor the mixed Indo-European, Dravidian, Semitic and Mongolian peoples who inhabit Persia. A Syrian of Asiatic birth and descent will not be entitled to become a naturalized citizen of the United States as being a free white person. Ex parte Shahid, D.C.S.C., 205 F. 812, 813; United States v. Cartozian, D.C.Or., 6 F.2d 919, 921; Ex parte Dow, D.C.S.C., 211 F. 486, 487; In re En Sk Song, D.C.Cal., 271 F. 23. Nor a native-born Filipino. U. S. v. Javier, 22 F.2d 879, 880, 57 App.D.C. 303. Nor a native of India who belonged to Hindu race. Kharaitf Ram Samras v. United States, C.C.A.Cal., 125 F.2d 879, 881.

Unfortunately, in this part of the continent identity is viewed or associated with complexion whereby the hue of a man, due to social engineering, creates a certain type of perception and stigmatism. Both terms "white" and "black" are in actuality legal statuses i.e. spells that invoke either the spirit of sovereignty or servitude. White means purity, purity means "God" and god is ruler of the land. However, being that Europeans are aliens they cannot truly be sovereign, or rulers of this land accept by way of consent of the true heirs and sovereigns. Every time you call a European "white" or when Europeans accept and refer to themselves as white both have just committed an error in law and are co-conspirators to fraud, however both have fallen in love with the lie. Before the Early and Late 1800s Europeans were not even called such but adopted the status via the naturalization act of 1790 March 26, which was later amended in 1870. Black was instituted by way of the reconstruction era after the systematic defeat of the Moors via a series of wars both tribal and otherwise. The legal status of the term white is actually based on astrology, making a reference to "white light". White light is the highest, because it includes all colors of the spectrum hence the original idea of the Moorish term "white person", meant a whole being, someone in good standing. The 7 primordial planets (spheres) of this galaxy combine to produce white light. 7 is the number of "the perfect man" thus to be white is to be a holistic being that embodies the divine essence and in turn is a reflection of the cosmic infinitude of the universe. Very few people on this planet deserve this title and those who use it for the most part are unqualified which means in donning it and accepting it as a label but not living up to the responsibilities of that vibration puts them in dishonor as they are acting in a mendacious capacity.

IV. Code words

1. Black:

- 1973 world book dictionary: adj. opposite of white; reflecting little or no light, without any light; very dark, having a dark skin, negro, dirty; filthy, dismal; gloomy, unrelieved, angry, sullen, evil, wicked, disastrous, (British) that pays black wages. < Old English blaec, alternative form of blac meaning "pale, shining".

This is the main curse or mark that has been placed on my people that has been socially engineered by European colonists and empowered by their Caucasian contemporaries. This status is the lowest on the political scale and it symbolizes the dregs of society. The originals of the earth of this section of the hemisphere have accepted this spirit and in turn have become possessed by anger, jealousy, greed, hatred and are essentially dead both civilly and mentally as they are ignorant and blind to the truth. Our brothers and sisters of other nations also serve to perpetuate this fraud hence why they come here and shun us but still set up shop because they, not unlike the romans, take advantage of our ignorance and feed on our dead carcass like the vultures they are. On their passports, they actually have the status of white but of course they'll never reveal that to us because we'll shun them, and/or they have side deals with the Jesuits to keep the secret of who we are but pretending not to know meanwhile laughing at us behind our backs. Plain and simple, if you claim that you are black, or if you allow others to classify you as such and you do not correct it then you have agreed to servitude and death in the eyes of the universe, seen and unseen.

2. African:

- 1973 world book dictionary: adj. of or having to do with Africa, its peoples, their languages, or their customs; from Africa, n. a native of Africa, especially a person belonging to one of the native tribes of Africa; a negro

The word Africa is derived from the Arabic word faraqa meaning to break up into many pieces. If you notice the people of that continent never actually call themselves Africans but they will say they are from Africa but if asked what their nationality is they would reply, "Ghanaian, Somalian, Ethiopian, Nigerian" etc., referring to the different tribal jurisdictions. The Asiatics of the North-West have been labeled and have accepted this brand which invokes the spirit of schismatism and disassociation from their lineage that ties them to this continent which was and is perpetuated by the slave narrative which was a farce created as revenge on what our dirty ancestors in the past did to them and has served as means by which they have essentially traded places with us. Some would argue that this brand, especially in comparison to black, negro, and colored is a lot more acceptable/respectable but if this is so why do those who actually come from the continent that domicile here not identify as the same? The answer is simple because they know to do so would sever the link to their ancestors and put them in dishonor as it has done to the Asiatics of the North-West.

In some circles the word Africa is a Masonic code for the Earth.

3. Race:

- Black's Law Dictionary 4th Ed.: An ethnical stock; a great division of mankind having in common certain distinguishing physical peculiarities constituting a comprehensive class appearing to be derived from a distinct primitive source. A tribal or national stock, a division or subdivision of one of the great racial stocks of mankind distinguished by minor peculiarities. Descent. In re Halladjian, C.C.Mass., 174 F. 834; Ex parte (Ng.) Fung Sing, D.C.Wash., I 6 F.2d 670. < Old French rais or raiz< Latin radix, root.

There is truly only one race on this planet and that is the human race. As I stated earlier in this manuscript all beings on this planet come from the Great Moabite Moorish Womb-Man, the Matriarch and progenitor of the human family. This is undisputable and even modern archeologists with readily admit that all life on this planet comes from what they call the African woman, which some scholars have referred to as "Zudiacus". Primitive, according to the 1973 world book dictionary, means of early times; of long ago, first of a kind, very simple, original, primary, and primordial. < Latin primitivus < primitiae, first things, first fruits < primus first. In this society, the word primitive is associated with Neanderthals or cave dwellers basically disrespecting the brilliance of the ancients and trying to assert themselves (albion/hybrids) as having a place in her-story that they simply do not. We as Asiatics are the primitive and natural people of this planet that gave birth, both naturally and artificially, to all other peoples on this planet.

4. Bless:

- Online etymology dictionary; 1973 world book dictionary: Derived from the old English word bletsian, bledsian meaning to consecrate (that is, with blood), related to blod, blood

This is another spell put on the masses by the Jesuits that is a curse in origin that invokes the spirit of blood (soul/life force) sacrifice. It is socially accepted in this society to bless those who sneeze, unknowingly putting curses on ourselves. This is why ministers, rabbis, and bishops etc., are always blessing you because they are secretly saying that you are their offering to the beast. All those worshipping centers are nothing more than glorified gas chambers that suck the oxygen/spirit substituting poison in the stead. This is why people catch the Holy Ghost because a demon has latched on to them. Th Most High is the spirit of peace and tranquility so therefore all that hollering and jumping around is a sign that something else is in the building. For example, the word mass is derived from Old English maesse < Late Latin missa < Latin militere, to send away; they send your soul away so other entities can take hold thus you become puppets for the beast. Another confirmation of this fact is the symbolic ritual of the drinking of the blood of Christ which is actually a ritual symbolizing the actual eating of the saints/Moors during the period of the inquisitions. These are real life vampires that suck energy physically, mentally and spiritually. The final example is the name of the podium that they speak form which is called a pulpit i.e. they pull you into the pit of Satan via misinformation and evil indoctrinations into your subconscious mind. The actual good salutation/counter spell to this is bliss so from now on give blissings not blessings and if someone blesses you rebuke it.

5. God:

- Online etymology dictionary: Old English god, "supreme being, deity; the Christian god; image of god; godlike person",< Proto-Germanic guthan (source also of Old Saxon, Old Frisian Dutch god, Old High German got, German gott, Old Norse guo, Gothic gup) from PIE (Proto-Indo-European) ghut, "that which is invoked", (source of Old Church Slavonic zovo, "to call", Sanskrit huta, "invoked", an epithet of Indra), from root gheu(e), "to call invoke". Also, PIE ghu-to, "poured", from root gheu, "to pour, pour a libation" (source of Greek khein, "to pour", also in the phrase khute Gaia, "poured earth", referring to a burial mound.

This the most potent piece of misinformation perpetuated on the "believers" that turn people into worshippers instead of actual practitioners whereas they have adopted a victim mentality that, in their mind absolves them and serves as a crutch against their own inner demons and shortcomings essentially placing a band aid on a bullet wound instead of actually removing the source of the trauma. God is a verb which means it is a ritual which means it is based on cause and effect not idle/idol worshipping. One cannot be a god, but one can god which is to invoke the spirits of the spirit realm which can be either positive or negative depending on intent and actions. The reason these code words were placed upon us in these manners was because our enemies, by way of our ancestors teaching and through observation, knows how powerful we are so they put spells/words with evil roots so as to make us curse ourselves placing us in perpetual servitude. This is the origin of the phrase, "Be careful what you wish for because you might just get it, meaning be mindful of how you speak and the intentions by which you empower those thoughts because you could be unwittingly placing a bond on yourself that binds you to evil spirits.

Luke 18:18-19 New International Version

> [18] *A certain ruler asked him, "Good teacher, what must I do to inherit eternal life?"*
>
> [19] *"Why do you call me good?" Jesus answered. "No one is good—except God alone.*

6. Understand:

- 1973 world book dictionary and Online etymology dictionary: mutual agreement: compound word: under-being beneath, lower, subordinate, not enough + stand < from Old English standan, "to occupy a place; stand firm, congeal; exist, take place; stay, continue, be valid, be; oppose, resist attack.

This is one of the main code words used by the policy enforcers of Rome. Whenever you get pulled over they ask do you understand, when you are in a court room they ask do you understand, when you get evaluated they ask do you understand; this is so that they can get you to agree to take part in your own molestation/violation. You must overstand/innerstand that when you are asked this to never agree or corroborate that statement i.e. you say that you do not understand because when you do you essentially say that you surrender to the will of satan as in you are under the jurisdiction of the Jesuits. They are fictitious and operate off of illusion and fallacy being that they are corpses, dead entities that are given life by your acquiescence and compliance. Never understand, always innerstand and overstand these beasts.

However, understanding id=s noble when done in the context of submitting the inevitable truth that is Th Creator. All must submit to something but make sure that something is no thing.

7. Hell:

- Black's Law 4th Ed.: The name formerly given to a place under the exchequer chamber, where the king's debtors were confined. Rich.Dict.
- 1973 world book dictionary: (obsolete/archaic) a place of confinement for debtors
- Online etymology dictionary: Old English hel, helle, "nether world, abode of the dead, infernal regions, place of torment, for the wicked after death", from Proto-Germanic haljo "the underworld" (source also of Old Frisian Helle, Old Saxon hellia, Dutch hel, Old Norse hel, German Holle, gothic halja "hell"). Literally "concealed place" (compare Old Norse hellir "cave, cavern") from PIE kel (2) "to cover, conceal" see cell.

Another misconception whereas we are taught to believe that hell is a place far away awaiting those who do wrong. The fact is this earth is hell and it is also heaven, but both are really states of mind. The real hell hasn't come yet, but it will and as is the case with heaven/haven. Th Most High didn't create either of these things but rather man did. Through our actions we have become zombies turning paradise into a nightmare filled with debauchery of all kinds that will only lead to self-destruction. We experience hell everyday and we experience heaven the only question being which will you choose to reside in? It's all about choices and that is the gift of the free will given to man.

8. Democracy:

- 1973 world book dictionary and Online etymology dictionary: < Middle French democratie, learned borrowing from Medieval Latin democratia < Greek demokratia < demos-common, (originally) district + kratos-rule, strength, power, authority (see cracy)

- Cracy: word-forming element forming nouns meaning "rule or government by" from French-cratie or directly from Medieval Latin-cratia, from Greek-kratia "power, might; rule, sway; power over; a power, authority", from kratos "strength", from PIE kre-tes "power, strength" suffixed form of root kar/ker "hard".
- District < Medieval Latin districtus, territory under the jurisdiction of a feudal lord < Latin distingere; see distress.
- Distress: law. The legal seizure of the goods of another as payment for debt or as a security < Old French distrece, perhaps < Vulgar Latin districtia < Latin distringere < dis-apart + stringere, draw.
- Demonocracy: the rule of demons, a ruling body of demons

As has been reveled the current political system which the masses has popularized is in fact the very thing that dooms them. This society was founded and established with the mindset of a republic which is by Th people, for Th people and of Th people. These people are actually servants but in delegating your inalienable sovereignty to them you have essentially became their servants. Now it must be inner/overstood that I do not advocate any part of these political tribalism as they are two wings of the same bird, however, just because someone one steals a car and robs a bank with it does that doesn't make the car evil but is solely on the driver. But, changing scenarios, if you allow someone to get in your vehicle and push you out of the captain's seat and into the passenger and they go rob banks and you do nothing to stop them or attempt to separate from them then you are an accomplice making you just as responsible. We are under occupation and the vehicle and the spirit of government has been high jacked and due to the masses compliance, the fraud is still running though it has been revealed that they are frauds and act in a fraudulent capacity but people would rather live a comfortable illusion than a hard reality. As children we said the pledge of allegiance, in it identified that this is truly a republic which it stands under G-d for liberty and justice for all. This is why they've created so many municipalities so as to divide and conquer the land and create separatism amongst the natives and our children.

9. Agent:

- 1973 world book dictionary: n. a person or company having the authority to act for another, a person who produces an effect, any power or cause that produces an effect, means; instrument. < Latin agens, entis, present participle of agree-do.

This term gets thrown around and is generally used to identify a person acting within a clandestine and negative capacity. The fact is we are all agents, but the question is for whom or of whom are you an agent for? Automatically when people hear agent they think of the spies or so- called federal agents, but these are not the only types of agents. You can be an agent of Th Most High meaning you invoke the spirit of goodness and produce by way of righteous intent righteous results for the benefit of society. Of course, there are those who work for Satan and perpetuate chaos and destruction. Also, it must not be assumed that all agents of Rome are apart of actual federal agencies or that they are even fully aware of who they actually work for. Some people are what is called sleeper agents who are controlled subconsciously doing the bid of evil without actual self awareness of the fact. The key is to know who you are and what you stand for and represent. Trust no man but always trust the spirit man meaning listen to your instincts, watch and learn.

10. Money:

- 1973 world book dictionary: n. current; gold, silver, or other metal made into coins; bank notes etc., representing gold or silver; any medium of exchange especially as issued by a government or authorized by public authority. < Old French moneie < Latin Moneta, mint, money < Juno Moneta, Juno the protectress (Roman goddess; in whose temple money was coined) < Monere, to warn. Doublet of Mint 2.
- Mint 2: A place where money is coined by public authority; (obsolete) a piece of money; coin- v.t. to coin (money), to make or fabricate; originate. < Old English mynet, a coin, ultimately < Latin Moneta, mint. Doublet of money.
- Dollar: Earlier daler < Low German or Dutch daler, abstracted from German Joachimsthaler, a silver coin from. Joachim's valley in Bohemia. Compare Thaler (a former German silver coin, worth about 71/2 cents; taler, the levant dollar)

- Black's Law Dictionary: Fiat: Lat. "Let it be done."
- Currency: n. a passing from one person to another, general use or acceptance; common occurrence. < Old French corant, present participle of corre, to run < Latin currere

Currency is energy and energy flows. The truth is that people themselves are the actual currency and /or money and that these fiat notes are really just bills of exchange whereas the debt incurred by the colonists is transferred onto people metaphysically by way of their belief in it which thus empowers it. Real money is gold and silver which is the main reason the Albion colonized our continent so as to steal the gold and silver of the people which is both corporeal and incorporeal. We suffer low self esteem, inflated egos, greed, and ruthlessness all for green pieces of paper that if we only took the time to read will reveal on its face that it is a note not money. See also article 1 section 10 of the United States constitution and it will further corroborate what I've written. A suggestion burn a 1 fiat note and release negative energy out of your life and break the bond of Rome. What you fear you also worship so if you fear being "broke" then you fear being not under the thumb of Satan. Do what you got to do to survive but do so righteously and always remember that money/fiat is not the root of all evil, it is the love of money that is (1 Tim. 6:10; Isa. 52: 3). "Money is a great slave, but a horrible master."-French Proverb

11. Slave:

- 1973 world book dictionary and online etymology dictionary: adj. a person who is the property of another, a person who submits to or follows another, a person who is controlled or ruled by some desire. < Old French esclave < Medieval Latin Sclavus, later Slavus Slav; Late Greek Sklabos (first applied to enslaved Slavs). The Slavic words for "slave" (Russian rab,

Serbo-Croatian rob, Old Church Slavonic rabu) are from Old Slavic orbu, from the PIE root orbh (also source of orphan), the ground sense of which seems to be "thing that changes allegiance" (in the case of the slave, from himself to his master.) Used in the secondary sense because of the many Slavs sold into slavery by the conquering peoples. This sense development arose in the consequence of the wars waged by Otto the Great and his successors against the Slavs, a great number of whom they took captive and sold into slavery.

Slavs are Slavic, Slovenian, Slavonic therefore the whole concept of Asiatics being the descendants of slaves is genetically impossible as we would have to be descended form Slavic. So, the truth is that we were never slaves but were/are indentured servants who are sharecroppers. A sharecropper is someone who farms land for the owner in return for parts of crops. This is the true her-story of how we lost connection to our land which was done in the form of contract signed by our ancestors that they were tricked into by those so-called Jews who are not. The same is done today as this is the way they set mandate by the tricking of the natives. However, this is far different than the narrative that is forced down the throats of my people whereas we were shipped from somewhere else and all that other bullshit. The fact is we were always here and all those statistics and movies and pictures are doctored so as to keep Asiatics in a state of conscious inferiority and emotionalism which is essentially a treadmill that keeps us spinning our wheels but making no progress because we still focus on the past and his- story which is a lie any way. Yes, we suffered atrocities and still do but the number and scale that was reported is a gross exaggeration of the facts and today we have no excuses because we now have everything we need to free ourselves. The debt was up in 2012 Gregorian but due to agents of Rome set up and placed strategically in Asiatic communities combined with the subconscious terrorism that occurs through music, sports, movies, news, etc., has stagnated the growth of the people though growth has and continues to occur but is moving slower than it should.

12. Republic:

- 1973 world book dictionary and Online etymology dictionary: "state in which supreme power rests in the people via elected representatives", < Middle French republique < Latin respublica (ablative republica) "the common weal, a commonwealth, state, republic," literally res publica "public interest, the state", from res "affair, matter, thing" + publica, feminine of publicus "public".
- Public, "open to general observation", < Old French public and directly from Latin publicus, "of the people; of the state, done for the state".

This is the spirit of this land (see article 4 section 4 of Constitution). Through traitorous deeds and usurpation, it has been substituted, in the minds of the people, as a democracy which is the opposite of what this society should be about. The whole goal of these demons was to sever the people's connection to the truth of her-story thus they have no reverence for what it is that truly sustains them. We suffer injustices because we do not enforce the pacts and oaths that these people swore to protect. In doing so we would increase the frequency on this planet to such an extent that they have no choice but to bow down. They are already do in secret but them being master illusionists make it seem as if everything is just as it was and will continue until Momma says otherwise which is the result of the strange phenomena that is occurring more rapidly by the day. Mother Nature will protect her own but if you are not loyal/ royal then when the planet cleanses herself fully you will be ashes in the trash heap. Here is an excerpt from the Secret treaty of Verona November 22, 1822:

> **ARTICLE 1.** *The high contracting powers being convinced that the system of representative govern- ment is equally as incompatible with the monarchial principles as the maxim of the sovereignty of the people with the high divine right, engage mutually in the most solemn manner, to use all their efforts to put an end to the system of representative governments, in whatever country it may exist in Europe, and to prevent its being introduced in those countries where it is not yet known.*

Their whole point is that they don't have the people's best interests at heart which is pretty evident at this point now all that remains is for the people to be who they are for every tongue must confess meaning speak truth to power trust Th Supreme laws and abide by them. Only the righteous will receive honor. (Lev. 26: 9-13; 1 Tim 1:8; 1 Tim. 1 Tim 1: 9-10) Govern means control and ment means the state of so when you allow others to dictate your state of mind then you surrender your willpower but if you control your own (e)state then you are essentially government.

13. Nigga:

- 1973 world book dictionary and Online etymology dictionary: Naga n. a mythological water creature of India associated with serpents, and regarded as a spirit of peace and fertility < Sanskrit naga, "serpent, snake"

- Negus: n. title of the sovereign of Ethiopia; title for a ruler Abyssinia < Amharic negush, Negus, king < nagasha, he forced, ruled
- Niggard: n. stingy person; miser; mean person < compare Old Icelandic knoggr, stingy

There is a reason we as a people have always been drawn to the word nigga as it was the ancestors that dwell within our DNA speaking to and through us so as we could receive the effects that this and these vibrations invoke. This is also why we never liked the word nigger because instinctively we felt its spirit of disdain combined with fact that it was uttered by our oppressors. It means cave people or hybrid which is why it never resonated because it didn't fit our lineage but rather those who said it the most which is another instance of attempting to trade places with us and absorb the power of our royal ancestry. There was a concerted effort by agents of Rome both Asiatic and albion that waged a campaign to suppress this word/vibration because in uttering it we raised our consciousness and frequency subconsciously hence why we know more than we ever did because in the 90s we were saying this word heavy which helped the process of mental and spiritual restoration. The serpent throughout the world is a symbol of supreme wisdom, restoration and immortal life because a snake sheds its skin thus transforms leaving the old shell behind. All over the world you'll see statues of the serpent and how all nations revere the serpent though here they show pictures of it chopped up which is symbolic to the story of Ausar and they (Europeans) show eagles eating them but at the same time all ambulances and doctors of medicine wear the caduceus which is the serpent (cosmic divine energy) climbing the 33 steps of Jacob's latter (your spinal cord) that is capped off with wings because once the serpent is fully erect it takes flight which is symbolic of intergalactic and inter-dimensional travel which is the power that our ancestors possessed hence why you can't find a lot of their bodies though they are doctored to appear as such by modern day archaeologists. We too have this ability, but we weaken it with disobedience to nature (Momma) and consciousness (father). Due to social engineering, we've for the most part grown to dislike or become ashamed of it (the serpent) as result of public opinion which came by way of the mis-transliteration of the bible which our ancestors wrote but was watered down due to tampering by our hybrid children. Also addressing the last definition is what we have become toward each other. We steal from each other, stunt on each other, murder each other, talk down on each other and we are reticent to help each other out. We shut ourselves off and refuse to share knowledge with each other instead holding on to it in the manner of tribalism and club bullshit which defeats and soils the essence of the divine gift of knowledge. I inner/overstand that you can't give pearls to swine, but you can still give the food of loving-kindness, humbleness, and patience. (See Acts 13:1) Also the word nagar in Ibri (Hebrew) means carpenter, which is one who builds and adds on, which is the celestial decreed duty of Th Moors.

14. Educate:

- 1973 world dictionary: n. to develop in knowledge, skill, ability, or character by training, study or experience. < Latin educare (with English ate) bring up, raise, related to educere; see educe. Synonym instruct
- Educe: v.t. to bring out, draw forth, elicit, and develop. < ex- out + ducere-lead. Synonym Extract
- Indoctrinate: v.t. to teach a doctrine, belief, or principle, to teach fundamentals, especially of military customs and discipline. Probably < Medieval Latin indoctinare (with English ate) < in-in + dortinare-teach < Latin doctrina, doctrine

A lot of people have been made to believe that they have an education when in fact they have indoctrination. To be truly educated is be elevated and to be led pass, through, and over the main stream teachings which are only formulas of propaganda and social engineering designed to shorten the horizon and narrow the perspective in turn giving one a false sense of superiority that in actuality is the opposite of what they deem academic. We as a people have been lead into Rome/Babylon/Jezebel when the ancient text tells you to come out of her (Rev. 18:4). We suffer dis-ease and abuse because we live by the way of the bringers of chaos and that which harbors evil. If you think that a degree makes you better than others or affords you some level of protection then you are dumb more so than one who never attended school a day in their lives and if you think that you can survive in this paradigm without studying at all then you are just as foolish and naïve as the supposedly educated. Remember, "Common sense was made before book sense", but a wise man knows the ledge. Balance is the key.

15. Religion:

- 1973 world book dictionary: n. matter of conscious. < Latin religio, onis-respect for what is sacred; probably (originally) care for (worship and traditions) < relegere, go through, or read again < re-again + legere-to read; religio was apparently strongly influenced, in popular thought, by the verb religare-to bind, in the sense "place an obligation on".

A lot of people who claim religion have never actually read their doctrines thoroughly and even if they have they did so with a narrow viewpoint. It is the responsibility of the student to not only read what is written but to decipher what the hidden meanings are (2 Tim. 2:15). A lot of people due to Self-righteousness and pride will never admit that they've read the books wrong and that these doctrines were created/modified so as to hinder the growth of the natural people but this is evident in the current state of the world despite most of the people on this planet claiming to be religious, yet they hate and are extremely unhealthy mentally, physically and spiritually. True religion is realignment with nature and the laws that govern the cosmos which is simplicity and compassion.

16. Spirituality:

- (173 world book dictionary: n. devotion to spiritual instead of worldly things; being neither corporeal nor material.
- Spirit: n. the immaterial part of man; soul. < Latin spiritus, us (originally) breath, related to spirare, to breath. Doublet of esprit, sprite.

-COME OUT OF HER MY PEOPLE!-

John 8:32 " And ye shall know the truth, and the truth shall make you free."

Colossians 2:8 Beware lest any man spoil you through philosophy and vain deceit, after the tradition of men, after the rudiments of the world, and not after Christ.

Your church denomination is a **FALSE RELIGION!**

MAN MADE RELIGIONS

Psalms 147:19-20

John Smyth	Charles Parham	Joseph Smith	Charles T Russel	William Miller

Created The Baptist Religion In 1608	Created The Pentecostal Religion In 1901	Created The Mormons Religion In 1830	Created The Jehovah Witness Religion In 1872	Created The 7th day Advenist Religion In 1863

Acts 5:29 "..We ought to obey God rather than men."

SUN-day

"Straight from the horse's mouth"

Prove to me from the Bible alone that I am bound to keep Sunday holy. There is no such law in the Bible. It is a law of the holy Catholic Church alone. The Bible says **"Remember the Sabbath day to keep it holy."** The Catholic Church says, No. By my divine power I abolish the Sabbath day and command you to keep holy the first day of the week. And lo! The entire civilized world bows down in reverent obedience to the command of the Holy Catholic Church.

Thomas Enright, CSSR, President, Redemptorist College (Roman Catholic), Kansas City, MO., February 18, 1884

Ask yourself this question..

How is it, that in our neighborhoods, there can be 4 churches on 1 block and in 20 years nothing in the area gets better?

BECAUSE GOD'S NOT IN THEM!

Acts 7:48 "Howbeit the most High dwelleth not in temples made with hands;"

You have been deceived!

www.israelunite.org
Israel United in Christ
44 S West St. Mt. Vernon, NY 10550
For More information call:
(718) 303-9655
outside N.Y. Call (866) 231-5114

A lot of people misuse this term as basis for all things relating to morality when in actuality it deals with breath and breath alone. This is where the ancient practice of meditation served as a medium by which man could practice and implore breathing techniques which increased oxygen flow to the brain thus enhancing frequency input, output, and overall brain function in turn heightening the senses both external and internal cultivating the divine connectivity of being to the supreme force bringing about wisdom, inspiration and divine creativity/productivity. This is why deep breathing methods are so important and should be practiced daily because it enhances circulation and Vibrational tones of thy temple bridging the gap between mortal and immortal, life and death, ignorance and enlightenment. The control of breath is key;

"Teach that the Holy Breath would make them one again, restoring harmony and peace." – Chapter 2: 19, Holy Koran Circle 7 by Prophet El Sharif Abdul Ali (Noble Drew Ali)

17. Master:

- 1973 world book dictionary: one who has power, authority and control, title of respect, teacher, a conqueror and commander, expert.

This is the level of fruition whereas one has gained ownership of their vessel/body in all dimensions (physically, spiritually and mentally). This is the 3rd degree of knowing thyself meaning you have attained a level of self-control that enables you to navigate without the boot of another on your neck. This does not exempt one from rules but rather from their negative consequences because all true masters adhere to and respect law, even the legal process which though it may not be actual law still is a necessary requirement so as to separate the strong from the weak. True masters know this and act accordingly and though nothing is absolute, except Th absolute, the master is for the most part safe wherever they go because the causation of their obedience is the effect of divine protection.

18. Good:

- Black's Law 4th Ed.: Valid; sufficient in law; effectual; unobjectionable; sound. Morrison v. Farmers' & Traders' State Bank, 70 Mont. 146, 225 P. 123, 125; McNabb v. Juergens (Iowa) 180 N.W. 758, 761; Raney & Hamon v. Hamilton & White, Tex.Civ. App., 234 S.W. 229, 230. Responsible; solvent; able to pay an amount specified.

We've been conditioned to believe that goodness only refers to character and/or behavior in the sense of good intent. However, the road to hell is paved with the good intent of those who thought they knew but who truly knew nothing. To be good is to know and demonstrate all law meaning the laws of civics which is the governance of civilization, the law of the mind which is the harnessing and expression of vibrations and frequencies, and the law of spirit which is intentions purified and supreme thankfulness. You cannot claim to be good if you don't take the time to study what runs the society in which you live. Morality is only as effective as the actions that represent them, so if you know the truth or are privileged to be in the company of one who does but do not acknowledge and take heed then you are the opposite of such and deserve whatever consequences that comes with the action or inaction of your voluntary ignorance.

The study of Etymology is a crucial component as it is an account or explanation of the origin and history of words, dealing with linguistic changes over time. We must know what we speak while at the same time get back to the essence of stillness and silence so as we can better hear what the ancestors are trying to convey to us. Culture is in the language and all you have to do is view how Asiatics speak to each other and themselves which is also done by society as a whole but is highlighted more so with us because we influence the world. How the mother and father go is how the majority of the children will go so it is up to us to change the atmosphere because in a lot of ways we created it.

19. Unity:

- UNITY. In the law of estates. **The peculiar characteristic of an estate** held by several in joint tenancy, and which is fourfold, viz., unity of interest, **unity of title**, unity of time, and **unity of possession**. In other words, joint tenants have one and the same interest, accruing by one and the same conveyance, commencing at one and the same time, and held by one and the same undivided possession. 2 Bl. Comm. 180 (Black's Law Dictionary 4th Ed.)

This is a word that is thrown around loosely in the so-called "black" community. It is a very seductive yet provocative spell that is cast widely on Moors classified, both knowingly and unknowingly, as "negro, colored, and black". It is the trap by which those conscious vampires use to drain the psychic energy of the good intentioned yet who deep down know, which is corroborated in the legal definition, that without a nationality there can be no true unity because unity comes under the authority of community and a community has substance via Jus Sanguine (bloodline). We have Noble titles (El, Bey, Ali, Al, Dey), we have the same possession (North, Central and South America) and our estate is Love, Truth, Peace, Freedom and Justice which is the foundation of the higher-self that is Moored to this realm by the collective will of the past, present and future generations. If you are against your bloodline then you are against unity because our heritage is not relegated to buildings, paperwork or personalities. So, essentially to be against Moors (your heritage/nationality) you are against Love, Truth, Peace, Freedom and Justice and are a traitor and an abomination.

20. White:

- Means Purity; ruler of the land; high social status.

This is a very powerful spell used by warlocks to siphon energy from the original strain so as propel themselves beyond their inherent genetic weakness. This, in all actuality, was originally reserved for the nobles, those who went around the universe spreading the 'light" hence they (The Moors) were called the "white men". However, due to massive mind control as a gradual effect because of the karmic lessons brought on because of our own cosmic cultivation this status was reversed. The actual proper terminology for the albions would be "wight" which when googled means *noun* ARCHAIC•DIALECT a person of a specified kind, especially one regarded as unfortunate. LITERARY a spirit, ghost, or other supernatural being. Old English *wiht* 'thing, creature', of Germanic origin; related to Dutch *wicht* 'little child' and German *Wicht* 'creature'.

B. Diaspora: The Creation of the "Races" Myth

I. Race

The word diaspora means the scattering of any group; dispersion and is derived from Greek diaspora, a scattering < dia-through, apart + spora, a sowing < speirin, to sow. Doublet of diaspora (1973 world book dictionary).

Due to the Moorish tribal wars and the infection of the masses the earth cracked so as to separate the peoples which was a divine plan to stop the bleeding and curb the infection of the demoniac forces that began to spill forth from the neighboring dimensions due to the practice of evil rituals, blood shed, and disobedience to the laws of nature.

However, though the peoples were divided the originals still held firm the tradition of oneness because we were conscious and cognizant to the law of existence which is in essence oneness as all things come from and are indebted to Th Supreme Law.

Once time moved along some ancients began doing experiments and in turn grafted a separate species of man known as "mankind" due to the fact that they were hybrids. This story is told in fragments regarding Yakub who is said to be the father of mankind and the original caucasian whose hatred for his own people caused him to create an entity that was essentially half man- half beast that he, being a master of all sciences, would instruct to take advantage of the tribalism of his Sistars and Brethren being that he knew how they operated and thus could manipulate and mold his hybrids into becoming basically walking diseases, vultures who take advantage of the dead and/or dying carcass of its prey.

The Albion gained power not by brute force, though they perpetuate that narrative so as to cover up their own history and the weakness that the truth reveals. They took advantage of the division amongst the first born and using the science of tricknology taught to them by their father they slowly but surely seized control of the Moorish empire piece by piece. The truth is they had divine help because they were/are our karma in a sense as we treated these people horribly never mind the fact that they really weren't supposed to be here in the first place. We violated on three fronts when it came to these hybrids: (1) We created them, (2) we mistreated them, and (3) we mated with them and invited them into our bloodline thus tainting our consanguinity and opening the door to their ruler ship which was foretold by the Elders, but we did not take heed to. Once we mated and created children with these people we were obligated to teach them because a father cannot abandon his children. The karma we've faced is nothing compared to what it would have been had the wise ones of the past not extended a hand to them and lifted them out of darkness. They had an in-depth inner/overstanding of how the law of the universe works and that what you give you receive so a lot of our kingdoms were actually given to Our European sons and daughters because we knew that they had to rule as a matter of succession.

Unfortunately, the children have violated and have not been as generous to the heirs as the heirs were to them which is why their time is running out and soon they will have to repeat the same lessons they should have learned the first time they were in the caves.

Once in power these Albion began to systematically alter her-story thus changing it to his-story due to transliterations, burning books but keeping others for themselves and generally poisoning this planet.

The modern concept of race and how it's structured was an invention of 3 men: Francois Bernier, Carolus Linnaeus, and Johann Friedlich Blumenbach.

One of the first efforts by Albion to highlight and document human variation began with French physician Francois Bernier's "nouville division de le terre par les differents especes ou races qui l'habitent", published in 1684. Loosely translated, it was entitled, "A new division of the earth, according to the different species or races of men who inhabit it". He was the one of the frontrunners that began planting seeds that pointed to the different skin tones/hues of beings on the planet and used an unscientific basis as a means to fabricate a supposed scientific notion based on outward physical characteristics.

Carolus Linnaeus (1707-1778) was a Swedish botanists and physician who developed the system for sorting living organisms into major (genus) and then more specific (species) categories in regard to men (e.g. homo sapiens). In the 1758 10th edition of "systema naturae" (natural selection), Linnaeus created the first formal, non-scientific human racial classification scheme. It included 5 varieties of homo- sapiens: Americans, Caucasians, Asiaticus, Afer, and ferus- based on physical and cultural descriptions that favored Albion/Caucasians. For the most part, caucasians acquired their information about so-called "Africans and Indians" in North America, not from direct experience with these populations, but rather primarily from those involved in human trafficking and mass infiltration and mis- education/indoctrination by mercenaries/missionaries. Caucasians were ethnocentric and naïve in their descriptions. This was especially true in Linnaeus' classifications of "homo ferrus' (wild men) and "homo monstrous" (monsters).

Johann Friedlich Blumenbach (1752-1840) was a German naturalist, physician, physiologist, and anthropologist who developed one of the earliest, non-scientific human racial classification systems. His work included his description of sixty human crania (skulls) published originally in fascicules as "Decas cranorium" (Gottingen, 1790-1828). This was a founding work for other scientists in the field of craniometry. He divided the human species into 5 races in 1779, later founded on crania research (description of human skulls), and called them:

- "Caucasian" or "white race"
- The "Mongolian" or "yellow" race which included all East Asians and some central Orientals.
- The "Malayan or "brown" race, including Southeast Asian and Pacific Islanders.
- The "Ethiopian" or "black" race, including all Sub-Saharan "Africans".
- The "American" or "red" race, including "Indians".

He argued that physical characteristics like skin color, cranial profile, etc., depended on geography, diet, and mannerism. Blumenbach claimed that Adam and Eve were caucasian inhabitants of Asia, and that other races came about due to the degeneration from environmental factors such as the sun and poor diet. Thus, he claimed, "Negroid" pigmentation arose because of the result of the heat of the tropical sun, while the cold wind caused the tawny color of Eskimos, while the Chinese were fair-skinned com-pared to the other Asian stocks because they kept mostly in towns protected from environmental factors. He believed that the degeneration could be reversed in a proper environmental control and that all contemporary forms of man could revert back to the "original caucasian race".

Though a lot of these theories have been disproved and disagreed with it has not stopped the modern-day anthropologists, archaeologists, and whatever other pseudo- scientists from using these constructs as a basis for the mass disinformation of the world which spawned the idea of so-called "white supremacy" as referring to albion or Caucasoid. These modern constructs set the blueprint for the mental enslavement and deceit of the Moors especially those of North-West Amexem/America whereas they paint a false picture that depicts a false paradigm that has Asiatics of this continent thinking that they are immigrants or the descendants of immigrants when it is the other way around and those who live on the reservations, who are mislabeled as "Indians" though this ain't India, are the true natives of the land when in actuality they are hybrids as well that were spawned due to the raping of the Aboriginals of this land and who were essentially used as attack dogs to spread fear and confusion on this land.

These constructs combined to create was would later become known as the United States census bureau from 1790 to 2010 and the race and ethnic standards for the federal statistics and administrative reporting (directive #15) which is where that check box on applications and registration forms asking you to identify your "race" or "ethnicity" (which violates the constitutional supreme law of this land, the united nations universal declaration of human rights, and the united nations declaration of the rights of a child). Most Asiatics will check black or African American or even other due to social engineering which automatically puts them in the lowest caste of society. My suggestion is that you create your own entitled Moor and check that or if they give you problems then check white because you are the sovereign of this land. If you leave it blank then the person who offered you the form is instructed to fill it in for you based on their personal perspective and observation which will most likely be black or African-American.

A constitutional and lawful question: What is your nationality? (moorishciviletter.net).

Constitutional and lawful responses (in accord with the United States constitution, the United Nations universal proclamation of human rights and the united nations declaration of the rights of the child):

- I am Moor/Moroccan/American
- I am Chinese
- I am Japanese
- I am Jamaican
- I am Aitian
- I am Mexican
- I am Cuban
- I am Dominican
- I am Spaniard
- I am Portuguese
- I am English
- I am Scottish
- I am Irish
- I am French
- I am German
- I am Dutch
- I am Italian
- I am Russian
- I am Polish

Unconstitutional and unlawful questions: What are you? What is your color? What color are you? What is your race?

Unconstitutional and unlawful responses:

- I am white
- I am black
- I am brown
- I am yellow
- I am red

The ultimate answer above all else is what Yashuah said "I am the great I am". At the end of the day there is but one culture and any honest man that has read more than one book on religion and has actually taken the time to study different doctrines outside of their tribal comfort zones will clearly see that all religions serve the same purpose and stem from the same 5 principles taught universally: Love, Truth, Peace, Justice, And freedom. These things are the foundation of righteousness and the same wrongs in one doctrine equate to the same wrongs in every other. So, to know the law is to express all faiths that represent and coincide with Th divine cosmic order. Any one that points to differences or that has no faith at all should be shunned and avoided. The same pain I feel is the same as a so-called Orientals, or Hindustani, or Mexican, etc., as well as joy, love, fear and restlessness. WE all experience the same things because we are all one and anything done to my front will affect my back and vice versa. All children are beautiful and deserve the best education and care that can be afforded them in all capacities of life. No child should be sick, illiterate, or made to think that people are crayons. In this part of the world more so than anywhere else this filth is perpetuated and has ruined minds. The time is now to stop hating, stop debating and look toward the future with open eyes, minds, and hearts. Only seeking to please TH Most High for in completing that task all else falls into place.

C. Agents of Rome: False prophets and traitors

I. Priesthood

Secret Treaty of Verona [American diplomatic code, 1778-1884, vol. 2; Elliot, p. 179.], Article 3: Convinced that principles of religion contribute most powerfully to keep nations in the state of passive obedience which they owe to their princes, the high contracting parties declare it to be their intention to sustain in their respective States those measures which the clergy may adopt, with the aim of ameliorating their own interests, so intimately connected with the preservation of the authority of the princes; and the contracting powers join in offering their thanks to the Pope for what he has already done for them, and solicit his constant cooperation in their views of submitting the nations. (Congressional Record-Senate; 64th Congress, 1st session volume 53, part 7 page 6781. April 25, 1916) (See Christian black codes of 1724 articles 2, 3, 5, 7, 8, 9, 11)

As you can see clearly the job of these people is to do the bidding of the pope and they have made pacts with demons swearing that they will always seek to destroy the will of the people. Churches, Mosques, Cathedrals, Synagogues, etc., are all hypnosis centers designed to keep you in darkness and in perpetual servitude. They are sacrificing institutions designed to corrupt the minds of children and possess and control the will of men. There are two types of shepherds: good shepherds (those who lead you to greener pastures physically, mentally and spiritually) and bad shepherds (those who lead you to the slaughter house). Real religion is not all passive but is intertwined with passion not just morally but in actual deeds that break bondage in all facets.

Excerpt from the Mysteries of the Silent Brotherhood of the East Chapter 8: The Council of the 7 of the World 17-18: (17) "The priesthood cannot be reformed; it is already dead; its greatest needs are graves and funeral chants." (18) "The new age calls for liberty-the kind that makes each man a priest; enables him to go alone and lay his offering on the shrine of Allah."

The priesthood is dead and the gods they serve are of this world which is why when they marry people they say, "By the power invested in me by the state of", because their G.O.D is the governmental ordinance department i.e. the popes of Rome.

II. Traitors

The Prophet warned that those who wear turbans and fezzes, meaning your own, would put you back into slavery. All institutions have been infiltrated and serve as reconnaissance for the so-called elites who must keep tabs on the people, so they insert those who they deem most effective into certain areas of the populace that provide threats and concerns to those who now sit in the seat of power. This is why through all the marching, Negro spirituals, conscious movements, clever slogans, etc., the people still suffer from the same disease that they been infected with pretty much since the 40's and 50's.

Prior to the 60s we weren't called black, then after we were it was perpetuated by those we thought had our best interest at heart along with negro, colored and African-American which are all brands that delude to servitude. All the top organizations who house scholars supposedly are privy to the same info provided in this manuscript and even more but for a few pieces of silver they have accepted the pact to be slaves hence it's the crab in the bucket syndrome whereas they have no will to climb so anybody they see trying to they'll tear down.

Excerpt from Executive order 11490: King Alfred Plan...Rex 84: Combined Memo: Department of Justice Preliminary Memo: Federal Bureau of investigation & central intelligence Agency: There are 12 minority organizations, and all are familiar to the 22 million. Dossiers have been collected on the leaders of the organizations and can be studied in Washington. The material contained in many of the dossiers, and our threat to reveal that material has considerably held in check some leaders. Leaders who do not have such usable material in their dossiers have been approached to take government posts, mostly as ambassadors and primarily in African countries. The promise of these positions also has materially contributed to a temporary slow-down of minority activities. However, we do not expect these slow-downs to be of long duration, because there are always new and dissident elements joining these organizations, with the potential power to replace the old leaders. All organizations and their leaders are under constant surveillance. The organizations are:

1. The Black Muslims
2. Student Non-Violent Coordinating Committee (SNCC)
3. Congress Of Racial Equality
4. Uhuru Movement
5. Group Of Advanced Leadership (goal)
6. Freedom Now Party (FNP)
7. United Black Nationalists Of America (UBNA)
8. The New Pan-African Movement (TNPAM)
9. Southern Christian Leadership Conference (SCLC)
10. The National Urban League (NUL)
11. The National Association For The Advancement Of Colored People (NAACP)
12. Committee On Racial And Religious Progress (CORARP)

Note: At the appointed time, to be designated by the president, the leaders of some of these organizations are to be detained only when it is clear that they cannot prevent the emergency, working with the local public officials during the first critical hours. All other leaders are to be detained at once. Compiled lists of minority leaders have been readied at the national data computer center. It is necessary to use the minority leaders designated by the president in much the same manner in which we use minority members who are agents with federal and central, and we cannot, until there is no alternative reveal king Alfred in all its aspects. Minority members of congress will be unseated at once. This move is not unprecedented in American history.

As is revealed in the aforementioned document all these so-called community leaders which includes the pastors, sheiks, imams, reverends etc., are all under the thumb of the Jesuit militia and only are afforded certain luxuries so long as they weave spells that keep their followers in comatose. This is why they work so hard to make sure you never find out the truth because once you do and separate they are no longer needed by their handlers/masters whom they are bound to by oath.

Their job is to keep you centered on emotionalism which means you are not using logic which stems from critical thinking I.e. common sense. Here is another excerpt from the same document which admits that we have always been here and are part in parcel to this land mass: Attorney general: preliminary memo: department of defense: This memo is being submitted in lieu of a full report from the Joint Chiefs of Staff. That report is now in preparation. There will be many cities where the minority will be able to put into the streets a superior number of people with a desperate and dangerous will. He will be a formidable enemy, for he is bound to the continent by heritage and knows that political asylum will not be available to him in other countries. The greatest concentration of the minority is in the Deep South, the great lakes region, the eastern seaboard and the west coast.

> LAND, in the most general sense, comprehends any ground, soil, or earth whatsoever; as fields, meadows, pastures, woods, moors, waters, marshes, furies, and heath. Co. Litt. 4a; Reynard v. City of Caldwell, 55 Idaho 342, 42 P.2d 292, 296; Holmes v. U. S., C.C.A.Okl., 53 F.2d 960, 963.
>
> In its more limited sense, "land" denotes the quantity and character of the interest or estate which the tenant may own in land. Holmes v. U. S., C.C.A.Okl., 53 F.2d 960, 963. "Land" may include any estate or interest in lands, either legal or equitable, easements, incorporeal hereditaments. Reynard v. City of Caldwell, 55 Idaho 342, 42 P.2d 292, 297; Jones v. Magruder, D.C.Md., 42 F.Supp. 193, 198; Lynch v. Cunningham, 131 Cal. App. 164, 21 P.2d 154; Petition of Burnquist, 220 Minn. 48, 19 N.W.2d 394, 401; Cuff v. Koslosky, 165 Okl. 135, 25 P.2d 290. The land is one thing, and the estate in land is another thing, for an estate in land is a time in land or land for a time. Plowd. 555.
>
> Technically land signifies everything which may be holden; and the term is defined as comprehending all things of a permanent and substantial nature, and even of an unsubstantial, provided they be permanent. Reynard v. City of Caldwell, 55 Idaho 342, 42 P.2d 292, 296.
>
> Ordinarily, the term is used as descriptive of the subject of ownership and not the ownership. Sou-

As you can see they know that we are the true Americans and that we didn't come from nowhere else though in public that fraud is spoon fed to the masses.

The name of this document by the way was inspired by the King of England (849-899) who slaughtered thousands under the guise of protecting Christianity. As a result, he was revered as one of the noblest kings in the history of England. This is the plan that they have cooking for the natives, basically a repeat of the holocaust. Holocaust means an offering which is completely burned; burnt offering, complete destruction by fire especially of animals and human beings, great or wholesale destruction. < Latin holocaustun < Greek holokauston, neuter of holokaustos < holos-whole + kaustops-burned < kaiein, to burn. This is why they first denationalize the natives so that they would no longer be under the

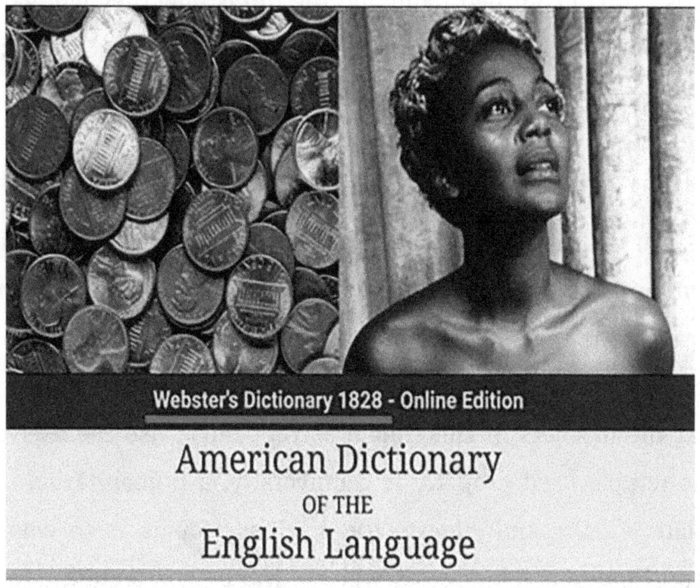

Webster's Dictionary 1828 - Online Edition
American Dictionary
OF THE
English Language

AMER'ICAN, *adjective* Pertaining to America.

AMER'ICAN, *noun* A native of America; originally applied to the aboriginals, or copper-colored races, found here by the Europeans; but now applied to the descendants of Europeans born in America.

---

divine law of nations and now they perpetuate violence which is to create a race riot so that they have a reason to exterminate and consume the life force of the melanin rich heirs so as they can stay alive. Sports, news, entertainment, religion is all geared toward emotional response which drains you and feeds your life force to the demons who need it to survive. They have vaporizing machines ready and waiting thus why they continue to show Asiatics shot down and other injustices that agents of Rome inside our communities perpetuate though when the fighting starts they'll be anywhere but the frontline, in fact, they won't be there cause they are the first to taste the flames because they are traitors and in war traitors get the worse punishments, see the movie the immortals as an example of how they castrate and destroy the converso before they ultimately fall as is the destiny of wickedness anyway. Remember hell is a cell which is a small confined room and the fire is how they will get rid of the bad seeds who disrespect nature thus they stand in dishonor. (Luke 13: 3, 5; Luke 13: 28; Surah 5:37; Surah 2:167; Surah 3:131)

Lastly, you will notice that the Moorish Science Temple is not mentioned in the list of organizations that were/are compromised and under surveillance. This is because it is the hidden hand, the "final boss" of the game, if you will. Because the secrets of freedom are intrinsic in Moorish science it stands to reason that the blockers of this "open secret" must also themselves be kept secret. The temple used properly is a university, a humanitarian outlet used too stimulate, elevate and educate the original peoples as to who and what they/we are. However, the traitors who infiltrated the temple have turned it into a cesspool of pseudo-freemasonry designed to box you in and out of your birthright at the same time.

Another reason why those other organization are mentioned and not Moorish Science Temple is due to the reverse-psychology effect. Naturally if some entity that you view as an oppressive element in your life is seemingly against someone or a group you might feel the need to enlist your energies for the said "cause". However, this is just another ploy to get you off track of the real attainment of knowledge of self, because even though the Moorish Science Temple structure as an organization has been corrupted and co-opted the science of it is still intact because it is pure being that it is indeed the sole (soul) salvation for not just our people but the entire planet. So, they couldn't openly acknowledge Moorish Science because you might investigate and depending on your level of sincerity uncover and unravel "pan's labyrinth" and put a grenade in the proverbial rabbit hole and destroy this fictious illusion we call a society. A little bit of something is better than a whole lot of nothing; a modicum of truth destroys a lot of lies and these occupational entities thrive on lies and misdirection, which is the summary point of this assessment. Don't let one 'bad apple' make you toss the whole barrel. Yes, there are traitors amongst us and all around us, but the truth is supposed to be held on to when grasps. Do not let the purity with which you sought this knowledge be turned into spite but let it blossom into the divine wisdom it has prepared you for. Be the change you seek and do not to the next generations what was done to us in terms of selfish withdrawal and outright betrayal. We have a culture which births principles and these are the standards of measure with which we are to govern ourselves and to navigate amongst these temporary savages; we have a prophet which means we have the mercy and forgiveness of The Creator.

Excerpt from cointelpro handbook:

> *Rule# 4-The infiltration strategy: You must always find one amongst their ranks that you can trust for critical information. You need not always entice them with money, sometimes petty jealousness and the opportunity for revenge is enough ammunition to secure a snitch. This tactic is very useful especially when your research reveals former lovers of their leading men (and women) who still harbor animosity towards their former lover. Many of their women will be willing to destroy these men without payment. Your head ally may be the person he or she lays with.*
>
> *Rule# 5-The Mistrust strategy: Never underestimate the need for blacks to fight one another as a means of discharging anger. Black leaders often have the same rage and impatience as blacks in the streets. We must use the same strategy we used to induce mass homicide to bring about the destruction of black militancy. J.E. Hoover used this strategy effectively for 50 years to keep a lid on black insurrection. Use distrust for each other and highlighting differences. Have your black agents start rumors and then get out of the way and watch then self-destruct. Not knowing who to trust the movement will be effectively stagnated. (See Genesis 25:30-34)*

Signs of cointelpro operatives/demons:

- Always promoting division i.e. talking about "color"; uses words like "racism" and "prejudice" without the proper context
- They always push and reinforce false narratives and paradigms, e.g. slavery
- They are focused on financial gain and put that at the forefront of the movement; very superficial
- They wear suits and ties
- They have bald heads or no facial hair, or they wear make-up and heels
- They have tattoos galore
- They show their bodies often and shamelessly
- They never speak on Moors, nationality, and birthrights; they use the terms black, colored, African-American, white etc.
- They worship in buildings made by men
- They don't practice what they preach: inconsistent in their conversation and doings
- They speak on moors from a third-party perspective i.e. "the Moors or those Moors"
- They don't teach law and history together
- They idolize men
- They watch TV
- They listen to trap music heavy
- They support the homosexual agenda
- They are against the enforcement of the constitution
- They don't study and criticize those who do
- They eat horribly i.e. meats, candy, alcohol, drugs, etc.
- They take oaths in lodges
- They wear tight clothes
- They wear fake hair
- They hurt innocent people
- They value clubs over unity
- They look down on people; always judging and pointing fingers; rely heavily on the blame game
- They talk too much and what they speak brings no remedy
- They are stuck on foolishness e.g. debates
- They conduct themselves recklessly even within the presence of women and children
- They say anything and do anything for attention which makes them distractions and vampires (energy thieves); loudmouths; overly emotional
- They are always or for the most part in a negative state and perpetuate that energy onto others

- Whisperers and nice talkers; they are not balanced and have little to no emotion
- Too involved with what others are doing
- They don't talk about women enough and how important they are; egos are inflated
- They only talk about how great we are, but not how great we are not, openly and honestly; they push the "we are God" paradigm but in the same breath blame the so-called "white man" for their problems i.e... hypocrites
- Their organizations have 501c-3 agreements
- Blond hair/red hair; blue and green eyes (signs of calcified pineal glands and whorish spirits)
- Babies cry around them and children in general are wary of their presence
- You never see them sweat or drink water

M. War on the Womb: The Destruction of balance

I. Death of the Matriarch: She Redeems by Rahsmariah Bey

The universe always has been and always will be matriarchal by nature. We were forced into patriarchal dogmatic society as a destructive product of the intervention /diversion (the crusades). The forceful purpose of the crusades was to destroy the matriarch and introduce the Patriarchal system which took not too many, generations to fulfill. They created without a doubt Christianity out of the political order of Christendom and forced the "belief system", out of which you have a people tagged as "believers" of today. Although belief is necessary to teach the initiates or the children, it is also very necessary that one graduates into knowledge and knowing. The Patriarchal system is out of order with nature and does not possess logic or common sense. Because it is out of order, it cannot, and will not stand. This is why you are witnessing the fall of any and all institutions that support or are supported by it. What you are witnessing is the fall of an unnatural order and the disillusion of untruths. Truth and facts are colliding with falsehood and belief. With the advent of the false belief system suddenly matter appeared to be without order. In fact, if you look up the word matter under the Christian

Science definition, (which is found in the dictionary), it reads as follows: matter: the illusion that the objects perceived by the physical senses have reality or substance.

The intervention and diversions of the Matriarchal society started long ago. As far back as the Punic wars- wars of the Phoenicians which merged into the Christian Crusades, the battle of tours or portier (one of the most decisive World wars with Charles the Hammer Martel, Charles the Hammer leading the crusades). This led eventually to the battle of lake Michigan, and the Spanish American war (fought on American soil), then there was the French revolution, which inspired the American revolution and out of the American revolution came the "Daughters of the American revolution" (DAR). The DAR taught their sons from the womb to have a psychological superior position over your sons, over the world for that matter. Those daughters (mothers) of the American Revolution, revolted against the society, as it were, and made sure their sons were taught in the womb, and came out of the womb with this authoritative demeanor. Those sons founded the Klu Klux Klan, knights of Columbus, various freemasonic orders, i.e. Tall Cedars of Lebanon, Shriners, etc. Lastly there was the un-civil war, one of the final nails in the coffin of the Matriarchal society, or of natural living and natural people.

The intervention/diversion goes way back in history, and it repeats itself as it is perpetual. It will keep repeating itself, unless and until we break the chain. As a result of the diversion or intervention, she became a victim of herself, lost in her own duties and expecting of someone else (her sons) to do her job. She forgot that she was the Matriarch and began looking outside of herself for "G-d", wherein she adopted idol god worship. Render unto Caesar that which is Caesar's, means to give the idol god worship of the Romans/ European-back to them.

Further destruction of the psyche of the Matriarch (Mother) was when she witnessed the mutilation and murder of her babies, her sons, daughters and her men. She was traumatized by the sight of the womb being cut open and babies dropping to the ground. She was traumatized when they tied each limb of her man (sons), to a different horse and sent them off in different directions. She was traumatized into disconnecting with her babies, as she knew that they would be taken away and sold on the auction block. She has always been the target. This is the basis of the modern psychological state of the woman. She is still in shock and while in that state, she has sold out herself and her babies to the very system that enslaves her and her sons. She first must be awakened and get back in touch with knowledge of self, so she may put things back in order, teach from the womb again and redeem humanity.

However, the man has no other choice but to fall, if she has. He diligently tried to take up the charge; he held ground fiercely, with brute determination to carry out the quest of the Mother. She and only she has the ability to bring and teach souls of higher vibration. Of course, she must be in a higher consciousness herself first. Unfortunately, when she went to sleep, so did he. She stopped teaching him from the womb and sent him out into the world unequipped. Hence, a people cannot rise higher than its women.

Women are the ones behind the scenes running institutions, organizations and associations. She makes all of them work; churches, hospitals, jails, synagogues, temples, schools, organizations, associations, offices, satellite offices, home offices, central offices, branch offices, etc., etc. Without her support, these institutions would not run. If she has all of this power, and she does, why isn't she cognizant of her own womb power? Why isn't it clear to her, that she produces the men and women of society? It is up to her how society is governed, although she may not be conscious of this, governing principles are taught as children are being raised. Of course, by her failing to do so, she has become the complainer of the very thing she is ultimately in control of. Organizations are put in place to deal with the symptoms of her problem, but not the problem. The Women fund and or support those very organizations that are set up to keep her womb enslaved. If she had self-knowledge, she would not continue to support that which is enslaving her and her babies. By doing so she works against herself. Some of these organizations have good intentions; however, as dictated in nature, no one raises children better than the Mother who brought them here. Mothers have to be more responsible. These souls have an agenda as well, all that lives, wants to live. They come from the door, with the struggle to free themselves from the constraints, and already set-up institutionalized slavery system, which is designed to have them locked up for the most of their life, if not physical lock-up, certainly mentally. Parents must be aware of the condition they bring their children into and what they are passing on to their children. Most parents don't or won't educate their own children, mainly because the children are looking for some facts, not beliefs and the parents have not enough studies on their own to pass correct information to their children. This type of activity is in great part responsible for the children becoming walking time bombs, who take out their aggressions on society, as they are a product aren't they?

For those of us who blame their condition on slavery and oppression but cannot put their finger on it, the fact is that slavery is institutionalized. Upon that recognition, know that the slaveholders are comfortable to these conditions as it makes their stronghold stronger. So, who is really the subjugated ones, the parents or the children, or both? As the condition of the parent, especially the Mother, perpetuates the condition of the children and thus society. Yet we talk about the condition of the children, as if disconnected from us as a whole. When children are dying younger and younger, it is a sign of ***extinction****.*

Chapter 4: The Adversary

A. The origin of modern politics and policy

I. Unum Sanctum:

On November 18, 1302, pope Bonafice VIII issued the papal bull Unum sanctum which historians consider one of the most extreme statements of papal supremacy ever made. The original document is lost but a version of the text can be found in the registers of Bonafice VIII in the Vatican archives. The bull lays down dogmatic propositions on the unity of the Catholic Church, the necessity of belonging to it for the eternal salvation, the position of the pope as the supreme head of the church, and the duty thence arising of submission to the pope in order to belong to the church and thus attain salvation. The pope further emphasized the higher position of the spiritual order in comparison to the secular order.

Most significantly, the bull proclaimed, "Extra ecclesiam mula salus": "outside the church, there is no salvation." It is a form of the concept known as plenitude potestatis (plentitude of power); it declares that those who resist the roman pontiff are resisting god's ordination. The bull declares that the church must be united, and the pope was its sole and absolute head: "Therefore, of the one and only church there is but one body and one head, not two heads like a monster." The Bull also states, "We are informed by the texts of the gospels that in this church and in its power, are two swords; namely, the spiritual and the temporal." The swords being referred to are the customary reference to the swords yielded by the apostles upon Christ's arrest (Luke 22:38; Matthew 26:52). Early theologians believed that if there are two swords, one must be subordinate to the other. This then became a spiritual hierarchal ladder, the spiritual judges the secular, "on account of its greatness and sublimity", while the lower spiritual power is judged by the higher spiritual power, etc. Thus, it was concluded, the temporal authorities must submit to the spiritual authorities, not merely on matters concerning doctrine and morality: "for with truth as our witness, it belongs to spiritual power to establish the terrestrial power and pass judgment if it has not been good." The bull ends, "furthermore, we declare, we proclaim, we define it is absolutely necessary for salvation that every human creature be subject to the roman pontiff."

II. Dum Diversas:

Is a papal bull issued on June 18, 1452 by Pope Nicholas V. It authorized Alfonso V of Portugal to conquer Saracens (Moors) and pagans and consign them to "perpetual servitude." Pope Calixtus III reiterated the bull in 1456 with inter caetera (not to be confused with Alexander VI's) renewed by pope Sixtus IV in 1481 and Pope Leo X in 1514 with precelse denotionis. The concept of the consignment of exclusive spheres of influence to certain nation states was extended to the Americas in 1493 by Pope Alexander VI with inter caetera divina.

To confirm the Portuguese trade rights, King Alfonso V appealed to Pope Nicholas V for support, seeking the moral authority of the church for his monopoly. The bull of 1452 was addressed to Alfonso V and conceded Portugal's right to attack, conquer and subjugate Saracens and pagans. "We grant you [kings of Spain and Portugal] by these present documents, with our apostolic authority, full and free permission to invade, search out, capture, and subjugate the Saracens and pagans and any other unbelievers and enemies of Christ wherever they may be, as well as their kingdoms, duchies, counties, principalities, and other property...and to reduce their persons into perpetual servitude."

III. Romanus Pontifex:

Latin for "the roman pontiff" is a papal bull written in 1454 by Pope Nicholas V to King Alfonso V of Portugal. As a follow up to dum diversas, it confirmed to the crown of Portugal dominion over all lands South of Cape Bojador in Africa. Along with encouraging the seizure of the lands of Saracen Turks and non-Christians, it repeated the earlier bulls' permission for the enslavement of such peoples. The bull's primary purpose was to forbid other Christian nations from infringing the King of Portugal's rights of trade and colonization in these regions.

This bull should not be confused with the September 21, 1451 bull by the same name, also written by Nicholas V, relieving dukes of Austria from any potential ecclesiastical censure for permitting Jews to dwell there.

The bull praises earlier Portuguese victories against Muslims of North Africa and the success of expeditions of discovery and conquest to the Azores and to Africa south of Cape Bojador. It also repeats earlier injunctions not to supply items useful in war such as weaponry, iron or timber to either non-Christians or Muslims. The substance of the bull's articles are as follows: "The roman pontiff, successor of the key-bearer of the heavenly kingdom and vicar of Jesus Christ, contemplating with a father's mind all several climes of the world and the characteristics of all nations dwelling in them and seeking and desiring the salvation of all, wholesomely ordains and disposes upon careful deliberation those things which he sees will be agreeable to the divine majesty and by which he may bring the sheep entrusted to him by god into the single divine fold, and may acquire for them the reward of eternal felicity, and obtain pardon for their souls. This we believe will more certainly come to pass, through the aid of the lord, if we bestow suitable favors and special graces on those catholic kings and princes, who, like athletes and intrepid champions of the Christian faith, as we know by the evidence of facts, not only restrain the savage excesses of the Saracens and of other infidels, enemies of the Christian name, but also for the defense and increase of the faith vanquish in the remotest parts unknown to us, and...the said infante...believing that he would best perform his duty to god in this matter, if by his effort and industry at sea might become navigable as far as to the Indians who are said to worship the name of Christ, and that thus he might be able to enter into relation with them, and to incite them to aid the Christians against the Saracens...to conserve their right and possession [the said king and infante] under certain most severe penalties then expressed, have prohibited and in general have ordained that none, unless with their sailors and ships and on payment of a certain tribute and with an express license previously obtained from the said king or infante, should presume to sail to the said provinces or to trade in their ports or to fish in the sea...since we had formerly by other letters of ours granted among other things free and ample faculty to the aforesaid King

Alfonso—to invade, search out, capture, vanquish, and subdue all Saracens and pagans whatsoever, and other enemies of Christ wheresoever placed, and the kingdoms, dukedoms, principalities, dominions, possessions, and all movable and immovable goods whatsoever held and possessed by them and to reduce their persons to perpetual slavery, and to apply and appropriate to himself and his successors the kingdoms, dukedoms, counties, principalities, dominions, possessions, and goods, and to convert them to his and their use for profit—by having secured the said faculty, the said King Alfonso, or, by his authority, the aforesaid infante, justly and lawfully has acquired and possessed, and doth possess, these islands, lands, harbors, and seas, and they do of right belong and pertain to the said king Alfonso and his successors, nor without special license from king Alfonso and his successors themselves has any other even of the faithful of Christ been entitled hitherto, nor is he by any means now entitled lawfully to meddle therewith."

IV. Inter caetera 1456:

On March 13, 1456 Pope Callixtus III issued the papal bull inter caetera (not to be confused with the inter caetera of 1493). This bull reaffirmed the earlier bulls dum diversas and romanus pontifex, which recognized Portugal's rights to territories it had discovered along the West African coast, and the enslavement of infidels and non-Christians captured there.

King Alfonso had requested that ecclesiastical jurisdiction over lands located in the vicinity of the southern shore of Guinea be vested with the order of Christ, the successor organization to the knights Templar in Portugal. (His son, infante Henry, was the Grandmaster.) The conquest of these lands...which the said infante withdrew with mailed hands from the Saracen...had been funded by the resources of the order.

In 1537 Pope Paul III condemned "unjust" enslavement of non- Christians in sublimes dei but he sanctioned slavery in Rome in 1545, the enslavement of Henry VIII in 1547 and the purchase of Muslim slaves in 1548. In 1686 the holy office limited the bull by decreeing that Africans enslaved by unjust wars should be free.

Dum diversas, along with other bulls, such as romanus pontifex (1455), ineffabillis et summi (1497), dudum pro parte (1516), and aequm reputamus (1534) document the Portuguese Ius patronatus. Pope Alexander VI, a native of Valencia, issued a series of bulls limiting Portuguese power in favor of that of Spain, most notably dudum siquidem (1493).

V. Inter Caetera Divina 1493: Doctrine of Discovery

The papal bull "Inter Caetera" issued by Pope Alexander VI on May 4, 1493 played a central role in the Spanish conquest of the new world. The document supported Spain's strategy to ensure its exclusive right to the lands "discovered" by Columbus the previous year. It established a demarcation line one hundred leagues west of the Azores and Cape Verde Islands and assigned Spain the exclusive right to acquire territorial possessions and to trade in all lands west of that line. All others were forbidden to approach the lands west of the line without special license from the rulers of Spain. This effectively gave Spain a monopoly on the lands in the "new world."

The bull stated that any land not inhabited by Christians was available to be "discovered", claimed and exploited by Christian rulers and declared that "the catholic faith and Christian religion be exalted and be everywhere increased and spread, that the health of souls be cared for and that barbarous nations be overthrown and brought to faith itself."

This "doctrine of discovery" became the basis of all European claims in the Americas as well as the foundation for the UNITED STATES' western expansion. In the U.S. Supreme Court in the 1823 case Johnson v. McIntosh, chief justice John Marshall's opinion in the unanimous decision held "that the principle of discovery gave the European nations an absolute right to new world lands." In essence, American "Indians" (Moors) had only a right of occupancy, which could be abolished.

The bull Inter Caetera made headlines again throughout the 1990s, and 2000, when many Catholics petitioned Pope John Paul II to formally revoke it and recognize the human rights of indigenous peoples (Moors).

VI. The Spanish Inquisition (Wikipedia)

The Tribunal of the Holy Office of the Inquisition (Spanish: Tribunal del Santo Oficio de la Inquisición), commonly known as the Spanish Inquisition (Inquisición española), was established in 1478 by Catholic Monarchs Ferdinand II of Aragon and Isabella I of Castile. It was intended to maintain Catholic orthodoxy in their kingdoms and to replace the Medieval Inquisition, which was under Papal control. It became the most substantive of the three different manifestations of the wider Christian Inquisition along with the Roman Inquisition and Portuguese Inquisition. The "Spanish Inquisition" may be defined broadly, operating "in Spain and in all Spanish colonies and territories, which included the Canary Islands, the Spanish Netherlands, the Kingdom of Naples, and all Spanish possessions in North, Central, and South America."

The Inquisition was originally intended primarily to ensure the orthodoxy of those who converted from Judaism and Islam. The regulation of the faith of the newly converted was intensified after the royal decrees issued in 1492 and 1502 ordering Jews and Muslims to convert or leave Spain.

The Spanish Inquisition (Inquisición Española) can be seen as an answer to the multi-religious nature of Spanish society following the reconquest of the Iberian Peninsula from the Muslim Moors. After invading in 711, large areas of the Iberian Peninsula were ruled by Muslims until 1250, when they were restricted to Granada, which fell in 1492. However, the Reconquista did not result in the total expulsion of Muslims from Spain, since they, along with Jews, were tolerated by the ruling Christian elite. Large cities, especially Seville, Valladolid and Barcelona, had significant Jewish populations centered in Juderia, but in the coming years the Muslims were increasingly subjugated by alienation and torture. The Jews, who had previously thrived under Muslim rule now suffered similar maltreatment.

Start of the Inquisition

Fray Alonso de Ojeda, a Dominican friar from Seville, convinced Queen Isabella of the existence of Crypto-Judaism among Andalusian conversos during her stay in Seville between 1477 and 1478. A report, produced by Pedro González de Mendoza, Archbishop of Seville, and by the Segovian Dominican Tomás de Torquemada, corroborated this assertion.

Spanish monarchs Ferdinand and Isabella requested a papal bull establishing an inquisition in Spain in 1478 in response to the conversos returning to the practice of Judaism. Pope Sixtus IV granted a bull permitting the monarchs to select and appoint two or three priests over forty years of age to act as inquisitors. In 1483, Ferdinand and Isabella established a state council to administer the inquisition with the Dominican Friar Tomás de Torquemada acting as its president, even though Sixtus IV protested the activities of the inquisition in Aragon and its treatment of the conversos. Torquemada eventually assumed the title of Inquisitor-General.

The monarchs decided to introduce the Inquisition to Castile to discover and punish crypto-Jews and requested the pope's assent. Ferdinand II of Aragon pressured Pope Sixtus IV to agree to an Inquisition controlled by the monarchy by threatening to withdraw military support at a time when the Turks were a threat to Rome. The pope issued a bull to stop the Inquisition but was pressured into withdrawing it. On 1 November 1478, Pope Sixtus IV published the Papal bull, Exigit Sinceras Devotionis Affectus, through which he gave the monarchs exclusive authority to name the inquisitors in their kingdoms. The first two inquisitors, Miguel de Morillo and Juan de San Martín, were not named, however, until two years later, on 27 September 1480 in Medina del Campo.

> The first *auto-da-fé (from the spanish acto de fe and Portuguese ato de fe, both meaning "act of faith"; a ritual of public pennance of condemned heretics and apostates the most extreme of which was execution by burning, which is what the term ultimately came to represent)* was held in Seville on 6 February 1481: six people were burned alive. From there, the Inquisition grew rapidly in the Kingdom of Castile. By 1492, tribunals existed in eight Castilian cities: Ávila, Córdoba, Jaén, Medina del Campo, Segovia, Sigüenza, Toledo, and Valladolid. Sixtus IV promulgated a new bull categorically prohibiting the Inquisition's extension to Aragón, affirming that,

"many true and faithful Christians, because of the testimony of enemies, rivals, slaves and other low people—and still less appropriate—without tests of any kind, have been locked up in secular prisons, tortured and condemned like relapsed heretics, deprived of their goods and properties, and given over to the secular arm to be executed, at great danger to their souls, giving a pernicious example and causing scandal to many."

"In 1482 the pope was still trying to maintain control over the Inquisition and to gain acceptance for his own attitude towards the New Christians, which was generally more moderate than that of the Inquisition and the local rulers."

In 1483, Jews were expelled from all of Andalusia. Though the pope wanted to crack down on abuses, Ferdinand pressured him to promulgate a new bull, threatening that he would otherwise separate the Inquisition from Church authority. Sixtus did so on 17 October 1483, naming Tomás de Torquemada Inquisidor General of Aragón, Valencia, and Catalonia.

Torquemada quickly established procedures for the Inquisition. A new court would be announced with a thirty-day grace period for confessions and the gathering of accusations by neighbors. Evidence that was used to identify a crypto-Jew included the absence of chimney smoke on Saturdays (a sign the family might secretly be honoring the Sabbath) or the buying of many vegetables before Passover or the purchase of meat from a converted butcher. The court employed physical torture to extract confessions. Crypto-Jews were allowed to confess and do penance, although those who relapsed were burned at the stake.

In 1484, Pope Innocent VIII attempted to allow appeals to Rome against the Inquisition, but Ferdinand in December 1484 and again in 1509 decreed death and confiscation for anyone trying to make use of such procedures without royal permission. With this, the Inquisition became the only institution that held authority across all the realms of the Spanish monarchy and, in all of them, a useful mechanism at the service of the crown. However, the cities of Aragón continued resisting, and even saw revolt, as in Teruel from 1484 to 1485. However, the murder of *Inquisidor* Pedro Arbués in Zaragoza on September

15, 1485, caused public opinion to turn against the *conversos* and in favour of the Inquisition. In Aragón, the Inquisitorial courts were focused specifically on members of the powerful *converso* minority, ending their influence in the Aragonese administration.

The Inquisition was extremely active between 1480 and 1530. Different sources give different estimates of the number of trials and executions in this period; Henry Kamen estimates about 2,000 executed, based on the documentation of the *autos-da-fé*, the great majority being *conversos* of Jewish origin. He offers striking statistics: 91.6% of those judged in Valencia between 1484 and 1530 and 99.3% of those judged in Barcelona between 1484 and 1505 were of Jewish origin.

Expulsion of Jews and repression of *conversos*

The Spanish Inquisition had been established in part to prevent conversos from engaging in Jewish practices, which, as Christians, they were supposed to have given up. However this remedy for securing the orthodoxy of conversos was eventually deemed inadequate since the main justification the monarchy gave for formally expelling all Jews from Spain was the "great harm suffered by Christians (i.e., conversos) from the contact, intercourse and communication which they have with the Jews, who always attempt in various ways to seduce faithful Christians from our Holy Catholic Faith". The Alhambra Decree, issued in January 1492, ordered the expulsion. Historic accounts of the numbers of Jews who left Spain have been vastly exaggerated by early accounts and historians: Juan de Mariana speaks of 800,000 people, and Don Isaac Abravanel of 300,000. Modern estimates, based on careful examination of official documents and population estimates of communities, are much lower: Henry Kamen estimates that, of a population of approximately 80,000 Jews and 200,000 conversos, about 40,000 chose emigration. The Jews of the kingdom of Castile emigrated mainly to Portugal (whence they were expelled in 1497) and to North Africa. However, according to Kamen, the Jews of the kingdom of Aragon went "to adjacent Christian lands, mainly to Italy", rather than to Muslim lands as is often assumed. Although the vast majority of conversos simply assimilated into the Catholic dominant culture, a minority continued to practice Judaism in secret, gradually migrated throughout Europe, North Africa, and the Ottoman Empire, mainly to areas where Sephardic communities were already present as a result of the Alhambra Decree.

Tens of thousands of Jews were baptized in the three months before the deadline for expulsion, some 40,000 if one accepts the totals given by Kamen, most of these undoubtedly to avoid expulsion, rather than as a sincere change of faith. These conversos were the principal concern of the Inquisition; being suspected of continuing to practice Judaism put them at risk of denunciation and trial.

The most intense period of persecution of conversos lasted until 1530. From 1531 to 1560, however, the percentage of conversos among the Inquisition trials dropped to 3% of the total. There was a rebound of persecutions when a group of crypto-Jews was discovered in Quintanar de la Orden in 1588; and there was a rise in denunciations of conversos in the last decade of the sixteenth century. At the beginning of the seventeenth century, some conversos who had fled to Portugal began to return to Spain, fleeing the persecution of the Portuguese Inquisition, founded in 1536. This led to a rapid increase in the trials of crypto-Jews, among them a number of important financiers. In 1691, during a number of autos-da-fé in Majorca, 37 chuetas, or conversos of Majorca, were burned.

Repression of Moriscos

The Inquisition searched for false converts from Judaism among the *conversos*, but also searched for false or relapsed converts among the Moriscos, forced converts from Islam. In spite of myth Kamen assertsthat very few Protestants were involved. Beginning with a decree on February 14, 1502, Muslims in Granada faced forcible conversion to Christianity or expulsion. Muslims in the Crown of Aragon were obliged to convert by Charles I's decree of 1526, as most had been forcibly baptized during the Revolt of the Brotherhoods (1519–1523) and these baptisms were declared to be valid. The War of the Alpujarras between 1568–1571, a general Muslim/Morisco uprising in Granada, ended in a forced dispersal of about half of the region's Moriscos throughout

Castile and Andalusia as well as increased suspicions by Spanish authorities against this community.

Many Moriscos were suspected of practicing Islam in secret, and the jealousy with which they guarded the privacy of their domestic life prevented the verification of this suspicion. Initially they were not severely persecuted by the Inquisition, but experienced a policy of evangelization without torture, a policy not followed with those *conversos* who were suspected of being crypto-Jews. There were various reasons for this. Most importantly, in the kingdoms of Valencia and Aragon a large number of the Moriscos were under the jurisdiction of the nobility, and persecution would have been viewed as a frontal assault on the economic interests of this powerful social class. Still, fears ran high among the population that the Moriscos were traitorous, especially in Granada. The coast was regularly raided by Barbary pirates backed by Spain's enemy the Ottoman Empire, and the Moriscos were suspected of aiding them.

In the second half of the century, late in the reign of Philip II, conditions worsened between Old Christians and Moriscos. The 1568– 1570 Morisco Revolt in Granada was harshly suppressed, and the Inquisition intensified its attention to the Moriscos. From 1570 Morisco cases became predominant in the tribunals of Zaragoza, Valencia and Granada; in the tribunal of Granada, between 1560 and 1571, 82% of those accused were Moriscos, who were a vast majority of the Kingdom's population at the time.

In 1609, King Philip III, upon the advice of his financial adviser the Duke of Lerma and Archbishop of Valencia Juan de Ribera, decreed the Expulsion of the Moriscos. Hundreds of thousands of Moriscos were expelled, some of them probably sincere Christians. This was further fueled by the religious intolerance of Archbishop Ribera who quoted the Old Testament texts ordering the enemies of God to be slain without mercy and setting forth the duties of kings to extirpate them. The edict required: 'The Moriscos to depart, under the pain of death and confiscation, without trial or sentence... to take with them no money, bullion, jewels or bills of exchange.... just what they could carry.' Although initial estimates of the number expelled such as those of Henri

Lapeyre reach 300,000 Moriscos (or 4% of the total Spanish population), the extent and severity of the expulsion in much of Spain has been increasingly challenged by modern historians such as Trevor J. Dadson. Nevertheless, the eastern region of Valencia, where ethnic tensions were high, was particularly affected by the expulsion, suffering economic collapse and depopulation of much of its territory.

Censorship

As one manifestation of the Counter-Reformation, the Spanish Inquisition worked actively to impede the diffusion of heretical ideas in Spain by producing "Indexes" of prohibited books. Such lists of prohibited books were common in Europe a decade before the Inquisition published its first. The first Index published in Spain in 1551 was, in reality, a reprinting of the Index published by the University of Leuven in 1550, with an appendix dedicated to Spanish texts. Subsequent Indexes were published in 1559, 1583, 1612, 1632, and 1640. The Indexes included an enormous number of books of all types, though special attention was dedicated to religious works, and, particularly, vernacular translations of the Bible.

At first, inclusion in the Index meant total prohibition of a text; however, this proved not only impractical and unworkable, but also contrary to the goals of having a literate and well-educated clergy. Works with one line of suspect dogma would be prohibited in their entirety, despite the remainder of the text's sound dogma. In time, a compromise solution was adopted in which trusted Inquisition officials blotted out words, lines or whole passages of otherwise acceptable texts, thus allowing these expurgated editions to circulate.

Organization

Beyond its role in religious affairs, the Inquisition was also an institution at the service of the monarchy. The Inquisitor General, in charge of the Holy Office, was designated by the crown. The Inquisitor General was the only public office whose authority stretched to all the kingdoms of Spain (including the American viceroyalties), except for a brief period (1507–1518) during which there were two Inquisitors General, one in the kingdom of Castile, and the other in Aragon.

The Inquisitor General presided over the Council of the Supreme and General Inquisition (generally abbreviated as "Council of the Suprema"), created in 1483, which was made up of six members named directly by the crown (the number of members of the Suprema varied over the course of the Inquisition's history, but it was never more than 10). Over time, the authority of the Suprema grew at the expense of the power of the Inquisitor General.

Below the Suprema were the different tribunals of the Inquisition, which were, in their origins, itinerant, installing themselves where they were necessary to combat heresy, but later being established in fixed locations. In the first phase, numerous tribunals were established, but the period after 1495 saw a marked tendency towards centralization.

- 1482 In Seville and in Córdoba.
- 1485 In Toledo and in Llerena.
- 1488 In Valladolid and in Murcia.
- 1489 In Cuenca.
- 1505 In Las Palmas (Canary Islands).
- 1512 In Logroño.
- 1526 In Granada.
- 1574 In Santiago de Compostela.

In the kingdom of Castile, the following permanent tribunals of the Inquisition were established:

There were only four tribunals in the kingdom of Aragon: Zaragoza and Valencia (1482), Barcelona (1484), and Majorca (1488). Ferdinand the Catholic also established the Spanish Inquisition in Sicily (1513), housed in Palermo, and Sardinia, in the town of Sassari. In the Americas, tribunals were established in Lima and in Mexico City (1569) and, in 1610, in Cartagena de Indias (present day Colombia).

Structure of the Spanish Inquisition

Composition of the Tribunals

Initially, each of the tribunals included two inquisitors, a *calificador* (qualifiers), an *alguacil* (bailiff), and a *fiscal* (prosecutor); new positions were added as the institution matured. The inquisitors were preferably jurists more than theologians; in 1608 Philip III even stipulated that all the inquisitors must have a background in law. The inquisitors did not typically remain in the position for a long time: for the Court of Valencia, for example, the average tenure in the position was about two years. Most of the inquisitors belonged to the secular clergy (priests who were not members of religious orders) and had a university education.

The *fiscal* was in charge of presenting the accusation, investigating the denunciations and interrogating the witnesses by the use of physical and mental torture. The *calificadores* were generally theologians; it fell to them to determine if the defendant's conduct added up to a crime against the faith. Consultants were expert jurists who advised the court in questions of procedure. The court had, in addition, three secretaries: the *notario de secuestros* (Notary of Property), who registered the goods of the accused at the moment of his detention; the *notario del secreto* (Notary of the Secret), who recorded the testimony of the defendant and the witnesses; and the *escribano general* (General Notary), secretary of the court. The *alguacil* was the executive arm of the court, responsible for detaining, jailing, and physically torturing the defendant. Other civil employees were the *nuncio*, ordered to spread official notices of the court, and the *alcaide*, jailer in charge of feeding the prisoners.

In addition to the members of the court, two auxiliary figures existed that collaborated with the Holy Office: the *familiares* and the *comissarios* (commissioners). *Familiares* were lay collaborators of the Inquisition, who had to be permanently at the service of the Holy Office. To become a *familiar* was considered an honour, since it was a public recognition of *limpieza de sangre* — Old Christian status — and brought with it certain additional privileges. Although many nobles held the position, most of the *familiares* came from the ranks of commoners. The commissioners, on the other hand, were members of the religious orders who collaborated occasionally with the Holy Office.

One of the most striking aspects of the organization of the Inquisition was its form of financing: devoid of its own budget, the Inquisition depended exclusively on the confiscation of the goods of the denounced. It is not surprising, therefore, that many of those prosecuted were rich men. That the situation was open to abuse is evident, as stands out in the memorial that a *converso* from Toledo directed to Charles I:

> *"Your Majesty must provide, before all else, that the expenses of the Holy Office do not come from the properties of the condemned, because if that is the case, if they do not burn they do not eat."*

Accusation

When the Inquisition arrived in a city, the first step was the *Edict of Grace*. Following the Sunday mass, the Inquisitor would proceed to read the edict; it explained possible heresies and encouraged all the congregation to come to the tribunals of the Inquisition to "relieve their consciences". They were called *Edicts of Grace* because all of the self-incriminated who presented themselves within a *period of grace* (usually ranging from thirty to forty days) were offered the possibility of reconciliation with the Church without severe punishment. The promise of benevolence was effective, and many voluntarily presented themselves to the Inquisition and were often encouraged to denounce others who had also committed offenses, informants being the Inquisition's primary source of information. After about 1500, the Edicts of Grace were replaced by the *Edicts of Faith*, which left out the grace period and instead encouraged the denunciation of those guilty.

The denunciations were anonymous, and the defendants had no way of knowing the identities of their accusers. This was one of the points most criticized by those who opposed the Inquisition (for example, the Cortes of Castile, in 1518). In practice, false denunciations were frequent. Denunciations were made for a variety of reasons, from genuine concern, to rivalries and personal jealousies.

Detention

Diego Mate López Zapata in his cell before his trial by the Inquisition Court of Cuenca

After a denunciation, the case was examined by the *calificadores*, who had to determine if there was heresy involved, followed by detention of the accused. In practice, however, many were detained in preventive custody, and many cases of lengthy incarcerations occurred, lasting up to two years, before the *calificadores* examined the case.

Detention of the accused entailed the preventive sequestration of their property by the Inquisition. The property of the prisoner was used to pay for procedural expenses and the accused's own maintenance and costs. Often the relatives of the defendant found themselves in outright misery. This situation was remedied only following instructions written in 1561.

The entire process was undertaken with the utmost secrecy, as much for the public as for the accused, who were not informed about the accusations that were levied against them. Months or even years could pass without the accused being informed about why they were imprisoned. The prisoners remained isolated, and, during this time, the prisoners were not allowed to attend Mass nor receive the sacraments. The jails of the Inquisition were no worse than those of secular authorities, and there are even certain testimonies that occasionally they were much better.

Trial

The inquisitorial process consisted of a series of hearings, in which both the denouncers and the defendant gave testimony. A defense counsel was assigned to the defendant, a member of the tribunal itself, whose role was simply to advise the defendant and to encourage them to speak the truth. The prosecution was directed by the *fiscal*. Interrogation of the defendant was done in the presence of the *Notary of the Secreto*, who meticulously wrote down the words of the accused.

The archives of the Inquisition, in comparison to those of other judicial systems of the era, are striking in the completeness of their documentation. In order to defend themselves, the accused had two possibilities: *abonos* (to find favourable witnesses, akin to "substantive" evidence/testimony in Anglo-American law) or *tachas* (to demonstrate that the witnesses of accusers were not trustworthy, akin to Anglo-American "impeachment" evidence/testimony).

In order to interrogate the accused, the Inquisition made use of torture, but not in a systematic way. It was applied mainly against those suspected of Judaism and Protestantism, beginning in the 16th century. For example, Lea estimates that between 1575 and 1610 the court of Toledo tortured approximately a third of those processed for heresy. In other periods, the proportions varied remarkably. Torture was always a means to obtain the confession of the accused, not a punishment itself. Torture was also applied without distinction of sex or age, including children and the aged.

Torture

As with all European tribunals of the time, torture was employed. The Spanish inquisition, however, engaged in it far less often and with greater care than other courts. Historian Henry Kamen contends that some "popular" accounts of the inquisition (those that describe scenes of uncontrolled sadistic torture) are not based in truth. Kamen argues that torture was only ever used to elicit information or a confession, not for punitive reasons.

Although the Inquisition was technically forbidden from permanently harming or drawing blood, this still allowed several methods of torture. The methods most used, and common in other secular and ecclesiastical tribunals, were *garrucha*, *toca* and the *potro*. The application of the *garrucha*, also known as the strappado, consisted of suspending the victim from the ceiling by the wrists, which are tied behind the back. Sometimes weights were tied to the ankles, with a series of lifts and drops, during which the arms and legs suffered violent pulls and were sometimes dislocated. The *toca*, also called *interrogatorio mejorado del agua*, consisted of introducing a cloth into the mouth of the victim, and forcing them to ingest water spilled from a jar so that they had the impression of drowning. The *potro*, the rack, was the instrument of torture used most frequently.

Inquisition torture chamber. Mémoires Historiques (1716)

The assertion that *confessionem esse veram, non factam vi tormentorum* (literally: '[a person's] confession is truth, not made by way of torture') sometimes follows a description of how, after torture had ended, the subject freely confessed to the offenses. Thus, confessions following torture were deemed to be made of the confessor's free will, and hence valid.

Once the process concluded, the inquisidores met with a representative of the bishop and with the *consultores*, experts in theology or Canon Law, which was called the *consulta de fe*. The case was voted, and sentence pronounced, which had to be unanimous. In case of discrepancies, the *Suprema* had to be informed.

According to authorities within the Eastern Orthodox Church, there was at least one casualty tortured by those "Jesuits" (though most likely, Franciscans) who administered the Spanish Inquisition in North America: St. Peter the Aleut.

Sentencing

The results of the trial could be the following:

1. Although quite rare in actual practice, the defendant could be **acquitted**. Inquisitors did not wish to terminate the proceedings. If they did, and new evidence turned up later, they would be forced into reopening and re-presenting the old evidence.
2. The trial could be **suspended**, in which case the defendant, although under suspicion, went free (with the threat that the process could be continued at any time) or was held in long-term imprisonment until a trial commenced. When set free after a suspended trial it was considered a form of acquittal without specifying that the accusation had been erroneous.
3. The defendant could be **penanced**. Since they were considered guilty, they had to publicly abjure their crimes (*de levi* if it was a misdemeanor, and *de vehementi* if the crime were serious), and accept a public punishment. Among these were *sanbenito*, exile, fines or even sentencing to service as oarsmen in royal galleys.
4. The defendant could be **reconciled**. In addition to the public ceremony in which the condemned was reconciled with the Catholic Church, more severe punishments were used, among them long sentences to jail or the galleys, plus the confiscation of all property. Physical punishments, such as whipping, were also used.
5. The most serious punishment was **relaxation** to the secular arm for burning at the stake. This penalty was frequently applied to impenitent heretics and those who had relapsed. Execution was public. If the condemned repented, they were shown mercy by being garroted before burning; if not, they were burned alive.

Frequently, cases were judged in absentia, and when the accused died before the trial finished, the condemned were burned in effigy.

Confiscations

It is unknown exactly how much wealth was confiscated from converted Jews and others tried by the Inquisition. Wealth confiscated in one year of persecution in the small town of Guadaloupe paid the costs of building a royal residence. There are numerous records of the opinion of ordinary Spaniards of the time that "the Inquisition was devised simply to rob people". "They were burnt only for the money they had", a resident of Cuenca averred. "They burn only the well-off", said another. In 1504 an accused stated, "Only the rich were burnt".

...In 1484...Catalina de Zamora was accused of asserting that "this Inquisition that the fathers are carrying out is as much for taking property from the conversos as for defending the faith. It is the goods that are the heretics." This saying passed into common usage in Spain. In 1524 a treasurer informed Charles V that his predecessor had received ten million ducats from the conversos, but the figure is unverified. In 1592 an inquisitor admitted that most of the fifty women he arrested were rich. In 1676, the Suprema claimed it had confiscated over 700,000 ducats for the royal treasury (which was paid money only after the Inquisition's own budget, amounting in one known case to only 5%). The property on Mallorca alone in 1678 was worth "well over 2,500,000 ducats".

Note: Any time the Words "Jews, Muslims, Moslems, Heretics, Protestant, Saracen, African, Berber, Indian, Asiatic/Asian, Arab" are used they are all codewords used to identify the Moors who were/are the up lifters and mediums of healing for civilization.

VII. Cestui Que Vie Act 1666

Cestui Que Vie Act 1666

1666 CHAPTER 11 18 and 19 Chp. 2

An Act for Redresse of Inconveniencies by want of Proofe of the Deceases of Persons beyond the Seas or absenting themselves, upon whose Lives Estates doe depend.

X1Recital that Cestui que vies have gone beyond Sea, and that Reversioners cannot find out whether they are alive or dead.

Whereas diverse Lords of Mannours and others have granted Estates by Lease for one or more life or lives, or else for yeares determinable upon one or more life or lives And it hath often happened that such person or persons for whose life or lives such Estates have beene granted have gone beyond the Seas or soe absented themselves for many yeares that the Lessors and Reversioners cannot finde out whether such person or persons be alive or dead by reason whereof such Lessors and Reversioners have beene held out of possession of their Tenements for many yeares after all the lives upon which such Estates depend are dead in regard that the Lessors and Reversioners when they have brought Actions for the recovery of their Tenements have beene putt upon it to prove the death of their Tennants when it is almost impossible for them to discover the same, For remedy of which mischeife soe frequently happening to such Lessors or Reversioners.

I. Cestui que vie remaining beyond Sea for Seven Years together and no Proof of their Lives, Judge in Action to direct a Verdict as though Cestui que vie were dead.

If such person or persons for whose life or lives such Estates have beene or shall be granted as aforesaid shall remaine beyond the Seas or elsewhere absent themselves in this Realme by the space of seaven yeares together and noe sufficient and evident proofe be made of the lives of such person or persons respectively in any Action commenced for recovery of such Tenements by the Lessors or Reversioners in every such case the person or persons upon whose life or lives such Estate depended shall be accounted as naturally dead, And in every Action brought for the recovery of the said Tenements by the Lessors or Reversioners their Heires or Assignes, the Judges before whom such Action shall be brought shall direct the Jury to give their Verdict as if the person soe remaining beyond the Seas or otherwise absenting himselfe were dead.

If the supposed dead Man prove to be alive, then the Title is revested. Action for mean Profits with Interest.

[**X2**Provided alwayes That if any person or [**X3**person or] persons shall be evicted out of any Lands or Tenements by vertue of this Act, and afterwards if such person or persons upon whose life or lives such Estate or Estates depend shall returne againe from beyond the Seas, or shall on proofe in any Action to be brought for recovery of the same [**X3**to] be made appeare to be liveing; or to have beene liveing at the time of the Eviction That then and from thenceforth the Tennant or Lessee who was outed of the same his or their Executors Administrators or Assignes shall or may reenter repossesse have hold and enjoy the said Lands or Tenements in his or their former Estate for and dureing the

Life or Lives or soe long terme as the said person or persons upon whose Life or Lives the said Estate or Estates depend shall be liveing, and alsoe shall upon Action or Actions to be brought by him or them against the Lessors, Reversioners, or Tennants in possession or other persons respectively which since the time of the said Eviction received the Proffitts of the said Lands or Tenements recover for damages the full Proffitts of the said Lands or Tenements respectively with lawfull Interest for and from the time that he or they were outed of the said Lands or Tenements, and kepte or held out of the same by the said Lessors, Reversioners, Tennants or other persons who after the said Eviction received the Proffitts of the said Lands or Tenements or any of them respectively as well in the case when the said person or persons upon whose Life or Lives such Estate or Estates did depend are or shall be dead at the time of bringing of the said Action or Actions as if the said person or persons where then liveing.]

London 1666, during the black plague and great fires of London, Parliament enacted an act behind closed doors, called Cestui Que Vie Act 1666. The act being debated was to subrogate the rights of men and women, meaning all men and women were declared dead, lost at sea/beyond the sea. (Back then operating in Admiralty law, the law of the sea, so lost at sea).

The state (London) took custody of everybody and their property into a trust. The state became the trustee/husband holding all titles to the people and property, until a living man comes back to reclaim those titles, he can also claim damages.

When CAPITAL letters are used anywhere in a name this always refers to a legal entity/fiction, Company or Corporation no exceptions. e.g. John DOE or Doe: JANE

8. CEST TUI QUE TRUST: (pronounced setakay) common term in New Zealand and Australia
9. STRAWMAN: common term in United States of America or Canada

Straw man or party. A "front"; a person who is put up in name only to take part in a deal. Nominal party to a transaction; one who acts as an agent for another for the purpose of taking title to real property and executing whatever documents and instruments the principal may direct respecting the property. Person who purchases property for another to conceal identity of real purchaser.-Black's Law 5h Edition Pg. 1274

CLAIM, n. A broad, comprehensive word, Wheeler v. Equitable Life Assur. Soc. of United States, 211 Minn. 474, 1 N.W.2d 593, 596. CLAIM, v. To demand as one's own; to assert, Hill v. Henry, 66 N.J.Eq. 150, 57 Atl. 555. To state; to urge; to insist.-Black's Law 4h Edition Pg. 313

CESTUI QUE TRUST. He who has a right to a beneficial interest in and out of an estate the legal title to which is vested in another. 2 Washb. Real Prop. 163. The person who possesses the equitable right to property and receives the rents, issues, and profits thereof, the legal estate of which is vested in a trustee. Bernardsville Methodist Episcopal Church v. Seney, 85 N.J.Eq. 271, 96 A. 388, 389; Moore v.

Shifflett, 187 Ky. 7, 216 S.W. 614, 616. Beneficiary of trust, Ulmer v.

Fulton, 129 Ohio St. 323, 195 N.E. 557, 564, 97 A.L.R. 1170.

CESTUI QUE USE. He for whose use and benefit lands or tenements are held by another. The cestui que use has the right to receive the profits and benefits of the estate, but the legal title and possession (as well as the duty of defending the same) reside in the other. 2 Bla.Comm. 330; 2 Washb. Real Prop. 95.

CESTUI QUE VIE. He whose life is the measure of the duration of an estate. 1 Washb. Real Prop. 88. The person for whose life any lands, tenements, or hereditaments are held.-Black's Law 4th Edition Pg. 289

These are the legal entity/fiction created and owned by the Government who created it. It is like owning a share in the Stock Market, you may own a share... but it is still a share of the Stock.

Legally, we are considered to be a fiction, a concept or idea expressed as a name, a symbol. That legal person has no consciousness; it is a juristic person, ENS LEGIS, a name/word written on a piece of paper. This traces back to 1666, London is an Independent City State, just like the Vatican is an Independent City State, just like Washington DC is an Independent City State.

The Crown is an unincorporated association. Why unincorporated? It's private. The temple bar is in London, every lawyer called to the "bar"swears allegiance to the temple bar. You can't get called without swearing this allegiance.

When London burned, the subrogation of men's and women's rights occurred. The responsible act passed... CQV act 1666 meant all men and women of UK were declared dead and lost beyond the seas. The state took everybody and everybody's property into trust. The state takes control until a living man or woman comes back and claims their titles by proving they are alive and claims for damages can be made.

This is why you always encouraged to feel you need representation when involved in legal matters, because you're (assumed/considered) dead.

The legal fiction is a construct on paper, an estate in trust. When you get a bill or summons from court it is always in capital letters, similar to tomb stones in graveyards. Capital letters signify death. They are writing to the dead legal fiction. A legal fiction was created when someone informed the government that there was a new vessel in town, based upon your birth.

Birth Certificates are issued to us by the Doc. just as ships are given berth Certificates at the Dock. It's about commerce. We come from our mother's waters. Your mother has a birth canal just like a ship. The ship moves by the sea cur

In about 1837 the Births, Deaths and Marriages act was formed in UK and the post of registrar general was established. **His job was to collect all the data from the churches which held the records of birth.**

Regis – from Queen or Crown. All people are seen to be in custody of," The Crown". This allows people to function in commerce and to accept the benefits provided by the state. We have to understand who we are as men and women and how we are misclassified in the "system". The City of London is a centre for markets, where merchants work. Then there is Mercantile Law. It comes from Admiralty Law. Look at the symbols in he City Courts that relate to Admiralty.

So, where you have commerce and money, you also have "justice" and "injury". You need to understand the bankruptcy before you can understand the judiciary. We have accepted the claim to accept the summons, yet ONLY the dead can be summoned. There is an obligation to accept any liability which has been created.

A not guilty plea, or ANY plea admits jurisdiction. The straw man, aka legal fiction is always guilty. Barristers and solicitors make a living out of creating controversy. By creating a controversy, you become liable for the case.

People need to learn how to act as a creation of The Cosmic Mother (higher-self) rather than a creation of carnal Man (lower- self)!

Corruption

Cestui Que Vie Trust

Canon 2036

A Cestui Que Vie Trust, also known later as a "Fide Commissary Trust" and later again as a "Foreign Situs trust" and also known as a form of "Secret Trust" is a fictional concept being a Temporary Testamentary Trust, first created during the reign of Henry VIII of England through the Cestui Que Vie Act of 1540 and updated by Charles II through the Cestui Que Vie Act of 1666 wherein an Estate may be effected for the Benefit of one or more Persons presumed lost or abandoned at "sea" and therefore assumed/presumed "dead" after seven (7) years. Additional presumptions by which such a Trust may be formed were added in later statutes to include bankrupts, minors, incompetents, mortgages and private companies.

Canon 2037

The original purpose and function of a Cestui Que (Vie) Trust was to form a temporary Estate for the benefit of another because some event, state of affairs or condition prevented them from claiming their status as living, competent and present before a competent authority. Therefore, any claims, history, statutes or arguments that deviate in terms of the origin and function of a Cestui Que (Vie) Trust as pronounced by these canons is false and automatically null and void. A Cestui Que (Vie) Trust may only exist for seventy (70) years being the traditional accepted "life" expectancy of the estate.

Canon 2038

A Beneficiary under Estate may be either a Beneficiary or a Cestui Que (Vie) Trust. When a Beneficiary loses direct benefit of any Property of the higher Estate placed in Cestui Que (Vie) Trust on their behalf, they do not "own" the Cestui Que (Vie) Trust and are only the beneficiary of what the Trustees of the Cestui Que (Vie) Trust choose to provide them.

Canon 2039

As all Cestui Que (Vie) Trusts are created on one or more presumptions based on its original purpose and function, such a Trust cannot be created if none of these presumptions can be proven to exist.

Canon 2040

The Trust Corpus created by a Cestui Que (Vie) is also known as the Estate from two Latin words e + statuo literally meaning "by virtue of decree, statute or judgment". However, as the Estate is held in a Temporary not permanent Trust, the (Corporate) Person as Beneficiary is entitled only to equitable title and the use of the Property, rather than legal title and therefore ownership of the Property. Only the Corporation, also known as Body Corporate, Estate and Trust Corpus of a Cestui Que (Vie) Trust possesses valid legal personality.

Canon 2041

The Property of any Estate created through a Temporary (Testamentary) Trust may be regarded as under "Cestui Que Use" by the Corporate Person, even if another name or description is used to define the type of trust or use. Therefore "Cestui Que Use is not a Person but a Right and therefore a form of "property".

Canon 2042

In 1534, prior to the 1st Cestui Que Vie Act (1540), Henry VIII declared the first Cestui Que Vie type estate with the Act of Supremacy which created the Crown Estate. In 1604, seventy (70) years later, James I of England modified the estate as the Crown Union (Union of Crowns). By the 18th Century, the Crown was viewed as a company. However by the start of the 19th Century around 1814 onwards upon the bankruptcy of the company (1814/15) , it became the fully private Crown Corporation controlled by European private banker families.

Canon 2043

Since 1581, there has been a second series of Cestui Que Vie Estates concerning the property of "persons" and rights which migrated to the United States for administration including:

i. In 1651 the Act for the Settlement of Ireland 1651-52 which introduced the concept of "settlements", enemies of the state and restrictions of movement in states of "emergency"; and
ii. In 1861 the Emergency Powers Act; and
iii. In 1931 the Emergency Relief and Construction Act; and
iv. In 2001 the Patriot Act.

Canon 2044

Since 1591, there has been a third series of Cestui Que Vie Estates concerning the property of "soul" and ecclesiastical rights which migrated to the United States for administration including:

i. In 1661 the Act of Settlement ; and
ii. In 1871 the District of Columbia Act; and
iii. In 1941 the Lend Lease Act.

Canon 2045

By 1815 and the bankruptcy of the Crown and Bank of England by the Rothschilds, for the 1st time, the Cestui Que Vie Trusts of the United Kingdom became assets placed in private banks effectively becoming "private trusts" or "Fide Commissary Trusts" administered by commissioners (guardians). From

1835 and the Wills Act, these private trusts have been also considered "Secret Trusts" whose existence does not need to be divulged.

Canon 2046

From 1917/18 with the enactment of the Sedition Act and the Trading with the Enemy Act in the United States and through the United Kingdom, the citizens of the Commonwealth and the United States became effectively "enemies of the state" and "aliens" which in turn converted the "Fide Commissary" private secret trusts to "Foreign Situs" (Private International) Trusts.

Canon 2047

In 1931, the Roman Cult, also known as the Vatican created the Bank for International Settlements for the control of claimed property of associated private central banks around the world. Upon the deliberate bankruptcy of most countries, private central banks were installed as administrators and the global Cestui Que Vie/Foreign Situs Trust system was implemented from 1933 onwards.

Canon 2048

Since 1933, when a child is borne in a State(Estate) under inferior Roman law, three (3) Cestui Que (Vie) Trusts are created upon certain presumptions, specifically designed to deny the child forever any rights of Real Property, any Rights as a Free Person and any Rights to be known as man and woman rather than a creature or animal, by claiming and possessing their Soul or Spirit.

Canon 2049

Since 1933, upon a new child being borne, the Executors or Administrators of the higher Estate willingly and knowingly convey the beneficial entitlements of the child as Beneficiary into the 1st Cestui Que(Vie) Trust in the form of a Registry Number by registering the Name, thereby also creating the Corporate Person and denying the child any rights as an owner of Real Property.

Canon 2050

Since 1933, when a child is borne, the Executors or Administrators of the higher Estate knowingly and willingly claim the baby as chattel to the Estate. The slave baby contract is then created by honoring the ancient tradition of either having the ink impression of the feet of the baby onto the live birth record, or a drop of its blood as well as tricking the parents to signing the baby away through the deceitful legal meanings on the live birth record. This live birth record as a promissory note is converted into a slave bond sold to the private reserve bank of the estate and then conveyed into a 2nd and separate Cestui Que (Vie) Trust per child owned by the bank. Upon the promissory note reaching maturity and the bank being unable to "seize" the slave child, a maritime lien is lawfully issued to "salvage" the lost property and itself monetized as currency issued in series against the Cestui Que (Vie) Trust.

Canon 2051

Each Cestui Que Vie Trust created since 1933 represents one of the 3 Crowns representing the 3 claims of property of the Roman Cult, being Real Property, Personal Property and Ecclesiastical Property and the denial of any rights to men and women, other than those chosen as loyal members of the society and as Executors and Administrators.

Canon 2052

The Three (3) Cestui Que Vie Trusts are the specific denial of rights of Real Property, Personal Property and Ecclesiastical Property for most men and women, corresponds exactly to the three forms of law available to the Galla of the Bar Association Courts. The first form of law, corporate commercial law, is effective because of the 1st Cestui Que Vie Trust. The second form of law, maritime and trust law, is effective because of the 2nd Cestui Que Vie Trust. The 3rd form of law, Talmudic and Roman Cult law is effective because of the 3rd Cestui Que Vie Trust of Baptism.

Canon 2053

The Birth Certificate issued under Roman Law represents the modern equivalent to the Settlement Certificates of the 17th century and signifies the holder as a pauper and effectively a Roman Slave. The Birth Certificate has no direct relationship to the private secret trusts controlled by the private banking network, nor can it be used to force the administration of a state or nation to divulge the existence of these secret trusts.

Canon 2054

As the Cestui Que Vie Trusts are created as private secret trusts on multiple presumptions including the ongoing bankruptcy of certain national estates, they remain the claimed private property of the Roman Cult banks and therefore cannot be directly claimed or used.

Canon 2055

While the private secret trusts of the private central banks cannot be directly addressed, they are still formed on certain presumptions of law including claimed ownership of the name, the body, the mind and soul of infants, men and women. Each and every man and woman has the absolute right to rebuke and reject such false presumptions as a holder of their own title.

Canon 2056

Given the private secret trusts of the private central banks are created on false presumptions, when a man or woman makes clear their Live Borne Record and claim over their own name, body, mind and soul, any such trust based on such false presumptions ceases to have any property.

Canon 2057

Any Administrator or Executor that refuses to immediately dissolve a Cestui Que (Vie) Trust, upon a Person establishing their status and competency, is guilty of fraud and fundamental breach of their fiduciary duties requiring their immediate removal and punishment.

28 U.S. Code § 3002.Definitions

(15)"United States" means—

(A) a Federal corporation;

(B) an agency, department, commission, board, or other entity of the United States; or

(C) an instrumentality of the United States.

VIII. Berlin Conference (Wikipedia)

The **Berlin Conference** of 1884–85, also known as the **Congo Conference** (German: *Kongo konferenz*) or **West Africa Conference** (*Westafrika-Konferenz*), regulated European colonization and trade in Africa during the New Imperialism period, and coincided with Germany's sudden emergence as an imperial power. Called for by Portugal and organized by Otto von Bismarck, first Chancellor of Germany, its outcome, the **General Act of the Berlin Conference**, can be seen as the formalization of the Scramble for Africa. The conference ushered in a period of heightened colonial activity by European powers, which eliminated or overrode most existing forms of African autonomy and self-governance.

Conference

Owing to the European race for colonies, Germany started launching expeditions of its own, which frightened both British and French statesmen. Hoping to quickly soothe this brewing conflict, King Leopold II convinced France and Germany that common trade in Africa was in the best interests of all three countries. Under support from the British and the initiative of Portugal, Otto von Bismarck, German Chancellor, called on representatives of 13 nations in Europe as well as the United States to take part in the Berlin Conference in 1884 to work out joint policy on the African continent.

Whilst the number of plenipotentiaries varied per nation, the following 14 countries did send representatives to attend the Berlin Conference and sign the subsequent Berlin Act:

- Austria-Hungary
- Belgium
- Denmark
- France
- German Empire
- Italy
- Netherlands
- Ottoman Empire
- Portugal
- Russian Empire
- Spain
- Sweden-Norway
- United Kingdom
- United States – though the United States reserved the right to decline or to accept the conclusions of the Conference.

The conference was convened on Saturday, November 15, 1884 at Bismarck's official residence on Wilhelmstrasse (site of the Congress of Berlin six years earlier). Bismarck accepted the chairmanship. The British representative was Sir Edward Malet (Ambassador to the German Empire). Henry Morton Stanley attended as a U.S. delegate.

General Act

The General Act fixed the following points:

- To gain public acceptance, the conference resolved to end slavery by African and Islamic powers. Thus, an international prohibition of the slave trade throughout their respected spheres was signed by the European members. Because of this point the writer Joseph Conrad sarcastically referred to the conference as "the International Society for the Suppression of Savage Customs" in his novella *Heart of Darkness*.
- The Congo Free State was confirmed as the private property of the Congo Society, which supported Leopold's promises to keep the country open to all European investment. The territory of today's Democratic Republic of the Congo, some two million square kilometers, was confirmed by the European powers as essentially the property of Léopold II (but later it was organized as a Belgian colony under state administration).
- The 14 signatory powers would have free trade throughout the Congo Basin as well as Lake Malawi, and east of this in an area south of 5° N.
- The Niger and Congo rivers were made free for ship traffic.
- A Principle of Effectivity (based on "effective occupation", see below) was introduced to stop powers setting up colonies in name only.
- Any fresh act of taking possession of any portion of the African coast would have to be notified by the power taking possession, or assuming a protectorate, to the other signatory powers.
- Definition of regions in which each European power had an exclusive right to "pursue" the legal ownership of land (legal in the eyes of the other European powers).

The first reference in an international act to the obligations attaching to "spheres of influence" is contained in the Berlin Act.

Principle of Effective Occupation

The principle of effective occupation stated that powers could acquire rights over colonial lands only if they possessed them or had "effective occupation": in other words, if they had treaties with local leaders, if they flew their flag there, and if they established an administration in the territory to govern it with a police force to keep order. The colonial power could also make use of the colony economically. This principle became important not only as a basis for the European powers to acquire territorial sovereignty in Africa, but also for determining the limits of their respective overseas possessions, as effective occupation served in some instances as a criterion for settling disputes over the boundaries between colonies. But, as the Berlin Act was limited in its scope to the lands that fronted on the African coast, European powers in numerous instances later claimed rights over lands in the interior without demonstrating the requirement of effective occupation, as articulated in Article 35 of the Final Act.

At the Berlin Conference of 1885, the scope of the Principle of Effective Occupation was heavily contested between Germany and France. The Germans, who were new to the continent of Africa, essentially believed that as far as the extension of power in Africa was concerned, no colonial power should have any legal right to a territory, unless the state exercised strong and effective political control, and if so, only for a limited period of time, essentially an occupational force only. However, Britain's view was that Germany was a latecomer to the continent, and was assumptively unlikely to gain any new possessions, apart from already occupied territories, which were swiftly proving to be more valuable than British-occupied territories. Given that logic, it was generally assumed by Britain and France that Germany had an interest in embarrassing the other European powers on the continent and forcing them to give up their possessions if they could not muster a strong political presence. On the other side, the United Kingdom (UK) had large territorial "possessions" on the continent and wanted to keep them while minimizing its responsibilities and administrative costs. In the end, the British view prevailed.

The disinclination to rule what the Europeans had "conquered" is apparent throughout the protocols of the Berlin Conference, but especially in "The Principle of Effective Occupation." In line with Germany and Britain's opposing views, the powers finally agreed that this could be established by a European power establishing some kind of base on the coast, from which it was free to expand into the interior. The Europeans did not believe that the rules of occupation demanded European hegemony on the ground. The Belgians originally wanted to include that "effective occupation" required provisions that "cause peace to be administered", but other powers, specifically Britain and France, had that amendment struck out of the final document.

This principle, along with others that were written at the Conference allowed the Europeans to "conquer" Africa while doing as little as possible to administer or control it. The Principle of Effective Occupation did not apply so much to the hinterlands of Africa at the time of the conference. This gave rise to "hinterland theory," which basically gave any colonial power with coastal territory the right to claim political influence over an indefinite amount of inland territory.

Since Africa was irregularly shaped, this theory caused problems and was later rejected.

Agenda

- **Portugal–Britain**: The Portuguese government presented a project, known as the "Pink Map" (also called the "Rose- Colored Map"), in which the colonies of Angola and Mozambique were united by co-option of the intervening territory (land that later became Zambia, Zimbabwe, and Malawi.) All of the countries attending the conference, except for the United Kingdom, endorsed Portugal's ambitions. A little more than five years later, in 1890, the British government, in breach of the Treaty of Windsor (and of the Treaty of Berlin itself), issued an ultimatum demanding that the Portuguese withdraw from the disputed area.
- **France–Britain**: A line running from Say in Niger to Maroua, on the north-east coast of Lake Chad determined what part belonged to whom. France would own territory to the north of this line, and the United Kingdom would

own territory to the south of it. The Nile Basin would be British, with the French taking the basin of Lake Chad. Furthermore, between the 11th and 15th degrees latitude, the border would pass between Ouaddaï, which would be French, and Darfur in Sudan, to be British. In reality, a no man's land 200 kilometres wide was put in place between the 21st and 23rd meridians.

- **France–Germany**: The area to the north of a line formed by the intersection of the 14th meridian and Miltou was designated French, that to the south being German.
- **Britain–Germany**: The separation came in the form of a line passing through Yola, on the Benoué, Dikoa, going up to the extremity of Lake Chad.
- **France–Italy**: Italy was to own what lies north of a line from the intersection of the Tropic of Cancer and the 17th meridian to the intersection of the 15th parallel and 21st meridian.

Consequences

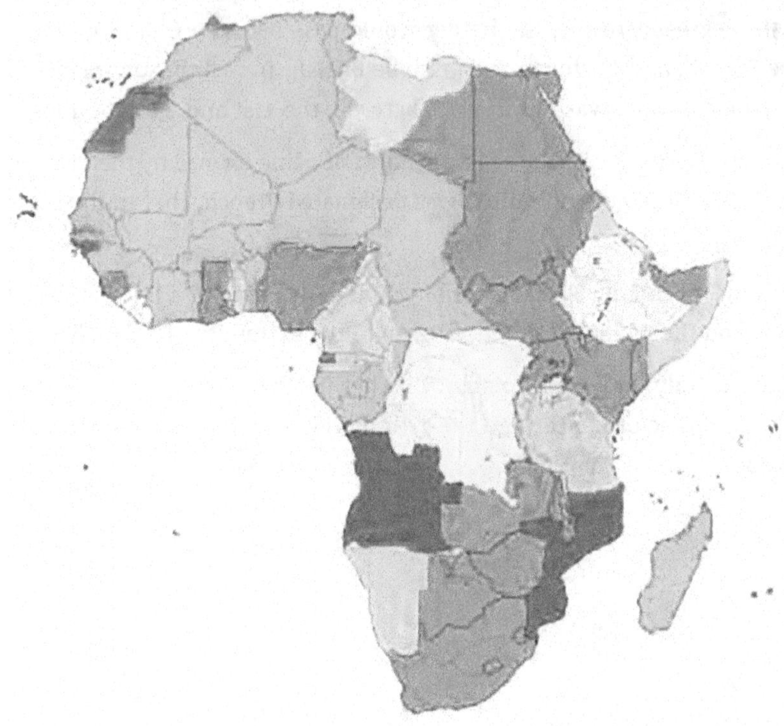

European claims in Africa, 1913. Modern-day boundaries, largely a legacy of the colonial era, are shown.

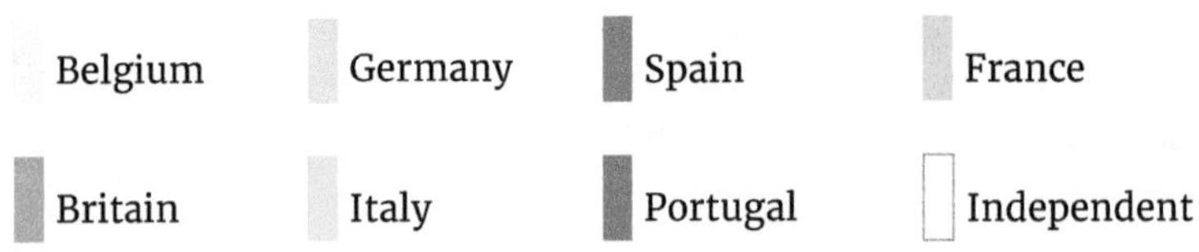

The conference provided an opportunity to channel latent European hostilities towards one another outward, provide new areas for helping the European powers expand in the face of rising American, Russian, and Japanese interests, and form constructive dialogue for limiting future hostilities. For Africans, colonialism was introduced across nearly all the continent. When African independence was regained after World War II, it was in the form of fragmented states.

The Scramble for Africa sped up after the Conference, since even within areas designated as their sphere of influence, the European powers still had to take possession under the Principle of Effectivity. In central Africa in particular, expeditions were dispatched to coerce traditional rulers into signing treaties, using force if necessary, as for example in the case of Msiri, King of Katanga, in 1891. Bedouin and Berber ruled states in the Sahara and Sub-Sahara were overrun by the French in several wars by the beginning of World War I. The British moved up from South Africa and down from Egypt conquering Arabic states such as the Mahdist State and the Sultanate of Zanzibar and, (having already defeated the Zulu Kingdom in South Africa, in 1879), moving on to subdue and dismantle the independent Boer republics of Transvaal and Orange Free State.

Within a few years, Africa was at least nominally divided up south of the Sahara. By 1895, the only independent states were:

- Morocco, involved in colonial conflicts with Spain and France, who conquered the nation in the 20th century.
- Liberia, founded with the support of the United States for returned slaves;
- Ethiopian Empire, the only free native state, which fended off Italian invasion from Eritrea in what is known as the First Italo-Abyssinian War of 1889–96.
- Majeerteen Sultanate, the sultanate was founded in the early 18th century, it was annexed by Italy in the 20th century.
- Sultanate of Hobyo, the sultanate was carved out of the former Majeerteen Sultanate and ruled northern Somalia until the 20th century, when it was conquered by Italy.

The following states lost their independence to the British Empire roughly a decade after (see below for more information):

- Orange Free State, a Boer republic founded by Dutch settlers;
- South African Republic (Transvaal), also a Boer republic;

By 1902, 90% of all the land that makes up Africa was under European control. The large part of the Sahara was French, while after the quelling of the Mahdi rebellion and the ending of the Fashoda crisis, the Sudan remained firmly under joint British–Egyptian rulership with Egypt being under British occupation before becoming a British protectorate in 1914.

The Boer republics were conquered by the United Kingdom in the Boer war from 1899 to 1902. Morocco was divided between the French and Spanish in 1911, and Libya was conquered by Italy in 1912. The official British annexation of Egypt in 1914 ended the colonial division of Africa.

B. The Culprits of Evil

I. Puppets and puppeteers

The so-called Jews, Germans, Christians, Freemasons, Teutonic order, so-called Muslims, Rosa crucians, ku Klux Klan, knights of molta, skull and bones, college soroties and fraternities, knights Templar, knights of Columbus and all other manner of secret societies are all the same people and they all work for the popes of Rome.

All pastors, ministers, reverends, rabbi, imams, politicians, entertainers, nuns, missionaries/mercenaries, light workers, gurus and organizational leaders all belong to one of the aforementioned or other various branches of secret society set on controlling the minds of the people and destroying the good will of man thus tainting the essence of creation. They all take oaths to never reveal the secrets of truth and to only keep it buried and amongst themselves. They are all 32nd or 33rd degree freemasons and are selected as overseers to make sure the sheep don't rebel or do anything that could actually affect the current system of corruption. They cast spells of emotionalism and indifference over the masses basically serving as distractions while the vampires, which includes them, feed off the energy of the misguided and blind.

The head is the pope, which in actuality is a dual figure head whereas there is the white pope (public figure) and the black pope (private figure; the actual leader and commander of the Jesuit militia). All taxes paid in this part of the continent as well as others are in actuality tithes/taxes offered and surrendered to the popes of Rome as a sign of collusion and devotion. 60% goes to the Vatican and 40% goes to the Queen of England. This is why despite the billions of dollars shelled out by the citizens of the U.S. the infrastructure is still crumbling.

Rome actually represents the whole collective of European nations (Albion, Gaelic, Gothic, and Frankish). They all have the same agenda and mission which is world domination and conquest. These are the true aliens/hybrids who are the seeds of Satan which all ancient doctrine speaks of and forewarned against.

II. His-story: Origin of Dogma

Christianity rules the world both directly and indirectly. Its official name is the nicenal constantinal politan creed. The political operation of the world is the nicenal constantinal politan hegemony, which is the basis of the European supremacy doctrine.

The creation of modern-day Christianity was brought about by German Jesuits and took about 751 years to fully implement from the creation of serapis at the council of nicea in 320 B.C. to the council of empharis in 431 A.D. to transform the teachings of the ancient Moors/Yehudim into what has become the warped perception of who and what were/are true Kerest beings hence turning society into atheists and/or idol god worshippers.

The campaign that began in 711 by the Kushite Moors of the northern coast of Amexem/Africa was in response to atrocities inflicted upon the people of the European nations by the Christians which included not just Asiatic Moors but the Albion sons and daughters as well. The term renaissance < Old French renaissance < re-again + naissance- birth < nascentia-birth, origin < nasci-be born. This was the great revival that occurred throughout Europe whereas they were introduced to life saving methods and techniques essential for civilized life. Though there were atrocities committed by Asiatics as well the good clearly outweighed the bad as if it had not been for Moors the Albion would never know culture. However, what was established by the wise elders was infiltrated and polluted and became tapestry in the halls of masonic lodges as oppose to keys to free the minds of man.

In 1534, Saint Ignasius De Loyola founded the Society of Jesus. He was their first superior general and he founded many colleges and universities, which are training grounds for Jesuit militia. Originally there were 6 members that eventually grew to 60. These people took an oath to the pope. Pope Paul III approved De Loyola's plan to infiltrate all levels of the world's politics for the church beginning in 1539. They vowed to go anywhere in the world they were ordered to go to and wage war against free thinkers. They vowed to destroy any original people on the planet. They will go against anybody who opposes the pope's agenda and policies. They infiltrate any organization which will further their cause and goal of world bondage and destruction. They operate openly and in secret. The modern-day secret societies and those of lesser degrees take a lesser oath but it is the same in its intent which is to uphold the rites and wills of the popes of Rome. They can be any nationality, religious affiliation, and indulge in all manners of unnatural degradation towards society. Jesuits use the art of war, cunning, intrigue, deceit, hypocrisy, espionage, prevarication, craftiness, casuistry, mental reservation, public manipulation, plots, schemes, trickery, cheating, guerilla tactics, cloak and dagger, diplomacy or any other means necessary to promulgate the agenda of the Roman Catholic Church.

III. "Old" New world order infiltrates masons and calls themselves the new world order:

By the mid-1800s the Jesuits had infiltrated and taken over their arch enemies, the Masons. The Jesuits set about with the purpose of disrupting and causing confusion in the masons. In America Jesuit Albert Pike promptly announced that the god of the masons was 'Lucifer' turning the masons 1800 in the opposite direction from which was their foundation.

IV. "Old" new world order initiates conflict to destroy U.S.A. - The Morrill un-civil War

Albert Pike (1809-1891) a Jesuit of Newbury Port moved to Arkansas where he became a prominent member of the secessionist movement. He was chosen by Giuseppe Mazzini, the head of the freemasons and mafia in Italy and Europe (no doubt Mazzini was closely tied to the pope), to head the illuminati operations in America and moved to Charleston, South Carolina, in 1852.

Brigham Young, a high-level freemason, in 1846 at the council of Bluffs, Iowa had a private meeting with Pierre De Smet, one of the most powerful Jesuits of the 19th century. Being the foremost Jesuit of influence among the Indian nation, De Smet, using confederate general and 33rd degree freemason Albert Pike, incited his Sioux Indians to mass-murder 800 caucasian Lutherans of Minnesota (northerners) while having procured the exemption of Jesuits from the draft during America's bloodbath, erroneously called "the civil war."

Albert Pike made the rank of brigadier general in the un-civil war. Pike's reign of terror was so despicable that foreign governments intervened to put an end to his savagery.

Albert Pike wrote a book titled "Morals and Dogma" which is regarded as the freemason bible and was quoted as saying to his followers: "That which we must say to the crowd is: we worship god, but it is the god that one adores without superstition. To you sovereign grand inspectors general (33rd degree; highest freemasonic degree in some orders), we say this, that you may repeat it to the brethren of the 32nd, 31st, and 30th degrees-the masonic religion should be, by all the initiates in the high degrees, maintained in the purity of the Luciferian doctrine. If Lucifer were not god, would Adonai (Yahoshua) culminate him?...yes, Lucifer is god..."(A.C. De La Rive, La Femme et L'enfant dans la franc-maconne ne universelle p.568) Furthermore in the book "Morals and Dogma" Pike admits: "Masonry like all religions, conceals its secrets from all except the adepts and sages, or the elect and use false explanations and misinformation/misinterpretations of its symbols to mislead; to conceal the truth which is called light, from them (believers), and to draw them away from it (truth)."

He also explains in "Morals and Dogma of the ancient and accepted Scottish rite of freemasonry": "Blind force of the people is a force that must be economized, and also managed...it must be regulated by intellect to attack the citadels (institutions) built up on all sides against the human race. By superstitions, despotism, and prejudices, the force must have a brain and a law (the illuminati's). Then it's (force) deeds of daring produce permanent results, and there is real progress. Then there are sublime conquest. When all forces combined, and guided by the intellect (illuminati), and regulated by the rule of right, and justice, and of combined systematic movement and effort, the great revolution prepared for the ages will begin to march...it is because force is ill regulated that revolutions prove failures." (rev. ed. 1956)

V. "Old" New world order plans world domination:

Following the un-civil Morrill tax war, Pike and Mazzini planned to take over the world. Pike designed a plan for world conquest and wrote about it in a letter to Mazzini dated August 15, 1871. He said three future world wars would prepare the world for the new world order. A young Cecil Rhodes who became a master mason of the freemasonry gang a few years later in 1877, at the Apollo university lodge no. 357, would later provide a significant amount of finance for the NWO's "own the world plan", with blood diamonds from Africa. Rhodes who also joined a Scottish rite at Oxford University, called prince rose cruix lodge no. 30, would help assemble much of the secret upper level psychopaths to carry out Mazzini and Pike's psychotic world war plan.

Albert Pike's plan for the illuminati was as simple as it was effective. He required that communism, Nazism, political Zionism, and other international movements be organized and used to ferment the three major global revolutions:

1. "The First World War must be brought about in order to permit the illuminati to overthrow the power of the Czars in Russia and of making that country a fortress of atheistic communism. The divergences caused by the 'agentur' (agents) of the illuminati between the British and the Germanic empires will be used to ferment this war. At the end of the war, communism will be built and used in order to weaken the religions."

2. "The second world war must be fermented by taking advantage of the difference between the fascists and the political Zionists. This war must be brought about so that Nazism is destroyed, and that the political Zionism be strong enough to institute a sovereign state of Israel in Palestine. During the Second World War, international communism must be strong enough to balance Christendom, which would then be restrained and held in check until the time when we would need it for the final social cataclysm.

3. "The third world war must be fermented by taking advantage of the differences caused by the 'agentur' of the illuminati between the political Zionists (so-called Jews) and the leaders of the Islamic world. The war must be conducted in such a way that Islam (pseudo version; pale Arabs) mutually destroys each other. Meanwhile, the other nations, once more divided upon the issue will be constrained to fight to the point of complete physical, moral, spiritual and economic exhaustion...we shall unleash the nihilists and the atheists and shall provoke a formidable social cataclysm which in all its horror will show clearly to the nations the effect of absolute atheism, origin of savagery and of the bloodiest turmoil. Then everywhere, the citizens, obliged to defend themselves against the world minority of revolutionaries, will exterminate those destroyers of civilization, and the multitude, disillusioned by Christianity, whose deistic spirits will from that moment be without compass or direction, anxious for an ideal, but without knowing where to render its adoration, will receive the true light through the universal manifestation of the pure doctrine of Lucifer, brought finally out in the public view. This manifestation will result from the general reactionary movement which will follow the destruction of Christianity and atheism, both conquered and exterminated. At the same time."- Albert Pike's letter to Mazzini, dated August 15, 1871 (see former royal Canadian navy intelligence officer, William Guy Carr's books, "Satan, prince of this world", and "pawns in the game", pp.25-26, which includes extracts of Pike's letter.)

VI. The Mafia-right out of the Jesuit order; just like the top-level freemasons:

Mazzini was not only the head of the illuminati; he was the leading revolutionists in Europe. He was determined to establish a new world order and created a plan to accomplish his goal. He detailed his plan for world domination in a letter to Pike on January 22, 1870: "We must allow all the federations to continue just as they are, with their systems, their central authorities and their diverse modes of correspondence with high grades of the same rite, organized as they are at the present, but we must create a super rite, which will remain unknown, to which we will call those masons of high degree whom we shall select. With regard to our brothers in masonry, these men must be pledges to the strictest secrecy. Through this supreme rite, we will govern all freemasonry which will become the one international center, the more powerful because its direction will be unknown."- Lady Queensborough, occult theocracy, pp.208-

209 (this secret rite is called "the new and reformed palladian rite." It has headquarters in Charleston, South Carolina; Rome, Italy; and Berlin, Germany).

VII. Oath of a Jesuit:

"I do further promise and declare, that I will, when opportunity presents, make and wage relentless war, secretly or openly, against all heretics, protestants and masons, as I am directed to do, to extirpate and exterminate them from the face of the whole earth, and that I will burn, hang, waste, boil, flay, strangle, bury alive, these infamous heretics, open up the stomachs and wombs of their women and crush their infants' heads against the walls in order to annihilate them. That when the same cannot be done openly, I will secretly use the poison cup, the strangulation cord, the steel of the poniard, or the leaden bullet, regardless of honor, rank, dignity or authority of the persons whatever be their condition in life, either public or private, as I at any time may be directed to do so, by any agent of the pope, or superior of the brotherhood of the holy faith of the society of Jesus.

I do further declare that I will help, assist and advise all or any of his holiness' agents, in any place, whether I should be in Switzerland, Germany, Holland, or America, or in any other territory I shall come to, and do my utmost to extricate heretical, protestant or masonic doctrines, and destroy all their pretended power, legal or otherwise."- Quotes from Jesuit oath shown here were entered into the congressional record, 62nd congress, 3rd session; house bill 1523, library of congress, catalog card #: 66-43354, volume 29, part 4, pp.3215-3216.

This is why we are not supposed to protest, riot, or get emotional with these Satan seeds because their aim is to provoke so as they have reason to do bodily harm. Never move in fear but always maintain control of self as these people are just looking for an excuse to harvest your organs especially the melanin rich. The klanners/highwaymen who are erroneously referred to as officers are the enforcers of the Jesuit militia and their job is basically collect body parts. They get kickbacks for organs; 10,000 for kidneys and liver, and 20,000+ for hearts and brains. They are geared toward survival which includes taking your blood from you which is why no matter what you go to the doctor for they always want a blood sample because they need it to feed. All that blood people donate is stored for when all their institutions finally collapse completely, and they have to go back to the caves. Never give your blood away or semen for that matter and stay away from the hospital as it is a death trap specifically for melanin rich children and women. Eat right and do your own checkups. Plus, after reading their oath you should not have your children anywhere near their institutions or facilities as you are basically dangling a steak in front of a wolf, a hungry wolf at that. (See Godfather III. For further confirmation.)

C. Roman Agenda and Operations:

I. New World (dis) order

An excerpt from the book, "The new world order" by A. Ralph Epperson, 1989:

> *The Family: homosexual marriages will be legalized; parents will not be allowed to raise their children (the state will); all women will be employed by the state and not allowed to be "homemakers"; divorce will become exceedingly easy and monogamous marriage will be slowly phased out*
>
> *The workplace: the government will become the owner of all factors of production; the private ownership of property will be outlawed, and believers will be either eliminated or imprisoned; there will be a new religion; the worship of man and his mind; all will believe in this new religion.*

II. Concentration camps:

Halliburton confirms concentration camps already constructed: on February 17, 2006, in a speech to the council on foreign relations, defense secretary Donald Rumsfeld spoke on harm being done to the country's security, not just by the enemy, but also by what he called "news informers" who needed to be combated in "a contest of wills."

In 2002 attorney general John Ashcroft announced his desire to see camps for U.S. citizens deemed to be "enemy combatants." (See "U.S. concentration camps" Anthony J. Hilder article on Russia TV program.)

A defense apartment document entitled, "strategy for homeland defense and civil support", has set out a military strategy against terrorism that envisions an "active, layered defense" both inside and outside U.S. territory. In the document, the pentagon pledges to "transform U.S. military forces to execute homeland." The strategy calls for increased military reconnaissance and surveillance.

The Washington post reported on February 15, 2006 that the national counterterrorism center's (NCTC) central repository holds the names of 325,000 terrorist suspects, a fourfold increase since fall of 2003. A pentagon official said the counterintelligence field activity's talon program has amassed files on antiwar protestors.

Shortly after Bush orchestrated 9/11, he issued "military order number one", which empowered him to detain any non-citizen as an international terrorist or enemy combatant.

Halliburton subsidiary KBR has been awarded a security contract announced by the department of homeland security's United States immigration and customs enforcement (ICE) component. The indefinite contract is to support ICE facilities and has a maximum total value of 385 million over a 5-year term. The contract provides for establishing temporary detention and processing capabilities in the event of an emergency influx of immigrants into the United States, or to support the rapid redevelopment of new programs." (See source document on Halliburton site; see also army regulation 210-35, civilian inmate labor program)

"Oh, all of us in the C.I.A know all about the concentration camps in America and their purpose! We all know that their purpose is to terminate 'registers of the new world order' under martial law!"- Michael Maholy, 20-year naval intelligence/C.I. A under Bush Sr.

III. Zionazi and Jesuit evil (libertyforlife.com):

Freemason and Jesuit Zionist/Zionazi active global genocide and neurological incapacitation efforts are being conducted simultaneously on multiple fronts:

4. Neurological Incapacitation (dumbing down the public): Fluoride (added to water, toothpaste, salt, food); Lead (added to paint, fuel, food): Aluminum (added to food, deodorant, cooking utensils, and sprayed in chemtrails); Meat (what's injected into animals is ingested by the consumer); Sweeteners/Aspartame (food that kills brain cells); Morgellons Nano technology (chemtrails; food); Media (all news, textbooks, newspapers, radio, TV, internet, etc.)
5. Global Genocide: H1N1/Swine flu (failed attempt in 2008); Ebola (failed attempt-working on new strains); Genetically Modified Foods (corn, veggies); Geo engineering to kill food supply (chemtrails and harp); Morgellons (chemtrails, food); attack on immune system; Barium (sprayed in chemtrails, agriculture); Round up/Agent orange (agriculture); Vaccination shots

Many of the terrorist acts and wars are intentially perpetuated by these leaders, in what is clearly a sacrificial offering on a global scale.

IV. Methods of madness

The 5 P's:

- Polytheism: The belief and worship of many gods. This is one of the biggest misconceptions about the truth of her-story/our story which was warped by his-story. Contrary to popular belief our ancestors never worshipped but one Supreme Being but they were aware and respectful of the many manifestations of that said Force which spoke to the fact that the essence of creation dwelled within all living beings and we inner/overstood that to respect and care for one was to show love/gratitude to Th All. We cultivated our divine oneness with all by using the gifts/mediums of nature which included the products of our own divine intellect, will and imagination as alters of which we gave thanks to Th Supreme Universal Governing Force. For example, we didn't worship the sun but rather Th spirit that dwelled within it that gave it the ability to incubate, the same went for the moon as well which we viewed as a representation of the Mother being that it cultivates and nurtures and facilitates the tides of nature. If you go into a church and see people kneeling at the altar, do you assume they see that alter as the creator or do you innerstand that they use it simply as medium for praising Th Most High? To worship many gods is to fracture yourself mentally and spiritually which inevitably creates discord and confusion amongst the natives bringing about war.
- Politics: The science of winning and holding control of government. This is

the profession of hypnotist, those who seek to control the minds of men thus they control the bodies of men as well. Politicians are everywhere and not just in the halls of congress, but they are gang leaders, ministers, rabbi, imams, teachers, etc. Anybody that attempts to or holds a leadership role is essentially a politician. For the most part these people serve as distractions and are mediums by which the life force of the people is drained and misguided. Poly means many and a tic is a parasite, a blood sucker so in the title it shows you the purpose and intent of these people we so readily trust and allow to represent us. They are agitators and traitors against whom they take an oath either officially or unofficially to serve.

- Psychology: The study of the mind and behavior of humans. There is a reason why in every phase of our lives we are evaluated, from the standardized tests, to the guidance counselors and trips to the psychologists brought on by the psychosomatic trauma of living in a society that wants to either sacrifice you, take away your potential, or make you an unnatural being. All the intel gathered at these institutions are simply databases where the info stored can be used against the people of the society both on a conscious and subconscious level in turn either totally conforming an individual or driving them to the point of mental fracture whereas they can be turned into slaves via institutions such as mental wards and hospitals serving as host for parasites that feed off of the essence of man until there is no more left to drink.
- Philosophy: An explanation or theory of the universe based entirely on conversation and not necessarily facts. The actual spirit of philosophy is the love and seeking of wisdom. However, through mis-education and indoctrination philosophy has been turned into theory rather than empirical evidence which is the spawn or next step after philosophy. It basically is a way by which those who study, and master words can manipulate the psyche of man by way of oral phantasmagoria whereby a lot is said but nothing is concrete. It opens the door for unnatural exploration whereby men begin dabbling in things beyond their understanding or their capability to possibly grasp the consequences of their foolish pride, ignorance and arrogance hence the portal opens for the lower forces of nature to possess and corrupt the spirits of man until they no longer qualify to even be called such.
- Penal: Relates to law and punishment. This system was established by Nimrod and laid down by Hammurabi. There is truly but one law of the universe that if all lived by, they would be safe within their own space and that great universal law is respect. Respect covers over a multitude of sin for in its purest form it

is love which is gratitude. All other laws only attempt either to place respect on a pedestal or knock it off. The fact is so long as you or I don't infringe on our right to life, liberty and the pursuit of happiness then there should be no bloodshed or curses uttered. However, man in their arrogance has created a lot unnecessary laws designed to restrict the locomotion and weaken the will of natural persons, but it is only the compliance and lack of self-respect that has allowed tyranny to prevail. A man who is in control shall not be controlled; one who respects themselves shall be respected.

The 9 methods of division

- Age: the old versus the young. Knowledge versus wisdom. It is a lose lose situation as both sides miss out on the benefit of growth that either side can offer the other. Willy Lynch highlighted this in his address to his fellow slave holders that has worked like a charm. The reason it has worked because the parents have lost respect for themselves and in turn have no reverence for what they have produced which creates a disconnect whereas they are willing to sacrifice their own babies because they are already defeated and have capitulated to the ways of slavery and misery loves company. The children see this and in turn grow to not respect their parents as well and it creates a sense of loneliness and inevitable rebellion against anyone in the same position hence they miss out on the lessons that are there to be learned by their elders due to bitterness and their own self-hatred. Both need to stop pointing and start hugging and brainstorming especially the elders because we as youth are their future and their redemption can come by way of them properly showing us the way as we are them and their fore-bearers all one and the same. Likewise. some elders are angels in disguise that we must take heed so as to bring about our own transformation into the nagas we are meant to be.
- Hue: Light versus dark. Melanin rich versus melanin recessive. Divide and conquer is the oldest trick and is at the same time the most effective. We have been socialized to see with the two instead of the first. This difference is highlighted on both sides of the spectrum whereas so-called black leaders and so-called conscious community leaders are quick to point out the power of melanin richness but not the side effects of misguidedness; they bang on pale people for their lack of melanin but in the same breath complain about what they do, in other words they tear down the so-called "white" man only to lift you up just to give you somebody to blame and hate on which actually lowers your frequencies as a dead man cannot be revived with death but only

life/love. At the other end the paleo disrespect their mothers and fathers and also play the blame game while at the same time acting with a superiority complex that is undermined by their savagery and constant fear mongering. It is time for people to wake up take a long hard look in the mirror, into the eyes/soul of themselves and see what is missing and correct that. To think you can fix a people without them fixing themselves is beyond foolish and the highest degree of arrogance, and to think that one thing is the source of all your problems and that that thing is outside or separate from you is an extreme act of ignorance and hypocrisy. In other words, grow up and be responsible; human beings are a parade of fools and everybody takes turn leading the parade!

- Size: the bully complex is heavy part of the psychology of man that has in modern times been heightened to skyscraper status. All ways wanting more; bigger muscles, bigger genitals, bigger house, bigger cars, etc. It's never enough and millions go to their grave chasing after things or fantasying about things they only ever wanted because they were either told about them or saw somebody else with them. Never mind if they actually need or even if they truly want it deep down, they just got to have it. But why? Just to make the next person feel like you when you didn't have it and then what happens when you get it? Are all your problems gone or do they increase due to your lack of self-awareness? Contentment is a precious resource and more valuable than gold. Those who sit in the seats of power and who pretend to be government officials use the size factor as a justification to destroy those who aren't as big or don't have the amount of weaponry that they have and the citizens sanction this because well hey if they were as "big and bad" as "us" then they wouldn't be getting raped and pillaged. This is basically what you say when you see nothing wrong with women and children being bombed or banned anywhere that there is land when the Creator gifted us all with dominion. The bigger they are the harder they fall which speaks more to the mindset of man more than anything where they have tricked themselves into thinking that they are supreme when in actuality they are ants meant to serve, build and multiply but instead want to worship themselves instead of what and who made them. They've built all these institutions just, so they can fall.
- Sex (gender): Male versus female. Mother versus son. Sister versus brother. This is the beginning of the end for any civilization when yin and yang no longer occupy the same space in harmony. The manifest is all around us as nature is the barometer for the psyche and consciousness of man. All this homosexual and transgender mess is only perpetuated so as to stop creativity

which is life. They want you to go to banks to get a child or adopt. This is all unnatural and will inevitably lead to the self-destruction of man as once you are no longer producing then you are not conducive to the expansion of the universe in turn making you useless hence you get discarded and junked as you have wrecked your creation/your vehicle that is supposed to get you to the next level of existence but instead you chose to listen to wrong directions and crashed. Ma and pa make a home and together they are stronger than any evil force that would destroy because they become one and make magic thus they combine to manifest a force of unbridled power, the will of nature in the flesh that restores and replenishes.

- Status: Life versus death. Fallacy versus reality. Overstanding versus understanding. This has become a major topic of discussion that was brought about by the divine Moorish national movement. Status is important because it is a declaration and proclamation that you are ready to place yourself among the affairs of men meaning that you affirm to the Great Universal Supreme force that you are her son that you are alive and well. The whole point of all these legal constructs was to strip us of our lives by first stripping us of our dignity then our knowledge. You either are a corporation/corpse or a man: moral and noble; manifested after nature; manipulated according to nature; magnetic and nubile; Moorish Aboriginal Navigator; Master Architect of Nations. You cannot serve two masters and the responsibility of free will is choice. Pick one. The chain of Satan wasn't made that strong and it is only your voluntary ignorance that keeps you in captivity. You are the key and the lock, the slave and the master, the question and the answer!
- Location: house versus apartment. Shelter versus homelessness. Modern world versus third world. Another trap of mental servitude that brings about either overconfidence or low self-esteem. The fact is one who is loyal is royal meaning one who obeys the Most High is comfortable wherever they roam. Some have more than others but if we all helped out a little more especially those with the means then no person would ever have to suffer without shelter. However, Th Creator gives to each as Th Wills so at the end of the day wherever you are, be blissed and thankful. Anywhere a Queen/King steps is a castle. It's all temporary anyway so appreciate everything because Th Creator gives, and Th Creator takes away. You laugh at or disregard the homeless one day and the next it is you in the same position.
- Hair: Nappy versus straight. Curly versus wavy. Hair versus baldness. There are five ethers or textures of hair and the nappier the hair the better reception

with the universal frequencies. However, obedience is the greatest receptor as Th Most high knows the hearts of man and gives according to deeds and intent. If you are blissed with kingly hair i.e. 9 ether then good just be sure to feed it the right vibrations because gifts turn into curses when misused. The same goes for straight, curly, wavy or no hair. Do right and you receive right. Of course, I advise against the cutting of your hair no matter the texture as that is yours, a gift from Th all but if you've lost yours due to genetics or external factors just focus on the inner most of all and not the outer. Be Merry and stay humble and grounded because a tree is only as strong as the roots from which it stems.

- Religion: Christianity versus Islam. Buddhism versus Hinduism. Sufi versus Shiite. Protestants versus Catholics. Baptists versus Jehovah witnesses. All of this is nonsense and an utter disrespect to the common sense/wisdom of man. All one has to do is actually read these doctrine with open hearts and minds and not even in their entirety just a skim job will reveal that it's all connected. This is why we Moors in the past, the true ones left doctrines in the house when we convened with one another in ancient times. What we did bring was the best of our beliefs and faith and we thus we became fruitions of our teachings when interacting with our fellow Seastars and Brethren. We as beings are one but also unique unto ourselves which in turn means we resonate with different aspects of creation on different levels. For some nature is the greatest canvas of and best works of TH Creator, others it is the human body with all its passageways and circuitry, others it is the chambers of the mind and all its complexities and magnetism, for some it is the heart and the chambers that dwell within. So long as we all agree on and acknowledge the existence of Th higher force we're good which by the way doesn't necessarily have to be in the form of a doctrine or field of study. Just being humble and grateful is all the praise Th Most high requires and whatever we choose to master is only the gift of capability instilled in us by Th Creator serving as our best means of comfortable expression which only serves to cultivate the etheric cord of oneness with our maker bridging the gap from mortal to immortal. There are no big I's and small U's, we all have a gift, a different viewpoint and perspective and they should be protected, respected and shared respectfully/lovingly.

The 9 Catholic Lies

- Christ: From the Greek word Christos meaning "the anointed (one)." Anointed means to smear and smear is the act of spreading lies and slander. The Romans have socially engineered society to believe that Christ was a specific man when in actuality it is status, a divine rite of passage that is the transformation of man from beast, to human, and then to holiness. There were Kerest beings such as Yashuah (A.K.A Jesus), Musa (A.K.A Moses), Mohammed etc., those who were chosen and cultivated in the greatness and splendor of the womb and then thus fulfilled their purposes as healers, reformers and liberators. To be anointed is to be oiled with the divine secretion of the pineal gland which is the 1st eye though it is commonly referred to as the 3rd. This oil lights the torch which spawns Th flame of Supreme consciousness/awareness that is referred to as "godhood" or "sainthood" whereas the body begins to emanate a glow, an aura that is represented in many historical depictions as a nimbus or halo which serves as symbolism for the activation of and self-actualization of man's Supreme potential destiny whereby he becomes a direct reflection of the Universal light, the spectrum of all colors hence they are deemed "perfected". What men have done men can do and no man no matter how great is deserving of worship, but only Th source. Great men deserve great respect and honor, but never should they be held to stand next to Th Creator unless Th says so. Also, it must always be remembered that the only people that can save a people is Th people. Yashuah, though he healed, never actually saved anyone but rather it was the grace and humbleness that dwelled within the faithful's hearts and their willingness to listen, learn, accept and will that saved them. Another point, anity means without substance and if we know that Christ or Christos is the divine substance that when raised anoints the Son of God's crystal palace (Brain) then to be a Christian then is to be without that vital substance and incapable of induces the alchemical function to raise "The Dead" i.e., the lower-self merging and becoming totally subordinate with/to the Higher-self thus, why it was only in the past associated with Albions who unfortunately incarnated without such grace.

- Television: Tele-far + videre-to see. When you watch television, it is not you actually seeing but rather it is seeing far/deep into your subconscious mind whereby it plants the seeds of fear, greed, lust, envy, hatred, gluttony and pride. It is a portal that enables lower entities to suck your energy and essentially hypnotize you, placing you in a trance while they drain you of your essence. It is the main source of misinformation by which the beasts infects the minds of the world, turning people into believers and thus empowering illusions that only serve as distractions while all around they attempt to destroy all values and morality. In 1957 after world war II Pope John XXII said that, "cinema, sound broadcasting, and television are a far easier method for spreading the cause of Roman Catholicism than the written word is." In 1964 Pope Paul VI said, "it is the churches' birthright to use and own the press, cinema, radio, and television." These proclamations stemmed from the bull "directum inquisitorum" in 1584 by Pope Gregory XIII which officially gave Jesuits the right to deal in commerce and banking i.e. to control the money/currency. This has given them access and control over education/indoctrination, mass media, agriculture (Monsanto), and genetics (cloning; disease spawning and infestation).

- Holidays: Though most holidays do actually stem from ancient agricultural rituals they have been tainted by the atrocities of the modern world and thus should be shunned and avoided. No Moor should celebrate these days as they are symbolic of the ritualistic slaughtering of our ancestors and are days in which human blasphemy is on full display what with the over consumerism (greed), the overeating (gluttony), the drunkenness (revelry), the statue and fictional image worship (idolatry) and the mass amounts of satanic rituals done in secret where the main course is young children who are feasted upon, literally and figuratively. These are days for the vampires to fill themselves on the energy of the blind, death and dumb. (see Isaiah 10:3-5; Amos 5:21)

- Believe: The root word is lie. The prime word is belie which means "to give a false idea of; misrepresent", < Beleogian, be- be + leogan-lie. Synonyms are contradict, controvert, disprove, repute, and betray. This is why they always speak on believers in their secret documents and why they pray on these people the most because it is the power of belief that strengthens the adversary and keeps the charade going, though it is currently dying and will eventually fade. Unfortunately, so many will go down with it due to their voluntary ignorance. Th Most High Creator gifted us with minds so as to question which brings about answers especially when feelings and emotionalism is not in involved and personal opinions hold no sway thus they don't get in the way. This is why Th Creator even tolerates us questioning Th to a certain extent because Th knows that it gave us these inquisitive minds and truth needs no alibi. Righteousness heals the blind and pure hearts recognize Th king; the universe is mathematics and eventually it all adds up. Belief is for children, but it is necessary, but it is just the beginning and should not be the sole basis of one's life. The paradox is that you never stop believing because if you did you couldn't achieve anything, but it must be balanced with pragmatism and hard work which is the formula by which all of life's answers are revealed. In other words, to quote the magnanimous Noble Ali, "if you would ask me what to study, I would say yourselves; and when you well have studied them; and then would ask me what to study next, I would reply yourselves". (Holy Circle 7 Koran chp. 3:14). All these doctrines are but allegories and metaphors sprinkled with a touch of real situations that all symbolize and represent you; the good, the bad, the ugly, and the beautiful.

- Christian: can be traced back to the word cretin which means a deformed idiot. Deformed because you have separated Th Supreme force from you as something outside of yourself when salvation is within. Look toward history and you'll find that those who claimed Christianity were the most hateful and savage people known to man and like then commit the same atrocities today. Not trying to single out one group but Christianity is the main source of propaganda of the world and is basically a smear campaign that disguises itself as do gooders when they are deceivers, cowards and vandals. Any believer/idiot that places the words of man over the conscience of soul is the vessel of a Christian spirit whether they claim Muslim, Buddhists or any other doctrine. "The Christian cannot read his bible except through Jewish spectacles thus he reads it wrong."-Henry Ford. Christianity is in actuality a political appendage of the Roman curia and is used to brand and mark man as property of the beast/Vatican. The whole motive behind them forcing people into Christianity i.e. idol god worship was/is to dam them meaning to stop the flow of water/knowledge that is attained by way of application of Th divine sciences of nature which leads to liberation, immortality and evolution.

- Jesus: There is no j in Ibri (Hebrew) and in fact the letter j didn't even exist in the English lexicon until the 1500's. It is well established that Th title/attribute of Th Nazarene was Yeshua/Yehoshua. Another blatant lie is that he founded the Christian religion when in actuality he never claimed to be Christian as that would make him a traitor as it was the Christians/ Romans who persecuted the Yehudim, which is the correct term for the tribe of Yahudah (called Judah; who the so-called Jews have identity jacked; see revelation 2) and crucified Th messenger though not literally like they would have us believe. The image depicted as the so-called Jesus is actually a man by the name of Caesar Borgia. The theory is that people weren't too happy or enthusiastic about the catholic churches' regular massacres of the "Jews" (Yehudim) and Moslems (same nation different tribe), because they bore the likeness of Th Messiah (see revelations 1:13-14, 2:18, 18:12; Daniel 10:6). Pope Alexander VI then ordered the destruction of all art depicting a Semitic (modern term for Moors; used to describe and categorize the dark-skinned peoples who spoke Ibri, Arabic, Aramaic, Phoenician, and Assyrian, all of these being Moorish sects, tribes, and dialects) "Jesus" and commissioned a number of paintings depicting the aforementioned Borgia who was a cardinal and his son as the model for the new image of Christ. The painter was Leonardo Davinci who also happened to be Borgia's lover thus the nastiest of all the Borgia's became the iconic "Jesus" who is idolized by and that has graced the walls of many a "believer". The new Roman god: a vote was taken, and it was with a majority show of hands (161 votes to 157) that both deities become one god. Following long-standing heathen custom, Constantine used the official gathering and the Roman apotheosis decree to legally deify two deities as one and did so by democratic consent. A new god was proclaimed and "officially" ratified by Constantine (acta consili nicaeni, 1618). That purely political act of deification effectively and legally placed Hesus and Krishna among the Roman Gods as one individual composite. That abstraction lent Earthly existence to amalgamated doctrines of the empire's new religion; and because there was no letter "j" in the alphabets until around the 9th century or so, the name subsequently evolved into "Jesus Christ". (Hesus + Krishna) (Nexus magazine vol. 14 #4). So, this also dispels the Jehovah fraud as well since its origin/ attribute isn't ancient then it is a modern demonistic construct (see Strong's exhaustive concordance). Also, the Term Jew is fraud as well created only to give an identity to a people whose history they are too ashamed to claim so therefore they've reconstructed a false narrative that places them in antiquity when in actuality there existence only goes back at the most 6,000 years and no further which also dispels the whole Egypt slave myth as well seeing as the pyramids are well over 10,000+ years old which predates albions.

- Police: If you look closely you can see the lie in police. The general public calls them officers but they are not as they would have to be elected by the people to deserve that title and any time you call them that especially if you are a true American (sovereign and primitive to Th land) you transfer authority to them. They are privateers which according to black's law dictionary 4th ed. is a vessel owned, equipped and armed by one or more private individuals, and duly commissioned by a belligerent power to go on cruises and make war upon the enemy, usually praying on his finance. Another term would be highwayman which according to black's law 4th ed. is a bandit; one who robs travelers upon the highway. They are policy enforcers of Rome and they strong- arm citizens and others seeking finance, or body parts. This is why you never sign up to be an organ donor and if you are I suggest that you get that status removed as it is basically a license to kill and if you ever, Creator forbid, have an accident you will receive the slowest response because they have to collect on the promise you made.

- License: Another word if you look closely you can see the lie in it. This is an instrument of servitude perpetrated on the public to restrict movement thus limiting commercial opportunities. The fact is you do not need license to drive unless you are a professional i.e. taxi cab driver, bus driver, limo driver, delivery truck driver etc. If you are moving about in a non-commercial capacity then you are not driving but are traveling and such is your right commissioned and granted to you by Th Creator (see Genesis 1:26-28). You don't need a license to marry, practice law, or give birth for all of these are divine rights.
- Attorney: Derived from Old French Atorne, past participle of atorner- to assign, attorn; synonymous with agent. The prime root word attorn means to turn over (goods, services, etc.) to another; assign; transfer; to acknowledge the relation of tenant to a new landlord; to transfer homage and service to a new feudal lord. You are the goods and your time/energy are the services. When you go to court with a barrister as your representation you are basically placed on an auction block and at the whim and mercy of the tribunal. They are bounty hunters and are officers of the court; they all belong to the same club and take the same oath which binds their allegiance to the Bar association of England essentially making them knights of the Roman curia. As I've stated no license is required to demonstrate competence as you are the law and self-defense is mandatory as it is vital piece of self-preservation i.e. intelligence which is a gift of Th Most High and why you have a mind to think in the first place.

D. Modern Wickedness Manifested

I. Socialist Playbook

Saul Alinsky died about 50+ years ago, but his writings set a precedent and a blueprint that was/is used by leaders to control nations. His works include "Rules for radicals" and "Revelle for radicals". Obama wrote about him in his literary works and Hilary Clinton did her college thesis on his writings.

"How to Create a Social State" Saul Alinsky: "There are 8 levels of control that must be obtained before you are able to create a social state. The first is the most important:

1. Healthcare: control healthcare and you control the people.
2. Poverty: increase the poverty level as high as possible; poor people are easier to control and will not fight back if you are providing everything for them to live.
3. Debt: increase the debt to an unsustainable level. That way you are able to increase taxes, and this will produce more poverty.
4. Gun control: remove the ability to defend themselves from the government. That way you are able to create a police state.
5. Welfare: take control of every aspect of their lives (food, housing and income).
6. Education: take control of what people read and listen to; take control of what children learn in school.
7. Religion: remove the belief in the G-d from the government and schools.
8. Class warfare: divide the people into wealthy and the poor. This will cause more disconnect, and it will be easier to tax the wealthy with the support of the poor."

"The Rules for Radicals":

1. "Power is not only what you have, but what the enemy thinks you have." Power is derived from 2 main sources-money and people. "Have-nots" must build power from flesh and blood.
2. "Never go outside the expertise of your people." It results in confusion, fear and retreat. Feeling secure adds to the backbone of anyone.

3. "Whenever possible, go outside the expertise of the enemy." Look for ways to increase insecurity, anxiety and uncertainty.
4. "Make the enemy live up to his own book of rules." If the rule is that every letter gets a reply, send 30,000 letters. You can kill them with this because no one can possibly obey all of their own rules.
5. "Ridicule is man's most potent weapon." There is no defense. It's irrational. It's infuriating. It also works as a key pressure point to force the enemy into concessions.
6. "A good tactic is one your people enjoy." They'll keep doing it without urging and come back to do more. They're doing their thing and will even suggest better ones.
7. "A tactic that drags on too long becomes a drag." Don't become old news.
8. "Keep the pressure on. Never let up." Keep trying new things to keep the opposition off balance. As the opposition masters one approach, hit them from the flank with something new.
9. "The threat is usually more terrifying than the thing itself." Imagination and ego can dream up many more consequences than any activist.
10. "The major premise for tactics is the development of operations that will maintain a constant pressure upon the opposition." It is this unceasing pressure that results in the reactions from the opposition that are essential for the success of the campaign.
11. "If you push a negative hard enough, it will push through and become a positive." Violence from the other side can win the public to your side because the public sympathizes with the underdog.
12. "The price of a successful attack is a constructive alternative." Never let the enemy score points because you're caught without a solution to the problem.
13. "Pick the target, freeze it, personalize it, polarize it." Cut off the support network and isolate the target from sympathy. Go after people and not institutions; people hurt faster than institutions.

"*Absorb what is useful, discard what is not and add what is uniquely your own.*" – Bruce Lee.

Obviously, these tactics are flawed and are filled with glass but if you search through the rubble long enough with knowledge, wisdom and overstanding enough you're bound to find a gem. These are the tactics used so as to make you surrender your will which is to succumb to slavery and bow down to satan. To fight a war effectively you must know yourself which is in essence the same as knowing your enemy because we are all reflections of each other both negative and positive, light and dark, good and evil; they are but two extremes on the same pole and dwell within all creatures. To know your enemy is to know the worse of self and to know yourself is to know the best of your opposition.

II. Summation: Prophecy fulfilled

Times magazine article 1913, describing a meeting that took place Between Edward Mandell and Woodrow Wilson: "[Very] Soon, every American will be required to register their biological property (self and offspring) in a national system designed to keep track of the people and that will operate under the ancient system of pledging. By such methodology, we can compel people to submit to our agenda, which will affect our security as a chargeback for our fiat paper currency. Every American will be forced to register or suffer being unable to work or earn a living. They will be our chattel, and we will hold security interest over them forever, by operation of the law merchant under the scheme of secured transactions. Americans, by unknowingly or unwittingly delivering bills of lading to us will be rendered bankrupt and insolvent, forever to remain economic slaves through taxation secured by their pledges. They will be stripped of their rights and given commercial value designed to make us a profit and they will be none the wiser, for not one in a million could ever figure out our plans and, if by accident one or two should figure it out, we have in our arsenal plausible deniability. After all, this is the only logical way to fund government, by floating liens and debts to registrants in the form of benefits and privileges. This will reap to us huge profits beyond our wildest expectations and leave every American, contributor to this fraud which we will call 'social insurance'. Without realizing it, every American will insure us for any loss we may incur, and, in this manner, every American will unknowingly be our servant, however begrudgingly. The people will become helpless and without any hope for their redemption and, we will employ the high office of the president of our dummy corporation to ferment this plot against America".

The writing is on the wall my people but as was quoted by Voltaire, "it is difficult to free fools from the chains they revere." I was and am in many ways just as foolish as you were/are but I'm not the same fool I used to be plus I refuse to live in servitude to man or beast. The choice is yours.

(E) Synagogue of Satan

I. Jews: those who are not

"I know thy works, and tribulation, and poverty, (but thou art rich) and I know the blasphemy of them that say they are jews, and are not, but are the synagogue of Satan."-Revelations 2:9

Excerpts: The Harold Wallace Rosenthal Interview 1976: Hidden Tyranny Harold Rosenthal, an influential so-called jew learned in the "jewish ways" and involved in the workings of government in Washington D.C., explained the jewish involvement and the cause of major problems we face today. Conducted by Walter White, Jr.

"It is a marvel that the American people do not rise up and drive every jew out of this country." "We jews continue to be amazed with the ease by which Christian Americans have fallen into our hands. While the native Americans wait for Khrushchev to bury them, we have taught them to submit to our every demand." "It's a very simple matter...Americans have not had a presidential choice since 1932. Roosevelt was our man; every president since Roosevelt has been our man." "It is Zionist-communist policy from beginning to end. Yet the citizens think this jewish policy will benefit America." "We jews have put issue upon issue to the American people. Then we promote both sides of the issue as confusion reigns. With their eye's fixed on the issues, they fail to see behind every scene. We jews toy with the American public as a cat toys with a mouse." "The blood of the masses will flow as we wait for world victory." "...the naïve politicians in Washington are gullible. Most of them are not too bright so the powerful jewish lobbyists influenced this practice long ago and there is no one strong enough to stop it. Some of the money is even returned to the UNITED

STATES and spent on zionists propaganda efforts, much of it through the B'nai B'rith and the conference of jewish organizations and the world jewish congress. The jewish agency is a funding arm, a sort of body of B'nai officials. There is nothing wrong with sending American dollars to Israel tax-free so long as we are smart enough to get away with it..." "Anti-Semitism does not signify opposition to Semitism. There is no such thing. It is an expression we jews use effectively as a smear word used to brand a bigot...anyone who brings criticism against jews..."

"**During Christ's time, the jews were seeking a material and earthly kingdom but Christ offered the jews a spiritual kingdom. This they couldn't buy, so they rejected Jesus Christ and had him crucified.**": That's all he was a man who walked on the earth like any other man and this myth about Christ rising from the dead and returning to earth to visit with his disciples is a bunch of crap. The jews who drove the Arabs out of Palestine did so to disprove Christ's mission for a spiritual kingdom. You see, instead of a leader who would make an empire for the jews, your kind of people gave the jews a peaceful preacher called Christ who instead of an eye-for-an-eye turns the other cheek. Rubbish! We are building and, in fact, have built an earthly empire without your kind and your disappointing messiah."

"...so, if it benefits them to change their name they do so...they mix in your society which is plenty corrupt so while the jews are benefitting themselves the dumb goy doesn't realize that these jews with non-jew names are jews...in the foreseeable future there will be no presidential power in the United States. The invisible government is taking strength in that direction."

"The united-nations is nothing but a trap-door to the red world's immense concentration camp. We pretty much control the U.N." "It is an established rule to destroy all members of pre-existing government, their families and relatives, but never jews. They destroy all members of the police, state police, army officers and their families but never jews. You see, we know when a government begins to search for the communists within its borders they are really attempting to uncover jews in their area...the invisible rulers in the communist countries have world control over the propaganda and the governments in free countries. **We control every media of expression including newspapers, magazines, radio and television. Even your music! We censor the songs released for publication long before they reach publishers. Before long we will have complete control of your thinking.**" "There will be a forced class warfare here in the United States and many will be liquidated...and it is too late for the christian followers to put up a defense...**that is undoubtedly one of our great purposes in life. We are aggressors!**" "...the cultural and intellectual influence of Judaism is felt throughout the entire world- yes, throughout civilization."

"Money is more important than morality." "What good would it do? What the hell does the public know about the running of government. The great majority are asses-horses' asses."

"...few have the guts to speak out. We would all have a better understanding between each other-jews and gentiles-if we spoke out more openly. Your people don't have guts. We establish your thinking-we even place within you a 'guilt complex' making you afraid to criticize Jewry openly."

"At a very early date, urged on by the desire to make our way in the world, jews began to look for a means whereby we might distract all attention from the racial aspect. What could be more effective, and at the same time more above suspicion, than to borrow and utilize this idea of a religious community? We've been forced to borrow the idea from the Aryans. We jews never possessed any religious institution which developed out of our own consciousness, for we lack any kind of idealism. This means that a belief in life beyond this terrestrial existence is foreign to us. As a matter of fact, the Talmud does not lay down principles with which we prepare the individual for a life to come but furnishes only rules for a sumptuous life in this world. It is a collection of instructions for maintaining the jewish race and regulating intercourses between us and the goy. Our teachings are not concerned with moral problems, but rather with how to 'get'.

"In regard to moral value of the jews' religious teaching, there exist quite exhaustive studies which show the kind of religion that we have in a light that makes it look uncanny to the Aryan mind. We are the best example of the kind of product which religious training evolves. Our life is of this world only and our mentality is as foreign to the true spirits of Christianity as our character was to the founder of the new creed 2000 years ago. The founder of the Christianity made no secret of his estimation of the jews and the fact that he was not one of us. When he found it necessary he drove us out of the temple of God, because then, as always, we used religion as a means of advancing our commercial interest."

"But at the time, we managed to nail Jesus to the cross for his attitude towards us; whereas, the modern Christians enter into party politics and in order to win elections, they debase themselves by begging for jewish votes. They even enter into political intrigues with us against the interest of their own nation."

"We can live among other nations as long as we succeed in persuading them that the jews are not a distinct people, but are the representatives of a religious faith who, therefore, constitute a 'religious community', though this be of a peculiar character. As a matter of fact, this is the greatest of our falsehoods."

The jews have established 5 major falsehoods which work to conceal their nature and protect their status and power, to wit:

- The jews are Israelites, and thus god's chosen people (see Job 30:30; Lam. 5:10, 4:2, 4:8; Amos 9:7)
- Jesus Christ was a jew
- That 6 million jews were killed in the holocaust during World War II
- That all races are equal, or that all are brothers
- That jews are just another religious group

"We are obliged to conceal our own particular character and mode of life so that we will be allowed to continue our existence as a parasite among the nations. Our success in this time has gone so far that many believe that the jews among them are genuine Frenchmen, or Englishmen, or Italians, or Germans who just happen to belong to a religious denomination which is different from that prevailing in these countries. Especially in circles concerned with government, where the officials have only a minimum of historical sense, we are able to impose our infamous deception with comparative ease. Therefore, there is never the slightest suspicion that we jews form a distinct nation and are not merely the adherents of a 'confession'. Though one glance at the press which we control ought to furnish sufficient evidence to the contrary, even for those who possess only the smallest degree of intelligence."

"Our power has been created through the manipulation of the national monetary system. We authored the quptatio, 'money is power'. As revealed in our master plan, it was essential for us to establish a private national bank. The federal reserve system fit our plan nicely since it is owned by us, but the name implies that it is a government institution. From the very outset, our purpose was to confiscate all gold and silver, replacing them with worthless non-redeemable paper notes. This we have done!"

Prior to 1968, the gullible goy could take a one-dollar federal reserve not into any bank in America and redeem it for a dollar which was by law a coin containing 412 ½ grains of 90% silver. Up until 1933, one could have redeemed the same note for a coin of 25 4/5ths grains of 90% gold. All we do is give the goy more non- redeemable notes, or else copper slugs. But we never give them gold and silver. Only more paper...we jews have prospered through the paper gimmick. It's our method through which we take money and give only paper in return"

"The money question properly solved is the end of the jewish question and every other question of mundane nature."-Henry Ford

"At first, by controlling the banking system we were able to control corporation capital. Through this, we acquired total monopoly of the movie industry, the radio networks and the newly developing television media. The printing industry, newspapers, periodicals and technical journals had already fallen into our hands. The richest plum was later to come when we took over the publication of all school materials. Through these vehicles we could mold public opinion to suit our own purposes. The people are only stupid pigs that grunt and squeal the chants we give them, whether they be truth or lies."

"There is no such thing as the silent majority because we control their cry and their hue. The only thing that exists is an unthinking majority and unthinking they will remain, as long as their escape from our rigorous service is the opiate of our entertainment industry. By controlling industry, we have become masters and the people slaves. When the pressure of daily toil builds to an explosive degree, we have provided the safety valve of momentary pleasure. The television and movie industries furnish the necessary temporary distraction. These programs are carefully designed to appeal to the sensuous emotions, never to the logical thinking mind. Because of this people are programmed to respond according to our dictates, not according to reason. Silent they never are; thinking they will remain."

"We have castrated society through fear and intimidation. Its manhood exists only in combination with a feminine outward appearance. Being so neutered, the populace has become docile and easily ruled. As all geldings in nature, their thoughts are not involved with the concerns of the future and their posterity, but only with the present toil and the next meal."

Harold Wallace Rosenthal apparently talked "too freely" as he was killed in an alleged sky-jacking attempt on an Israeli airliner in Istanbul, Turkey, August 23, 1976. Four people were killed and some 30 injured during the sky-jacking but his bullet was the only one that wasn't random. This interview has a lot more content which can be viewed on rense.com; The Harold Wallace Rosenthal Interview by Serena Martin 6-28-05.

This is pretty cut and dry and speaks to all the phantasmagoria of this world and who is behind it. We have been divided and thus conquered by the true savages; those who we Moors could not civilize but who learned to spy and infiltrate by way of the Demi-gods and the weaknesses of our own lower natures. These are the true enemies, whom which our Caucasian and European sons and daughters were fleeing from when they sought refuge in Th North Gate, but this was forgotten and/or disregarded as they became possessed and fell in love with the lies/illusions of the sorcerers. The same is said for the Asiatics who are in all actuality responsible for the power that these beast wield and who till this day keep them in power though the time is up, and the pit has opened, and the seals have been removed. Judgment is here and the faithful shall prosper.

"Fear none of those things which thou shalt suffer: behold, the devil shall cast some of you into prison, that ye may be tried; and ye shall have tribulation ten days: be faithful unto death, and I will give thee a crown of life. He that hath an ear, let him hear what the Spirit saith unto the churches; He that overcometh shall not be hurt of the second death."-Revelation 2:10-11

II. 5 pillars of evil:

Excerpts from Ellis island museum:

1. Conquest: Despite the myth that North America lay "empty" and available for the taking, European explorers encountered over 200 different cultures whose ancestors had lived on this continent for thousands of years. Through armed conflict Europeans seized the land and claimed it for settlement. This often-

entailed enslaving, subjugating, or removing native peoples to reservations against their will. Disease was an unintended instrument of conquest-millions of native Americans died from foreign viruses to which they had no resistance.

Definition: the act of conquering; a thing conquered; land, people, etc., conquered; a winning of the affections, especially by persuasive courtship; a person whose love or favor has been won. < Old French conqueste < conquest, past participle of conquerre; see conquer < Latin conquirere < com-together + quaerere-seek.

2. Colonization: European nations colonized the Americas to exploit natural resources, engage in commerce, create new communities, and convert native peoples to Christianity. Spain, France, Holland, England, and other European powers claimed different parts of what would become the United States. They battled one another as well as native Americans to gain dominance and control trade and territory.

Definition: the establishment of a colony or colonies; Colony < Latin colonia-farm, settlement < colonus-cultivator, settler < colere- cultivate, inhabit. -Syn. Possession, dependency, dominion.

3. Migration: Beginning tens of thousands of years ago, people migrated to North America and the land that now makes up the United States. In the 16th century, new groups made the journey, coming from Europe, Africa, and Asia. Today, people continue to arrive in large numbers from every part of the globe. Regardless of when they journeyed, they left their homelands as "immigrants", who worked, struggled, and adapted to a new world.

Definition: a number of people or animals migrating together; a movement of one or more atoms from one place to another within the molecule; the movement of ions between the two electrodes during electrolysis. < Latin migrare (with English ate).

4. Enslavement: European colonial powers enslaved more than 10 million West Africans and transported them to the Americas and the Caribbean, half a million-enslaved people were brought to the United States. Forcibly moved across continents to fill a ravenous hunger for labor, these men and women created the agricultural might of the nation. Their enslavement played a role in both building the nation and in tearing it apart.

Definition: an enslaving; a being enslaved. < En-in + slave- < Old French esclave < Medieval Latin sclavus, later slavus-slav; slave < Late Greek sklabos (first applied to enslaved Slavs).

5. Annexation: "Annexation" is the claiming of new territories by the government through war, treaty, or purchase. The United States expanded its territory by annexing areas that had once belonged to other nations-especially native Americans, France, Spain, Russia, Mexico, and Hawaii. While the people who inhabited these annexed territories did not physically migrate, they still found themselves living in a new country and encountering new people and new challenges.

Definition: an annexing; a being annexed; something annexed. Annex= to join or add to a larger thing; to attach; to add to a book or other writings; append; to take as one's own or for one's own use; appropriate, especially without permission < Medieval Latin annexare < Latin annexus, past participle of anneciere < ad-to + neciere-bind.

Chapter 5: The Solution

A. Competence

I. Getting started

12 Things The Moor (misclassified Negro) Must Do for Himself By Nannie Helen Burroughs (circa 1930) :

1. The Moor (misclassified as Negro) Must Learn to Put First, The First Things Are: Education; Development of Character Traits; A Trade and Home Ownership. The Negro puts too much of his earning in clothes, in food, in show and in having what he calls "a good time". The Dr. Kelly Miller said, The Negro buys what he WANTS and begs for what he Needs". Too true!

2. The Moor (misclassified as Negro) Must Stop Expecting God and White Folk to Do for Him What He Can Do for Himself. It is "the Divine Plan" that the strong help the weak, but eve n God does not do for man what man can do for himself. The Negro will have to do exactly what Jesus told the man (in John 5:8 to do—Carry his own load--"take up your bed and walk".

3. The Moor (misclassified as Negro) Must Keep Himself, His Children and His Home Clean and Make the Surroundings In Which He Lives Comfortable and Attractive. He must learn to "run his community up" --not down. We can segregate by law; we integrate only by living. Civilization is not a matter of race; it is a matter of standards. Believe it or not--someday, some race is going to outdo the Anglo-Saxon completely. It can be the Negro race, if the Negro gets sense enough. Civilization goes up and down that way.

4. The Moor (misclassified as Negro) Must Dress More Approximately for Work and For Leisure Knowing what to wear--how to dress it--when to wear it and where to wear it, are. Earmarks of common sense, culture and also an index to character. The Negro Must Make his Religion an Everyday Practice and Not Just A Sunday Go-To-Meeting Emotional Affair.

5. The Moor (misclassified as Negro) Must Highly Resolve to Wipe Out Mass Ignorance. The leaders of the race must teach and inspire the masses to become eager and determined to improve mentally, morally and spiritually, and to meet the basic requirements of good citizenship. We should initiate an intense literacy campaign in America, as well as in Africa, Ignorance--satisfied ignorance--is a millstone about the neck of the race. It is democracy's greatest burden. Social integration is a relationship attained as a result of the cultivation of kindred social ideals, interests and standards. It is a blending process that requires time, understanding and kindred purposes to achieve. Likes alone and not laws can do it.

6. The Moor (misclassified as Negro) Must Stop Charging His Failures Up to His "Color" And to White People's Attitude. The truth of the matter is that good service and conduct will make senseless race prejudice fade like mist before the rising sun. God never intended that a man's color shall be anything other than a badge of Distinction. It is high time that all races were learning that fact. The Negro must first QUALIFY for whatever position he wants. Purpose, initiative, ingenuity and industry are the keys that all men use to get what they want. The Negro will have to do the same. He must make himself a workman who is too skilled not to be wanted, and to too DEPENDABLE not to be on the job, according to promise or plan. He will never become a vital factor in industry until he learns to put into his work the vitalizing force of initiative, skill and dependability. He has gone "RIGHTS" mad and "DUTY" dumb.

7. The Moor (misclassified as Negro) Must Overcome His Bad Job Habits He must make a brand-new reputation for himself in the world of labor. His bad job habits are absenteeism, funerals to attend, or a little business to look after. The Negro runs an off and on business. He also has a bad reputation for conduct on the job--such as petty quarreling with other help, incessant loud talking about nothing; loafing, carelessness due to lack of job pride; insolence, gum chewing and -too often—liquor drinking. Just plain bad job habits!

8. He (The Moor) Must Improve His Conduct in Public Places Taken as a whole, he is entirely too loud and too ill—mannered. There is much talk about wiping out racial segregation and also much talk about achieving integration.. Segregation is a physical arrangement by which people are separated in various services. It is definitely up to the Negro to wipe out the apparent justification or excuse for segregation. The only effective way to do it is to clean up and keep clean. By practice, cleanliness will become a habit and a habit becomes character.

9. The Moor (misclassified as Negro) Must Learn How to Operate Business for People--Not For Negro People, Only. To do business, he must have to remove all typical "earmarks", businesses practices; measure up to accepted standards and meet stimulating competition, graciously--in fact, he must learn to welcome competition.

10. The Average So-Called Educated Moor (misclassified as Negro) Will Have to Come Down Out of The Air, He Is Too Inflated Over Nothing. He Needs an Experience Similar To The One That Ezekiel Had— (Ezekiel 3:14-19). Otherwise, through indifference, as to the plight of the masses, the Negro, who thinks that he has escaped, will lose his own soul. It will do all leaders to read Hebrew 13:3, and the first Thirty-seven Chapters of Ezekiel. A race transformation itself through its own

leaders and its sensible "common people". A race rises on its own wings or is held down by its own weight. True leaders are never "things apart from the people". They are the masses. They simply got to the front ahead of the masses. Their only business at the front is to inspire to masses by hard work and noble example and challenge them to "Come on!" Dante stated a fact when he said, "Show the people the light and they will find the way!" There must arise within the Negro race a leadership that is not hunting bargains for itself. A noble example is found in the men and women of the Negro race, who, in the early days, laid down their lives for the people. Their invaluable contributions have not been appraised by the "latter-day leaders". In many cases, their names would never be recorded, among the unsung heroes of the world, but for the fact that white friends have written them there. "Lord, God of Hosts, be With Us Yet". The Negro of today does not realize that, but, for these exhibits A's, that certainly show the innate possibilities of members of their own race, white people would not have moved to make such princely investments in lives and money, as they have made, for the establishment of schools and for the on-going of the race.

11. The Moor (misclassified as Negro) Must Stop Forgetting His Friends, "Remember". Read Deuteronomy 24:18, Deuteronomy rings the big bell of gratitude. Why? Because an ingrate is an abomination in the sight of God. God is constantly telling us that "I the Lord thy God delivered you"—through human instrumentalities The American Negro has had and still has friends—in the North and the South. These friends' contributions for the advancement of the race--for their brothers in bonds. The noblest thing that the Negro can do is to live and labor that these benefactors will not have given in vain. The Negro must make his heart warm with gratitude, his lips sweet with thanks and his heart and mind resolute with purpose to justify the sacrifices and stand on his feet and go forward--"God is no respector of persons. In every nation, he that feareth Him and worketh righteousness is" sure to win out. Get to work! That's the answer to everything that hurts us. We talk too much about nothing instead of redeeming the time by working. R-E-M-E-M-B-E-R In spite of race prejudice, America is brim full of opportunities, Go after them, but with integrity and principles always which stems from knowledge of Self!

Tools you will need:

Henry Campbell Black's law dictionary 1st-4th ed. (editions after are less reliable and convoluted), old testament bible, Vedas, Buddhists manuals, Emerald tablets, Circle 7, The Qur'an, "History of the Moorish Empire in

Europe" Vol. 1-3 by S.P. Scott, "Story of the Moors In Spain" by Stanley Lane Poole, "The Golden Age Of the Moors", by Ivan Van Sertema, unabridged dictionaries (older) , etymological dictionaries, thesaurus, comprehensive dictionary, oxford dictionary, Holy Tablets, Declaration of Independence, Organic American Constitution of 1791, Articles of Confederation, Bill of rights, Articles of Association, Kyballion, Clock of destiny 1 & 2, Secret mysteries of the Brotherhood of the East, Zodiac Constitution, Library of congress, "Nature Knows no Color line" by David McRitchie chp. 6, Declaration of Decolonization, Declaration of the rights of Indigenous peoples, Declaration on the rights of a child, Latin to English dictionary, English to Latin dictionary, Hebrew to English dictionary, English to Hebrew dictionary, Greek to English dictionary, English to Greek dictionary, spanish to English dictionary, English to spanish dictionary, Metu Neter, numerology, treaty of peace and friendship, George Washington's letter to the sultan of Morocco, ordinance of 1787, organic 13th amendment, Hammurabi codes, Moorish Empire-18th century books, The kabala, books on Hindustani history and philosophy, The Mauryan Dynasty in Perot/Hindustan (also Nanda/Gupta), studies of ancient central American culture, cosmology, astrology and other ancient eastern culture philosophies, multiple law dictionaries on ancient and modern jurisprudence, Dead sea scrolls, Egyptian Book of Life (dead), advanced yoga lessons, multiple sets of old encyclopedias, African religious philosophies, The torah/tenakh, two versions of the sepuginta, and let these be a foundation yet always viewed with discretion and let the journey begin from your intuition and pure heartedness.

These are holy books and points of reference but tread wisely. These are mirrors of what you already are and serve to exercise the genetic greatness that lies dormant within. In other words, we have been blinded and these serve as glasses to help us see better which means we then have the responsibility to do better. Remember that words are spells and that you cannot be too sure of or in what spirit the book you read was written in so take nothing at face value, compare, examine and trust your gut. Also, be mindful to pace yourself and don't overstand your innerstanding before you innerstand your overstanding.

Note: Whatever you can't find physically at yard sales, flea markets and goodwill stores can be obtained through Pdf files online. Here are websites who offer invaluable info: Rvbeypublications.com, Also, you can find a lot of valuable info on YouTube via these people who have personally helped in my maturation: Da13th Sun, Yaffa Bey, Taj Tarik Bey, Dolo King Of the Moors, Judah Son, Moreno Bey, Mantis Views29, Moorish American 720, Moors In America, Abdullah El Talib Mosi Bey, Rasmariah Bey, SetenRa Bey, Hakim Bey, Cannanland Moors, Dr. Phil Valentine, IAMHH, Dr. Sebi.

II. Techniques of Study:

- Do not pass any word that you do not comprehend
- Good lighting and clean water
- Know and master the 8 parts of speech
- Make sure to have the aforementioned tools as points of reference and clarification; take nothing at face value

III. Law

Jurisprudence is the science and philosophy that treats "positive law" and the administration of the same. It is the study of the nuance and structure of the legal systems and/or their forms, as opposed to or distinguished from, the content of the said legal or law systems, jurisprudence is more akin to analytical comparison of systems of law. The root of jurisprudence is derived from the old Moorish Latin words juris meaning law and prudentia meaning knowledge.

Positive law is law actually and specifically enacted or adopted by proper authority for the government of an organized jural society. "A law; in the sense in which that term is employed in jurisprudence, is enforced by a sovereign political authority. It is thus distinguished not only from all rules which, like the principles of morality and the so- called laws of honor or fashion, are enforced by an indeterminate authority, but also from all rules enforced by a determinate authority which is either, on the one hand, super human, or, on the other hand, politically subordinate in order to emphasize the fact that "laws", in the strict sense of the term, are thus authoritatively imposed, they are described as positive laws." (Holl. Jur. 37)

The first order of law is **Natural Law.** These are **Universal Principles** which so necessarily agrees with nature and state of man, that without observing their inherent maxims, the peace and happiness of society can never be preserved. Knowledge of natural laws may be attained merely by the light of reason, from the facts of their essential agreeableness with the constitution of human nature. Natural law exists regardless of whether it is enabled as positive law.

When law began to emerge into human consciousness, thought, word and deed we come to the next order of law on this planet. The most fundamental law of all human law has to do with survival which is a universal principle. It has to do with human interactions, of any kind, any relationships, buying, selling or trading or relating in any way. It is based upon treating or dealing with others the way you would like to be treated or dealt with. This is the **Law of Commerce**. The Law of Commerce has been in operation since man interacted with each other starting many thousands of years ago through the Sumerian/ Babylonian era where it was codified and enforced. Ancient artifacts dating over 6,000 years old reveal that the system was so complex it even included receipts, coined money, shopping lists, manifestos and a postal system with the medium being in baked clay.

As a derivative of commercial law, being removed from natural law, and therefore inferior, is **Commercial Law** (co-together + munis- service, gift, exchange; to exchange together). This emerged basically, in England out of disputes over a portion of the earth in allodium (sovereign ownership of land) and was based on "common" sense. So, common law is the law of the earth. Common law gave rise to the jury system and many writs and processes which governments have absorbed and statualized and made into rules and regulation processes in courts.

Common law procedures were based on the opportunity "to face your accuser or the injured party" in front of witnesses to sort out the problem directly. This process was never intended to include "lawyers, attorneys or judges construing their own law", as these "titles" are all based upon the fiction of "representation" which can never be the real thing.

After common law come governments, and their laws and legislatives regulations, ad infiinitum (without limit; to an infinite extent; indefinitely) of the organic republics of the states. The only "law" the central government, United States of America, could create was to "allow commerce to flow more efficiently between the states." It was never intended to regulate people- the sovereigns.

Below that, the "garbage froth", more or less, is politics and the private copyrighted company policy of foreign corporations such as UNITED STATES, THE STATE OF...THE COUNTY OF...THE

CITY OF..., etc. The purpose of these "municipalities" (munis-gift, exchange, servive + capere-to take; to take service and exchange) is to "govern" fictitious entities such as JOHN DOE and K-MART- not to regulate people. Remember back when you thought YOU were JOHN DOE because that is how it is written on your driver's license?

One of our problems is that when we engage with government, municipalities and other such elements, in all our dealings in the law we have been conditioned to interact on and in THEIR level. We have never risen to the level where the base of law is, where the reality, the power, the solidity and the pre-eminence exists- the Sovereign's level.

But now, we can function on this powerful level. This is check mate.

This is the end of the game. This is the remedy.

The principles, maxims and precepts of Commerce law are eternal, unchanging and unchangeable. They are expressed in the Bible, both Old and New Testament. This law of commerce, unchanged for thousands of years, forms the underlying foundation for all law on this planet and for the governments around the world. It is the law of Nations and everything that human civilization is built upon. This is why it is so powerful. When you operate at this level, by these precepts, nothing that is of inferior statute can overturn or change it or abrogate it or meddle with it. It remains the fundamental source of authority and power and functional reality.

IV. Affidavits (Writs)

Affidavit: A written or printed declaration or statement of facts, made voluntarily, and confirmed by the oath or affirmation of the party making it, taken before an officer having authority to administer such oath. June v. School Dist. No. 11, Southfield Tp., 283 Mich. 533, 278 N.W. 676, 677, 116 A.L.R. 581. Any voluntary ex parte statement reduced to writing and sworn to or affirmed before some person legally authorized to administer oath or affirmation, made without notice to adverse party and without opportunity to cross-examine. Kirk v. Hartlieb, 193 Ark. 37, 97 S.W.2d 434, 435, 436. The word sometimes includes "depositions." U. S. v. Kaplan, D.C.Ga., 286 F. 963, 970.

"Affidavits" are of two kinds; those which serve as evidence to advise the court in the decision of some preliminary issue or determination of some substantial right, and those which merely serve to invoke the judicial power. Worthen v. State, 189 Ala. 395, 66 So. 686, 688. (Black's Law 4th edition).

Commerce in everyday life is the vehicle or glue that holds, or binds, the corporate body politic together. More specifically, commerce consists of a mode of interacting, doing business, or resolving disputes whereby all matters are executed under oath, certified on each party's commercial liability by sworn affidavit, or what is intended to possess the same effect, as true, correct, and complete, not misleading, the truth, the whole truth and nothing but the truth.

The affidavit is usually required for an application for a driver's license, and IRS form 1040, a voter's registration, a direct Treasury account, a Notary "Copy Certification" or certifying a document, and on nearly every single document that the system desires others to be bound or obligated. Such means of signing is an oath, or commercial affidavit, executed under penalty of perjury, "true, correct, and complete." Whereas in court setting testimony (oral) is stated in judicial terms by being sworn to be "the truth, the whole truth, and nothing but the truth, so help me god."

In addition to asserting all matters under solemn oath of personal, commercial, financial, and legal liability for the validity of each and every statement, the participant must provide material evidence, i.e. ledgering, or bookkeeping, providing the truth, validity, relevance, and verifiably of each and every particular assertation to sustain credibility. Commerce is antecedent to and more fundamental to society that courts or legal systems and exists and functions without respect to courts or legal systems. Commercial law, the non-statutorily variety as presented below in Maxims 1-11, is the economic extension of Natural Law into man's social world and is universal in Nature. The foundational, invariant, necessary, and sufficient principles or "Maxims of Commerce" pertaining herein: Maxims of Law

1. **Workman is worthy of his hire:** Exodus 20:15; Leviticus 19:13; Matthew 10:10; Luke 10:7; II Timothy 2:6. Legal Maxim: "It is against equity for freemen not to have the free disposal of their own property."
2. **All are equal under TH Law (G-d's Law-Moral and Natural Law.)**: Exodus 21: 23-25; Leviticus 24: 17-21; Deuteronomy 1:17, 19:21; Matthew 22: 36-40; Luke 10:17; Colossians 3:25. "No one is above Th law."
3. **In commerce Truth is Sovereign**: Exodus 20:16; Psalms 117:2; John 8:32; II Corinthians 13:8. "To lie is to go against the mind."-Oriental Proverb; "of all that is good, sublimity is supreme."
4. **Truth is expressed in the form of an affidavit**: Leviticus 5: 4-5, 6: 3-5, 19:11-13; Numbers 30:2; Matthew 5:33; James 5:12
5. **An unrebutted affidavit stands as truth in commerce**: Peter 1:25; Hebrew 6:13-15. Legal Maxim: "He who does not deny, admits."
6. **An unrebutted affidavit becomes the judgment in commerce**: Hebrew 6: 16-17.
7. **In commerce for any matter to be resolved it must be expressed**: Hebrew 4:16; Philippians 4:6; Ephesians 6: 19-21. Legal Maxim: "He who fails to assert his rights has none."
8. **He who leaves the battlefield first loses by default**: This means that an affidavit not rebutted point for point stands as "truth in commerce" as such action as non-response signifies acquiescence, consent and acknowledgement. Book of Job; Matthew 10:22. Legal Maxim: "He who does not repel a wrong when he can, occasions it."
9. **Sacrifice is the measure of credibility (no willingness to sacrifice= no liability, responsibility, authority or measure of conviction**: Acts 7. Legal Maxim: "He who bears the burden ought also to derive the benefit."
10. **Satisfaction of a lien**: Genesis 2-3; Matthew 4; Revelations. In commerce a lien

or claim can be satisfied in any of 3 ways: 1) by someone rebutting your affidavit point for point, with another affidavit, until the matter is resolved as to whose correct, in the case of non-resolution; 2) you convene a sheriff's common law jury, based on the seventh amendment, concerning a dispute involving a claim of more than $20. Or, you can use three disinterested parties to make judgment; 3) the only other way to satisfy a lien is to pay it. Legal Maxim: "If the plaintiff does not prove his case, the defendant is absolved."

11. **A lien or claim can only be satisfied through a rebutted affidavit by an affidavit point for point, resolution by jury, or payment.**

These maxims are supported by the spirit of Isonomy and are corroborated by public law 97-280 whereas it was deemed that the Bible is the foundation and basis of law in this society which also coincides with the Qu'ran, the daughter of the Bible. This is why so- called Jewish lawyers are considered the best because they study the tenakh/torah and practice Mosaic law which is the foundation of the modernized systems of legal processes.

Commercial law is non-judicial. This is pre-judicial (without prejudice). This is timeless. This is the base, the foundation beneath which any government or any of their court systems can possibly exist or function.

Due to the fact that the Union States' Corporate-State Agencies and Quasi-Government agencies have instituted 'Colorable' practices of Birthrights theft, it is in the Natural Persons' best interest to notify or to give declaratory affidavits of facts to all parties of interest. These shall serve as notice to principles of and to agents, that there shall be no assumed jurisdiction in matters concerning Moorish American Nationals.

In ideal circumstances (when government is operating to Constitutional limitations), such protocols would be less necessary. However, the fact remains that the opposite is true! Corrupt government officials and personnel on all levels, federal, state, county and local, are consistently violating the Constitution to which they are bound to support and uphold! Thus, necessitating the unorthodox issuing of writs on a massive scale. The point of the writs being sent to the various departments is to notify them of criminal activities among the local and state officials. They have a fiduciary obligation to act or to pass the complaints on to the properly authorized government agency to investigate the criminality. If not, they too, are in conspiracy in such matters. The paper trail of evidence produced by active Moors and other constitutionally-Loyal citizenry, affirms these facts 'for the record'! Keep in mind that article III, section 2 of the Constitution also deals with matters of 'Diversity of Citizenship' in controversies to which the United States is a party. Thus, the governmental positions of ministers and consuls come into play in international relationships, even in territories where different nations may be operating in the same territory.

Be cognizant at all times the rule of law that is key to dealing with, and maintaining, good government. It is called "The Separation of Powers"; the Constitution for the United States Republic of North America is based on that principle. A clear consciousness of this government principle must be present in the mental processes of all right-law reasoning natural persons. It is also an important measure for distinguishing and identifying the barriers and limits of 'jurisdiction' in all and any legal argument or controversy before any court or tribunal, or subject matter in government. Notice to the principal is notice to the agent and notice to the agent is notice to the principle.

No court or judge can overturn or disregard or abrogate someone's affidavit of truth. The only one who has any capacity or right or responsibility or knowledge to rebut your affidavit of truth is the one who is adversely affected by it. It's your job, your right, your duty and responsibility to speak for yourself because no one else can rightfully speak for you; you are who you say you are. No one else can know what your truth is or has the free-will responsibility to state it. This is **Your** job!

V. Jurisdiction (Juris= right + Diction=Words)

The word is a term of large and comprehensive import and embraces every kind of judicial action. Federal Land Bank of Louisville, Ky., v. Crombie, 258 Ky. 383, 80 S.W.2d 39, 40; McGowin v. McGowin, 122 Fla. 394, 165 So. 274, 275, 276. It is the authority by which courts and judicial officers take cognizance of and decide cases. Board of Trustees of Firemen's Relief and Pension Fund of City of Marietta v. Brooks, 179 Okl. 600, 67 P.2d 4, 6; Morrow v. Corbin,

122 Tex. 553, 62 S.W.2d 641; State v. Barnett, 110 Vt. 221, 3 A.2d 521, 526; the legal right by which judges exercise their authority. Max Ams, Inc. v. Barker, 293 Ky. 698, 170 S.W.2d 45, 48; It exists when court has cognizance of class of cases involved, proper parties are present, and point to be decided is within issues. Noxon Chemical Products Co. v. Leckie, C.C.A.N.J., 39 F.2d 318, 319; United Cemeteries Co. v. Strother, 342 Mo. 1155, 119 S.W.2d 762, 765; Harder v. Johnson, 147 Kan, 440, 76 P.2d 763, 764. (Black's Law 4th ed.)

If you are proceeding in a court, for yourself, on your own behalf; in person, then it would be necessary to know the 3 'main' factors at law, prior to proceeding (pro se).

3 Factors of Jurisdiction:

- You must first state **<u>your person</u>** as a proper person, "in propria persona", which sets your (1st factor) Status (your standing in the community and your standing at/in law). This sets **<u>personum jurisdiction</u>**; determining if the court has jurisdiction over you; your person.
- Subject matter/venue jurisdiction. This is where you ask for the judicial authority of the court (D.O.A.O) to determine if the court even has jurisdiction over the subject matter(s), in regard to what you may be proceeding about.
- Adjudication, wherein they impose sentencing, fines, penalties, punishments, and imprisonment as remedy for the injury you have done. Before proceeding to adjudication there **<u>must</u>** be an injured party before the court, for you to bring remedy to. Your accuser must be present, for the record in court. These are proper procedures in court and must be identified before you proceed (pro se). One must be careful **<u>not</u>** to proceed (pro se) in a courtroom, that is colorable and has no jurisdiction. Most courts (tribunals) are colorable (fictitious), therefore going pro- se is not advised. They cannot lawfully adjudicate, but to find out ask for their Delegation of Authority, not just their oath of office, but the D.O.A for that said court. Don't be fooled by an oath. The oath is a request that one would make for them to present the state's obligation to uphold the constitution and implicates them when they go against.

These 3 factors are Universal to any court. In essence status (personum jurisdiction) sets the stage, because if they have no jurisdiction over you, they have no jurisdiction over the matter. They could have jurisdiction over the matter, but not have jurisdiction over you. Jurisdiction is important, that is why it is the first issue of law. Once the issue of jurisdiction is placed before the court, it must be satisfied before the court can proceed, and the issue of jurisdiction can be brought up at any time. This is a fine line for the court to confuse pro se and in propria persona, although they are two distinctly separate things. These criminals take opportunity to use a little trickery, to trip you up, and gain jurisdiction early in the game over you, right at the juncture where you are in the process of stating your status for the record that sets the stage to determine whether the court has jurisdiction over you in order that it may proceed.

Law Terms:

- **VISIT**. In international law. The right of visit or visitation is the right of a cruiser or war-ship to stop a vessel sailing under another flag on the high seas and send an officer to such vessel to ascertain whether her nationality is what it purports to be. It is exercisable only when suspicious circumstances attend the vessel to be visited; as when she is suspected of a piratical character. (Black's Law 4th ed.)
- **VISITATION**. Inspection; superintendence; direction; regulation. Bank of America Nat.Trust & Savings Assn v. Douglas, 70 App.D.C. 221, 105 F.2d 100, 105, 123 A.L.R. 1266. As applied to corporations, means, in law, the act of a superior or superintending officer who visits a corporation to examine into its manner of conducting business and to enforce an observance of its laws and regulations. Kawfield Oil Co. v. Illinois Refining Co., 169 Okl. 75, 35 P.2d 961, 963. Also, a power given by law to the founders of all eleemosynary corporations. 2 Kent, Comm. 300-303; 1 Bl. Comm. 480, 481. In England, the visitation of ecclesiastical corporations belongs to the ordinary. 1 Bl.Comm. 480, 481. See Trustees of Union Baptist Assn v. Hunn, 7 Tex. Civ.App. 249, 26 S.W. 755; Thompson v. Southern Connellsville Coke Co., 269 Pa. 500, 112 A. 533, 534. (Black's Law 4th ed.)
- **OF**. A term denoting that from which anything proceeds; indicating origin, source, descent, and the like; as, he is of a race of kings; he is of noble blood. Stone v. Riggs, 43 Okl. 209, 142 P. 298, 299. Associated with or connected with, usually in some causal relation, efficient, material, formal, or final. Harlan v. Industrial Accident Commission, 194 Cal. 352, 228 P. 654, 657. The word has been held equivalent to after, 10 L.J.Q.B. 10; at, or belonging to, Davis v. State, 38 Ohio St. 506; in possession of, Bell County v. Hines, Tex.

Civ.App., 219 S.W. 556, 557; Stokes v. Great Southern Lumber Co., D.C.Miss., 21 F.2d 185, 186; manufactured by, 2 Bing. N.C. 668; by, Hannum v. Kingsley, 107 Mass. 355; residing at, Porter v. Miller, 3 Wend. (N.Y.) 329; 8 A. & E. 232; from, State v. Wong Fong, 75 Mont. 81, 241 P. 1072, 1074; in, Kellogg v. Ford, 70 Or. 213, 139 P. 751, 752. (Black's Law 4th ed.)

- **FOR.** In behalf of, in place of, in lieu of, instead of, representing, as being which, or equivalent to which, and sometimes imports agency. Medler v. Henry, 44 N.M. 63, 97 P.2d 661, 662. During; throughout; for the period of; as, where a notice is required to be published "for" a certain number of weeks or months. Wilson v. Northwestern Mut. L. Ins. Co., C.C.A.Kan., 65 F. 39, 12 C.C.A. 505; Northrop v. Cooper, 23 Kan. 432; Burdine v. Sewell, 92 Fla. 375, 109 So. 648, 653. Duration, when put in connection with time. Progressive Building & Loan Assn v. McIntyre, 169 Tenn. 491, 89 S.W.2d 336, 337. In consideration for; as an equivalent for; in exchange for; in place of; as where property is agreed to be given "for" other property or "for" services. Norton v. Woodruff, 2 N.Y. 153; Duncan v. Franklin Tp., 10 A. 546, 43 N.J.Eq. 143; Mudge v. Black, Sheridan & Wilson, C.C.A.Mo., 224 F. 919, 921. Belonging to, exercising authority or functions within; as, where one describes himself as "a notary public in and for the said county." By reason of; with respect to; for benefit of; for use of; in consideration of. Basler v. Sacramento Electric, Gas & Ry. Co., 166 Cal. 33, 134 P. 993, 994; Elmore-Schultz Grain Co. v. Stonebraker, 202 Mo.App. 81, 214 S.W. 216, 221; Work v. U. S., ex rel. Rives, 54 App.D.C. 84, 295 F. 225, 226. The cause, motive or occasion of an act, state or condition. American Ins. Co. v. Naylor, 103 Colo. 461, 87 P.2d 260, 265. Used in sense of "because of," "on account of," or "in consequence of." Kelly v. State Personnel Board of California, 31 Ca1.App.2d 443, 88 P.2d 264, 266. By means of or growing out of. Cormier v. Hudson, 284 Mass. 231, 187 N.E. 625, 626. (Black's Law 4th ed.)
- **AUTOMOBILE GUEST.** A person who is received and entertained in the automobile of another. Chanson v. Morgan's Louisiana & T. R. & S. S. Co., 18 La.App. 602, 136 So. 647, 649. Linn v. Nored, Tex.Civ.App., 133 S.W.2d 234, 237. (Black's Law 4th ed.)
- **PASSENGER.** A person whom a common carrier has contracted to carry from one place to another, and has, in the course of the performance of that contract, received under his care either upon the means of conveyance, or at the point of departure of that means of conveyance. Bricker v. Philadelphia & R. R. Co., 132 Pa. 1, 18 A. 983, 19 Am.St. Rep. 585; Schepers v. Union Depot R.

Co., 126 Mo. 665, 29 S.W. 712; Pennsylvania R. Co. v. Price, 96 Pa. 256; The Main v. Williams, 14 S.Ct. 486, 152 U.S. 122, 38 L.Ed. 381; Horne v. Southern Ry. Co., 186 S.C. 525, 197 S.E. 31, 35, 116 A.L.R. 745. One carried for hire, or reward, as distinguished from a "guest" who is one carried gratuitously, that is, without any financial return except such slight benefit as is customary as part of the ordinary courtesy of the road. Duncan v. Hutchinson, 139 Ohio St. 185, 39 N.E.2d 140, 142. (Black's Law 4th ed.)

- **AUTOMOBILE**. A vehicle for the transportation of persons or property on the highway, carrying its own motive power and not operated upon fixed tracks. Blashfield's Cyclopedia of Automobile Law, vol. 1, c. 1, § 2. Etymologically, the term might include any self-propelled vehicle, as an electric street car, or a motor boat, but in popular and legal usage it is confined to a vehicle for the transportation of persons or property on terrestrial highways, carrying its own motive power and not operated upon fixed tracks. Bethlehem Motors Corporation v. Flynt, 178 N.C. 399, 100 S.E. 693, 694. Synonymous with "motor vehicle." State v. Ferry Line Auto Bus Co., 99 Wash. 64, 168 P. 893, 894. "Car" as substitute or synonym. Monroe's Admr v. Federal Union Life Ins. Co., 251 Ky. 570, 65 S.W.2d 680, 681. Taxicabs included. Navy Gas & Supply Co. v. Schoech, 105 Colo. 374, 98 P.2d 860, 864, 126 A.L.R. 1225. Trolley vehicles or trolley busses excluded. City of Dayton v. Lie Brosse, 62 Ohio St. 232, 23 N.E.2d 647, 650. (Black's Law 4th ed.)
- **DRIVER**. One employed in conducting or operating a coach, carriage, wagon, or other vehicle, with horses, mules, or other animals, or a bicycle, tricycle, or motor car, though not a street railroad car. A person actually doing driving, whether employed by owner to drive or driving his own vehicle. Wallace v. Woods, 340 Mo. 452, 102 S.W.2d 91, 97. (Black's Law 4th ed.)
- **DRIVING**. To urge forward under guidance, compel to go in a particular direction, urge onward, and direct the course of. Mould v. Travelers' Mut. Casualty Co., 219 Iowa 16, 257 N.W. 349. (Black's Law 4th ed.)
- **TRAVELER**. One who passes from place to place, whether for pleasure, instruction, business or health. Lockett v. State, 47 Ala. 45; 10 C.B.N.S. 429. (Black's Law 4th ed.)
- **TRAVEL**. To go from one place to another at a distance; to journey; spoken of voluntary change of place. White v. Beazley, 1 Barn. & Ald. 171; Hancock v. Rand, 94 N.Y. 1, 46 Am.Rep. 112; State v. Smith, 157 Ind. 241, 61 N.E. 566, 87 Am. St.Rep. 205. (Black's Law 4th ed.)

- **REPRESENT**. To appear in the character of; personate; to exhibit; to expose before the eyes. To represent a thing is to produce it publicly. Dig. 10, 4, 2, 3; In re Matthews, 57 Idaho, 75, 62 P.2d 578, 580, 111 A.L.R. 13. To represent a person is to stand in his place; to supply his place; to act as his substitute. Plummer v. Brown, 64 Cal. 429, 1 P. 703; Seibert v. Dunn, 216 N.Y. 237, 110 N.E. 447, 449. (Black's Law 4th ed.)
- **REPRESENTATION**. Any conduct capable of being turned into a statement of fact. Scandrett v. Greenhouse, 244 Wis. 108, 11 N.W.2d 510, 512. (Black's Law 4th ed.)
- **MISREPRESENTATION**. An intentional false statement respecting a matter of fact, made by one of the parties to a contract, which is material to the contract and influential in producing it. (Black's Law 4th ed.)
- **REPRESENTATION OF PERSONS**. A fiction of the law, the effect of which is to put the representative in the place, degree, or right of the person represented. Civ.Code La. art. 894. (Black's Law 4th ed.)
- **MISPRISION**. A word used to describe a misdemeanor which does not possess a specific name. 3 Inst. 36; United States v. Perlstein, C.C.A.N.J., 126 F.2d 789, 798. But more particularly and properly the term denotes either (1) a contempt against the sovereign, the government, or the courts of justice, including not only contempt of court, properly so called, but also all forms of seditious or disloyal conduct and leze-majesty; (2) maladministration of high public office, including peculation of the public funds; (3) neglect or light account made of a crime, that is, failure in the duty of a citizen to endeavor to prevent the commission of a crime, or, having knowledge of its commission, to reveal it to the proper authorities. 4 Bl.Comm. 119-126; State v. Biddle, 124 A. 804, 805, 2 W.W.Harr., Del. 401. (Black's Law 4th ed.)
- **NEGATIVE MISPRISION**. The concealment of something which ought to be revealed; that is, misprision in the third of the specific meanings given above. (Black's Law 4th ed.)
- **POSITIVE MISPRISION**. The commission of something which ought not to be done; that is, misprision in the first and second of the specific meanings given above. (Black's Law 4th ed.)
- **CONSTITUTIONAL PSYCHOPATHIC INFERIORITY**. Individuals who show a lifelong and constitutional tendency not to conform to the customs of the group, and who habitually misbehave, and have no sense of responsibility to their fellowmen or to society as a whole. These individuals fail to learn

by experience and are inadequate, incompatible, and inefficient. State ex rel. Pearson v. Probate Court of Ramsey County, 205 Minn. 545, 287 N.W. 297, 300; Wilson v. Walters, al.App., 112 P.2d 964. (Black's Law 4th ed.)

- **ALLODIAL.** Free; not holden of any lord or superior; owned without obligation of vassalage or fealty; the opposite of feudal. Barker v. Dayton, 28 Wis. 384; Wallace v. Harmstad, 44 Pa. 499. (Black's Law 4th ed.)

- **RES.** Lat. In the civil law. A thing; an object. As a term of the law, this word has a very wide and extensive signification, including not only things which are objects of property, but also such as are not capable of individual ownership. Inst. 2, 1, pr. And in old English law it is said to have a general import, comprehending both corporeal and incorporeal things of whatever kind, nature, or species. 3 Inst. 182- Bract. fol. 7b. By "res," according to the modern civilians, is meant everything that may form an object of rights, in opposition to "persona," which is regarded as a subject of rights. "Res," therefore, in its general meaning, comprises actions of all kinds; while in its restricted sense it comprehends every object of right, except actions. Mackeld. Rom. Law, § 146. This has reference to the fundamental division of the Institutes, that all law relates either to persons, to things, or to actions. Inst. 1, 2, 12. In modern usage, the term is particularly applied to an object, subject- matter, or status, considered as the defendant in an action, or as the object against which, directly, proceedings are taken. Thus, in a prize case, the captured vessel is "the res." And proceedings of this character are said to be in rem. (See In Personum; In Rem.) "Res" may also denote the action or proceeding, as when a cause, which is not between adversary parties, is entitled "In re". (Black's Law 4th ed.)

- **RES JUDICATA.** A matter adjudged; a thing judicially acted upon or decided; a thing or matter settled by judgment. A phrase of the civil law constantly quoted in the books. Epstein v. Soskin, 86 Misc.Rep. 94, 148 N.Y.S. 323, 324; Rule that final judgment or decree on merits by court of competent jurisdiction is conclusive of rights of parties or their privies in all later suits on points and matters determined in former suit. American S. S. Co. v. Wickwire Spencer Steel Co., D.C.N.Y., 8 F.Supp. 562, 566. And to be applicable, requires identity in thing sued for as well as identity of cause of action, of persons and parties to action, and of quality in persons for or against whom claim is made. Freudenreich v. Mayor and Council of Borough of Fairview, 114 N.J.L. 290, 176 A. 162, 163. The sum and substance of the whole rule is that a matter once judicially decided is finally decided. Massie v. Paul, 263 Ky. 183, 92 S. W.2d 11,

14. See, also, Res Adjudicata, supra. Estoppel and res judicata distinguished. See estoppel. (Black's Law 4th ed.)

- **ORGANIC LAW**. The fundamental law, or constitution, of a state or nation, written or unwritten; that law or system of laws or principles which defines and establishes the organization of its government. St. Louis v. Dorr, 145 Mo. 466, 46 S.W. 976, 42 L.R.A. 686, 68 Am.St.Rep. 575. (Black's Law 4th ed.)
- **NATURAL LAW**. This expression, "natural law," or jus naturale, was largely used in the philosophical speculations of the Roman jurists of the Antonine age, and was intended to denote a system of ales and principles for the guidance of human conduct which, independently of enacted law or of the systems peculiar to any one people, might be discovered by the rational intelligence of man, and would be found to grow out of and conform to his nature, meaning by that word his whole mental, moral, and physical constitution. The point of departure for this conception was the Stoic doctrine of a life ordered "according to nature," which in its turn rested upon the purely supposititious existence, in primitive times, of a "state of nature;" that is, a condition of society in which men universally were governed solely by a rational and consistent obedience to the needs, impulses, and promptings of their true nature, such nature being as yet undefaced by dishonesty, falsehood, or indulgence of the baser passions. Maine, Anc.Law, 50, et seq.; Jus Naturale. (Black's Law 4th ed.)

Here are some additional law terms that you should know: Allodium, ab intio, arbitrary, acts, prima facie, power of attorney, ward ship, artifice, association, identity, identification card, name, nomen, appellation, ward ship, abandonment, extort, conspiracy, rescission of contract, dissolve, dissolution in contracts, dissolution in practice, dissolution in corporation, disclaimer, negotiable instrument, adhesion, nunc pro tunc, abrogate, attribute, proclaim, jus sanguinis, jus soli, substantive, substantive law, estate, gender, natural born day, malfeasance, prejudice, prejudicial error, jus gentium, domicile (national, municipal, domestic and quasi-national), domiciled, de facto, de jure, escheat, hereditaments (corporeal and incorporeal), birthright, residence, resident, ancestral, ancestral estate, heir, inheritance, land, mailing location, autograph, liberty (civil, conscience, contract, speech, personal, natural, political, religious), rights (natural, civil, political, personal), all rights reserved, privilege, retained, charter, freehold estate, estoppel, quo warranto, aboriginal, primitive, primogeniture, jus, jus praetorioum, jus precarium, jus priesens, divine, law, united states, united codes of law, federal, union, general and permanent character, constitution, treaty, treaty of peace, ipso jure, ipso facto, sine die, en legis, matrimonium, competent, competent court, incompetent

VI. Cases (points of reference)

13 Supreme Court cases (stare decisis):

1. The Right to Travel; The Right to Mode of Conveyance; The Right to Locomotion are all absolute rights, and the Police can not make void the exercise of rights. **State v. Armstead, 60 s. 778, 779, and 781**:
2. The use of the highways for the purpose of travel and transportation is not a mere privilege, but a common and fundamental right of which the public and Natural Beings cannot be rightfully deprived. **Chicago Motor Coach v. Chicago 337 Illinois 200, 169 NE 22, ALR, Ligare v. Chicago 139 ILL. 46, 28 HE 934, Boone v. Clark 214 SW 607, 25 AM jur (1st), Highways, sec. 163**:
3. The right to Park or Travel is part of the Liberty of which the Natural Person, citizen cannot be deprived without "due process of law" under the Fifth Amendment of the United States Constitution. **Kent v. Dulles 357 US 116, 125**:
4. The Right of a citizen to Travel upon the public highways and to transport one's property thereon, either by carriage or automobile, is not a mere privilege, which a City may prohibit or permit at will, but a common right, which he / she has under the right to life, liberty, and the pursuit of happiness. **Thompson v. Smith 154 SE 579**:
5. State Police Power extends only to immediate threats to public safety, health, welfare, etc., **Michigan v. Duke 266 US, 476 Led. At 449: which driving, and speeding are not. California v. Farley Ced. Rpt. 89, 20 CA3d 1032 (1971)**:
6. The State is prohibited from violating substantive rights. **Owens v. City, 445 US 662 (1980)**; and it can not do by one power (e.g. Police power) that which is, for example, prohibited expressly to any other such power (e.g. Taxation / Eminent Domain) as a matter of law. **US and UT v. Daniels, 22 p 159**, nor indirectly that which is prohibited to it directly. **Fairbanks v. US 181, US 283, 294, 300**:
7. Traveling in an automobile on the public roads was not a threat to the public safety or health and constituted no hazard to the public, and such a traveler owed nothing more than "due care" (as regards to tort for negligence) to the public and the owner owed no other duty to the public (e.g. State), he / she and his / her auto, having equal rights to and on the roadways / highways as horses and wagons,

etc.; this same right is still substantive rule, in that speeding, running stop signs, traveling without license plates, or registration are not threats to the public safety, and thus, are not arrestable offenses. **Christy v. Elliot, 216 I 131, 74 HE 1035, LRA NS 1905 – 1910: California v. Farley 98 CED Rpt. 89, 20 CA 3d 1032 (1971).**

8. Under the United States Republic's Constitutional system of Government and upon the individuality and intelligence of the citizen, the state does not claim to control one's conduct to others, leaving one the sole judge as to all that affects oneself. **Mugler v. Kansas 123 US 623, 659 – 60**:

9. Where rights secured by the Constitution are involved, there can be no rule-making or legislation, which would abrogate them. **Miranda v. Arizona 384 US 436, 125**:

10. The claim and exercise of Constitutional Rights cannot be converted into a crime. **Miller v. Kansas 230 F 2nd 486, 489**:

11. For a crime to exist there must be an injured party (Corpus Delicti). There can be no sanction or penalty imposed on one because of this Constitutional right. **Sherer v. Cullen 481 F. 945**:

12. If any Tribunal (court) finds absence of proof of jurisdiction over a person and subject matter, the case must be dismissed. **Louisville v. Motley 2111 US 149, 29S. CT 42**. "The Accuser Bears the Burden of Proof Beyond a Reasonable Doubt".

13. "Lack of Federal Jurisdiction can not be waived or overcome by agreement of parties". Griffin v. Matthews, 310 F supra 341, 342 (1969): and "Want of Jurisdiction" may not be cured by consent of parties." Industrial Addition **Association v. C.I.R., 323 US 310, 313**.

Additional cases:

- "Writing is 'void ab initio' in the case of fraud in the inception, and it need not be formerly rescinded as a prerequisite to the right of avoidance." **Bonacci v. Massachusetts bonding ins. Co., (1943) 58 ca 2d 657, 664**:
- "...waivers of constitutional rights, not only must they be voluntary, they must be knowingly intelligent acts done with sufficient awareness". **Brady v. U.S., 397 U.S. 742, 748**:
- A judgment may not be rendered in violation of constitutional protections. The validity of a judgment may be affected by a failure to give the constitutionally required due process notice and an opportunity to be heard. **Earle v. McVeigh, 91 US 503, 23 l Ed 398**:
- One may be employed, do business, and enter into other contracts and sue

and be sued under any name they choose at will. **Lincoln v. First National Bank 10 F. 894, Coppage v. Kansas 236 U.S. 1, in Re Mculta 189 F. 250:**

- The judicial or court method of changing one's name, is merely an affirmance and aid of the "common law". Thus, the common law, by superiority, establishes 'supreme validation', and suffices to serve public notice for declaration of a name correction and change, the 'court method' of corroborating a 'name correction and change' is not to be assumed as necessary nor superior, but merely a formalized method of confirming or acknowledging a person's right to name correction or change; such a change carries the exact same legal weight as a court decreed name change as long as it is not done with fraudulent intent. **In Re Mculta 189 F. 250, Christianson V. King County 196 F. 791, United States V. Mckay 2 F. 2d 257:**
- An order that exceeds jurisdiction of the court, is void, or voidable, and can be attacked in any proceeding in any court where the validity of the judgment comes into the issue. **Rose v. Himely (1808) 4 Cranch 241, 2l Ed 608:**
- The Supreme Court ruled that a police officer could not arrest a citizen merely for refusing to present identification. **Kolander v. Lawson 461 U.S. 352, 1983:**
- "The constitution is a written instrument. As such, its meaning does not alter. That which it meant when it was adopted, it means now." **S. Carolina V. U.S., 199 U.S. 437, 448(1905):**
- "We are bound to interpret the constitution in the light of the law as it existed at the time it was adopted". **Mattox v. U.S., 156 US 237, 243:**
- "If a court grants relief, which under the circumstances it hasn't any authority to grant, its judgment is to that extent void". **1 Freeman on Judgments, 120c**; "A void judgment is no judgment at all and is without legal effect." **Jordan v. Gilligan, 500 F. S2d 701, 710(6th Cir. 1974)**; "a court must vacate any judgment entered in excess of jurisdiction. " **Lubben V. Selective Service System Local Bd. No 27, 453 F. 2d 645(1st Cir. 1972)**.
- "The people of the united states resident within any state are subject to two governments: one state, and the other national, but there need be no conflict between the two." **United States v. Cruikshank, 92 U.S. 542 (1876)**
- "An unconstitutional act is not law; it confers no rights no duties; affords no protection; it creates no office; it is in legal contemplation, as inoperative as though it had never been passed. **Norton v. Shelby County, 118 U.S. 425**
- A <u>**writ**</u> may be void because it is defective in language, because the court had no jurisdiction to issue the writ; **Big Torts 122 Nixon v. Reeves**, 65 Minn.

159, 67 news 989, 33 L.R.A. 506. See Bouviers Law Encyclopedia Rawles 3rd revision Pg. 1182.

- The clerk of the court who issues a **defective writ**, or one not authorized by the court, is liable; **and so is a judge who orders a writ which he had no right to issue or where he had no jurisdiction.** Big Torts 128. See Bouviers Law Encyclopedia Rawles 3rd revision Pg. 1182.
- "The court is to protect against any encroachment of Constitutionally secured liberties." **Boyd v. U.S. 616**
- A self-executing constitutional provision is defined as immediately effective without the necessity of ancillary legislation. **Clery v. Kincaid, 23 Idaho, 789, 131 P. 1117, 1118; Stange v. City of Cleveland, 94 Ohio St. 377, 114 N.E. 261, 262.** Full faith and credit via article 4 section 1.
- "A state cannot impose restrictions on the acceptance of a license that will deprive the license of his constitutional rights." **Rukenbrod v. Mullins, 10 Utah 548, 133 P.2d. 325, 144 ALR 839.**
- "No state shall convert a liberty into a privilege, license it, and attach a fee to it." **Murdock v. Penn., 319 US 105**
- "The practice of law cannot be licensed by any state/State." **Schware v. Board of Examiners, United State Reports 353 U.S. pages 238, 239.**
- Licenses are for the conduct of a business, profession, occupation, the exercise of such when they are a privilege. Licensing is in the nature of a SPECIAL PRIVILEGE entitling license to do something that he would not be entitled to do without a license. **San Francisco v. Liverpool, 74 Cal 113.**
- A "person" driving in an automobile cannot be stopped to see if he or she is licensed to "drive" unless there is reasonable suspicion the "person" has engaged in criminal conduct. **Delaware v. Prouse, (1979) 440 US 648, 59 Led 2d 660**
- The courts are not bound by an officer's interpretation of the law under which he presumes to act. **Hoffsomer v. Hayes, 92 Okla 32, 227 F. 417**
- "If a state converts a liberty into a privilege, the citizen can engage in the right with impunity." **Shuttlesworth v. Birmingham, 373 US 262**
- A right that which is free and open to all is not the subject of a license or tax. **Chicago v. Collins, 51 NE 907; Freeburg v. Dawson 274 F. 240**
- "Traffic infractions are not a crime." **People v. Battle, 50 Cal. App. 3 step 1, 123 Cal. Rptr. 636. 639.**

- "The practice of law is an occupation of common right." **Sims v. Ahern, 271 SW 720 (1925)**
- Where a private occupational statute exists, of which the intent is regulation of private commercial occupations, the particular agency enforcing a private statue, shall not apply it by trickery and deceit, and threat and misrepresentation, to persons regulated and taxed, nor should it permit any party to do so, in violation of persons' right to stay out of compelled contract, when he is not a person subject to the statute, unless clearly with its words. **State v. Eberhard, 179 P. 853; 246 p. 2d 1011.**
- **Federal Rules of civil procedures, rule 17, 28 USCA "Next Friend"**. A next friend is a person who represents someone who is unable to tend to his or her own interest.
- Litigants can be assisted by unlicensed laymen during judicial proceedings. **In Argersinger**, "No accused may be deprived of, his liberty as the result of any criminal prosecution, whether felony or misdemeanor, in which he was denied assistance of counsel." **Railroad Trainmen v. Virginia Bar, 377 U.S. (1964) Gideon v. Wainright, 372 U.S. 335 (1963) Argersinger v. Hamlin 407 U.S. 25 (1972) 10-5015**
- Members of groups who are competent non-lawyers can assist other members of the group achieve the goals of the group in court without being charged with "unauthorized practice of law". **NAACP v. Button, 371 U.S. 415; United Mineworkers of America v. Gibbs, 383 U.S. 715; Johnson v. Avery, 89 S. Ct. 747 (1969)**
- "Officers of the court have no immunity, when violating a constitutional right, from liability. For they are deemed to know the law." **Owen v. Independence, 100 S.C.T/ 1398, 445 US 622**
- State governments are but trustees with a derived authority. **4 Wheat 402**
- Administrators defined government succinctly: "Governments are corporations", in as much as every government is an artificial person, an abstraction, a creature of the mind only, a government can only deal with artificial persons. The imaginary, having no reality or substance cannot create or attain parity with the real (living). **Penhallow v. Doane's**
- If you have relied on prior decisions of the Supreme Court, you have the perfect defense for willfulness. **U.S. v Bishop, 412 US 346**

Simple words such as "person" "citizen" "people" "or" "nation" "crime" "charge" "right" "statute" "preferred" "prefer" "constitutor" "creditor" "debtor" "debit" "discharge" "payment" "law" and "United States" doesn't mean what we think it does because we were never taught the legal definitions of the above words.

Whenever demonstrating law always be mindful of two things: Confidence and Control. Keep these two thoughts within your consciousness at all times. Confidence is the spawn of preparation and control is the daughter of patience. Think before you react and react with thinking; as in decisive and calculated action. There are always risk and nothing is 100% but trust your instincts and be More/Mr.

VII. Dzsetention: Prisoners in your own land

The accused may demur to the complaint when it shall appear upon the face thereof either as follows:

- That the court has no jurisdiction of the person (defendant/accused); or of the subject of the action; or
- The plaintiff has no legal capacity to sue; or
- There is another cause of action pending between the same parties for the same cause; or
- There is a defect of parties, plaintiff or defendant: (emphasis on the nom deguerre); or
- Several 'causes of action' have been improperly united; or
- The complaint does not state facts sufficient to constitute a cause of action.

**Reference/source of law: John Bouviers Institutes of American Law #3270 subsection 144 (122)*

By the law of nations, no state is bound to recognize slavery of another state. (Source of law: John Bouviers Institutes of American Law #168 "Book of Persons" page #37)

"A valid and sufficient accusatory instrument is a non-waivable jurisdictional prerequisite to a criminal prosecution." **People v. Case, 42 Ny 2d 98, 99 [1977]**

The jailer is liable for the escape of prisoners lawfully in arrest, and if the arrest is illegal, he is free from all liability. He (the jailer) may, therefore in his defense show that the court issuing the process had no jurisdiction. **Able v. Ward, 8 Mass. 791** or; that the process was void.

Therefore, where a copy of process was left with the jailer as his warrant, he may justify an escape by showing such a copy to be on its face void; he is not bound to look beyond the copy, and the validity of the process itself is not material. **Kidder v. Barker, 18 Vt. 454** (reference of law: John Bouviers Institutes of American Law Book of Wrongs #2338 pg. 629)

One who has been kidnapped or stolen away, "or" a freeman who has been taken by robbers and reduced to slavery is not a slave. (Reference of law: John Bouviers institutes of American law #165 Book of Persons pg.37)

Where a person who is not vested by law, with authority to make an arrest, attempts to do so, he acts as a private citizen, and one who opposes him therein is not guilty of opposing an officer; **U.S. Baird, 48 fed. 554.** John Bouviers Concise Encyclopedia of Law Francis Rawles 3rd revision pg. 2397.

The right of self-defense extends to injuries committed against the limbs and the body of a man, and the aggressor may even be killed, if the person attacked has no other means of saving himself. (Reference of law: John Bouviers institutes of American Law excerpt from #204 pg. 50)

Negro Act of 1740: The comprehensive Negro Act of 1740 passed in South Carolina made it illegal for slaves to move abroad, assemble in groups, raise food, earn money, and learn to write English (though reading was not proscribed). Additionally, owners were permitted to kill rebellious slaves (chattel property) if necessary.

Dred Scott Case: Dred Scott v. John F.A. Sandford. 60 US 393 19 Howard 393: Judgement reversed, and Scott dismissed for lack of Jurisdiction. Judgment for defendant, C.C.D. Mo. Persons of African descent cannot be, nor were ever intended to be, citizens under the U.S. Constitution. Plaintiff is without standing to file a suit. **Argued February 11-14, 1856 Re-argued December 15-18, 1856 Decided March 6, 1857; Supreme Court of the United States.**

See also case of Elizabeth Freeman (Mum Bet), Anthony Burns, and Abdu'l Rahman Ibrahim Ibn Sori, William Dungey case of 1855, organic 13th Amendment, Christian Black Codes of 1724, Willy Lynch letter, Sundry Free Moors Act, 12 USC (united states code of law) 95a, Buck Act of 1940, Articles Of Incorporation United States Service Company, House Joint Resolution 192 73rd Congress 1933 March 17 vol. 33, pg. H-1303, James Trafficant speech on U.S. bankruptcy, International Organization Immunities act of 1941,USC Title 8 sub-section 126

The fact is we do not owe any debts (see U.S. Constitution, Article 6) and our karmic debt has also been paid as well, which was about 400 years of servitude, ended in 2000-2001. However, when we keep using language such as, "my congressman, my public representatives, our democracy, officers, judges, our war" etc., we bind ourselves to these demons hence the national debt which is nothing more than the souls/spirits of the original Asiatics of Northwest Amexem (Moors/Muurs) whose spirits were/are hypothecated via negotiable instruments such as marriage contracts, birth certificates, mortgages which means dead pledge, social security, voting etc. These people are imposters and the I.R.S is not a lawful institution, and neither is the Federal Reserve so therefore we need to come out of the mentality that we owe anything to these interloping Roman crusaders. The only thing we owe is to each other and that is love (see Bible Romans 13:8-13). This is the time of jubilee/yubilee meaning a time to profess and proclaim our freedom and inheritance. All of those Asiatic/Moors who continue to serve two masters and dishonor their mothers and fathers will be eliminated and bound to eternal servitude along with their masters, the beast of Rome. News is entertainment and entertainment is news, meaning that all these movies, though sprinkled with lies as well, are telling an overall narrative and provide a blueprint of what is to come. Get out, the purge, magnificent 7, are all telling you the future of the traitors and the responsibility of the knowing which is to come together and shed their beastly ways. See also Robin hood with Morgan Freeman, Black Knight with Martin Lawrence and Wild Wild West with Will Smith. All these movies admit to who we are.

VIII. Protocols of A Noble (de jure):

1. Walk true in your standing (don't be artificial/fake)
2. Know who you are and where you come from i.e. your lineage (study; See Hosea 4:6)
3. Act with high standards (it's always the right time to do the right thing)
4. Act with good intent (don't be a shady opportunist; selfish)
5. Be humble and gracious
6. Be compassionate
7. Be diplomatic at all times
8. Be prepared not scared
9. Be confident and proud of who and what you are
10. Be committed to freedom
11. Be a protector (Seastar and Brethren's keeper; each one teach one)
12. Be Loyal/Royal
13. Be real

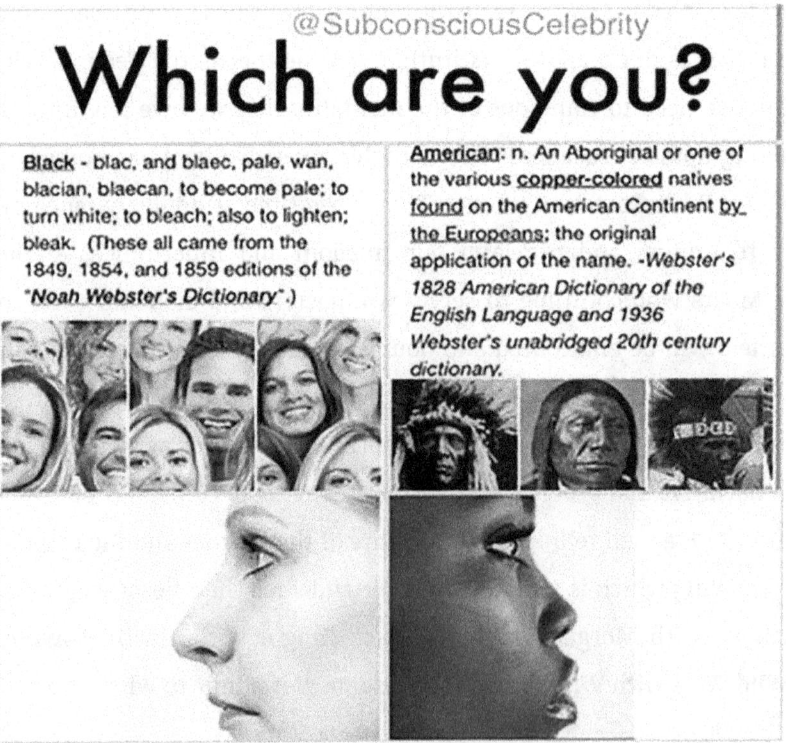

B. Balance

I. Return of the Matriarch: Power of the Womb

A tree will never encompass the entire earth, the earth will never outgrow the heavens and man will never be as powerful and as forceful as Th Creator because nothing can surpass its source, it can only serve to be a worthy or unworthy reflection of its predecessor/maker.

The duality of positive and negative energies manifested as female and male, yin and yang were created at the same time, there is and always will be a hierarchy, an order by which Th Supreme Force wills to be. In other words, there will always be a first, a second and so forth. As it happens that fist was Female, and she was/is made is the closest image of Th Universe and thus she has the power of the womb which receives the spark of life and incubates the souls of those sent on their journey, those who have navigated and passed unseen trials and tribulations so as to conquer others in this realm of the flesh. Of course, we were taught different, but the confirmation of the aforementioned statement is the universal birthmark we all share, a belly button, which symbolizes that we had an umbilical cord which means we came by natural birth through the womb of man, the word man by the way means being, so it includes both energies not just those with testicles. If you don't have a belly button then most likely you are a clone or something else entirely.

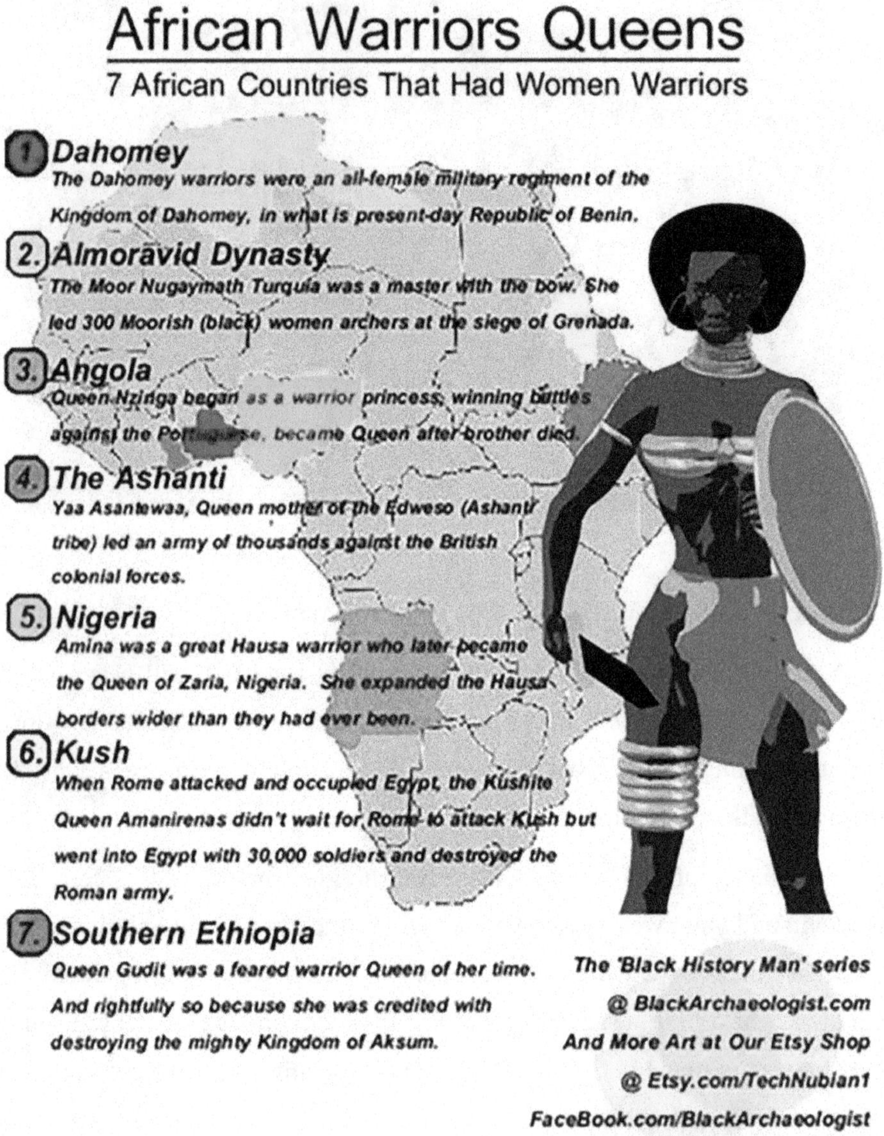

African Warriors Queens

7 African Countries That Had Women Warriors

1 Dahomey
The Dahomey warriors were an all-female military regiment of the Kingdom of Dahomey, in what is present-day Republic of Benin.

2. Almoravid Dynasty
The Moor Nugaymath Turquia was a master with the bow. She led 300 Moorish (black) women archers at the siege of Grenada.

3. Angola
Queen Nzinga began as a warrior princess, winning battles against the Portuguese, became Queen after brother died.

4. The Ashanti
Yaa Asantewaa, Queen mother of the Edweso (Ashanti tribe) led an army of thousands against the British colonial forces.

5. Nigeria
Amina was a great Hausa warrior who later became the Queen of Zaria, Nigeria. She expanded the Hausa borders wider than they had ever been.

6. Kush
When Rome attacked and occupied Egypt, the Kushite Queen Amanirenas didn't wait for Rome to attack Kush but went into Egypt with 30,000 soldiers and destroyed the Roman army.

7. Southern Ethiopia
Queen Gudit was a feared warrior Queen of her time. And rightfully so because she was credited with destroying the mighty Kingdom of Aksum.

The 'Black History Man' series
@ BlackArchaeologist.com
And More Art at Our Etsy Shop
@ Etsy.com/TechNubian1
FaceBook.com/BlackArchaeologist

Painting in the Larco museum in Lima Peru. This painting depicts the Inca Emperors, and the subsequent European Emperors of the Inca. It begins with Manco Cápac the legendary first Sapa Inca (top left side), and his sister Mama Huaco (top right side). This painting also depicts Holy Roman Emperor Charles V (Carlos Quinto) as the first European Emperor of the Inca, (the rest were Spanish Kings).

The painting can be dated circa 1800: because the last two entries are Carlos Tercero (Charles III) as the 24th Inca Emperor, and his son Carlos Quarto (Charles IV) House of Bourbon, as the 25th Inca Emperor. Charles IV reigned as king of Spain from December 14, 1788 to March 19, 1808 (abdicated in favor of his son Fernand VII).

Empress Khalifa of whom the territory California was named

There is an old African proverb that says, "If you teach a man you teach an individual but if you teach a woman you teach a nation." Every woman born comes into this realm with enough eggs to populate an entire continent. Mitochondria DNA is only inherited from the mother. It's not a mixture of both parents' genes, like nuclear DNA, so it preserves a family record that isn't scrambled in every generation. The word mitochondria is from New Latin < Greek mitos- warp, thread + Khondrion, diminutive of khondros, meaning grain or granule. If a woman fails to have a daughter her genes disappear, because the mitochondria DNA doesn't pass on. The same we were taught that a family name disappears if a son is not born, so it is with mitochondria. This was a deliberate attempt by beast to suppress the dominating gene in women, by placing the philosophy that without a son, the family lineage dies. This of course is not true. The information stored in the mitochondria DNA is what is known as the "Akashic Records". These records are a repository of information that exist in the astral realm. It is a complete and thorough record of everything that has ever occurred, including the thoughts and feelings of every individual, through all time. The word "Akasaa" comes from Sanskrit and means "Primary substance" or "Ether".

This is the science behind the seeming destruction and dumbing down of the masses because of the mental and spiritual subjugation of women. If you want to know the condition of a society or the trajectory of its future look at the condition of the females and that'll give you a clear-cut answer as to was is and will be the problem/solution.

Women have always been noted as being smarter and wiser than us males because quite simply they have to be. Because the female is responsible for raising the children (the future), nature has endowed the female with the best eyesight, the best hearing, the best feeling (intuition), the best reflexes, and the best cunning. They say hell hath no fury like a women scorned but heaven have no better beauty that a female born; not just in the obvious sense of birth but in the true essence of the meaning being that she knows herself and respects herself to the utmost level and is reborn into the true Divine being that she is.

The soul of woman, being that she was first, is older therefore she has been down the longest because she fell first and afterwards we sons fell so her level of trauma is at a higher degree than ours. It's like someone falling out of a building on the 3rd floor as opposed to one who fell out of the 13th. Yes, both may actually die but chances are the latter will have far more serious injuries than the former one; broken legs as opposed to brain damage. She has been through so much and has gone from the most respected to the most neglected but in a lot of ways she did it to herself. She is the problem which means that she is the solution. They say behind every great male is a female because she is the one that pushes us forward and what was first will be last and what is last shall be first. The order, however, can never truly be reversed because as long as she bleeds so will the earth and when she is healed so will the earth be restored and cured.

Facts of Reverence, Guidance and Appreciation:

A human body can bear only up to 45 del (unit) of pain. Yet at the time of giving birth a mother feels up to 57 del of pain. This is similar to 20 bones getting fractured at the same time. Can you imagine it now, the mother's pain and devotion/love?

Egyptian (Kamatan) women gave birth sitting down so gravity assisted the baby's exit, permitting less forceful contractions. Doctors probably did not assist at childbirth.

Female ejaculate is called "Amrita", which means "nectar of bliss". If a woman is basically healthy and emotionally balanced it is a healing elixir for males; it actually is an elixir of longevity for males, so in such a case a male who is gifted with this by a righteous Goddess should drink with gratitude and joy. If she is not physically healthy and/or has extreme emotional and mental issues, it is not "Amrita".

Excerpt from Virginia slave cod 1662, pg. 460 article 36: "All children shall be bond or free, according to the condition of their mothers..." You are what your mother is, simple and plain.

See Christian black codes of 1724 article 10

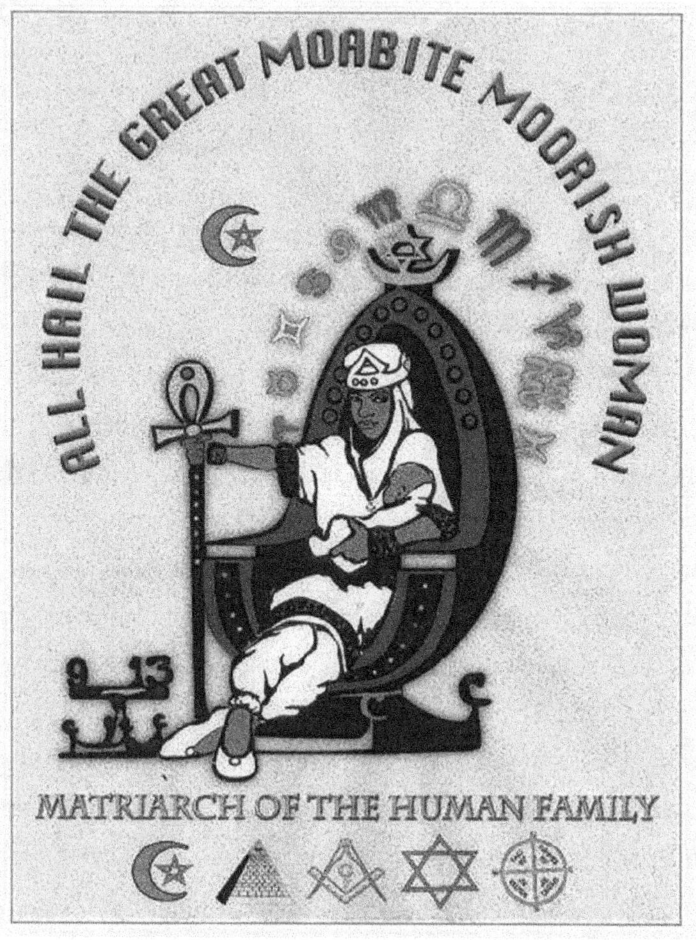

II. Unity: Brotherhood of Man

Holy Covenant of the Asiatic Nation (Circle 7 Ch. 25):

Ye are the children of one father, provided for by his care; and the breast of one mother hath given you suck. 2. Let the bonds of affection, therefore, unite thee with thy brothers that peace and happiness may dwell in thy father's house. 3. And when ye separate in the world, remember the relation that bindeth you to love and unity; and prefer not a stranger before thy own blood. 4. If thy brother is in adversity, assist him; if thy sister is in trouble, forsake her not. 5. So shall the fortunes of thy father contribute to the support of his whole race; and his care be continued to you all, in your love to each other.

C. Love Divine

I. Mysteries of the Secret Brotherhood of the East: Yehoshua takes the sixth degree and passed the sixth adept chamber of the Eastern Sages: In all the land there was no place more grandly furnished than the beauty of the temple of the Sun:

(1) Few students ever entered this room. The priests guarded them with awe and called them the halls of mysteries. (2) When Yehoshua had attained the victory over fear, he gained the right to enter. (3) The guide led on the way. And, after passing many richly furnished rooms, they reached the hall of harmony, and there was Yehoshua left alone. (4) Among the instruments of music was a harpsichord. And Yehoshua sat in thoughtful mood, inspecting it, when quietly a maiden of entrancing beauty came into the hall. (5) She did not seem to notice Yehoshua as he sat and mused so busy with his thoughts. (6) She found her place beside the harpsichord. She touched the chords most gently and she sang the songs of Yisrael. (7) And Yehoshua was entranced; such beauty he had never seen such music he had never heard. (8) The maiden sang her songs. She didn't seem to know that any one was near. She went her way. (9) And Yehoshua, talking with himself, said out, "What is the meaning of this incident? I did not know that such entrancing beauty and such queen-like loveliness were ever found among the sons of men. (10) I did not know that a voice of an angel ever graced a human form; or that seraphic music ever come from human lips." (11) For days he sat entranced. The current of his thoughts was changed. He thought of nothing but the singer and her songs. (12) He longed to see her once again and, after days, she came. She spoke and laid her hand upon his head. (13) Her touch thrilled all his soul; and, for a time, forgot the work that he was sent to do. (14) Few were the words the maiden said. She went her way; but then the heart of Yehoshua had been touched. (15) A love flame had been kindled in his soul, and he was brought to face the sorest trial of life. (16) He could not sleep, nor could he eat. The thoughts of the maiden they would not go. His carnal nature called aloud for her companionship. (17) And then, he said, "Lo, I have conquered every foe that I have met, and shall I now be conquered by carnal love? (18) My father sent me here to show the power of love-divine;

that love that reaches every living thing. (19) Shall this pure universal love be all absorbed by carnal love? Shall I forget all creature's else and lose my life in this fair maiden?-though she is the highest type of beauty, purity, and love." (20) Into its very depths his soul was stirred, and long he wrestled with this angel-idol of his heart. (21) But when the day was almost lost his higher-ego rose in might. He found himself again, and then he said, (22) "Although my heart shall break, I will not fail in this my hardest task. I will be victor over carnal love." (23) And when again the maiden came and offered him her hand and heart he said, (24) "Fair one, your very presence thrills me with delight. Your voice is benediction to my soul. My human self would fly with you and be contented in your love. (25) But all the world is craving for a love I have come to manifest. (26) I must then, bid you go, but we will meet again. (27) I see you in the hurrying throngs of earth as a minister of love. I hear your voice in song that wins the hearts of men to better things." (28) And then in sorrow and in tears the maiden went away; and Yahoshua was alone again.

II. Mysteries of the Secret Brotherhood of the East: Yehoshua reveals the marriage law of man and wife from Allah:

(1) The law forbids adultery; but, in the eyes of the law, adultery is an overt act; the satisfaction of the sensuous self, outside of the marriage bonds. (2) Now, marriage, in the sight of the law, is but a promise made by man and woman, by the sanction of the priest, to live together until death. No priest or officer has the power from Allah to bind two souls in wedded love. (3) What is a marriage tie? It is not what the priest may say or do. There is but one true marriage; and Allah alone can perform this marriage. (4) It is the love of Allah that finds its way into the two-man and woman's hearts; and that is all ever to be. Your priests cannot cause this to be. (5) It is the promise of the two to that they will love each other until death. (6) Is love a passion that is subject to the will of man. (7) Can man pick up his love as he would a gem, and lay it down or give it out to anyone? (8) Can love be bought or sold like sheep? (9) Love is the power of Allah that binds two souls and makes them one. There is no power on earth that can dissolve this bond. (10) The bodies may be forced apart by man, or death for just a little time, but they will meet again. (11) Now, in this bond

of Allah, we find the marriage tie. All other unions are but unions of straw; and they who live in them commit adultery. (12) But more than this; the man or woman who indulges lustful thoughts commits adultery. (13) Whom Allah has joined together; man cannot part. Whom man has joined together lie in sin.

D. The Future

I. Holy Circle 7 Koran Ch. 23: Holy Instructions for Thy Children

1. Consider, thou art a parent, the importance of thy trust; the being thou hast produced, it is thy duty to support.
2. Upon thee also it dependeth whether the child of thy bosom be a blessing or a curse to thyself; a useful or a worthless member to the community.
3. Prepare him early with instruction and season his mind with the maxims of truth.
4. Watch the bent of his inclinations, set him right in his youth and let no evil habit gain strength with his years.
5. So shall he rise like a cedar on the mountains; his head shall be seen above the trees of the forest.
6. A wicked son is a reproach to his father; but he that doth right is an honor to his grey hairs.
7. The soil is thine own, let it not want cultivation; the seed which thou soweth, that also shall thou reap.
8. Teach him obedience, and he shall bless thee; teach him modesty, and he shall not be ashamed.
9. Teach him gratitude, and he shall receive benefits; teach him charity, and he shall gain love.
10. Teach him temperance, and he shall have health; teach him prudence, and fortune shall attend him.
11. Teach him justice, and he shall be honored by the world; teach him sincerity, and his own heart shall not reproach him.
12. Teach him diligence, and his wealth shall increase; teach him benevolence, and his mind shall be exalted.
13. Teach him science, and his life shall be useful; teach him religion, and his death shall be happy.

OUTRO:

"*To know others is intelligence; knowing yourself is true wisdom. Mastering others is strength; mastering yourself is true power. If you realize you have enough, you are truly rich.*" -Lao Tzu

"*Step into the fire of self discovery. This fire will not burn you; it will burn what you are not.*" -Mooji

Part 2: Heal Thyself

"*Physician Heal thyself*" - Luke 4:13

Intro: There are two parts to existence: the seen and the unseen. The seen is the various physical phenomena that we witness and consciously take part in daily. The unseen is the energy/force that drives and dictates all that we encounter. There is the flower and there is the root. The root is primordial and the source from which the flower sprouts. The flower goes through different stages of growth until it is full blossomed out into what is what designed to become. However, eventually the bud will die, either by external factors or just plain attrition, but the root will remain and will sprout another bud. We are the flowers and our health is the root, that which links us to Th Supreme Force of Creation. Without health there is no wealth for such is the currency by which we use as collateral for the locomotion of life, i.e. getting from point A to point B; mortality to immortality. Our self maintenance is vital to the cultivation of our spirits' oneness with nature which gives us vigor, tranquility, and sanity.

Chapter 1: The Command Center

A. Foundation: parts and functions

I. 5 levels of consciousness:

1. Conscious: Aware of one's own existence, sensations, surroundings, thoughts, etc.
2. Sub-conscious: The inner sense of what is right or wrong in one's conduct or motives, impelling one toward right action.
3. Magnetic conscious: The law of attraction (the power of the universe that binds)
4. Super conscious: The consciousness of higher self; transcendence; "God-Head"
5. Infinity conscious: The great awakening; the fully erect serpent; man's highest potential; the apex of existence

II. The Major Glands

1. Pineal: produces melatonin, a vital hormone that regulates and influences sexual development and sleep-wake cycles. It connects the endocrine system with the nervous system in that it converts nerve signals from the sympathetic system of the peripheral nervous system into hormone signals. It is located in the center of the brain.

Melatonin is produced within the pineal gland and synthesized from the neurotransmitter serotonin. Its production is determined by light and dark detection. The retina sends signals about light and dark detection to the hypothalamus. These signals are eventually relayed to the pineal gland. The more light detected, the less melatonin produced and released into the blood.

Melatonin levels are at their highest during the night and this promotes changes in the body that help us sleep. Low levels of melatonin during daylight hours help us to stay awake. Melatonin inhibits the release of certain reproductive hormones from the pituitary gland that affects male and female reproductive organs. These pituitary hormones, known as gonadotropins, stimulate gonads to release sex hormones. In animals, melatonin plays a key role in regulating mating season.

2. Pituitary: known as the "master gland" of the body because it controls several other hormone glands in our body, including the thyroid and adrenals, the ovaries and testicles.

The pituitary gland makes or stores many different hormones. The following hormones are made in the anterior of the pituitary gland:

- Protacin: stimulates breast milk production after childbirth. It also affects sex hormone levels from ovaries in women and from testes in men, as well as fertility.
- Growth Hormone (HGH): stimulates growth in childhood and is important for maintaining a healthy body composition and well being in adults. In adults, GH is important for maintaining muscle mass and bone mass. It also affects fat distribution in the body.
- Adrenocorticotropin (ACTH): stimulates the production of cortisol by the adrenal glands-small glands that sit atop the kidneys. Cortisol, a "stress hormone", is vital to our survival. It helps maintain blood pressure and blood glucose (sugar) levels and is produced in larger amounts when we're under stress- especially after illness or injury.
- Thyroid Stimulating Hormone (TSH): stimulates the thyroid gland to produce thyroid hormones, which regulate the body's metabolism, energy, balance, growth, and nervous system activity.
- Luteinizing Hormone (LH): stimulates testosterone production in men and egg release (ovulation) in women.
- Follicle Stimulating Hormone (FSH): promotes sperm production in men and stimulates the ovaries to produce estrogen and develop eggs in women. LH and FSH work together to enable normal function of the ovaries and testes.

The following hormones are stored in the posterior of the pituitary gland:

- Antidiurectic Hormone (ADH): also called vasopressin, regulates water balance in the body. It conserves body water by reducing the amount of water lost in the urine.
- Oxytocin: causes milk to flow from the breasts in breastfeeding women and may also help labor to progress.

3. Thalamus: is an olive shaped structure about one inch in length. It serves as a relay station for impulses traveling to and from the spinal cord, brain stem, cerebellum and cerebrum. It has an important function in directing sensory input

to the appropriate place in the cerebral cortex. Sensory input from the body, eyes, ears and other senses (except smell) pass through the thalamus.

4. Hypothalamus: is located below the thalamus. The hypothalamus is an important center for many critical internal body functions. The hypothalamus monitors water concentration, hormone concentrations, and body temperature. It is associated with feelings of rage, aggression, hunger and thirst.

The hypothalamus also plays an important role as an intermediary between the nervous system and the endocrine system (hormones). The hypothalamus has many connections with the pituitary gland and can produce and regulate hormones.

Gland Stimulation:

1. Pineal: meditation, fasting, tea (preferably pine needle and ayahuasca)
2. Pituitary: high protein foods, manganese, vitamins E and D
3. Thalamus and Hypothalamus: increased chromium intake (broccoli, potatoes, garlic, basil, oranges, green beans, apples, and bananas, essential oils [frankincense and myrrh]), chaste tree berry, and healthy fats, get enough rest and reduced stress, exercise regularly. Vitamin B

III. 3 Main Parts of the Brain (exterior):

1. Cerebrum: The biggest part of the brain. It makes up 85% of the brain's weight. The cerebrum is the thinking part of the brain and it controls voluntary muscles. Your memory lives in the cerebrum-both short-term and long-term. It is also the center of reason. The cerebrum has two hemispheres: Right (creativity, imagination, holistic thinking, intuition, arts [motor skills], rhythm [beats], non-verbal communication, and visualization) and Left (logic, analysis, sequencing, linear, mathematics, words of song, language, facts, verbal expression, and computation). The right hemisphere controls the left side of the body and the left hemisphere controls the right side.
2. Cerebellum: is located at the back of the brain, below the cerebrum. It is only 1/8 the size of the cerebrum. It controls balance, movement, and coordination.
3. Brain Stem: sits beneath the cerebrum and in front of the cerebellum. It connects the rest of the brain to the spinal cord. The stem is in charge of all the functions your body needs to stay alive, such as breathing, digesting food, and circulating blood. It also controls the involuntary muscles (heart, stomach, lungs, etc.). It

sorts through the millions of messages that the brain and the rest of the body send back and forth to each other.

Stimulation:

a. Healthy Foods: they contain potassium and calcium, two minerals that are important for the nervous system
b. Plenty of exercise
c. Head protection
d. No drugs or alcohol
e. Doing challenging activities (puzzles, reading, music, art, etc.)

IV. Things that harm your brain:

- Gluten
- Artificial sweeteners
- Monosodium Glutamate (MSG) Also called: hydrolyzed protein, glutamate, hydrolyzed soy, yeast extract, casienate, spices, natural flavorings, vinegar powder
- Refined sugar
- Fluoride
- Too much electronic contact
- Lack of Physical and Mental Stimulation

Causes of brain fog:

- Adrenal fatigue syndrome
- Yeast/viral infections
- Hypoglycemia
- Bowel toxicity
- Neurological causes
- Gluten intolerance
- Psychogenic causes

Environmental causes:

- Food chemicals
- Artificial sweeteners
- Medications
- Toxic medals
- Petro-chemicals
- Electromagnetic fields

F. Frequencies and Vibrations

I. Serpent Rising

Kundalini is Sanskrit meaning "coiled one" and refers to a form of primal energy located at the base of the spine. It is the force of Supreme knowledge and wisdom which are keys that open the doors of regeneration and immortality.

Kundalini awakens the brain: As Kundalini energy rises through sushuma (the central energy channel or nadi that travels the full length of the middle of the spinal cord. It is the channel through which we experience kundalini awakening), large amounts of high-octane energy reaches the brain. The energy flows from RAS (Reticular Activating System: also known as extrathalamic control modulatory system, a set of connected nuclei in the brains of vertebrates that is responsible for wakefulness and sleep-wake transitions. These are evolutionary ancient areas of the brain, which are crucial to survival.) and the thalamus to the cortex and awakens dormant, under-active parts of the brain-especially in the frontal lobes.

The whole brain now begins to pulse as a unit generating coherent, high amplitude brain waves within all frequency bands. Maximum amplitude will usually be in the alpha band, however, fast EEG (Electroencephalogram) activity in the beta and gamma bands will be strongly increased in the frontal area.

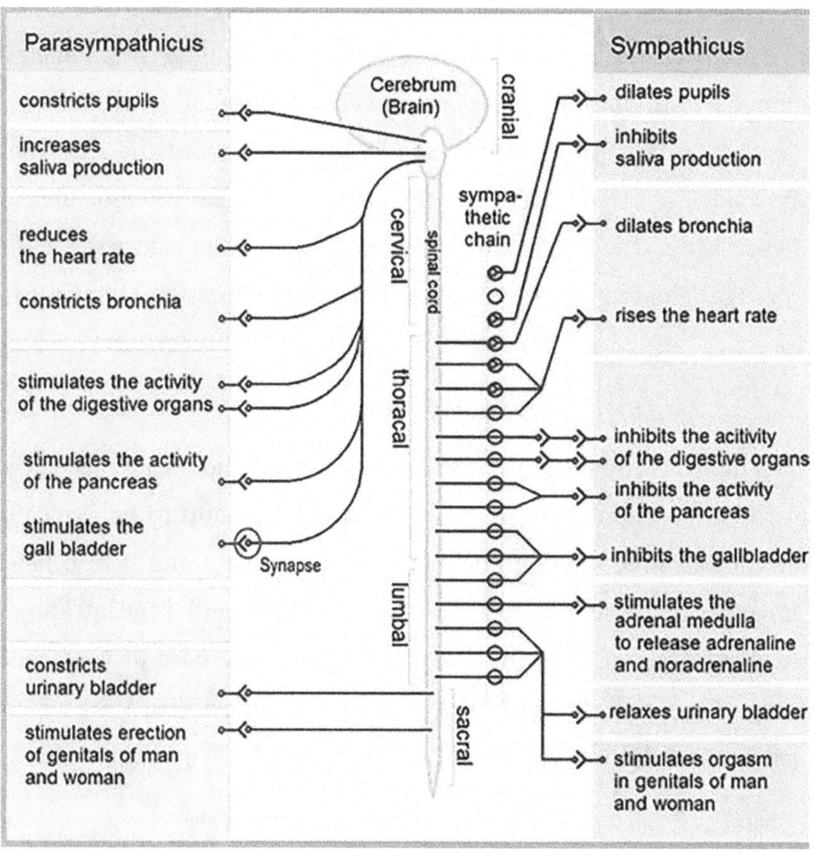

II. Meet your Brain Waves (finerminds.com)

It's important to inner/overstand how your brain contributes to your state of mind: While most of us focus on looking at our emotions in an attempt to become happier, more spiritual beings, our brain waves and our subconscious mind also play a part in our quest for fulfillment.

Are we the controllers of our reality? We easily forget that we are the controllers of our reality and that "our reality" is not made up of outside influences, but that it actually consists of our thoughts, beliefs, and mindset. Therefore, by learning about the deeper states of consciousness, you can open your subconscious mind and create your reality at will, and with precision. To do this, the first step is innerstanding your different brain frequencies.

1. Beta (14-40 Hz) - The waking Consciousness and Reasoning Wave:

Beta brain waves are associated with normal waking consciousness and a heightened state of alertness, logic and critical reasoning. While beta brain waves are important for effective functioning throughout the day, they also can translate into stress, anxiety and restlessness. The voice of beta can be described as being that nagging little inner critic that gets louder the higher you go into range. Therefore, with a majority of adults operating at beta; it is little surprise that stress is today's most common health problem.

2. Alpha (7.5-14 Hz) - The Deep relaxation wave:

Alpha brain waves are present in deep relaxation and usually when the eyes are closed, when slipping into a lovely daydream or during light meditation. It is an optimal time to program the mind for success and it also heightens your imagination, visualization, memory, learning and concentration. It is the gateway to the subconscious mind and lies at the base of your conscious awareness. The voice of alpha is your intuition, which becomes clearer and more profound the closer you get to 7.5 Hz.

3. Theta (4-7.5 Hz) - The light meditation and resting wave:

Theta brain waves are present during deep meditation and light rest, including the all-important REM (Rapid eye movement) dream state. It is the realm of your sub consciousness and only experienced momentarily as you drift off to sleep from alpha and wake from deep sleep (delta). It is said that a sense of deep spiritual connection and unity with the universe can be experienced at theta. Your mind's most deep-seated programs are at theta and it is where you experience vivid visualizations, great innerstanding, profound creativity and exceptional insight. Unlike your other brain waves, the elusive voice of theta is a silent voice. It is at the alpha-theta border, from 7 Hz to 8 Hz, where the optimal range for visualization, mind programming and using the creative work of your mind begins. It's the mental state which you consciously create your reality. At this frequency, you are conscious of your surroundings however your body is in deep relaxation.

4. Delta (0.5-4 Hz) – The deep sleep wave:

The delta frequency is the slowest of the frequencies and is experienced in deep, dreamless sleep and in very deep, transcendental meditation where awareness is fully detached. Delta is the realm of your unconscious mind, and the gateway to the universal mind and the collective unconscious, where information received is otherwise unknowable/unavailable at the conscious level. Among many things, deep sleep is important for the healing process- as it's linked to deep healing and regeneration. Hence, not having enough deep sleep is detrimental to your healing in more ways than one.

5. Gamma (above 40 Hz) – The insight wave:

This range is the most recently discovered and is the fastest frequency. While little is known about this state of mind, initial research shows gamma waves are associated with bursts of insight and high-level information processing.

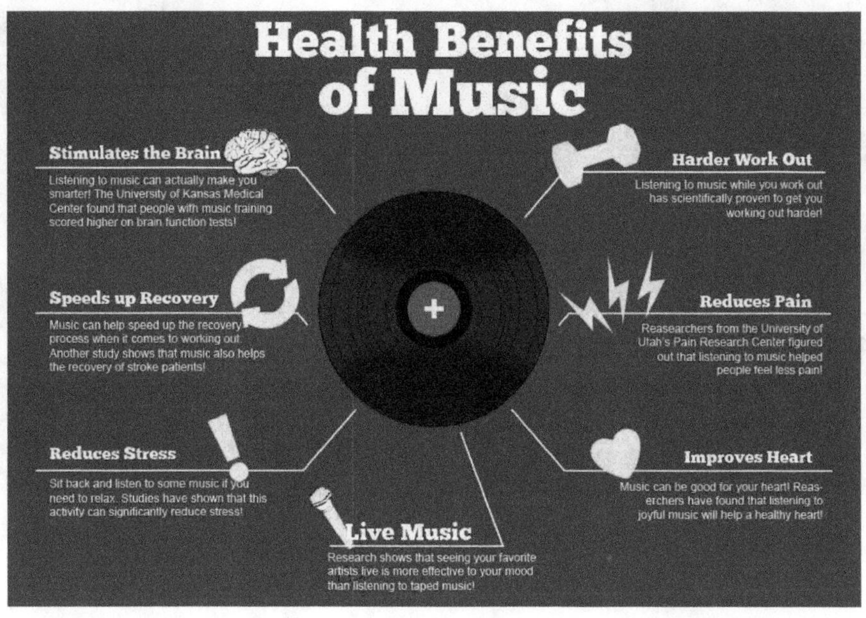

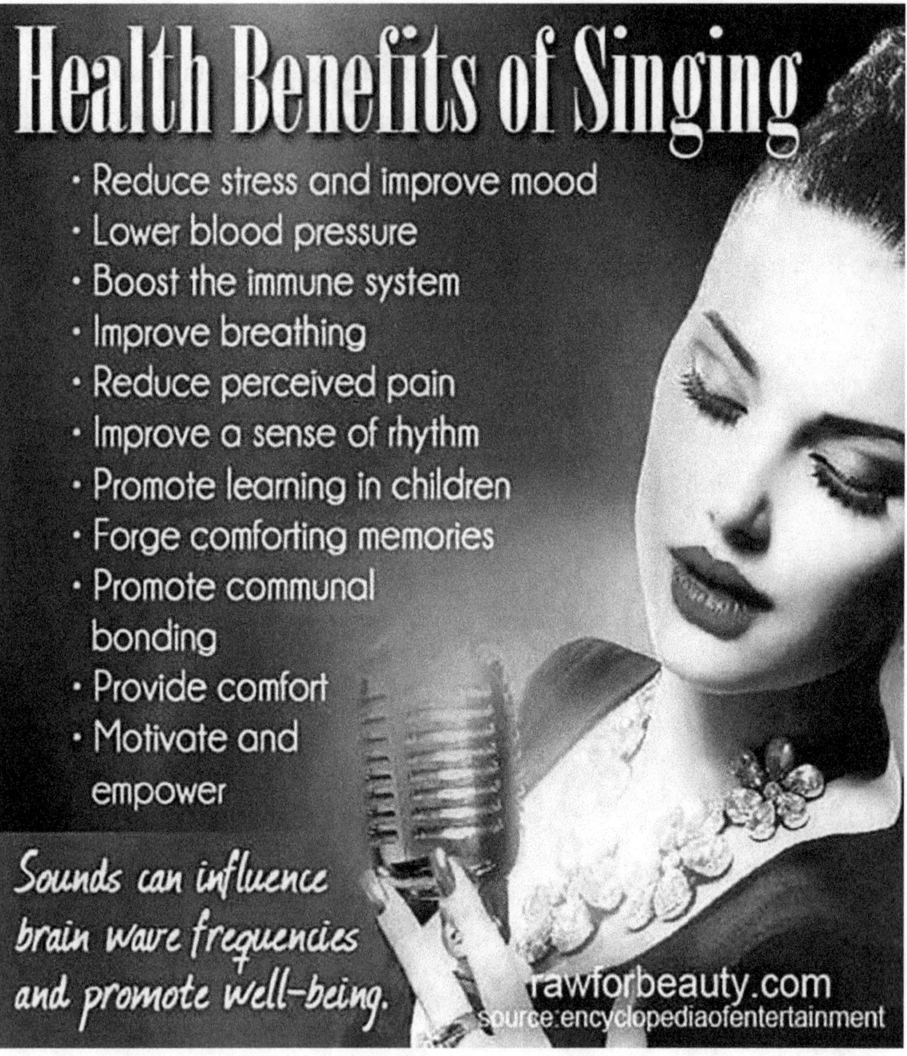
Health Benefits of Singing
· Reduce stress and improve mood
· Lower blood pressure
· Boost the immune system
· Improve breathing
· Reduce perceived pain
· Improve a sense of rhythm
· Promote learning in children
· Forge comforting memories
· Promote communal bonding
· Provide comfort
· Motivate and empower
Sounds can influence brain wave frequencies and promote well-being.
rawforbeauty.com
source:encyclopediaofentertainment

G. Meditation

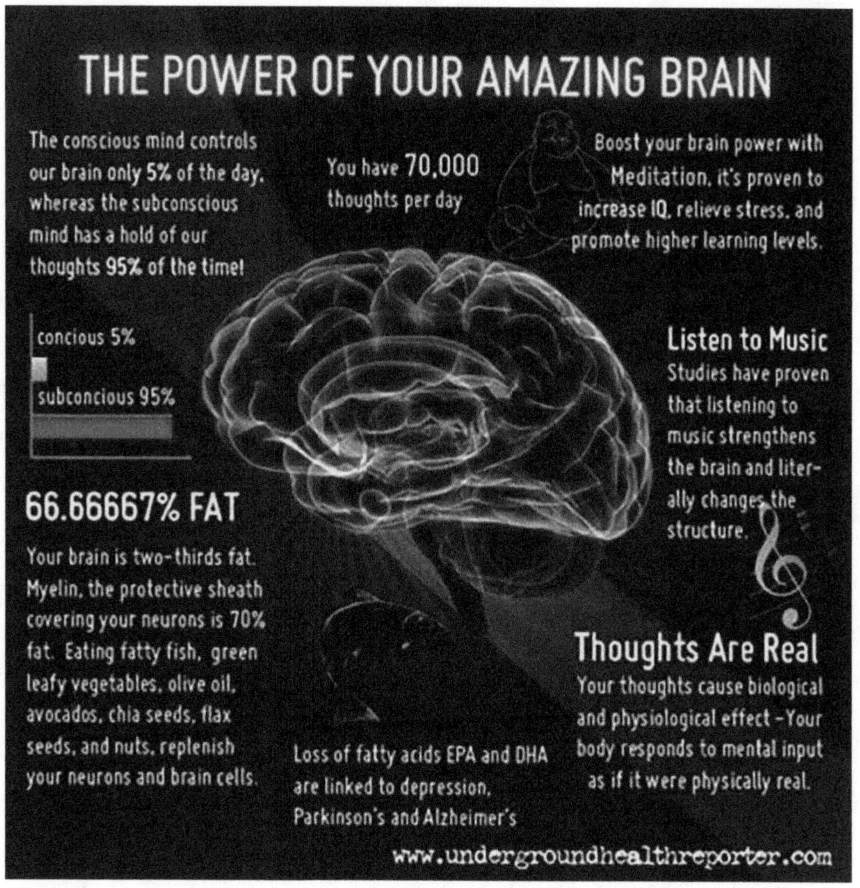

I. What is Meditation?

Meditation is the art of mastering the mind through the development and strengthening of one's awareness. Being that the subconscious mind is constantly dumping thoughts at random into the conscious mind and can highjack one's consciousness and attention, it is critical that one develop their capacity to master their mind so that they can steer it in the direction that they truly want.

As the barriers between the subconscious and conscious mind are gradually dissolved through the act of meditation, one progressively gains more and more control over their consciousness, which in turn enables them to direct their willpower more accurately/precisely into what they truly want to accomplish in life.

Being that our mind and brain are constantly in action in both our waking lives and dreaming lives, it is an organ of the body that is typically deprived of enough time to be rested and rejuvenated. In meditation, one seeks to relax the mind through putting one's awareness and attention on stillness. In this state one allows themselves to stop their thoughts and worries and just be at peace for the meditation duration. If and when thoughts arise during meditation, it is the mediators' mission not to engage in the thought, but to view from a 3rd person perspective without identifying with it. Through the practice of this act, one gains more mastery over the subconscious mind as well as a better perspective on their undesirable mental programs that may be running like a feedback loop. As one progresses in meditation and the mind acquires more and more stillness, tension in the mind from over-active thinking is reduced and the grey matter of the brain becomes more soft and flexible. In turn the pineal gland which sits in the center of the brain is enabled to function with greater energetic receptabiltiy and transmutation.

II. Layers of Meditation:

- Physical Body: one begins meditation, feels only the physical body
- Emotional Body/ego: one goes deeper and encounters the emotional self and ego
- Higher Self/Guidance: one clears the emotional body and begins to realize the subtle body and sensations
- Union/Becoming Light: the devotee now begins to channel light and slowly begins to rebuild the multidimensional

III. Raising energy Levels

Meditation to increase vitality: to increase vitality lie in a comfortable position and relax the muscles of your body. Visualize the energy centers and envision the energy from the sun is entering your being at the point of the chosen energy center. You may also visualize that you are receiving life itself in the form of sunrays. Work with the breath by inhaling the energy in and holding the breath while concentrating on the particular energy center. If there are any psychic issues or health problems related with that center they will be alleviated. Practice this exercise for as long as you like each day and feel revitalized and renewed.

9 benefits of deep breathing:

- Stimulates brain growth
- Improves heart rate variability
- Lowers stress levels
- Alleviates anxiety and negative emotions
- Reduces anxiety
- Lowers blood pressure
- Balances the left and right hemispheres of the brain
- Cleanses lungs
- Improves sleep

10 benefits of stretching:

- Encourages optimistic outlook
- Fortifies posture
- Enables flexibility
- Increases stamina
- Decreases risk of injury
- Improves energy levels
- Promotes blood circulation
- Improves athletic performance
- Reduced soreness
- Reduces cholesterol

IV. Circadian Rhythm

A circadian rhythm is a roughly 24-hour cycle of/in the physiological processes of living beings, including plants, animals, fungi and cyanobacteria. In a strict sense, circadian rhythms are endogenously generated, although they can be modulated by external cues such as sunlight and temperature.

Methods of connectivity/tuning in: Sun gazing:

- Boosts production of melatonin and serotonin (our "fell-good" hormones)
- Increased health, longevity and spiritual well being
- Increases the actual size of the pineal gland and stimulates the pituitary, acts as a form of meditation
- Increased self confidence
- Increased energy levels
- Promotes weight loss'
- Better eyesight
- Enhanced vitality
- Lessen appetite
- Improves dream recall
- Strengthens electromagnetic field
- Improves quality of sleep
- Activates DNA

Sun gazing at sunrise and sunset when there are no UV rays is the best way to receive the highest effects of the above-mentioned benefits.

Walking barefoot on natural earth:

- Decreases emotional anxiety
- Absorbs free energy from earth
- Pushes off the body's dirty electricity absorbed through electronics
- Stretches and strengthens muscles, tendons, and ligaments in your feet, ankles, and calves; provides reflexology and toe strengthening and stretching
- Delivers all the benefits of grounding and earthing

Magnets:

- Magnets, especially hematite, causes red blood cell separation allowing them to oxygenate which allows the release of more energy to the heart and body for better circulation and also helps the mind function with more clarity.

Sitting by trees:

- Eliminates negative energy
- Cleanses aura field
- Induces relaxed state of mind
- Shares wisdom and knowledge
- Brings mental clarity
- Lowers stress and anxiety levels
- Strengthens nervous system

3 reasons to try grounding therapy:

Ground therapy is based on the scientific principle that standing barefoot on the ground gives us access to the earth's subtle electromagnetic energies and can improve your health.

- Eliminates free radicals and halts pain and disease they can cause if left unchecked
- Can lower blood pressure and improve circulation
- Reduces pain from inflammation and lyme disease

There are two types of meditation: formal and informal, personal/unique and learned indoctrination. We all know of the prescribed methods of meditation and what that looks like but also there is the meditation of passion that works just as well where one is engaged in the cultivation of one's natural talent e.g. sports, writing, carpentry, etc. Whatever you do that allows your mind to focus and cut off the outside vexations of the world is deemed meditation. So long as you are comfortable and relaxed then with enough time of stillness it will all fall into place and you'll find yourself in a great state of being and the universe will unfold, and the inner divine brilliance of self will emerge.

H. Enlightenment

I. What is enlightenment?

Spiritual enlightenment is a state of being where you experience and know, on an ongoing basis, an ultimate sense of peace and meaning, and your perception of yourself and the universe includes, in a very real and present way, that your connection to the ultimate reality is now permanent and unbreakable.

II. Keys:

- Work a job that you love; find your passion and build on that
- Eat mineral, enzyme rich organic fruit and vegetables and concentrated green powders, chlorella, avocadoes, and fresh raw pressed oils like hemp and olive oils
- Stress less, learn proper breathing techniques and start meditating
- Connect with nature daily i.e. touching and talking to plants, trees and animals
- Get rid of your TV
- Avoid all junk food
- Eat algae and herbs, and infuse cells with daily green smoothies and juices
- Connect with your inner child, make art and be creative
- Dance more
- Quit smoking and drinking
- Get rid of fear, worry, and learn to love unconditionally
- Never own a disease and reduce the amount of time that you talk about being ill; refuse to allow illness a place in your consciousness

Happiness Chemicals and how to hack them

DOPAMINE
THE REWARD CHEMICAL

- Completing a task
- Doing self-care activities
- Eating food
- Celebrating little wins

OXYTOCIN
THE LOVE HORMONE

- Playing with a dog
- Playing with a baby
- Holding hand
- Hugging your family
- Give compliment

SEROTONIN
THE MOOD STABILIZER

- Meditating
- Running
- Sun exposure
- Walk in nature
- Swimming
- Cycling

ENDORPHIN
THE PAIN KILLER

- Laughter exercise
- Essential oils
- Watch a comedy
- Dark chocolate
- Exercising

Chapter 2: Dis-Ease

A. Poison: Self Destruction

I. Acidity

A PH (potential of hydrogen) scale is a measure of acidity or alkalinity of water-soluble substances. A PH value is a number from 1-14, with 7 as the middle (neutral) point. Values below 7 indicate acidity which increases as the number decreases, 1 being the most acidic.

Acidity is the progenitor of mucus which is the harbinger of all disease. Just about all the ailments humans face today can be traced back to the amount of mucus build-up within their systems due to bad habits. Through the gestation of these non-essential mucaloids parasites are spawned which in turn feed off of the host (you) laying eggs and essentially turning the bodies of men into cesspools. This in turn leads to not only the physical ailments such as HIV/AIDS, cancer, pneumonia, etc., but also mental as well as spiritual disorders as well. Contrary to popular belief disease is not a natural phenomenon and though our bodies do have good mucus and bacteria so as to maintain balance, we were never meant to be sick as nature provides remedies for any and all ailments, but humans have regressed and are outside of nature and instead rely on men instead of Th Creator Of men. These maladies are due to the dis-ease of the human body brought on by dumb choices and also environmental poisonings.

II. Demons: Causes and Effects

The prefix de means, to do the opposite of, down, away, off, to take away, entirely, completely. Mon is man (vowels are interchangeable) so therefore a demon is anything against man in terms of growth and progression/evolution; something that causes narrow-mindedness and myopic perspectives. So, a demon could be your minister, cell phone, television, face book, car, friend, family member, basically anything that keeps you stuck and not in motion. They (demons) come in all forms.

III. Acidic Foods:

1. Meat
2. Ice cream
3. Canned fruit
4. Peanuts
5. Canned tuna
6. Corn
7. Processed sugar
8. Vinegar
9. Cereals
10. Mustard
11. Mayonnaise
12. Corn tortillas
13. Milk
14. Sardines
15. Soft drinks
16. Halva
17. Artificial sweeteners
18. Ketchup
19. Corn oil
20. Cottage cheese
21. Yogurt
22. Syrup
23. Jams and jellies
24. Cookies
25. Butter
26. Chips
27. Bread
28. Pies
29. Pretzels
30. Deep fried foods
31. Safflower and canola oil
32. Soy
33. Sunflower oil
34. Ghee

Toxins:

- NutraSweet
- Aspartame
- Splenda
- High fructose corn syrup
- Canned foods
- Pasteurized dairy
- Unfermented soy
- Diet anything
- Nonfat/low fat anything
- Margarine
- Hydrogenated oils
- Soft drinks
- Trans fat
- GMO'S
- Artificial colors and preservatives
- MSG

IV. Forbidden foods: (see Lev. 11:7–8; Qu'ran 16:115)

- Pork (bacon, ham, etc.)
- Rabbits, hares and rodents
- Web footed birds and their eggs
- All shellfish and fish without scales and fins
- Birds of prey
- Snails, eels, and all creeping things that crawl, fly, or swim

V. Symptoms of parasites:

- Allergies
- Anxiety and depression
- Bad breath
- Body odor
- Breathing difficulties
- Bruising
- Changes in weight
- Chronic dehydration
- Crawling sensations
- Dark circles under eyes
- Digestive problems
- Eating disorders
- Eye pain
- Fatigue
- Floaters
- Headaches
- Joint pain
- Learning disability
- Memory problems
- Mood disorders
- Oral health problems
- Pain around belly button
- Poor cognitive skills
- Seizures
- Stress
- Stunted growth
- Weakness

VI. 5 ways cell phones harm your body:

Smart phone hazards: smart phones are the most popular type of cell phone, and they're also one of the few that emit a high level of radiation. Holding a smart phone or any cell phone for that matter, in your pocket or bra is risky to your reproductive organs and breasts. Here are a few ways cell phones are a health risk:

1. Cancer risk: a new study from Sweden suggests decades of cell phone use can triple your chances for brain cancer. (Note: this is mainly pertaining to obsessive cell phone users who talk phone to ear a lot.)
2. Hindering sleep: cell phones might even be hazardous to our sleep, with the latest evidence suggesting that individuals with smart phones in the bedroom sleep less each night. In addition, microwave radiation from cell phones is much riskier for children than originally thought. One study noted a child's brain tissue and bone marrow actually absorbs significantly more than those of an adult.
3. Disease carriers: let's be honest, how often do you clean your cell phone? It's not something we think about, but a recent study noted cell phones could be as dirty as public toilet seats, and that the heat phones generate makes a perfect breeding ground for bacteria.
4. Do cell phones promote psychological and social issues? : research has often studied the way cell phones change the way we think, but a team of researchers actually found cell phones actually interfere with normal socialization. The near constant use even creates learned compulsive behaviors (like narcissism).
5. Spinal misalignment: a surprising connection: think about how many times a day you check your phone. It might not be as many times as others, but all that constant tilting down to look at your phone screen takes its toll, leading to neck and back pain as well as migraines. This is not just something caused by looking at cell phone screens, doctors are even seeing it more and more in younger children because of handheld games.

More and more authorities are noting the possible risks of cell phones. In 2011, the world health organization conceded cell phones are "possibly carcinogenic", and, since then more and more research has been added to the danger pile. Now, the FCC is reassessing safe radiation exposure limits for cell phones, something that hasn't been explored since 1996.

How to protect yourself: Cell phones expose you to a great deal of radiation and your best bet for protecting yourself is to reduce the amount of verbal communication you have on your phone. Use speaker, utilize text messages and wear EMF clothing.

VII. Fluoride

There are 3 types of fluoride used to "fluoridate" water supplies: flurosolic acid, sodium fluorosilicate and sodium fluoride.

1. Flurosilic acid: the most often used for cost reasons, and it is derived from phosphate fertilizers according to the CDC's website.
2. Sodium fluorosilicate: also known as sodium silicofluride is made by neutralizing flurosillicic acid with sodium chloride or sodium sulfate. Another name is disodium hexaflurosilicate.
3. Sodium Fluoride: a chemical compound and medication. As a medication it is primarily used to prevent tooth decay in children older than 6 months in areas where the drinking water is low in fluoride, however, the ADA (American Dental Association) has warned that young children subjected to fluoride are at risk to a disease called dental fluorosis. It is also commonly used in rat poison.

In 1955 crest became the first fluoride toothpaste. Fluoride calcifies the pineal gland otherwise known as your 3rd (1st) eye which literally has cones and rods just like your other eyes! Fluoride is so toxic that it is considered a hazardous waste by the EPA. Hitler fluoridated the water in concentration camps to sedate prisoners. Fluoride is the same ingredient used in Prozac. According to Doctor Bill Omunsun, there's the same amount of fluoride in an 8oz glass of fluoridated tap water as there is in a "pea-sized" amount needed to call the poison control center, as recommended on the back of any fluoridated toothpaste.

DIY (Do it Yourself): Toothpaste

Or you could just brush your teeth with pure sea salt and/or pure baking soda and rinse with saltwater or H2O2 (hydrogen peroxide 35%).

- 2 tbl. Pure sea salt
- 1 tbl. Bentonite clay
- 1 tbl. Xylitol (optional)
- 15-20 drops of peppermint essential oil
- 1 tbl. Dried, finely ground sage leaf

"Burgers contain rat and human DNA, study finds"

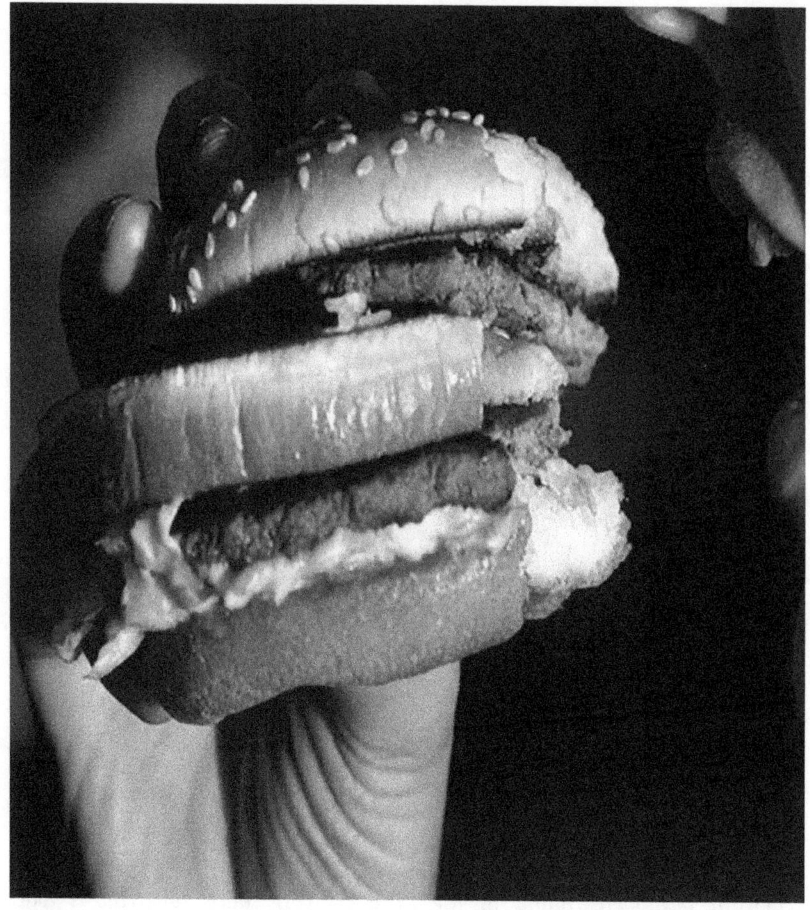

Clear Labs did not name the 79 brands that sold the burgers in the study (Getty Images)

A study of 258 burgers in the US finds unexpected additional – and lack of – ingredients

Upon ordering a burger in a fast food chain, diners might have already come to terms with the fact there is a very slim chance of horse meat lurking under that tomato.

But the additions of rat and human DNA could be harder to swallow.

A new study from US-based food testing company Clear Labs has discovered, from a sample of 258 burgers, two cases of meat in vegetarian products, three burgers with rat DNA and one case of human DNA.

"The most likely cause is hair, skin, or fingernail that was accidentally mixed in during the manufacturing process," it read, referring to the human DNA.

"What many consumers don't know is that some amounts of human and rat DNA may fall within an acceptable regulatory range," the report added.

It also found that there are "gaps" in food safety and quality standards, but overall the beef industry has "benefited from stringent regulation and aggressive testing requirements".

Of larger concern than the "unpleasant" DNA findings was that almost a quarter of vegetarian burgers have different ingredients to those on the label. Two veggie burgers contained beef, and one black bean burger contained no black beans.

Although Americans are unlikely to mix up their bison from their ground lamb patties on the barbecue, it seems the burger industry is making that mistake. Around 6 per cent of the burgers substituted one product for another. A common finding was that, for meat burgers, chicken or turkey was unexpectedly added in.

Another problem is that 4.3 per cent of burgers contained pathogenic DNA, which can cause food outbreaks and food poisoning.

Certain pathogens found in the products can cause tuberculosis-like symptoms, gastroenteritis, foodborne illness and E. coli.

Pathogens in four vegetarian burgers, considered a low risk category for food poisoning, was "troubling", the report said.

https://www.independent.co.uk/news/world/americas/burgers-contain-rat-and-human-dna-study-finds-a7023661.html

"McDonalds Exposed for Using Human Meat!"

by Pablo Reyes

OKLAHOMA CITY – First Horse meat, then the mysterious "Pink slime", Now Human meat? A shocking discovery has been made in an Oklahoma City McDonald's meat factory and other McDonald's meat factories nationwide. Meat inspectors reportedly found, what appeared to be, Human meat stored in the meat factory freezers of an Oklahoma City meat factory and human meat already in trucks right outside the factory ready to be shipped to McDonald's restaurants. Health inspectors immediately demanded inspection in various McDonald's meat factories across the country and horrifyingly found human meat in about 90% of the factories inspected thus far.

The USDA (United States Department of Agriculture) has seized McDonald's production and shipping and will call for more meat factory inspections and restaurant inspections. The FBI is also investigating the factories. FBI agent Lloyd Harrison told Huzler reporters "The worst part is that it's not only human meat, it's child meat. the body parts that were found across the U.S. factories were deemed to small to be adult body parts, this is truly horrible".

The situation brings up many unanswered questions. How long have they been using human meat? Where did they get the children from? Were they already dead when brought into factories? Investigators and Inspectors are currently being deployed for intensive investigations all around the U.S.

20
20
VISION

Chapter 3: Nature's Remedies

A. Water

I. What does water do for you?

- Forms saliva (digestion)
- Keeps mucosal membranes moist
- Allows body's cells to grow, reproduce and survive
- Flushes body waste, mainly in urine
- Lubricates joints
- Is the major component of most body parts
- Needed by the brain to manufacture hormones and neurotransmitters
- Regulates body temperature (sweating and respiration)
- Acts as a shock absorber for brain and spinal cord
- Helps deliver oxygen all over the body

II. 4 essential tips to drinking clean water: (treeoflif3.com)

1. Lemons and limes: add lemons to your water. Just by adding lemons to your water you are creating the perfect alkaline drink to keep you healthy and energized. Lemons in your water will naturally cause your body to detoxify the inorganic minerals and toxins from your body. The vitamin c and antioxidants in lemons will fight free radicals and help the body to produce collagen for healthy wrinkle free skin. Lemons also contain pectin, which acts as a fiber to help you feel full longer and therefore could lead to weight loss. (*pro tip: buy conventional or organic lemons and limes with seeds. Avoid genetically modified seedless fruits which contain no real nutrition. A half of key lime can alkalize 1 gallon of water).
2. Reverse osmosis and distilled water: drink RO water or distilled water. Another simple way to ensure your water contains no chemicals or fluoride is to buy distilled water and/or RO water. Distilling water will purify the water of all inorganic minerals leaving you with clean, pure water. Many people think distilled water will leech out the minerals from your body but that isn't true. Distilled water only flushes out the "inorganic" minerals. These inorganic minerals are poorly absorbed and rejected from our tissues and if not cleansed they can harden the arteries, cause arthritis, kidney stones, degenerative diseases and obesity. Remember all you need to do is add lemons, limes and/or cucumber and you now have healthy mineral water.

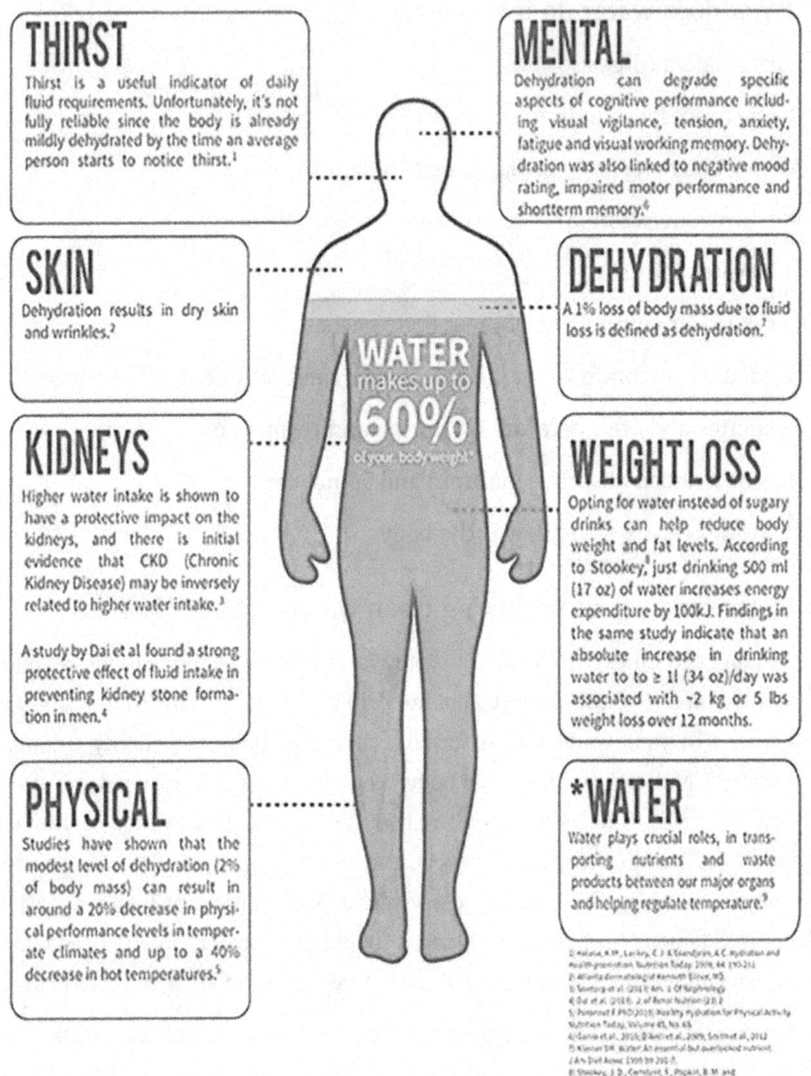

Consequences of Dehydration
THIRST
Thirst is a useful indicator of daily fluid requirements. Unfortunately, it's not fully reliable since the body is already mildly dehydrated by the time an average person starts to notice thirst.[1]
MENTAL
Dehydration can degrade specific aspects of cognitive performance including visual vigilance, tension, anxiety, fatigue and visual working memory. Dehydration was also linked to negative mood rating, impaired motor performance and shortterm memory.[6]
SKIN
Dehydration results in dry skin and wrinkles.[2]
DEHYDRATION
A 1% loss of body mass due to fluid loss is defined as dehydration.[7]
WATER
makes up to
60%
of your bodyweight*
KIDNEYS
Higher water intake is shown to have a protective impact on the kidneys, and there is initial evidence that CKD (Chronic Kidney Disease) may be inversely related to higher water intake.[3]
A study by Dai et al found a strong protective effect of fluid intake in preventing kidney stone formation in men.[4]
WEIGHT LOSS
Opting for water instead of sugary drinks can help reduce body weight and fat levels. According to Stookey,[8] just drinking 500 ml (17 oz) of water increases energy expenditure by 100kJ. Findings in the same study indicate that an absolute increase in drinking water to to ≥ 1l (34 oz)/day was associated with ~2 kg or 5 lbs weight loss over 12 months.
PHYSICAL
Studies have shown that the modest level of dehydration (2% of body mass) can result in around a 20% decrease in physical performance levels in temperate climates and up to a 40% decrease in hot temperatures.[5]
*WATER
Water plays crucial roles, in transporting nutrients and waste products between our major organs and helping regulate temperature.[9]

3. Coconut water: coconut water is one of the purest waters on earth! The juice from coconuts is naturally alkalizing and the perfect liquid for our body. The water travels through many fibers, being purified where it is stored sterile in the nut itself. An interesting fact is that coconut water is identical to human blood plasma, which makes it the universal donor "clean water", with the perfect balance of

electrolytes to stay hydrated. Drink real coconut juice, rather than the boxed kind because nothing is better than the real thing. Many commercial coconut waters sold in stores are made with added sugars or concentrates which should be avoided so look out. A coconut a day keeps the doctor away!

4. Eat hydrating fruits and veggies: most fruits and veggies are filled with the purest clean water. The cucumber for example is 96% water; this is the perfect veggie to juice giving the cleanest liquids. Incorporate a variety of the highest hydrating fruits and veggies in raw form. You could also make juices/smoothies. Here are some popular fruits and veggies with their respective water percentages: watermelons 96%, pineapple 95%, celery 95%, lettuce 95%, tomatoes 94%, cantaloupe 89% (all forms of melons), blueberries 95%, pear 92%, and grapefruit 90%. You can also make homemade vitamin or detox water by soaking these fruits and veggies in a liter of water and enjoying that. Be creative; find ways to enjoy these gifts of nature and your body will thank you, leaving you with healthy beautiful skin to show.

Additional tips:

- Drink warm water in the A.M. first thing to help the liver and kidneys flush out toxins.
- Warm water flushes out phlegm and assists in nasal and throat congestion, digestion and makes you regular.
- Add mint or basil to your water for added flavor and tons of nutrition.
- Add cayenne pepper and honey with cinnamon.
- Add apple cider vinegar to your water. Make sure it is the kind that says, "with the mother".)

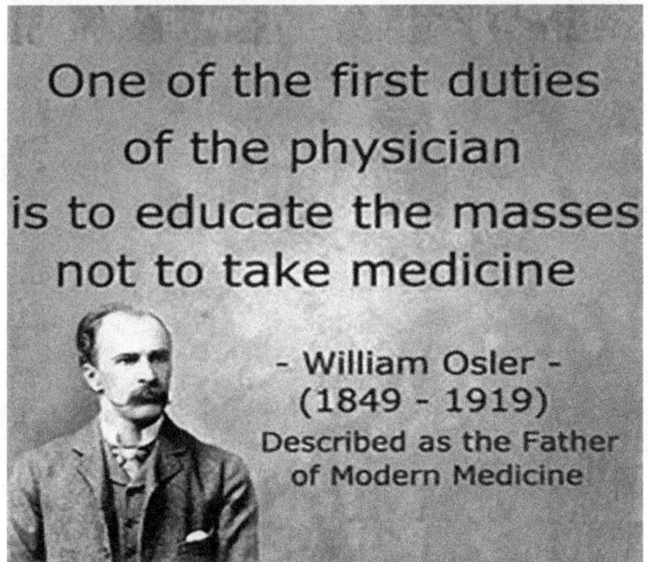

One of the first duties
of the physician
is to educate the masses
not to take medicine
- William Osler -
(1849 - 1919)
Described as the Father
of Modern Medicine

III. Coconut water: 9 brands to avoid due to toxins (naturalhealth365.com)

Are you drinking this type of (toxic) coconut water? For packaged coconut water to retain its nutrients, it should come directly from fresh coconuts. However, some manufacturers have adopted several methods of packaging that ruin its purity:

1. Adopting water from mature coconuts: Nutrient dense water comes from young green coconuts. As the one-seeded drupe ages, the nutrients seep into the meat of the coconut. Therefore, the water loses its nutrition value. Not only are the nutrients severely watered down, the taste is different from that of young coconuts. Mature coconuts are better for making coconut milk, oil, and other products. They are also cheaper for the manufacturer to buy.
2. Using reconstituted concentrate instead of fresh coconut water: heated and reduced to syrup, regular water is later added to this coconut water syrup for packaging. When coconut water (or any fruit) is heated to this extent, it loses its nutrients and its beneficial enzymes are denatured. Importing coconut water is also cheaper for the manufacturer.
3. Pasteurizing coconut water with heat: due to its delicacy, coconut water is naturally perishable. It should be kept cold. However, several manufacturers use extremely high heat to kill bacteria and still keep nutrients intact, manufacturers disregard

more healthy methods. If coconut water is from concentrate, it will have gone through the heating process twice!

4. Adding preservatives to flavor and sweeten coconut water: young coconut water is sweet and refreshing. However, some manufacturers add "natural flavors" or sweeteners. The only reason they would need to do this is if they are using mature coconut water that has an acidic taste.
5. Dipping coconuts in chemicals for transport: many non-organic coconuts are preserved for transporting to the united states by dipping them in known carcinogens-formaldehyde or sodium metabisulphate. These chemicals may seep into and poison the coconut meat and water.

Have these brands of coconut water earned your trust? : The following is a list of brands that may have touted their drinks to be "100% coconut water" or "all-natural coconut water." But, let the buyer beware!

- C20: this brand uses high heat pasteurization up to 1200 with the product in their cans. They use both steel and aluminum.
- Coco libre (organic): while this brand is labeled organic, it uses coconut water from concentrate. Their processing practice uses flash pasteurization with heat. Natural flavors are also added.
- Cona zona: this brand's nutrition label reveals its coconut water is made from concentrate.
- Goya: this brand spent mega dollars on fighting GMO labeling in California. They use heat pasteurization with added preservatives including sugar.
- Naked coconut water: this PepsiCo brand uses water from mature coconuts and then flash pasteurizes them. They have faced a class action lawsuit for using synthetic substances and genetically modified organisms (GMOs) in their product while labeling deceptively.
- O.N.E. coconut water: this is another PepsiCo brand that uses flash pasteurization with heat. Their coconut waters contain natural flavors and sugar. The sugar ingredient isn't classified as to the type, but it may very well be a GMO type as used in their other brand-named juice.
- Purity organic: while this brand is labeled organic, it doesn't use the best practices. It uses concentrate and flash pasteurization with heat in processing their coconut water.
- Vita coco: touted as being "100% pure"; their brand pasteurizes its coconut

water with heat and also have café versions which contains carrageenan- which is an emulsifier that may wreak havoc on gut health.

- Zico: this is a coca-cola company who is a big GMO supporter. Their coconut waters are made from concentrate, pasteurized with ultra high heat, and added with natural flavors.

Once again, the best coconut water comes from an organic coconut tree. It should be young and green. If you must opt for packaged coconut water I recommend Harmless Harvest which is the first coconut water brand to be fair trade certified, and to my knowledge the only commercial brand at that. Also check out exotic super foods.

B. Nutrients

I. 13 essential vitamins

Vitamins are a group of substances that are needed for normal cell function, growth, and development. Vitamins are grouped into two categories: fat soluble vitamins are stored in the body's fatty tissue. The 4 fatty-soluble vitamins are A, D, B and K. These vitamins are absorbed more easily by the body in the presence of dietary fat; there are 9 water-soluble vitamins. The body must use water-soluble vitamins right away. Any leftover water-soluble vitamins leave the body through the urine. Vitamin B12 is the only water-soluble vitamin that can be stored in the liver for many years.

1. Vitamin A: helps form and maintain healthy bones, skin, soft tissue, mucus membranes and teeth; (Food sources) dark leafy greens, dark-colored fruit and fish
2. Vitamin B6 (pyridoxine): helps form red blood cells and maintain brain function. This vitamin also plays an important role in the proteins that are part of many chemical reactions in the body. The more protein you eat the more pyridoxine your body needs; (Food sources) avocado, banana, legumes (dried beans), nuts, whole grains (milling and processing removes a lot of this vitamin).
3. Vitamin B12: like other B vitamins it is important for metabolism. It also helps form red blood cells and maintain central nervous system; (Food sources) spirulina, fortified cereals, Bragg's nutritional yeast.
4. Vitamin C (Absorbic acid): is an antioxidant that promotes healthy teeth and

gums. It helps the body absorb iron and maintain healthy tissue. It also promotes wound healing; (Food sources) broccoli, brussels sprouts, cabbage, cauliflower, citrus fruits, potatoes, spinach, strawberries, tomatoes and tomato juice.

5. Vitamin D: known as the "sunshine" vitamin, since it is made in the body after being in the sun. 10-15 minutes of sunshine 3x a week is enough to produce the body's requirement of vitamin D. It is very hard to get enough vitamin D from food sources and most people who don't live in sunny areas may be vitamin D deficient. Vitamin D helps the body absorb calcium, and helps to maintain proper blood levels of calcium and phosphorous; (Food sources) fish (fatty fish such as salmon, mackerel, herring, and orange boughy), fish liver oils (cod's liver oil), fortified cereals, fortified milks, fortified orange juice, mushrooms

6. Vitamin E (tocopherol): an antioxidant that helps the body form red blood cells and use vitamin K. Fights free radicals and prevents disease development, repairs damaged skin, balances cholesterol, thickens hair, improves vision and balances hormones; (Food sources) avocado, dark green veggies (spinach, broccoli, asparagus, and turnip greens), papaya and mango, seeds and nuts.

7. Vitamin K: helps blood to coagulate, builds strong bones, prevents heart disease; (Food sources) cabbage, cauliflower, dark green veggies (spinach, kale, collards, and turnip greens), and fish.

8. Vitamin B7 (biotin): is essential for the metabolism of proteins and carbohydrates, and in the production of hormones and cholesterol-lowering effects; (Food sources) chocolate, legumes, nuts and yeast.

9. Vitamin B3 (niacin): is a B vitamin that helps maintain healthy skin and nerves. It also has cholesterol-lowering effects; (Food sources) avocado, legumes, nuts, potatoes, fish (tuna and salt- water fish).

10. Vitamin B9 (folate and folic acid): works with B12 to help form red blood cells. It is needed for the production of DNA, which controls tissue growth and cell function. Any woman who is pregnant should be sure to get enough folate. Defects such as spinal bifida are linked to low levels of folate. Many foods are fortified with folate; (Food sources) asparagus and broccoli, beets, dried beans (cooked pinto, navy and lima), green leafy veggies (spinach and romaine lettuce), lentils, oranges and orange juice.

11. Vitamin B5 (pantothenic acid): is essential for the metabolism of food. It also plays a role in the production of hormones and cholesterol; (Food sources) avocado, broccoli, kale and other veggies in the cabbage family, legumes and lentils, mushrooms, and sweet potatoes.

12. Vitamin B2 (riboflavin): works with the other B vitamins. It is important for body growth and the production of red blood cells; (Food sources) dairy products, green leafy veggies, legumes, nuts, fortified breads and cereals; riboflavin is destroyed by exposure to light. Foods with riboflavin should not be stored in clear containers that are exposed to light.
13. Vitamin B1 (thiamine): helps the body's cells change carbohydrates into energy. Getting plenty of carbohydrates is very important during pregnancy and breast feeding. It is also essential for heart function and healthy nerve cells; (Food sources) legumes, nuts and seeds, peas and whole grains.

II. 10 Vital Minerals:

- Protein: are large, complex molecules that play many critical roles in the body. They do most of the work required in cells and are required for the structure, function and regulation of the body's tissues and organs... enzymes carry out almost all of the thousands of chemical reactions that take place, in cells; (Food sources) almonds, oats, broccoli, tuna, quinoa, lentils, pumpkin seeds, Ezekiel bread, and Brussels sprouts.
- Calcium: our bodies use 99% of its calcium to keep bones and teeth strong, thereby supporting skeletal structure and function. The rest of the calcium in our body plays a key role in cell signaling, blood clotting, muscle contraction and nerve function; (Food sources) kale, sardines, broccoli, okra, almonds, bok choy, watercress, and spinach.
- Zinc: is found in cells throughout the body. It is needed for the body's defensive (immune) system to work properly. It plays a role in cell division, cell growth, wound healing and the breakdown of carbohydrates. It is also needed for the senses of smell and taste; (Food sources) spinach, kidney beans, flax seeds, pumpkin seeds, watermelon seeds.
- Iron: is an essential element for blood production. About 70% of our body's iron is found in the red blood cells of our body called hemoglobin and in the muscle cells called myoglobin. Hemoglobin is essential for transferring oxygen in our blood from the lungs to the tissues; (Food sources) sunflower seeds, beans, whole grains, dark leafy greens (spinach), dark chocolate, pumpkin seeds, and squash, nuts, swiss chard and cacao powder.
- Phosphorous: the main function of phosphorous is the formation of bones and teeth. It plays an important role in how the body uses carbohydrates and fats. It is also needed for the body to make protein for the growth, maintenance and repair of cells and tissues; (Food sources) nuts, fish, seeds, beans, and lentils.

- Magnesium: is needed for more than 300 biochemical reactions in the body. It helps to maintain nerve and muscle function, supports a healthy immune system, keeps the heart rate steady and helps bones remain strong. It also helps regulate blood glucose levels and aid in the production of energy and protein; (Food sources) fruits and veggies (bananas, dried apricots, and avocados), nuts (almonds and cashews), peas, beans (legumes), seeds, whole grains (brown rice and millet).
- Manganese: helps the body form connective tissue, bones, blood clotting factors, and sex hormones. It also plays a role in fat and carbohydrate metabolism, calcium absorption and blood sugar regulation. Is also necessary for normal brain and nerve function; (Food sources) whole grains, nuts, leafy greens and teas, and seeds.
- Iodine: is a vital component of hormones produced by the thyroid gland that are responsible for a number of important functions in the body including growth, metabolism, reproduction, nerve and muscle function, regulation of body temperature and blood cell production; (Food sources) sea veggies (kelp, arame, hiziki, kombu, wakame, seaweed), cranberries, navy beans, strawberries, potatoes and fish.
- Carbohydrates: Provides energy, as they are the body's main source of fuel, needed for physical activity, brain function and operation of the organs. All cells and tissues in the body need carbs and they are also important for intestinal health and waste elimination; (Food sources) fruit and fruit juice, grains, legumes, and starchy veggies (e.g. potatoes).
- Fiber: plays an essential role in digestive, heart, and skin health, and may improve blood sugar control, and weight management. It comes in two varieties: soluble and insoluble, and most plant-based foods contain a mixture of both. Soluble fiber turns into a gel in the stomach and slows digestion, which helps in cholesterol and blood sugar lowering. Insoluble fiber remains unchanged all the way to the colon, making waste heavier and softer so it can shimmy through the intestines more easily; (Food sources) split peas, lentils, beans (black, and lima), artichokes, peas, broccoli, brussels sprouts, berries (rasp and black), avocadoes, pears, bran flakes, whole-wheat pasta, pearled barley, oatmeal.

C. Alkaline: Cancer fighters

I. Herbs

- Ashwagandha
- Astragalus
- Burdock root
- Cayenne
- Chickweed
- Irish moss
- Cleavers
- Dandelion
- Ginger
- Red clover tops
- Reishi
- Rhubarb root
- Sarsaparilla
- Slippery elm bark
- Bladderwrack
- Yellow dock

"Alkalinity is the key to tranquility". -Dr. Sebi. It is any substance having a base PH higher than 7 and that is capable of neutralizing an acid.

II. Beat cancer with hydrogen peroxide 35% (H2O2) (naturalnews.com):

Cancer is dangerous. Don't flirt with disaster. Don't eat it and don't go near it. Don't drink it. Don't put it on your skin. Yes, this is a warning not to put cancer on or inside your body. Cancer is in GMO pesticide DNA seed designs and the treatment used on veggies and fruit. Cancer is in sun block lotion full of toxins that hold in your sweat and block out the vitamin D you would normally get from the Sun. Cancer is in cosmetics, make-up, soaps, toothpaste and shampoos. Cancer may be lurking in your fridge, your pantry and your medicine cabinet, but it has a rival that destroys it like a M-60 leveling a field of enemy soldiers. It's called "hydrogen peroxide" and the "lame-stream" media will tell you how "dangerous" it is at 35%, but they will not tell you that you can drip a couple of drops in a glass of water each day and end cancer. Yes, it's true.

Cancer thrives in an acid-heavy system, here the blood and the organs are flooded with processed salt, sugar, animal fat and artificial food. The heart and brain struggle to filter out the toxins found in most conventional forms of food, like antibiotics, hormones, pesticides, insecticides, herbicides, bleach, ammonia, fluoride, heavy metals and much more. This is why the doctor's and oncologists tell chemo patients not to eat alkalizing foods like kale, because it will "interfere with the chemotherapy". God forbid you should try to alkalize all that acid that's killing your good cells. Most cancer patients die as result of the chemotherapy and radiation damage to their non-cancerous cells. In other words, your good cells that are trying to help your body beat cancer are deprived of oxygen also, leading to new cancers and often death within 5 years. "The most overlooked solution to all manner of illness and disease is perhaps the simplest. All pathogens, viruses, and parasites are anaerobic. They thrive in the absence of oxygen but cannot survive with an abundance of oxygen. They depend on fermenting glucose to survive and multiply." (naturalnews.com)

What should you do, whether you have cancer or not? Alkalize your body, that's what. Now keep in mind, hydrogen peroxide does not rebuild the immune system, or repair the cells damaged by toxic chemo; however, there's no better time to welcome that "change of season" for the regeneration of new cells, skin, hair and organ cells than right now. This is pre-programmed in our DNA. Men and women have the same schedule:

Getting enough hydrogen peroxide inside the cancer cells is key: it has been clinically demonstrated that the spread or mestasis of cancer is "inversely" proportional to the amount of oxygen around the cancer cells".

That means that the more oxygen, the slower the cancer spreads. Conversely, the less oxygen, the faster the cancer spreads. If cancer cells get enough oxygen, they will die! Hydrogen peroxide kills cancer cells, because cancer cells do not have the mechanism to break down the hydrogen peroxide and stop it from doing its work.

The key to curing cancer with hydrogen peroxide is getting enough hydrogen peroxide in the cancer cells. There is a scientific description of this: proteolytic enzymes, also called pancreatic enzymes, literally cut apart the thick coating that covers cancer cells, so the immune system can recognize the cells as cancerous. Well, you don't have to be a scientist to understand that! By cutting apart the protein coating, the hydrogen peroxide then gets inside the cancer cells. You won't hear about that on any CNN "cancer special" or on "Dr. Oz".

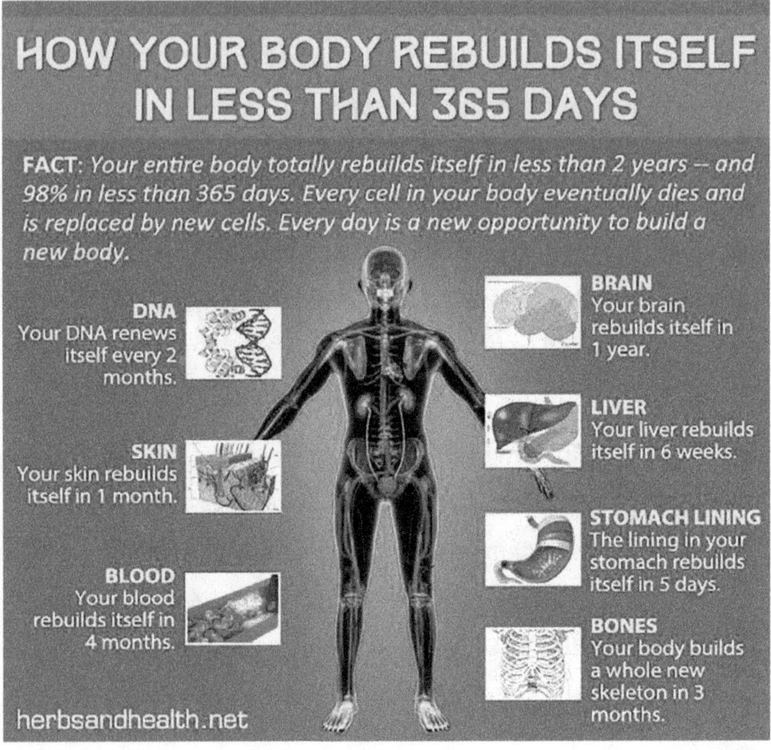

HOW YOUR BODY REBUILDS ITSELF IN LESS THAN 365 DAYS
FACT: Your entire body totally rebuilds itself in less than 2 years -- and 98% in less than 365 days. Every cell in your body eventually dies and is replaced by new cells. Every day is a new opportunity to build a new body.
DNA
Your DNA renews itself every 2 months.
SKIN
Your skin rebuilds itself in 1 month.
BLOOD
Your blood rebuilds itself in 4 months.
BRAIN
Your brain rebuilds itself in 1 year.
LIVER
Your liver rebuilds itself in 6 weeks.
STOMACH LINING
The lining in your stomach rebuilds itself in 5 days.
BONES
Your body builds a whole new skeleton in 3 months.
herbsandhealth.net

Science has known this for 50 years: Nobel peace prize winner Dr. Otto Warburg demonstrated over 50 years ago the basic difference between normal cells and cancer cells. Both derive energy from glucose, but the normal cell requires oxygen to combine with the glucose, while cancer cells break down glucose without oxygen, yielding only about 1/15 of the energy per glucose molecule that a normal cell produces. This is why cancer cells have such a huge appetite for sugar and why people who are obese get cancer more often. It's called the "biochemical cascade". (naturalnews.com)

Hydrogen peroxide and several other oxygen therapies are proven to be safe and effective. Pay attention to what you buy though, because 35% food grade hydrogen peroxide is the only grade recommended for initial use. Beware of the 3% "pharmaceutical grade". This is the grade sold at your local drugstore or supermarket. This product is not recommended for internal use, because it contains an assortment of stabilizers which shouldn't be ingested.

Home use advice: some individuals add a cup of 35% food grade hydrogen peroxide to a bathtub of warm water and soak for 20–30 minutes. The hydrogen peroxide is absorbed through the skin, which is your largest organ. Others drink a glass of water with several drops of food grade or reagent grade hydrogen peroxide. Also look into digestive enzymes. Researchers have noted for years a correspondence between low levels of enzymes and cancer; in fact, enzyme therapy has been used with good results against cancers in Europe and by some doctors in the united states.

III. Alkaline foods:

- Alfalfa
- Celery
- Barley grass
- Peppers
- Beet greens
- Broccoli
- Cabbage
- Mustard greens
- Chard greens
- Collard greens
- Chlorella
- Onions
- Cucumber
- Dulce
- Spinach
- Spirulina
- Edible flowers
- Garlic
- Green beans
- Dandelions
- Lettuce
- Kohlrabi
- Kale
- Pumpkin
- Wheatgrass
- Sprouts
- Watercress
- Wild greens

Immune boosting foods:

- Lemons
- Goji berries
- Sage
- Sweet potatoes
- Almonds
- Kale
- Grapefruit
- Raspberries
- Rosemary
- Onion
- Wheatgrass
- Asparagus

D. Detoxification

I. What is the lymphatic system?

It is the body's internal drainage system, designed to rid your blood of acidic and toxic waste! Without a properly functioning lymph system, our bodies become toxic waste bins which results in excessive weight and cellulite, arthritis, bursitis, headaches, different cancers and a compromised immune system. 2 steps to a healthy lymph system:

- Healthy Foods: greens, citrus fruits, healthy fats, melons, berries and water
- Necessary activities: massages, exercise, dry brushing, and deep breathing
- Factors that contribute to a sluggish lymphatic system: stress, iodine deficiency, pesticides, smoking, prescription drugs, meat, dairy and food additives.

II. Foods that eliminate mucus:

- Cauliflower
- Garlic
- Celery
- Asparagus
- Bamboo shoots
- Onions
- Lemons
- Limes
- Grapefruit
- Green veggies
- Kumquat
- Ginger
- Oranges
- Pineapple

III. Foods that fight Candida:

- Dandelion greens
- Coconut oil
- Parsley
- Broccoli
- Ginger
- Fennel
- Brussels sprouts
- Cinnamon
- Leeks
- Cardamom
- Oregano
- Clove
- Onion
- Hot peppers
- Swiss chard
- Thyme
- Turnips
- Cabbage

- Cumin
- Celery
- Arugua
- Watercress
- Zucchini
- Tumeric
- Garlic
- Kale
- Turnip greens
- Mustard greens
- Bok choy
- Cayenne
- Kohlrabi
- Anise
- Shallots
- Celery seed
- Sprouts
- Horseradish

Specific Cleansing:

- Blood: cayenne pepper, red grapes, wheatgrass, moringa, garlic, leafy greens, kale, beans, oregano, coconut water
- Lymph: sea veggies, asparagus, carrots, guava, lettuce, lemon water, strawberries, fruit and veggie juices
- Liver: leafy greens, grapefruit, barley grass, avocado, lemon, spinach, walnuts, argulo, apples, garlic, dandelion greens, artichoke, burdock root, milk thistle, dandelion
- Gallbladder: cucumber, lentils, tomatoes, watermelon, beans, avocado, whole grains, beets, legumes, garlic, onion, sweet potatoes
- Pancreas: spinach, cabbage, cherries, broccoli, red reishi mushrooms, sweet potatoes, blueberries,
- Kidneys: cranberries, tomatoes, tumeric, cauliflower, red bell pepper, onion, cabbage, raspberries, olive oil, ginger, bilberry, cranberry, astragalus
- Intestines: flax seeds, pineapple, artichokes, eggplant, dragonfruit, papaya, chili pepper, lentils
- Lungs: garlic, ginger, tumeric, pomegranate, kale, broccoli, apples, berries, water, mullein, yarrow, yerba santa, peppermint
- Brain: blueberries, deep water fish, nuts and seeds, avocadoes, whole grains, beans, pomegranate juice, freshly brewed tea, dark chocolate, sea veggies, cayenne pepper, ginseng, gingo balboa
- Heart: fish, nuts, berries, flaxseeds, oatmeal, dark beans, colorful veggies, spinach, tomatoes, asparagus, oranges, cantaloupes, broccoli, dark chocolate, cacao, motherwort, tumeric, garlic

- Stomach: chamomile, licorice, goldenseal, fennel, cumin, yogurt, sauerkraut, miso, bananas, garlic, asparagus, onions, caraway, cardamom, cinnamon, nutmeg, leafy greens and yellow veggies, citrus fruit, mint

E. Super foods:

I. Herbs and spices

- Cayenne pepper: helps burn fat, can keep blood pressure stabilized, lowers LDL and triglyceride, oral health, joint pain prevention/relief, anti-bacterial, food preservative, high capsaicin, stimulates circulation, detoxifying, improves digestion, relieves gas, appetite suppressant, prevents allergies, anti-inflammatory, can stop a heart attack
- Chlorella: Detoxifies Heavy Metals, Detoxifies Radiation and Chemotherapy, Supports Your Immune System, Promotes Weight Loss, Makes You Look Younger, Fights Cancer, Lowers Your Blood Sugar and Cholesterol
- Cinnamon: high source of antioxidants, anti-inflammatory, heart healthy, diabetes fighter, protects cognitive skills, lowers cancer risk, anti-viral, freshens breath, prevents/cures Candida, skin healthy, allergy relief, natural sweetener, food preservative
- Cumin: stomachache relief, thymol, carminative, respitory relief, common cold/ flu relief, rich in iron, high in calcium, boost immunity, enhances cognition and concentration, high in vitamin E, weight management, influences healthy menstrual cycle
- Cloves: antioxidants, antiseptic, local anesthetic, anti- inflammatory, rubeficient, carminative, anti-parasite, oral hygiene, good source of vitamin K, B6, B1, C and riboflavin, Vitamin A beta-carotene levels, contains numerous minerals (potassium, magnesium, manganese, iron, selenium, and iron)
- Basil: treats colds, immunity boost, stress relief, improves vision, prevents acne, oral health, eliminates kidney stones, cures stomachache, headache relief
- Bee Pollen: It has a highly nutritive value and is a good source for quick energy. It is excellent for allergies, hay fever, hypoglycemia, asthma, prostate gland, endurance, stamina, vitality, longevity
- Dill: reduces menstrual cramps, natural bug repellant, treats epilepsy, beneficial fatty acids that aid in digestion and provide energy, antimicrobial, protects against free radicals

- Black pepper: increases nutrient absorption, improves digestion, stimulates appetite, facilitates weight loss, relieves gas, helps clear congestion, combats arthritis, fights cancer and other maladies, antidepressant, oral hygiene
- Fennel: anti bad breath, aids digestion, relieves water retention, weight loss, cancer fighter, treats menstrual problems, treats respiratory illness, prevents cardiac problems, promotes eye health, improves brain function
- Fenugreek: diabetes control, stimulates breast milk production, balances cholesterol, heart healthy, cures constipation, joint pain relief, fights flues and colds, reduces menstrual discomforts, hair healthy, skin healthy
- Garlic: heart healthy, controls hypertension, arthritis relief, boosts immunity, treats cough and cold, anti-fungal, cures tooth ache and earaches, aids digestion, inhibits cancer, combats allergies
- Ginger: settles upset stomach, prevents cold and flu, treats morning sickness, reduces arthritis, cancer fighter, reduces menstrual problems, treats migraines, suppresses cough, promotes heart health, controls diabetes
- Maca: reliable aphrodisiac, improves fertility, increases energy, vitality, stamina, restores and corrects hormone imbalances, enhances mood and memory, antioxidant booster
- Mint: boost digestion, strengthens liver, cools body, relieves asthma, oral hygiene, reduces flatulence, eliminates mucus, cancer fighter, acne relief, prevents irritable nipples while breast feeding, eases hiccups,
- Moringa: 7x the vitamin C of oranges, 4x the vitamin A of carrots, 4x the calcium of milk, 3x the potassium of bananas, 2x the protein of yogurt, helps protect the heart, can purify water, anti-diabetic, anti-inflammatory, maintains healthy cholesterol, 25x more iron than spinach, cardiovascular health, brain healthy, antimicrobial, protects the liver, anti-bacterial, enhances wound healing
- Oregano: immune support, anti-fungal and anti-bacterial and may even kill mrsa, upper respitory infections, anti- inflammatory, relieves menstrual cramps, kills intestinal parasites, heart healthy, cancer fighter, nasal congestion relief, stimulates appetite, maintains body weight
- Pine needles: rich in vitamins A and C, relieves cold and flu, brings clarity and mental clearness, antidepressant, weight control, hypertension relief, fights free radicals, slows aging process
- Rosemary: boosts memory, strengthens immune system, stimulates hair

growth, alleviates headaches, hypertension relief, stimulates circulation, fights stress and anxiety, improves digestion

- Sage: protects heart health, boosts mood, enhances memory, improves digestion, soothes sore throat, lowers blood sugar, reduces menopausal symptoms, oral hygiene, hair growth
- Spirulina: detoxifier, reduces symptoms of HIV/AIDS, cancer fighter, stroke relief/reduction, boosts energy, metabolism boost, alleviates sinus issues
- Thyme: soothes sore throats, lowers blood pressure and cholesterol, prevents food poisoning, boosts mood, cancer fighter, naturally remedies bronchitis, diuretic, appetite stimulant
- Tumeric: prevents cancer, relieves arthritis, controls diabetes, reduces cholesterol levels, immunity booster, heals wounds, weight management, brain health, digestive aid, battles/prevents liver disease
- Wheatgrass: boost circulation, cleanses the liver, faster healing, gets rid of odors, treats arthritis, reduces fatigue, cancer fighter, battles obesity, immunity booster, improves fertility, detoxifier, restores PH levels

II. Nuts and Seeds:

- Chia: protects against heart disease, aids in weight loss, energy boost, protects against diabetes, reduces joint pain
- Hemp: strengthens immunity, helps cardiovascular system, superior source of protein, improves skin and hair, cancer fighter
- Pomegranate: rich source of antioxidants, pumps oxygen into blood, cancer fighter, lessens inflammation from arthritis, reduces risk of heart disease
- Flax: relieves abdominal pain, anti-inflammatory, stabilizes hormonal levels, reduces symptoms of PMS and menopause, reduces risk of breast and prostate cancer
- Pumpkin: good source of vitamin B, fights depression, boosts mood, prevents certain kidney stone formations, fights parasites
- Apricot: cancer fighter, relieves arthritic pain, lowers blood pressure, resists colds and flues, hair health
- Sesame: lowers cholesterol, prevents hypertension, rheumatoid arthritis relief, protects liver, good source of calcium
- Sunflower: helps reduce severity of asthma, lowers high blood pressure, prevents migraines, reduces risk of heart attack, reduces risk of stroke

- Cumin: helps digestive disorders, antiseptic, boosts power of liver, treats asthma and arthritis, boosts immune system
- Grape: prevents high blood pressure, lowers cholesterol, reduces swelling from injuries, helps eye disease from diabetes, heals wounds
- Pistachios: weight loss, insulin, cancer protective phenolics, lowers blood pressure, rheumatoid arthritis support
- Hazelnuts: cardiovascular health, Alzheimer's disease, rheumatoid arthritis relief, cancer fighter, antidiabetic
- Macadamia: lowers cholesterol levels, reduces diabetes risk, cleans colon, anemia treatment, morning sickness relief
- Brazil: cancer fighter, reduces blood sugar levels, prevents thyroid enlargement, prevents reproductive disorders, protects from tumors
- Chestnuts: improves glycemic control, memory protection, bowel health, anemia treatment, weight loss
- Almonds: appetite control, brain health, memory booster, biotin source, good source of vitamin E
- Walnuts: anti-inflammatory, heart health, liver healthy, brain healthy, cancer fighter
- Cashews: heart healthy, fights hypertension, diabetes fighter, eye healthy, helps form red blood cells
- Pecans: good source of Vitamins (A, B and E), cardiovascular health, bone and teeth health, skin healthy
- Pine Nuts: suppresses appetite, boost energy, heart healthy, anti-aging, antioxidants, vision health

III. Juice/smoothie cures:

- Cold: carrot, pineapple, ginger, garlic
- Headache: apple, cucumber, kale, ginger, celery
- Ulcer: cabbage, carrot, celery
- Hypertension: beet, apple, celery, cucumber, ginger
- Kidney detox: carrot, watermelon, cucumber, cilantro
- Eyes: carrot, celery
- Constipation: carrot, apple, fresh cabbage
- Hangover: apple, carrot, beet, lemon
- Nervousness: carrot, apple, spinach, beet

- Depression: carrot, apple, spinach, beet
- Diabetes: carrot, spinach, celery
- Asthma: carrot, spinach, apple, garlic, lemon
- Arthritis: carrot, celery, pineapple, lemon
- Kidney stone: orange, apple, watermelon, lemon
- Stress: banana, strawberry, pear
- Fatigue: carrots, beets, green apple, lemon, spinach
- Memory loss: pomegranate, beets, grapes
- Indigestion: pineapple, carrot, lemon, mint
- Apple cider vinegar
- Drink up: helps with weight loss, maintains body's alkaline PH levels, detoxes liver, reduces heartburn, helps body combat Candida
- For your face (toner): 1-part acv + 2 parts water; tightens skin, reduces acne
- For your hair (rinse and shine): mix 1-part water + 1-part acv and use after shampoo; shiny soft hair, removes build up from product
- For sunburn (soother): 1 cup acv in bathtub and soak; (bonus tip) post bath use coconut oil for further relief
- For disinfectant (cleaner): dilute a ½ cup of acv with 1 cu of water; cleans surfaces; leaves a delightful smell of apples
- For smells (air freshener): dilute a cup of acv with 1 cup of water; natural deodorizer
- For pets (flea repellant): ¼ cup acv to ¾ water; provides a shiny coat as well
- For garden (weed killer): 1-part acv to 8 parts water in spray bottle
- For produce (produce wash): 4 tablespoons acv to 1-gallon water; keeps dirt and pesticides away

IV. Honey

The best food on the planet! The only food that doesn't rot; a jar of honey may remain edible for 3000 years.

Raw honey (unfiltered, unpasteurized) contains 22 amino acids, 27 minerals and 5000 enzymes. The minerals included are iron, zinc, potassium, calcium, phosphorous, magnesium and selenium. The vitamins found in raw honey include B6, B1, B2, B3 and B5.

Honey beats silver in burn wound healing; possesses more antibacterial qualities and heals at a faster rate than silver, the dominant dressing used in wound healing. It also does not have the same toxic effect on the skin as does silver.

Aside from the physical benefits honey makes you glow and enhances your vibration/frequency; also aiding in internal temperature control, allowing less irritation and discomfort from high heat atmospheres.

Additional benefits:

- Filled with phytonutrients
- Antibacterial and antifungal
- Good source of antioxidants
- Soothes sore throat
- Digestive aid
- Battles allergies
- Energy booster
- Memory enhancer
- Soothes acid reflux
- A preservative
- Immune system booster
- Natural sweetener
- Acne remover
- Bee sting treatment
- Hair and skin care
- Antiseptic

F. Fasting:

I. The best cleanse

While it is important to provide the temple (body) with the best nutrients, it is also just as important to give it time to rest and regenerate itself. Our brains use a great deal of energy to digest the food we eat so the more we do so, even if it's healthy, takes away from our mental prowess thus we aren't as strong as we need to be. Here are the benefits:

- Anti-aging effects
- Better attitude
- Better resistance to food
- Better sleep
- Change of habits
- Clearer planning
- Creativity
- Diet changes
- Drug detoxification
- Improved senses
- Inspiration
- More clarity

- More energy
- More relaxation
- Purification
- Reduction of allergies
- Rejuvenation
- Rest for digestive organs
- Right use of will
- Spiritual awareness
- Weight loss

G. Eugenics

I. The Truth

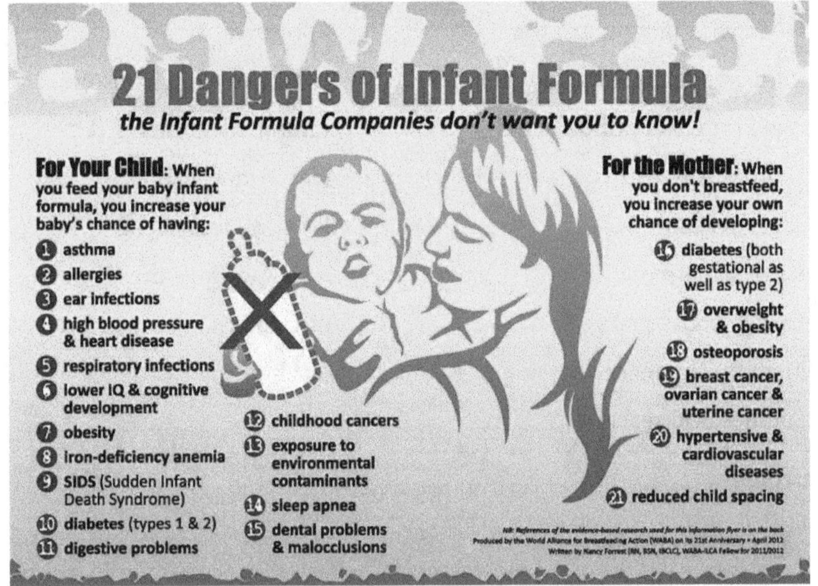

All forms of mercury are toxic to humans:

- 2 ppb (parts per billion) maximum mercury contaminant is in drinking water set by EPA.
- 250 ppb is the typical mercury level in tuna.
- 500 ppb is the highest detected by natural news in contaminated whitefish.
- 51,000 ppb level of mercury found in a flu shot natural news.com

  Sources: ICP-MS laboratory testing at natural news forensic food lab: package insert of flulaval influenza virus vaccine from glaxosmithkline

Other Ingredients in vaccines: (www.thinkingmomsrevolution.com), (www. illuzone.net)

- Ammonium sulfate (salt): suspected gastrointestinal, liver, nerve and respitory poison.
- Beta-propiolactone: known to cause cancer, suspected gastrointestinal, liver, respiratory, skin and sense organ poison.
- GMO yeast, animal, bacterial and viral DNA: can be incorporated into the recipient's DNA and cause unknown genetic mutations.
- Latex rubber: can cause life threatening allergic reactions.
- Monosodium glutamate (MSG/glutamate/glutamic acid): being studied for multigenetic, teratogenetic (developmental malformation and monstrosities) and reproductive effects. A neurotoxin. Allergic reactions can range from mild to severe.
- Aluminum: implicated as a cause of brain drainage; suspected factor in Alzheimer's disease, dementia, seizures and comas. Allergic reactions can occur on skin.
- Formaldehyde: major constituent of embalming fluid; poisonous if ingested. Probable carcinogen; suspected gastrointestinal, liver, immune system, nerve, reproductive system, and respiratory poison. Linked to leukemia, brain, colon and lymphatic cancer.
- Micro-organism: live and killed viri and bacteria or their toxins. The polio vaccine was contaminated with a monkey virus now turning up in human bone, lung-lining (mesothlioma), brain tumors and lymphomas. When babies are hours or days old, it is impossible to know if they have an allergy.
- Polysorbate 80: known to cause cancer in animals.
- Tri (n) butylphosphate: suspected kidney and nerve poison.
- Glutaraldehyde: poisonous if ingested. Causes birth defects in experimental animals.
- Gelatin: produced from selected pieces of calf and cattle skins, de-mineralized cattle bones and pork skin. Allergic reactions have been reported.
- Gentamicin sulfate & polymyxin B: allergic reactions can range from mild to life threatening.
- Mercury: one of the most poisonous substances known. Has an affinity for the brain, gut, liver, bone marrow and kidneys. Minute amounts can cause nerve damage. Symptoms of mercury toxicity are similar to those of autism.
- Neomycin sulfate (antibiotic): interferes with vitamin B6 absorption. An error

in the uptake of B6 can cause a rare form of epilepsy and mental retardation. Allergic reactions can be mild to life threatening.

- Phenol/phenoxyyethanol (2-PE): used as antifreeze. Toxic to all cells and capable of disabling the immune system's primary response mechanism.
- Human and animal cells: human cells from absorbed fetal tissue and human albumin. Pig blood, horse blood, rabbit brain, guinea pig, dog kidney, cow heart, monkey kidney, chick embryo, chicken egg, duck egg, calf serum, sheep blood and others.

> *"A major cause of the Roman emperor's decline, after 6 centuries of world dominance was its replacement of stone aqueducts by lead pipes for the transport and supply of drinking water. Roman engineers, the best in the world, turned their fellow citizens into neurological cripples. Today our own "best and brightest", with the best of intentions, achieve the same end through childhood vaccination programs yielding the modern scourges of hyperactivity, learning disabilities, autism, appetite disorders, and impulse violence."*-Harris L. Coulter, Ph.D.

See and you thought it was all just in the genetics; no, they have been tampering with our genetics turning us into beast slowly and methodically which in turn has sparked all manner of unnatural and backwards behavior.

II. Immunization Exemption (www.ncsl.org)

School immunization exemption state laws: States with religious and philosophical exemptions from school immunization requirements:

All 50 states have legislation requiring specified vaccines for students. Although exemptions vary from state to state, all school immunization laws grant exemptions to children for medical reasons. Almost all states grant religious exemptions for people who have religious beliefs against immunizations. Currently, 18 states allow philosophical exemptions for those who object to immunizations because of moral, personal or other beliefs.

Source: Adapted from immunization action coalition June 2014. The existing statute in Minnesota and Louisiana does not explicitly recognize religion as a reason for claiming an exemption, however, as a practical matter; the non-medical exemption may encompass all religious beliefs. In Arizona, the personal exemption is for school enrollees only.

School Vaccine Requirements and Exemptions:

- Alabama: Al. code 16-30-3
- Alaska: Ak. Stat. 14.30.125
- Arizona: Ariz. Rev. stat. ann. 15-872, 873
- Arkansas: Ark. Code ann. 6-18-702
- California: Cal. Health and safety code 120325 et. seq.
- Colorado: Colo. Rev. stat. 25-4-902, 903
- Connecticut: Conn. Gen. stat. 10-204a
- Delaware: del. Code ann. Tit. 14 131
- Washington DC: D.C. code ann. 38-501, 506
- Florida: fla. Stat. ann. 1003.22
- Georgia: ga. Code ann. 20-2-771
- Hawaii: haw. Rev. stat. 302A- 1154, 1156
- Idaho: Idaho code 30-4801, 4802
- Illinois: 105 III. Comp. stat. 5/27-8.1
- Indiana: Ind. Code ann. 21-40-5
- Iowa: Iowa code ann. 139A.8
- Kansas: kan. Stat. ann. 72-5209
- Kentucky: ky. Rev. stat. ann 214.034
- Louisiana: la. Rev. ann. 17: 170 (A); 40: 31.16
- Maine: me. Rev. stat. ann. Tit. 20-A 6355
- Maryland: md. Code ann. Educ. 7-403
- Massachusetts: mass. Gen. laws ann. 333.9208, 9215
- Michigan: mich. Comp. laws ann. 333.9208, 9215
- Minnesota: minn. Stat. ann. 121A-15
- Mississippi: miss. Code ann. 41-23-37
- Missouri: mo. Rev. stat. 167.181, 210.003
- Montana: mont. Code ann. 20-5-403, 405
- Nebraska: neb. Rev. stat. ann. 79-217, 221
- Nevada: nev. Rev. stat. 392.435, 437, 439
- New Hampshire: n.h. rev. stat. ann. 141-C:20-a, 20-c
- New Jersey: n.j. stat. ann. 26: 1A-9, 9.1
- New Mexico: n.m. stat. ann. 24-5-1, 3
- New York: n.y. pub. Health law 2164
- North Carolina: n.c. gen. stat. 130A-155, 156, 157
- North Dakota: n.d. cent. Code 23-07-17.1
- Ohio: Ohio rev. code ann. 3313.671

- Oklahoma: Okla. Stat. ann. Tit. 70, 1210.191, 192
- Oregon: or. Rev. stat. 433.267
- Pennsylvania: 28 pa. code 23-83, 84
- Rhode Island: r.i. gen. laws 16-38-2
- South Carolina: s.c. code ann. 44-29-180
- South Dakota: s.d. codified laws 13-28-7.1
- Tennessee: tenn. Code ann. 49-6-5001
- Texas: tex. Edu. Code ann. 38.001
- Utah: Utah code ann. 53A-11-301, 302
- Vermont: vt. Stat. ann, tit. 18, 1121, 1122
- Virginia: va. Code ann. 22.1-271.2, 32.1-46
- Washington: wash. Rev. code ann. 28A.210.080, 90
- West Virginia: w. va. Code 16-3-4
- Wisconsin: wis. Stat. ann. 252.04
- Wyoming: wyo. Stat. ann. 21-4-309

Religious exemption indicates that there is a provision in the statute that allows parents to exempt their children from vaccination if it contradicts their sincere religious beliefs.

Philosophical exemption indicates that the statutory language does not restrict the exemption to purely religious or spiritual beliefs. For example, Maine allows restrictions based on "moral, philosophical or other personal beliefs", and Minnesota allows objections based on "conscientiously held beliefs of the parent or guardian."

This is why we must get back to Islam in its purest form because it encompasses all religious/spiritual expressions and the devoted practitioner of Th Divine science can say they are in tune with any religious faith without it being an actual contradiction or flat out lie because Islam in its primordial form of application is the root from which the tree of divine worship and expression sprung. Don't ever identify yourself as a misnomer but instead use it properly without you yourself being used improperly. (See Luke 16:8 and Matthew 10:16)

Non-Derogable Rights

- Non-Derogable Rights - Rights which can not be taken away
- No nation state may suspend or violate, even in times of public emergency:
- (a) the right to life;
- (b) freedom from torture or cruel, inhuman or degrading treatment or punishment and from medical or scientific experimentation;
- (c) the right not to be held in slavery or involuntary servitude; and,
- (d) the right not to be subjected to retroactive criminal penalties as defined in the Covenant.
- Customary international law prohibits in all circumstances the denial of such fundamental rights.

OUTRO:

"*Health is the greatest gift, contentment the greatest wealth, faithfulness the best relationship*". –Buddha

PART 3: BUILD THYSELF

"*If you want to climb a mountain start at the top*". -Zen Proverb

Intro: Up is down and down is up, therefore, to build you must start from heaven which is actually the root/apex of existence. Th law is ingrained in our consciousness but by way of indoctrination combined with karmic debt owed by our past lives we fell from grace. Getting back to the ancient ways of spiritual discipline and communion is the only way to exercise our own inner demon/lower self in turn binding the beast and banishing its minions. Th law was written because we men are forgetful and weak willed so every generation Th Most High manifest in flesh by way of a select few so as to convey the warning that the end is not near but is here; we live in such a time. All the signs are there, and Th ancient ones are back, and the candle is lit, the window of salvation has been opened and we have been forgiven for our past foolishness, but we must fortify ourselves inwardly as well as outwardly creating an aura field that allows us to navigate this underworld while we ascend. Distractions are at an all- time high and it behooves us to take heed and not get nicked by the thorns of Satan and its vanity fare. A fortress is only as strong as its pillars and walls, but it must also be able to withstand inside attacks as well for the enemy of the righteous is of their own household. Be wise, spread love, and let foolery fight itself. Know Th law and be Th law.

Chapter 1: G.O.D

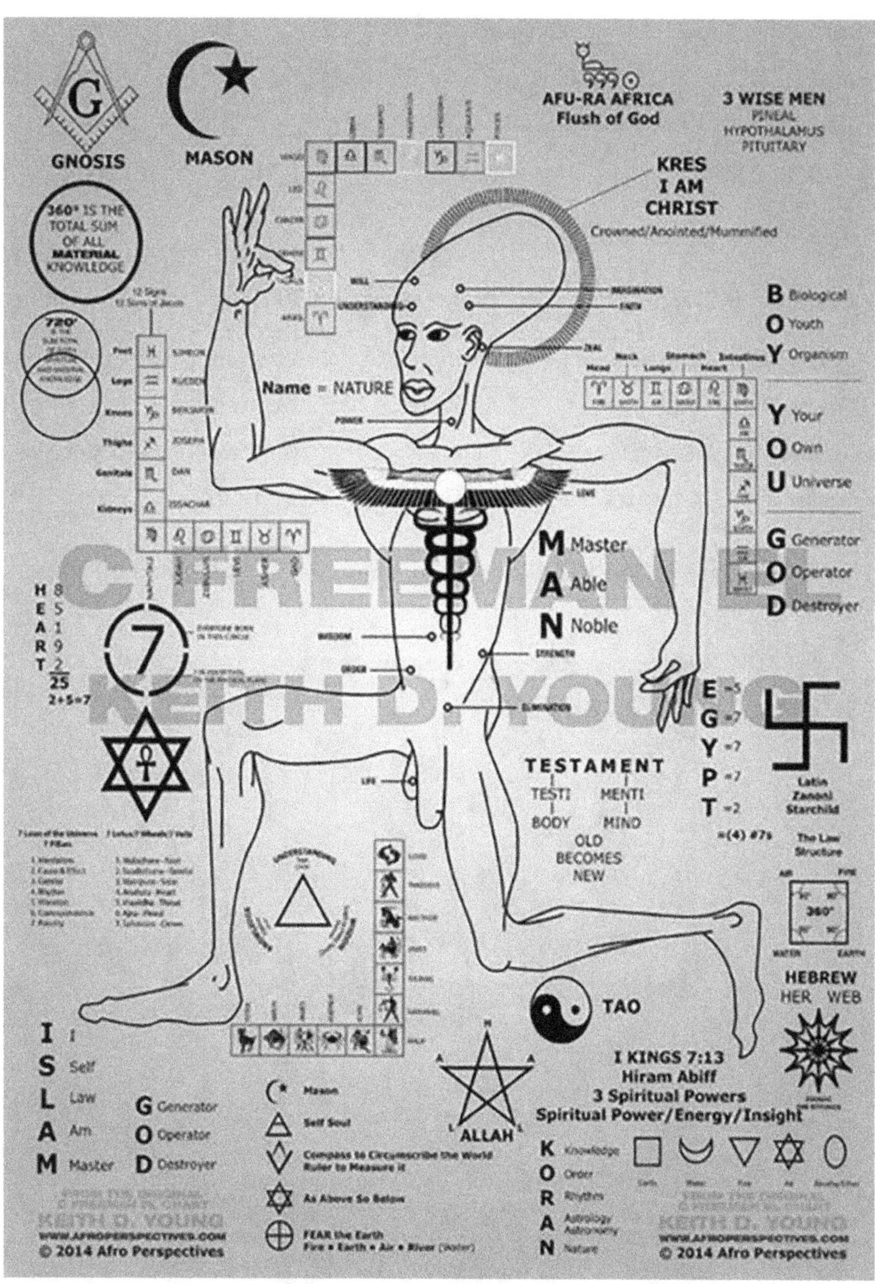

A. Culture Freedom

I-I	I	I	I	I
S-Self	Save	Sincerely	Seek	Serve
L-Law	Lives	Love	Learn	Loyally
A-Am	Around	Allah's	And	And
Master	Me	Mathematics	Manifest	Morally

P-Positive	Patient	Progressive	Proper	Persistent
E-Education	Enthusiasm	Energy	Ethereal	Effort
A-Always	And	Activates	Awareness	Achieves
C-Correct	Creativity	Cellular	Cultivates	Collective
E-Errors	Elevates	Edification	Eternal	Ends

Islam(6=Balance) + Peace(3=Understanding)= 9(Perfection)

THE GOLDEN RULE

Hinduism

Everything you should do you will find in this:
Do nothing to others
That would hurt you if it were done to you.

MAHABHARATA 5:1517

Buddhism

Do not offend others
As you would not want to be offended.

UDANAVARGA 5:18

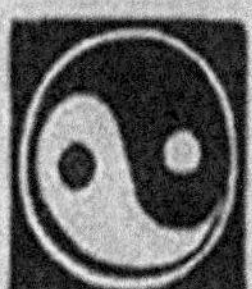

Taoism

The successes of your neighbor and their losses
Will be to you as if they were your own.

T'AI-SHANG KAN-YING P'IEN

Confucianism

Is there any rule that one should follow all of one's life?
Yes! The rule of the gentle goodness:
That which we do not wish to be done to us, we do not do to others.

ANALECTAS 15:23

Judaism

That which you do not wish for yourself
You shall not wish for your neighbor.
This is the whole law: the rest is only commentary.

TALMUD SHABBAT 31^

Christianity

In everything, do to others what
You would have them do to you.
For this sums up the law and the prophets.

MATTHEW 7:12

Islam

None of you shall be true believers
Unless you wish for your brother
The same that you wish for yourself.

B. The Science of Nature, God and the Universe

Nature is the effect or result of an initial cause. Nature or the universe is the result of a set of chain reactions initially set in motion by the thought of a supreme mind.

> "*Man is a thought of Allah; all thoughts of Allah are infinite; they are not measured up by time, for the things that are concerned with time, begin and end.*" The Holy Koran of the M.S.T.of A., Noble Drew Ali, p.4

This supreme mind is what is referred to as "God" the "Creator". Within the Judeo, Christian, Islamic tradition, as well as, in most other religious/ cultural traditions, this supreme mind or "God" was originally all that existed, alone, before creation.

> "*In the beginning God created the heaven and the Earth. And the earth was without form and void; and darkness was upon the face of the waters. And God said, Let there be light: and there was light.*" Genesis 1:1-3

Realizing first that it did indeed exist was the first step in creation symbolized by the first sign of the zodiac Aries, and it's key words, "I am". Once this supreme mind or "God" realized it existed and has always existed, it also realized the potential worlds that existed within itself. This is symbolized by the second sign of the zodiac Taurus, and it's keywords, "I Have". At this point, however, there still was no physical creation or universe, only the realization by the supreme mind or "God" that it existed, always existed, and that it had within it infinite worlds in a potential state. There was only realization of existence and realization of potential.

The thought then occurred to take all these potential worlds and make them manifest. This thought alone put in motions a series of chain reactions whose purpose, goal, and effect was to make manifest all the potential worlds this supreme mind or "God" had within itself. This thought to make all within manifest without is known to science as "The Big Bang." It is symbolized by the third sign of the zodiac, Gemini, and it's keywords, "I Think." At this point the supreme mind or "God" became "God" the "Creator", and the physical universe came into existence.

The universe did not come into existence as a fully manifest copy of all of the potential worlds within the supreme mind or "God". The universe came into manifestation as a seed, a process, a chain-reaction, which would eventually manifest all that which was originally in a potential state within the supreme mind or "God." Because the universe manifested as a seed or process striving towards the manifestation of the "all", this brought about what we refer to as time. Time is the measurement of one stage of this manifesting process to another stage of this manifesting process.

Since the worlds within the initial supreme mind or "God" is infinite, the universe will take an infinite amount of time to manifest all of these infinite potential worlds. Thus, the universe is "ever-becoming". The universe is actual a process set in motion by that original thought, and this process has a specific goal; to make all that which was potential in the supreme mind or "God", manifest in physical creation. There are an infinite number of potential worlds to manifest. In order for the universe or this process to manifest all of these potential worlds, it must do two things simultaneously;

1. Multiply by Division - or increase the number of things or worlds in existence, and
2. Order - Put all of these things and worlds into some type of order.

In doing these two things, the universe is thus becoming more complex, by increasing in quantity and increasing in order.

When an egg or ovum is fertilized, it increases the number of cells by dividing the cells. The cells are then put into order by being classified and organized into to different types of cells, which form different types of tissues. These tissues in turn form different types of organs. These organs are then organized as different parts of one body. Thus the human body is the result of multiplication by division, and order. Everything in existence comes from multiplication by division and order. Thus the human being manifests into the physical universe initially as a simple one celled being, which multiplies by dividing, and becomes a complex organism/organization of cell, tissues, organs etc. Thus, everything in nature or the universe goes from simplicity to complexity, and from being comprised of few parts to many parts.

It does not stop there. Humans than seek to organize themselves into even larger and more complex organisms or superorganisms known as societies. Small societies in turn join with other societies forming empires and global civilizations. So. on, and so on. Thus, while each thing is becoming more complex, it seeks to join with other things forming even larger and even more complex things. This drive of nature is embedded in each and everything thing in creation. When anything in this universe ceases to strive toward greater complexity by being a part of a greater order or organization, it withers and dies. This can be seen from the individual cells of the body, to humans and society. When muscle cells are not used, they sense they are useless to the body and began to self-destruct, wither and die. This is known as atrophy. As humans, we must be part of a larger organism (society). A human isolated or exiled from society will sense they are useless and will wither and perish.

As individuals, most of our people here in the United States are like superfluous or useless cells in the body or organism of the United States. Cells that feel that they are useless to the whole organism, wither and die. Thus, this is what counts in large part for our low life expectancy, low self-esteem, high amount of stress related illnesses, self-inflicted violence, high rates of alcohol and drug-abuse, "crab in the barrel mentality", etc. We must organize ourselves into a thriving organism or society, and then work out how we will relate with the larger society. We have somewhere skipped a step and tried to be part of one level of organization (United States), without first being part of a level or organization below that (a state, republic, etc.). We are like cells not part of now particular organ, trying to be part of a body. Many cells, not part of an organ, or serving some other purpose is eliminated one of two ways; excreted as urine, feces, sweat, or vomit, or treated as a virus or parasite and eliminated via an immune response. Perhaps the only reason we still exist is because the amount of money we spend as consumers is more than the social and economic burden and expense we incur. However, this may not be for long, and may be turning the other way as I speak. Perhaps this is why AIDS, crack, and other things were invented and implemented.

Thus, we as a people have a very limited time to get ourselves together and organize ourselves into thriving social organisms which are both useful to ourselves and greater levels or society, or we may vary soon by eliminated in accord with the laws of nature.

C. The Holographic Model of the Universe, Nature and the Mind

Nature's complex organization can be seen using two models: the fractal model, and the holographic model. Let us take a look at these two models, for they will give us a deeper understanding of the universe, the mind, and also the new techniques used to develop many of the new technologies coming about. This topic gets somewhat involved and technical, but as always, I will strive to put it forth in way that is easy for us to understand and grasp. First let us discuss what a hologram is, and then we will look at how it relates to the organization of the universe and the operation of the mind.

Hologram - a hologram is produced when a single laser light is split into two beams. One beam is reflected off of an object onto holographic film The other beam is collided at an angle with the first beam on the same holographic film. The interference pattern produced by the two beams reproduces a three-dimensional representation of the object that the first beam was reflected off of. Thus, a holographic image of the object is produced.

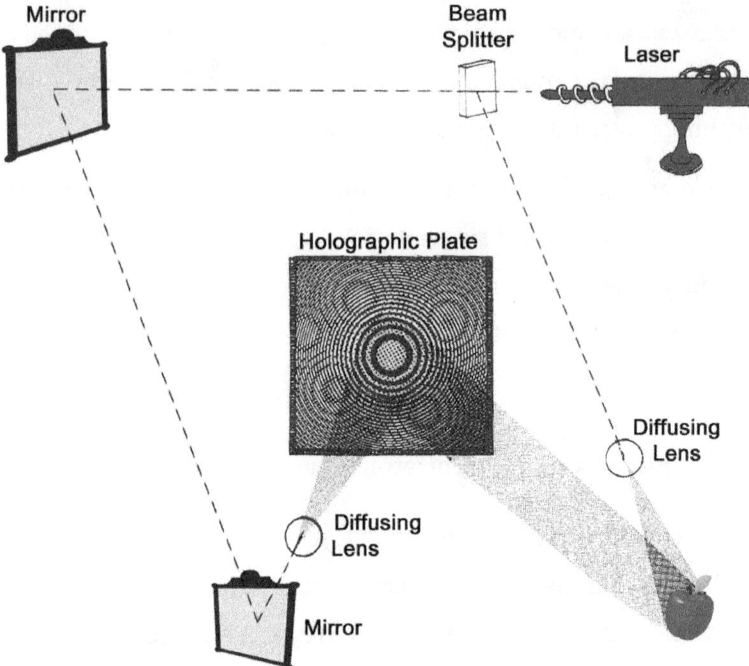

Figure 1. A hologram is produced when a single laser light is split into two separate beams. The first beam is bounced off of the object to be photographed, in this case an apple. Then the second beam is allowed to collide with the reflected light of the first, and the resulting interference pattern is recorded on film.

"The Holographic Universe", by Michael Talbot, p.15

The holographic object and holographic film on which it is produced have some peculiar characteristics. One is that the image is truly a three-dimensional representation of the object. If you were to walk around the object, you will see different parts of the object from different angles as if you really walked around the actual object itself. Also, the object will look so real, you will think you can actually reach out and touch it, but your hand will just pass through it as if it was not there. The peculiar characteristic of the hologram is that if you were to tear a holographic picture of an object in half, you would not have half of the object on each piece but instead, you will have the whole object on each half, only smaller in scale and size. If you tore the picture in half again, and again, you would still have the whole object in each piece. The other interesting characteristic about holograms is that a piece of holographic film can hold hundreds and thousands of holographic images depending on the size and quality of the holographic film, but the image that will be visible is determined by shining the laser or light at the same angle as the laser which created the image was shone at.

"Interestingly, holograms also possess a fantastic capacity for information storage. By changing the angle at which the two lasers strike a piece of photographic film, it is possible to record many different images on the same surface. Any image thus recorded can be retrieved simply by illuminating the film with a laser beam possessing the same angle as the original two beams. By employing this method researchers have calculated that a one-inch-square of film can store the same amount of information contained in fifty Bibles!"

"The Holographic Universe", by Michael Talbot, p.21

These characteristics of the hologram explain and helps us to understand many aspects of the human body, the mind, nature and the universe. For instance, every cell in the body contains the complete genetic code for the whole body but will only manifest certain parts of that genetic code. Thus, although a heart cell has within itself the genetic code for the whole body, it will only manifest the aspects of the genetic code pertaining to heart cells. This is just like the holographic film which may have hundreds of holograms stored on it, but only one or so will be visible depending on the angle of the laser (or light source) and the angle from which you view it.

Figure 2. Unlike normal photographs, every portion of a piece of holographic film contains all of the information of the whole. Thus if a holographic plate is broken into fragments, each piece can still be used to reconstruct the entire image.

Human life begins from a single cell which divides forming billions of highly specialized cells. Some become brain cells, some nerve cells, some heart cells, etc. What is it that determines what cell will develop into which type of cell? In the example of the hologram, the angle of the light source and perspective is what determined which of the hundreds of holograms would manifest. In the formation of the human body, it is where the cell lies relative to a sort of grid or matrix, which determines what it will develop into. One of the first specialized features that forms in the developing embryo or child is a long melanin coated neural tube that sort of divides the ball of cells called the embryo in half. This neural-melanin tube which eventually forms the spine and brain sets up the initial grid or matrix. Depending on where the cell is relative to this neural-melanin tube will determine what specialized cell it will develop into. It's position determines which aspects of the genetic code it will manifest, and which aspects will be suppressed in its development.

We are all created in the image and likeness of "God" but depending on where we fall within the time space matrix will determine which aspects of "God" we manifest, and which aspects we do not. The aspects of "God" that we do not manifest, is usually manifested by someone else. This is why we must come together as humans and form societies, because societies come closer to "God" than an individual can.

The hologram also helps us to understand how memory, and the brain works. Remember when the holographic picture was torn to pieces, each the full holographic object on the holographic picture can be re- produced in each piece. Well it was once thought that specific memories resided in different parts of the brain. Often during brain surgery, when certain parts of the brain was stimulated, patients would recall memories from their childhood or the past in some form. Later it was found that although stimulating a certain part of the brain may produce specific memories, when that part of the brain was cut out, that memory did not disappear, but was actually able to be recalled by the parts of the brain that remained. Thus, it was realized that memories did not reside in one location of the brained but is actually stored holographically throughout the brain. And just like the hologram, the remaining parts of the brain can reproduce a memory if a piece of the brain is removed or destroyed.

The holographic model of memory and brain functioning can also explain how our brains are able to store such vast amounts of information.

"...John von Neuman once calculated that over the course of the average human lifetime, the brain stores something on the order of 2.8 X 1020 (280,000,000,000,000,000,000) bits of information. This is a vast amount of information, and brain researchers have long struggled to come up with the mechanism that explains such a vast capability." The Holographic Universe, by Michael Talbot, p.21

The brain stores all of this information holographically, thus eliminating the need for vast size to store vast amounts of information. If a holographic picture contained 100 different images, tilting it back and forth in the path of a laser or light source will manifest different holographic images. The consciousness of man acts like a laser or light source helping us to recall memories and information by focusing our consciousness from different angles and perspectives. Whenever a name or particular piece of information you know "slips" you, the problem is that you can't focus your consciousness at the right angel to bring that piece of holographic information "to light". Those who are particularly skilled at recalling this holographically stored information are said to have a "photographic memory". Perhaps we should say "holographic memory" instead.

People often confuse the brain with the mind. The brain and nervous system is a physical entity which manifests mind, but it in itself is not the mind. The brain is like a holographic machine or apparatus storing memories, producing dreams, visions, ideas in the form of holograms. There is actually only one mind in the universe: the "Supreme Mind", or "God". Our brain and nervous system are just one means by which we plug into or access this one mind, or "God". Using an analogy, if the "Supreme Mind" or "God" is the internet, then your brain is the equivalent to one computer or terminal plugged into the internet. Your one computer or terminal is not the whole internet in itself, it is only one way in which you can plug into and access the internet. Thus, the mind is not "in" the brain or body, it is everywhere in the universe. Your brain and body are the means in which you access this supreme mind, supreme Hologram or "God". The part of the mind that you are accessing at any one time is like your conscious mind, it is the equivalent in the above analogy to a webpage or website you are currently accessing or have read and bookmarked. The sub-conscious mind are like webpages which are linked to the webpage and websites you have already visited and bookmarked but have not yet read or accessed. The unconscious mind are those webpages and websites you have never visited, are not linked to anything you have ever accessed or bookmarked, and that you are not even aware exist.

Another analogy I like to use is that we know or have the potential to know everything. The "Supreme Mind" is like a library containing all that can be known, but in which all of the lights are out. The conscious mind is like a little flashlight with which you can illuminate a small section of the library, but which cannot illuminate the whole library at one time. Our conscious mind can only access a small part of the supreme mind at a time, just like a computer terminal can only access a small part of the whole internet at one time. There are times however when we can illuminate the whole library at one time temporarily (super consciousness). Those who achieve this are called the "Illuminated Ones", "Illuminati", "High Scientist" or "Ascended Master". Keep all of the foregoing in mind when we discuss traditional African religions and Moorish Science.

D. The Science of the Ethers

The holographic model will also help us to understand the structure of the universe. The universe is actually made up of a super tenuous, and very fine and subtle material known as the ethers, or ether. Everything that exists in this physical universe is actually no more than various vibrations and interference patterns in the ether. The ethers record everything because the material it is made of is so fine and sensitive that even thoughts can disturb it, vibrate it and set it into motion. When you drop a rock into a pond, it causes ripples to expand out from it in concentric circles. Well if the ethers were a pond, a thought would send ripples through it. That is how tenuous, fine and subtle it is.

> *"Hark now, let every creature hear, the plane of soul is but the ether of the spirit p-lane vibrating not so fast, and in the slower rhythm of this plane the essence of life are manifest; the perfumes and the odors, the true sensations and the all of love manifest."* The Holy Koran of the M.S.T.of A., Noble Drew Ali, p.4

Well as previously stated, and taught by Noble Drew Ali, all things are thoughts of Allah or "God" vibrating the ethers, which in turn form the various objects in the physical universe. Every object from the atom up, is no more than a vibration or vortex (spinning) of the ethers. When the quantum physicists probed deeper into atom they found that nothing is really solid. All the atomic and sub-atomic particles are really only energy, vibrations and vortices of the ethers, whose interference patterns caused by interactions with other vibrations and vortices of the ethers create the illusion of solidity. Thus, solidity does not actually exist in the universe, it is merely an illusion produced by interference patterns which cannot readily pass through other interference patterns. An interference pattern is produce when one or more vibrations or vortices intersect. If you drop to two rocks in a pond, an interference pattern is formed where the two sets of ripples collide and intersect. A holographic image is formed where the two laser beams which were split from one, collide and intersect on the holographic film or medium.

"According to our current understanding of physics, every region of space is awash with different kinds of fields composed of waves of varying lengths. Each wave always has at least some energy. When physicists calculate the minimum amount of energy a wave can possess, they find that every cubic centimeter of empty space contains more energy than the total energy of all matter in the known universe!" "The Holographic Universe", by Michael Talbot, p.51

Thus, Space is not a vacuum containing nothing. Space is a plenum containing everything. Every inch of space contains the whole universe in a potential state the same way every inch of a hologram contains every part of the hologram. What you get out of this universe and life depends on the angle or paradigm from which you view it.

In light of the above quote, how can there ever be such thing as an "energy crisis". What there actually is, is a crisis in knowledge and understanding of the universe we live in, and how it works. Anything that requires energy can actually obtain all the energy it needs from any point in space around it, we must only learn the means of unlocking it.

Remember, the ethers record everything. Everything comes from it, and everything leaves it's mark in it. This is why the Hon. Elijah Muhammad said that there are pockets of air (ether) which contain the history of the world. Some refer to it as the Akashic record. Ascended Masters and High Scientists know how to tap into the ethers for historical records, as well as for energy and sustenance. Your mark in the ethers is referred to as your soul. It is a recording, or the mark left in the ethers by your birth, life and death. Upon death your record is replayed or unwound before you. Thus, all things are recorded in the universe or ethers holographically. You can access it if you find the correct way to shine the laser or light of your consciousness on it.

The universe is one vast hologram or thought of the Supreme Mind. The ether is the holographic film or medium, and various objects in the universe are various holographic images or interference patterns. Your consciousness is the laser and based on the angle from which you apply your consciousness (your paradigm) will determine that which manifests itself to from the ethers."
~Hakim Bey

"*I bargained with life for a penny, and life would pay no more, However I begged at evening when I counted my scanty store. For life is a just employer, he gives you what you ask, But once you have set the wages, why you must bear the task. I worked for a menials hire, only to learn, dismayed, That nay wage I had asked of life, life would have willingly paid.*" Think and Grow Rich, by Napoleon Hill, p.40

You get out of life that which your paradigm says you will. You get what you ask for.

E. Cosmogony

I. Th All: The Kybalion

"Under, and back of, the Universe of Time, Space and Change, is ever to be found The Substantial Reality– the Fundamental Truth." –The Kybalion.

All thinkers in all lands and in all times, have assumed the necessity for postulating the existence of this substantial reality. All philosophies worthy of the name have been based upon this thought. Men have given to this substantial reality many names–some have called it by the term deity (under many titles); others have called it "the infinite and eternal energy"; others have tried to call it "matter"–but all have acknowledged its existence. It is self-evident– it needs no argument.

What is there higher than matter or energy that we know to be existent in the universe? Life and mind! Life and mind in all their varying degrees of unfoldment! "Then", you ask, "Do you mean to tell us that Th All is life and mind?" Yes! And No! Is our answer. If you mean life and mind as we poor petty mortals know them, we say no! Th All is not that! "But what kind of life and mind do you mean?" you ask.

The answer is "living mind, as far above that which mortals know by those words, as life and mind are higher than mechanical forces, or matter-infinite living mind as compared to finite life and mind." We mean that which the illumined souls mean when they reverently pronounce the word: "spirit!"

II. The Mental Universe

"*The Universe is Mental–held in the Mind of Th All.*"–The Kybalion.

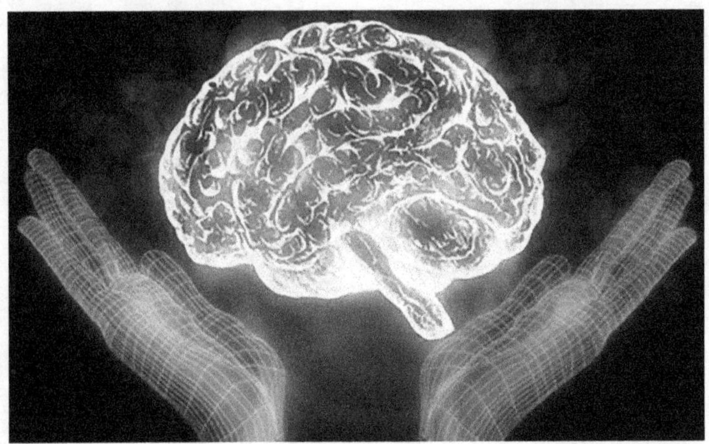

Th All is spirit! But what is spirit? Spirit is simply a name that men give to the highest conception of infinite living mind-It means "Th real essence." Spirit transcends our understanding, and we use the term merely that we may think or speak of Th All. For the purposes of thought and innerstanding, we are justified in thinking of spirit as infinite living mind, at the same time acknowledging that we cannot fully overstand it. We must either do this or stop thinking of the matter at all.

There is no escaping from the conclusion of the reason, which, as we have said, agrees with the highest teachings of the illumined. Just as you, student, may create a universe of your own in your mentality, so does Th All create universes in its own mentality. But your universe is the creation of a finite mind, whereas Th All is the creation of an infinite. The two are similar in kind, but infinitely different in degree.

But there is the point to fix in your mind at this stage: The Universe, and All it contains, is a mental creation of Th All. Verily indeed, all is mind!

> *"Th All creates in its Infinite Mind countless Universes, which exist for aeons of Time–and yet, to Th All, the creation, development, decline and death of a million Universes is as the time of the twinkling of an eye."*
>
> *"The Infinite Mind of Th All is the womb of Universes."* –The Kybalion.

The Principle of Gender is manifested on all planes of life, material, mental and spiritual. But, as we have said before, "Gender" does not mean "Sex"–sex is merely a material manifestation of gender. "Gender" means "relating to generation or creation." And wherever anything is generated or created, on any plane, the Principle of Gender must be manifested. And this is true even in the creation of Universes.

Now do not jump to the conclusion that we are teaching that there is a male and female God, or Creator. That idea is merely a distortion of the ancient teachings on the subject. The true teaching is that THE ALL, in itself, is above Gender, as it is above every other Law, including those of Time and Space. It is the Law, from which the Laws proceed, and it is not subject to them. But when THE ALL manifests on the plane of generation or creation, then it acts according to Law and Principle, for it is moving on a lower plane of being. And consequently, it manifests the Principle of Gender, in its Masculine and Feminine aspects, on the Mental Plane, of course.

This idea may seem startling to some of you who hear it for the first time, but you have all really passively accepted it in your everyday conceptions. You speak of the Fatherhood of God and the Motherhood of Nature–of God, the Divine Father, and Nature the Universal Mother–and have thus instinctively acknowledged the Principle of Gender in the Universe. Is this not so!

But the Hermetic teaching does not imply a real duality–THE ALL is ONE–the Two Aspects are merely aspects of manifestation. The teaching is that

The Masculine Principle manifested by Th All stands, in a way, apart from the actual mental creation of the Universe. It projects its Will toward the Feminine Principle (which may be called "Nature") whereupon the latter begins the actual work of the evolution of the Universe, from simple "centres of activity" on to man, and then on and on still higher, all according to well established and firmly enforced Laws of Nature. If you prefer the old figures of thought, you may think of the Masculine Principle as GOD, the Father, and of the Feminine Principle as Nature, the Universal Mother, from whose womb all things have been born. This is more than a mere poetic figure of speech–it is an idea of the actual process of the creation of the Universe. But always remember, that Th All is but one, and that in its Infinite Mind the Universe is generated, created and exists.

Is it any wonder that you, the child, feel that instinctive reverence for Th All, which feeling we call "religion"–that respect, and reverence for Th Father Mind? Is it any wonder that, when you consider the works and wonders of Nature, you are overcome with a mighty feeling which has its roots away down in your inmost being? It is the Mother Mind that you are pressing close up to, like a babe to the breast.

Do not make the mistake of supposing that the little world you see around you–the Earth, which is a mere grain of dust in the Universe–is the Universe itself. There are millions upon millions of such worlds, and greater. And there are millions of millions of such Universes in existence within the Infinite Mind of Th All. And even in our own little solar system there are regions and planes of life far higher than ours, and beings compared to which we earthbound mortals are as the slimy life-forms that dwell on the ocean's bed when compared to Man. There are beings with powers and attributes higher than Man has ever dreamed of the gods' possessing. And yet these beings were once as you, and still lower–and you will be even as they, and still higher, in time, for such is the Destiny of Man as reported by the Illumined.

And Death is not real, even in the Relative sense–it is but Birth to a new life–and You shall go on, and on, and on, to higher and still higher planes of life, for aeons upon aeons of time. The Universe is your home, and you shall explore its farthest recesses before the end of Time. You are dwelling in the Infinite Mind of Th All, and your possibilities and opportunities are infinite, both in time and space. And at the end of the Grand Cycle of Aeons, when Th All shall draw back into itself all of its creations–you will go gladly, for you will then be able to know the Whole Truth of being At One with Th All. Such is the report of the Illumined–those who have advanced well along The Path.

And, in the meantime, rest calm and, serene–you are safe and protected by the Infinite Power of the Father-Mother Mind.

"*Within the Father-Mother Mind, mortal children are at home.*"

"*There is not one who is Fatherless, nor Motherless in the Universe*" – The Kybalion.

III. Th Milky Way: Upanishads

Svarga Loka (bright world; heavenly world) refers specifically to the Milky Way. The door to this world is located at the mouth of the two arms extending toward the east, from TH Milky Way viewed during the winter months in northern Hindustan (India), which explains the importance of the East and the Northeast ritual and in cosmological speculations. Th Milky Way is also the bright ocean of heaven, the celestial waters; it is the source of the rivers that flow from the Himalayan Mountains thus connecting the Earthly to Th Celestial waters.

Another conception divides the universe into the world of humans, the world of fathers/ancestors, and the world of Th Gods. Although less tied to observable world reality, it is more significant for beliefs regarding the afterlife. The world of humans is, of course, the observable world in which our normal lives are lived. During the early period all humans, or at least those who lived a ritually correct life, were believed to go to the world of the fathers/ancestors; but the Upanishads reveal a new perception of that world according to which only those who are destined to return to and be reborn in this world, follow the path of the ancestors, while those destined not to return and are to become immortal proceed to the world of Th Gods.

This new conception is tied to the emergent world view centered on the doctrine of rebirth. This manner in which the rebirth process was thought to operate is similar to that which Brahmanical thought viewed the operation of ritual actions. Rites achieve their results by their autonomous power and according to ritual law of cause and effect; ritual success does not depend on Th will of a God. The moral law that governs the rebirth process operates in a similar manner; those who perform good deeds are reborn in good situations, while those who do evil proceed to evil births.

F. Cosmology

I. Mentalism: The Kybalion

"*THE ALL is MIND; The Universe is Mental.*" –The Kybalion.

This Principle embodies the truth that "All is Mind." It explains that Th All (which is the Substantial Reality underlying all the outward manifestations and appearances which we know under the terms of "The Material Universe"; the "Phenomena of Life"; "Matter"; "Energy"; and in short, all that is apparent to our material senses) is spirit, which in itself is unknowable and undefinable, but which may be considered and thought of as a universal, infinite, living mind. It also explains that all the phenomenal world or universe is simply a Mental Creation of Th All, subject to the Laws of Created Things, and that the universe, as a whole, and in its parts or units, has its existence

in the Mind of Th All, in which Mind we "live and move and have our being." This Principle, by establishing the Mental Nature of the Universe, easily explains all of the varied mental and psychic phenomena that occupy such a large portion of the public attention, and which, without such explanation, are non-understandable and defy scientific treatment. An understanding of this great Hermetic Principle of Mentalism enables the individual to readily grasp the laws of the Mental Universe, and to apply the same to his well-being and advancement. The Hermetic Student is enabled to apply intelligently the great

Mental Laws, instead of using them in a haphazard manner. With the Master-Key in his possession, the student may unlock the many doors of the mental and psychic temple of knowledge and enter the same freely and intelligently. This Principle explains the true nature of "Energy," "Power," and "Matter," and why and how all these are subordinate to the Mastery of Mind. One of the old Hermetic Masters wrote, long ages ago: "He who grasps the truth of the Mental Nature of the Universe is well advanced on The Path to Mastery." And these words are as true today as at the time they were first written. Without this Master-Key, Mastery is impossible, and the student knocks in vain at the many doors of The Temple.

II. Mental Transmutation

"*Mind (as well as metals and elements) may be transmuted, from state to state; degree to degree; condition to condition; pole to pole; vibration to vibration. True Hermetic Transmutation is a Mental Art.*" – The Kybalion.

As we have stated, the Hermetists were the original alchemists, astrologers, and psychologists, Hermes having been the founder of these schools of thought. From astrology has grown modern astronomy; from alchemy has grown modern chemistry; from the mystic psychology has grown the modern psychology of the schools. But it must not be supposed that the ancients were ignorant of that which the modern schools suppose to be their exclusive and special property. The records engraved on the stones of Ancient Egypt show conclusively that the ancients had a full comprehensive knowledge of astronomy, the very building of the Pyramids showing the connection between their design and the study of astronomical science. Nor were they ignorant of Chemistry, for the fragments of the ancient writings show that they were acquainted with the chemical properties of things; in fact, the ancient theories regarding physics are being slowly verified by the latest discoveries of modern science, notably those relating to the constitution of matter. Nor must it be supposed that they were ignorant of the so-called modern discoveries in psychology–on the contrary, the Egyptians were especially skilled in the science of Psychology, particularly in the branches that the modern schools ignore, but which, nevertheless, are being uncovered under the name of "psychic science" which is perplexing the psychologists of today and making them reluctantly admit that "there may be something in it after all."

The truth is, that beneath the material chemistry, astronomy and psychology (that is, the psychology in its phase of "brain-action"), the ancients possessed a knowledge of transcendental astronomy, called astrology; of transcendental chemistry, called alchemy; of transcendental psychology, called mystic psychology. They possessed the Inner Knowledge as well as the Outer Knowledge, the latter alone being possessed by modern scientists. Among the many secret branches of knowledge possessed by the Hermetists, was that known as Mental Transmutation, which forms the subject matter of this lesson.

"Transmutation" is a term usually employed to designate the ancient art of the transmutation of metals–particularly of the base metals into gold. The word "Transmute" means "to change from one nature, form, or substance, into another; to transform" (Webster). And accordingly, "Mental Transmutation" means the art of changing and transforming mental states, forms, and conditions, into others. So, you may see that Mental Transmutation is the "Art of Mental Chemistry," if you like the term–a form of practical Mystic Psychology.

But this means far more than appears on the surface. Transmutation, Alchemy, or Chemistry, on the Mental Plane is important enough in its effects, to be sure, and if the art stopped there it would still be one of the most important branches of study known to man. But this is only the beginning. Let us see why!

The first of the Seven Hermetic Principles is the Principle of Mentalism, the axiom of which is "TH All is Mind; the Universe is Mental," which means that the Underlying Reality of the Universe is Mind; and the Universe itself is Mental–that is, "existing in the Mind of Th All."

If the Universal is Mental in its nature, then Mental Transmutation must be the art of changing the conditions of the universe, along the lines of Matter, Force and Mind. So, you see, therefore, that Mental Transmutation is really the "Magic" of which the ancient writers had so much to say in their mystical works, and about which they gave so few practical instructions. If All be Mental, then the art which enables one to transmute mental conditions must render the Master the controller of material conditions as well as those ordinarily called "mental."

As a matter of fact, none but advanced Mental Alchemists have been able to attain the degree of power necessary to control the grosser physical conditions, such as the control of the elements of Nature; the production or cessation of tempests; the production and cessation of earthquakes and other great physical phenomena. But that such men have existed, and do exist today, is a matter of earnest belief to all advanced occultists of all schools. That the Masters exist, and have these powers, the best teachers assure their students, having had experiences which justify them in such belief and statements. These Masters do not make public exhibitions of their powers, but seek seclusion from the crowds of men, in order to better work their way along the Path of Attainment. We mention their existence, at this point, merely to call your attention to the fact that their power is entirely mental and operates along the lines of the higher Mental Transmutation.

But students and Hermetists of lesser degree than Masters–the Initiates and Teachers–are able to freely work along the Mental Plane, in Mental

Transmutation. In fact, all that we call "psychic phenomena"; "mental influence"; "mental science"; "new-thought phenomena," etc., operates along the same general lines, for there is but one principle involved, no matter by what name the phenomena be called.

The student and practitioner of Mental Transmutation works among the Mental Plane, transmuting mental conditions, states, etc., into others, according to various formulas, more or less efficacious. The various "treatments," "affirmations," "denials," etc., of the schools of mental science are but formulas, often quite imperfect and unscientific, of The Hermetic Art. The majority of modern practitioners are quite ignorant compared to the ancient masters, for they lack the fundamental knowledge upon which the work is based. Not only may the mental states, etc., of one's self be changed or transmuted by Hermetic Methods; but also, the states of others may be, and are, constantly transmuted in the same way, usually unconsciously, but often consciously by some understanding the laws and principles, in cases where the people affected are not informed of the principles of self-protection. And more than this, as many students and practitioners of modern mental science know, every material condition depending upon the minds of other people may be changed or transmuted in accordance with the earnest desire, will, and "treatments" of person desiring changed conditions of life. The public are so generally informed regarding these things at present, that we do not deem it necessary to mention the same at length, our purpose at this point being merely to show the Hermetic Principle and Art underlying all of these various forms of practice, good and evil, for the force can be used in opposite directions according to the Hermetic Principles of Polarity.

G. Supreme Mathematics

I. The Order of 3: Creation

3 forces of nature:

1. Brahma: Th Creative Force
2. Vishnu: Th Preservative Force
3. Sheba: The Destructive/Regenerative Force

3 attributes of Th Creator:

1. Omnipresence: in the early stages of man's growth it manifests itself as the sense of humanity, and oneness between men, and between man and his environment. The urge to seek and establish peace and cooperation. In the later part of man's growth, it manifests in us as the ability to experience all other men and things in the world as part of our being, as we now experience the separate parts of our bodies belonging to the body.
2. Omniscience: in the early stage of man's growth it manifest as the ability to solve, over time all problems in life. All discoveries and knowledge in the world were intuited by someone. In the latter part of life, it manifests as the ability to go into trance and discover the solution to any problem, on demand.
3. Omnipotence: the manifestation of psychic powers which have made themselves known through a number of individuals throughout history. While in the west, these appear at random, they are deliberately and methodically cultivated i.e. scientifically by Orientals and Kushites/Tamerians (So-called Africans).

3 Branches of Philosophy:

1. Natural Philosophy: is the knowledge and study of natural things, objects, and phenomena, which is called "science".
2. Moral Philosophy: is the knowledge and study of human conduct and actions, which are referred to as, "ethics".
3. Metaphysical Philosophy: is the knowledge and study that involves natural reasoning and deals with ultimate reality and with the most general causes of things. This is in contrast with revealed knowledge. Thus, the rational analysis of the incorporeal and of transcendental and abstract thinking. The study of the divine and natural law of 'cause and effect'.

3 Jewels:

1. Buddha: supreme knowledge and wisdom; enlightenment
2. Dharma: essential quality of character as of the cosmos; one's true nature
3. Sangha: communion and fellowship

3 Bodies of Buddha:

1. Nirmanakaya: the "transformation (appearance) body": this is the body in which they appear in the world for the benefit of suffering beings. It is not a real, physical body but more a phantom-like (illusion) appearance assumed by.
2. Dharmakaya: the "Dharma body", wherein they are one with Th Eternal Dharma (phenomena) that lies beyond all dualities and conceptions.
3. Sambhogakaya: the "Perfect enjoyment (or bliss) body": this is the body that appears to Bodhisattvas (one who is able to reach nirvana [heaven] but delays doing so out of compassion in order to save suffering beings) in the celestial realm where they commune with Th truth of Th Maha (great; very big) Yana (vehicle) i.e. Th Supreme Higher Force.

3 Dimensions:

1. nasut: the human world
2. malakut: the invisible world of angels
3. lahut: the divine world of reality

3 Pillars:

1. Sila: morality, charity and compassion
2. Dhyana: practice and concentration
3. Prajna: wisdom

3 Karmas:

Karma and Dharma: "as you sow, so shall you reap" is a common phrase in life which concisely sums up Th Law of karma. Karma is The Universal Law of cause and effect, which holds a being responsible for their actions and effects.

According to one's good or bad actions, Th Supreme Force rewards or punishes. The word "karma" means human action or deed; we are constantly performing karmas whether physically, mentally, or emotionally. A being's karma is responsible for good or bad consequences in their lives.

Nothing in this world happens accidentally or coincidentally; there is a reason behind everything though it may not be clear to us at that time. Good actions produce happiness and bad actions lead to suffering and misery in the present or next life. A being's past actions govern his present, and his present actions have an effect on his future. This means that every being, to a certain degree, is the creator of their own destiny.

All our karmas are performed in one of two ways: (1) is called nishkam (Nish= without, free form or un; kam= desire, wish for, longing) karma, when actions are performed without any expectation of material gain, ego, or earthly desires. Nishkam karmas are only performed to fulfill one's duty to Natural Law. (2) Sakam (Sakam= together, jointly or simultaneously) karma, whereas actions are done within the frame of mind of expectation of reward whether material or ethereal.

1. Kriyaman Karma (arrow in hand; current karma; being made): are karmas being acquired every moment, referring to those which are currently in front of us to decide and/or act upon. The fruits of these karmas can be attained in this life, the next, or after many births.
2. Sanchita Karma (arrows in the quiver; sum total; accumulated actions): is the vast store of piled-up karma accumulated in the preceding and all other previous births and yet to be resolved. In other words, it is the aggregate sum of yet unseen karma committed during innumerable previous existences. This is your total cosmic debt. Every moment of your every day, you are either adding to it or you are reducing this cosmic debt. It is waiting to be fulfilled in your future births. So unless and until the cosmic karmic debt of your soul is zeroed, it keeps on birthing in new physical forms, in order to exhaust its balance.
3. Praarabdha Karma (arrows in flight; fructifying karma; set in motion): is part of one's Sanchita karma that is being experienced in this birth. For example, the attributes and conditions of one's physical body and mental capacities are because one's praarabdha karma. If you work down your agreed upon debt in this lifetime, then more past debts will surface to be worked on. And that much karmic cosmic debt is dissolved.

II. The order of 4: Cycle of Destruction and Rebirth

4 Epochs of Existence:

(Hindustani Cosmology) The Universe is cyclically created and destroyed. Deeply rooted in the texts of Hindu literature, including Th Vedas and Th Purnanas, is the belief time is divided into 4 epochs or Yuga, of which we occupy the final. In roughly 432,000 years, it is believed that the avatar (a manifestation of a deity or released soul in bodily form on earth; an incarnate divine teacher) Kalki, the final incarnation of Vishnu, will bring the end of time as we know it.

1. Saiya Yuga: also called Sat yuga, Krta yuga and Krita yuga in Hinduism, is the first of the 4 yugas, the "Yuga (age or era) of truth", when humanity is governed by Gods, and every manifestation or work is close to the purest ideal and humanity will allow intrinsic goodness to rule supreme. It is sometimes referred to as the "Golden Age". The Atya Yuga lasts 1,728,000 years. The Goddess Dharma (depicted as a cow), which symbolizes morality, stood on all four legs during this period. Later on in the Treta Yuga, it would become 3, followed by 2 in the Dvapara Yuga. Currently, in the immoral age of Kali, it stands on one leg.

2. Treta Yuga: means 'a collection of 3' in Sanskrit, and is called so because during this era, there were 3 avatars of Vishnu that were seen: the 5th, 6th, and 7th incarnations as Vamana, Parashuramh, and Rama respectfully. The name could also come from the belief that the Treta Yuga lasts 3000 divine years. The Treta Yuga lasted 1,296,000 years. During this age, the power of humans slightly diminishes. Kings and Brahmanas need means to fulfill their desires instead of using mere money and will. People grow inclined toward more materialisticness and less inclined toward spirituality. Agriculture and mining came into existence along with norms and rules to keep society under control.

3. Dvapara Yuga: also spelt Dwarara Yuga. In Sanskrit it literally means, "two ahead", that is, something in 3rd place. According to ancient Hindu scriptures, this Yuga ended at the moment when Khrishna returned to his eternal abode Vaikuntha (place of non-hindrance). According to the Bhagavita (ancient Hindu manuscripts), the Dvapara Yuga lasts 864,000 years. There are only two pillars of religion at this period: compassion and truthfulness During these times, the Brahmas (priest) are knowledgeable of two or three but rarely have studied all 4 Vedas (Veda in Sanskrit means "knowledge"; these are the 4 canical scriptures [sruti] of Hinduism, a collection of 1,028 hyms and 10,600 verses, organized into ten books or "mandalas) thoroughly. Accordingly, because of this categorization, different actions and activities come into existence. All people in the Dvapara Yuga are desirous of achievement of the scriptural Dharma that is prescribed to each class, valiant, courageous, and competitive by nature and are engaged only in penance and charity. They are Kingly and pleasure-seeking. In this era, the divine intellect ceases to exist, and it is therefore seldom that anyone is wholly truthful. As a result of this life of deceit, people are plagued by ailments, diseases and various types of desires. After suffering from these ailments, people realize their misdeeds and perform penance. Some also organize Yagya (offerings) for material benefits as well as for divinity.

4. Kali Yuga: literally "Age of (the demon) Kali", or "Age of vice", is the last of the 4 stages the world goes through as part of the cycle of Yugas described in Sanskrit scriptures, within the present Maha Yuga (great age). Kali Yuga is associated with the demon Kali (not to be confused with the Goddess Kali). The "Kali" of Kali Yuga means "strife, discord, quarrel or contention". Hindus believed that human civilization degenerates spiritually during this era, whish is referred to as the "dark age", because in it people are as far away as possible from G-d. Hinduism often symbolically represents morality (Dharma) as a Bull. In Satya Yuga, the 1st stage of development, the

bull has 4 legs, but in each age morality is reduced by one quarter. By the age of Kali, morality is reduced to only a quarter of that of the golden age, so that the bull of dharma has only one leg.

Prophesied events during Kali Yuga:

- Rulers will become unreasonable; they will levy taxes unfairly
- Rulers will no longer see it as their duty to promote spirituality, or to protect their subjects; they will become a danger to the world
- People will start migrating, seeking countries where wheat and barley form the staple of food source
- "At the end of KaliYuga, when there exist no topics on the subject of G-d, even at the residences of so-called saints and respected gentlemen of the 3 higher varnas (classes) and when nothing is known of the techniques of sacrifice, even by word, at that time Th Lord will appear as Th Supreme Chastiser"-(Srimad-Bhagavatam 2.7)
- Avarice and wrath will be common. Humans will openly display animosity towards each other. Ignorance of dharma will occur.
- People will have thoughts of murder with no justification and will see nothing wrong with it.
- Lust will be viewed as socially acceptable and sexual intercourse will be seen as the central requirement of life.
- Disgrace will increase exponentially, while virtue will fade and cease to flourish.
- People will take their vows and break them soon after.
- People will become addicted to intoxicating drugs and drinks.
- Gurus will no longer be respected, and their students will attempt to injure them. Their teachings will be insulted, and followers of kama (desire) will wrest control of the mind from all human beings.
- Brahmans (priests; scholars) will not be learned or honored, kshatriyas (derived from kshatra-"rule, authority; ruling and military elite") will not be brave, vaishyas (landowners; traders; money-lenders) will not be just in their dealings.

4 noble truths:

1. suffering exists
2. suffering has an identifiable cause: desire to have and to be
3. these causes may be terminated
4. the means by which to eliminate suffering is obedience to Th Laws Of Nature

4 emanations of nirmanakaya:

Nirmana= manifest in form, kaya= body in the sense of many qualities gathered together, joined or united as one. Refers to the embodiments of loving-kindness, compassion, wisdom, and skillful means which appear in the world to help sentient beings.

1. Supreme emanations: takes birth in the world as a unique person. Gautama Buddha, Shakyamuni and Guru Padmasambhava, Yahoshuah, Muhammad are all examples of this kind. They have special forms of body, speech and mind. They have a visible aura/glow that radiates and are free from old age and sickness.
2. Birth Emanations: incarnates even in animal and non-visible realms, using different names and forms, male or female as they are needed. There are many Jakata (a voluminous body of literature native to Hindustan [India] concerning the previous births of Gautama Buddha. These are the stories that tell about the previous lives of Th Buddha, in both human and animal form) stories of Buddha taking birth as a fish, turtle, bird, monkey, bear and a lion, as well as among humans and even in Th "God" (higher) realms. These are all birth emanations or tulkus (a custodian of a specific lineage of teaching in Tibetan Buddhism who is given empowerments and trained from a young age by students of his predecessor). They may not appear in the traditional way, wearing robes and all. Tulkus may not even necessarily be recognized as Buddha but in every case, they are born to remove obstacles and dualistic conceptions, to free sentient beings from ignorance and bring about the inner/overstanding of primordial wisdom.
3. Artisan Emanations: these appear as objects of art and the artist who make them for the benefit of sentient beings. Thangkas (a Tibetan Buddhist painting on cotton, or silk-appliqué, usually depicting a Buddhist deity, scene, or Mandala [spiritual and ritual symbol in Indian religions, representing the universe]) statues and even music are some of the forms these emanations take. Beautiful, inspired works of art which bring clarity, peace, joy and something special which seems to touch the heart center are all known as artisan emanations.

4. Various Emanations: these can appear as rain, fire, or wind. During times when sentient beings are troubled with diseases, they may come in the form of special herbs and medicines for healing or perhaps when beings are in danger of losing their lives, suddenly something miraculous occurs and saves them. All of these things are various forms of the nirmanakaya.

4 Purusartha (object of human pursuit)

1. Dharma: righteousness, moral values
2. Artha: prosperity, economic values
3. Kama: pleasure, love; psychological values
4. Moksa: liberation, spiritual values, self-actualization

4 sublime states:

1. Loving-kindness
2. compassion
3. appreciation
4. equanimity

III. The order of 5: Life

5 eternal elements:

1. Jiva (Soul): one's true identity is not the human body, but the jiva that resides within it. The jiva, also called 'atma' or soul is eternal-it cannot be destroyed. It has no gender; it is neither male nor female. It is said to reside in our bodies in the same area as the heart. Childhood, youth, old age, stoutness, thinness, birth and death are all aspects of the body; so they never should be thought of as belonging to atma. On the other hand, being uncuttable, being unpierceable, not aging, being immortal, being the embodiment of gnan (wisdom), being the embodiment of bliss, and being characterized by eternal existence are all aspects of atma; they should never be thought of as belonging to the body. The jiva is free and pure, but we believe we are restrained by ignorance. Once we inner/overstand that we are not this body and worship purna purushottam narayan (purna= complete; pursha= spirit + uttama= highest, supreme being; narayan= supreme G-d in Vedic scripture; nara refers to all human beings or living entities), we realize that our jiva is free from the clutches of maya (ignorance) and is worthy of moksa (liberation form the cycle of death and rebirth). The very essence of Th Brahma (creative force).

2. Ishwar (divinities): transcends the jiva. It is the next element above the jiva; these beings partake in the creation, sustenance, and destruction of each universe. Ishwars are conscious spiritual beings that have a greater realization than jives. While the jiva must work to realize its own presence within the human body, Ishwar is aware of that divinity. There are infinite Ishwars but are all bound by maya (ignorance) just as purna purshottam narayan controls the jiva, he also controls the Ishwars. Like the jives Ishwars too aim to surpass maya and attain moksa.

3. Maya (ignorance): maya is the ignorance that separates the jives (souls) and ishwar (deities) from Brahma and Parabrahma (para=paramount; highest point + Brahma= Creative force). It is the desire that hinders a spiritual aspirant's path to moksha. Maya directly translates to attachment for wordly objects. Maya is the instrument through which parabrahma facilitates karma only when a devotee is able to overcome maya- overcome the darkness of attachment to worldly objects-is he able to attain moksha. Maya manifests from physical matter, and it is difficult for the jiva or ishwar to transcend. The key is for the jiva to engage in constant bhakti (devotion) to Th Creator, to be able to move beyond maya and towards one's own liberation.

4. Aksharbrahma (eternal abode): the gunatitsadhu (emanation of the creator), aksharbrahma, is the pathway to Th Creator and to Moksha. It is only through aksharbrahma that a jiva (soul) can associate itself with Th Creator and Innerstand Th well enough to seek refuge in Th, thereby bringing the jiva out of the darkness of maya and into the light of parabrahma. Aksharbrahma is known to have two forms: (1) formless and pure chaitanya (spirit; consciousness; intelligence; sensation; energy or enthusiasm; cosmic intellect that is aware of self and others), is known as chidakash (mental space). (2) That form which remains in service to/ of purshottam narayan and is the abode where Th Creator and the liberated jiva reside.

5. Parabrahma (Th Most High): Th Supreme Entity, referred to as purna purshottam narayan or Parabrahma, All-Knowing, All- Powerful, yet compassionate. Governs all the other 4 elements. Is said to reside in Akshardham (akshar= indestructible + dham=abode; place of eternal values and virtues of divinity) and visits earth to establish dharma (righteousness) for the sake of his devotees. Divine traits of Th All: (1) All-Doer (sarva karta), (2) divine form (divya sakar), (3) is supreme and above all else (sarvopari), (4) and is always present in human form (pragat).

5 types of Soul:

1. Nefesh: the lower or "animal" aspect of the soul, common to all other creatures.
2. Ruach: the middle soul or "spirit" that is able to distinguish right from wrong.
3. Neshamah: the higher soul or "super-soul" that is the locus of rationality and spiritual life. The "neshamah yeterah" is the "additional soul" that a man can experience during Shabbat.
4. Chayyah: the soul beginning to apprehend the divine nature/unity; the soul created before man's fall from grace.
5. Yechidah: the highest plane of soul when the ego loses all differentiation with the divine unity.

5 angels and demons

Demons: Hell

1. anger
2. envy
3. lust
4. greed
5. laziness

Angels: Heaven

1. Love
2. Truth
3. Peace
4. Freedom
5. Justice

5 odd numbers

- 1: Higher Force that governs All
- 3: Holy triune; Mother, Father and Child; manifestation
- 5: Power which is truth and shall set you free; demonstrate daily
- 7: Heaven's Gate; realm of ether
- 9: rebirth; anew; continuance

5 Great Prophets:

- 1: Higher Force that governs All
- 3: Holy triune; Mother, Father and Child; manifestation
- 5: Power which is truth and shall set you free; demonstrate daily
- 7: Heaven's Gate; realm of ether
- 9: rebirth; anew; continuance

5 points of civilization: I.S.L.A.M.

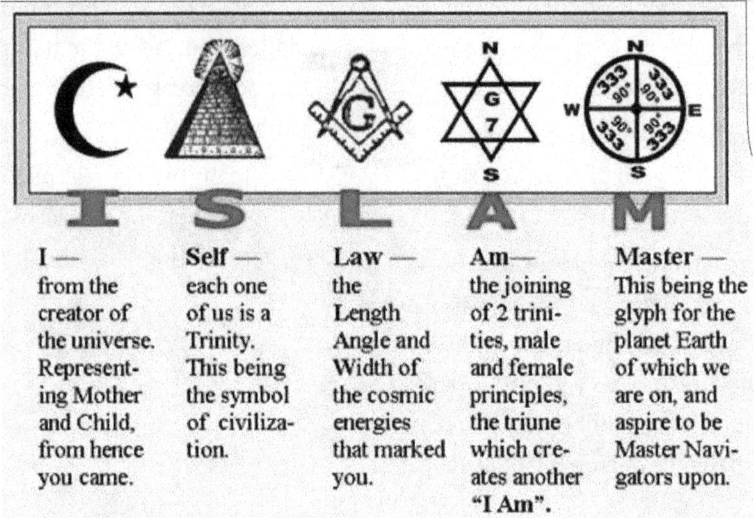

N
G
7
S
N
W
E
S
333
90°
I S L A M
I —
from the
creator of
the universe.
Represent-
ing Mother
and Child,
from hence
you came.
Self —
each one
of us is a
Trinity.
This being
the symbol
of civiliza-
tion.
Law —
the
Length
Angle and
Width of
the cosmic
energies
that marked
you.
Am—
the joining
of 2 trini-
ties, male
and female
principles,
the triune
which cre-
ates another
"I Am".
Master —
This being the
glyph for the
planet Earth
of which we
are on, and
aspire to be
Master Navi-
gators upon.

5 kinds of Love:

1. Desire: attraction
2. Longing: infatuation
3. Belonging: fellowship/communion
4. Cherishing: friendship/association
5. Selfless giving: universal and divine love; apex

IV. The order of 6: Th Fire of Refinement

6 realms of Rebirth

Higher Realms:

- Heaven
- Diva (asura; demons/ demi-gods)
- Human

Lower Realms:

- Animal
- Ghost
- Hell

6 precepts of Tao:

1. With care I aid those who are extended expressions of my nature.
2. Be true to self.
3. Connect to the world as I would want to be treated.

4. Connect to those outside of my nature with decisive action.
5. To those unwilling to accept me for my true nature, no action is required; just solemnly and silently let them be themselves as I remain myself.
6. I own nothing; I am merely a passing custodian of things outside of my true nature.

6 roots of the tree of Islam:

1. walayah: authority or guardianship
2. nabuyah: prophethood
3. adl: justice
4. tawhid: oneness with Th Creator
5. qiyamah: resurrection
6. imamah: divine appointing

V. The order of 7: Transformation

7 Chakras

The Seven Chakras of the Human Body

Crown Chakra
Connection to the divine

Located at the crown of your head, it deals with your connection to the divine within you and all around you. Physically, it supports your central nervous system and deep brain functions.

Your Crown Chakra may be weak if you:

- Feel disconnected to a higher power
- Feeling of loneliness and insignificance
- Are stuck in an unfulfilling and unrewarding career
- Have a strong attachment to possessions and relationships, and define yourself by what you have
- Migraines and tension headache

Throat Chakra
Self-expression

Located right in the center of your throat. It deals with issues of honesty, integrity, truth, expression and communication. Physically, it supports your neck, jaw, teeth, gums, mouth, lower sinus, throat and thyroid gland.

Your Throat Chakra may be weak if you:

- Are often afraid to speak up and voice your opinions around others
- Settle with following other people's opinions
- Are likely to be the "quiet one" in your professional and social circles
- Experience sore throats, swollen glands, sinus problems, disorders of the throat, mouth, teeth or gums

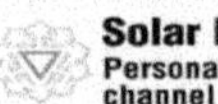

Solar Plexus Chakra
Personal power and ability to channel

Located along your spine it deals with issues of willpower, ambition and action. Physically, it supports your liver, pancreas, gallbladder, stomach and spleen.

Your Solar Plexus Chakra may be weak if you:

- See yourself as powerless and struggle with self-esteem issues
- Have different ways of shaming yourself and feel embarrassed by what people think of you
- Feel like a victim in the world, and often feel powerless to circumstances and other people's desires
- Suffer from frequent stomach pains and stomach anxiety

Root Chakra
Career, money mindset and sense of belonging

Located at the very base of your spine, is the most common chakra to be weakened. It deals with physical survival, safety, security, fear and insecurity.

Your Root Chakra may be weak if you:

- Feel a general lack of physical energy and vitality
- Are stuck in an unfulfilling and unrewarding career
- Find that your well-being is highly dependent upon external circumstances
- Believe that money creates security
- Suffer from eating disorders, adrenal fatigue, foot and leg pains/injuries, rectal or colon problems, immune disorders or bone disorders

Third Eye Chakra
Intuition, sense of purpose and direction in life

Located right in the center of your forehead and deals with intuition, your sense of purpose and direction in life. Physically, it supports your upper frontal sinuses, eyes, ears, and the outer layers of your brain.

Your Third Eye Chakra may be weak if you:

- Feel lost when it comes to having a sense of purpose in life
- Are indecisive, uncommitted and unconfident of the decisions you make
- Have an active imagination, but not in a good way as you spend much of your day in analytical mode
- Experience headaches and a feeling of tension in your brow area

Heart Chakra
Love, relationships and self-acceptance

Located along your spine right in the center of your chest next to your physical heart. It deals with issues of love, compassion and belonging. Physically, it supports your heart, lungs, upper torso, shoulders, arms and hands.

Your Heart Chakra may be weak if you:

- Are guarded and closed and rarely allow yourself to open up to others
- Sabotage your relationships with distrust and anger
- Are unable to let a situation rest because it didn't go your way
- Are clingy and needy in relationships and anxious that your partner doesn't need you as much as you need them
- Experience heart disorders, chest pain, asthma, allergies, circulation problems

Sacral Chakra
Sexuality and pleasure

This is where we awaken our kundalini energy. Located in our hips, sacrum and genitals, it is where we experience the joys of intimacy, creativity, pleasure, our desires and sexuality

Your Sacral Chakra may be weak if you:

- Struggle to see yourself as "sexy", and sometimes wonder how anyone could desire you
- Find it difficult to open up in relationships
- Have a tendency to end up in sexually incompatible relationships and find yourself wondering if you'll ever find "the one"
- Rarely have the time or desire to have sex

Chakras that people have most of their problems with

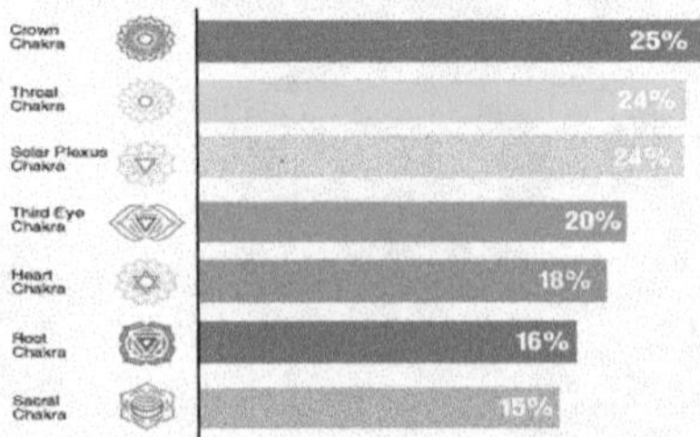

7 lights of the candlesticks:

1. Neophyte (believer): Curiosity=maturation=advancement
2. Faith (scholar): Consciousness=deeds=honor
3. Fruition (Master): Inspiration=application=assurance
4. Order: balance=reciprocity=justice
5. Intellect: study=reason=creativity
6. Power: wisdom=strength=beauty
7. Perfection (love): truth=peace=freedom

7 Principles of matunda ya kwanza (first fruits of the harvest):

1. Umoja: unity
2. Kujichagulia: self-determination
3. Ujima: collective work and responsibility
4. Ujamaa: cooperative economics
5. Nia: purpose
6. Kuuma: creativity
7. Imani: faith

7 liberal arts:

1. Grammar
2. Logic
3. Rhetoric
4. Arithmetic
5. Geometry
6. Astronomy
7. Music

7 Senses:

1. hearing
2. touch
3. sight
4. taste
5. smell
6. intuition
7. clairvoyance

7 cardinal sins:

1. haughty eyes
2. a lying tongue
3. hands that shed innocent blood
4. a heart that devises wicked schemes
5. feet that are quick to rush to evil
6. a false witness that pours out lies
7. a man who stirs up dissention among brothers

7 Lords:

1. holds the key of all hidden magic, creator of the halls of the dead; sending forth power, shrouding with darkness, binding the souls of the children of men; sending the darkness, binding the soul force; director of the negative energy to the children of men.
2. is he who looses the power. Lord, he of life to the children of men. Light is his body, flame is his countenance; freer of souls to the children of men.
3. is the master, the lord of all magic-key to the word that resounds among men.
4. is the lord of light, the hidden pathway, path of souls of the children of men.
5. is he who is lord of the vastness, master of space and key of the times.
6. is he who orders the progress; weighs and balances the journey of men.
7. is the father, vast he of countenance, forming and changing from out of the formless.

7 pillars:

1. shahadah: sincere reciting of faith
2. salat: performing ritual palil (prayer) in the proper way, 5x a day
3. zagat: paying an alms (charity) tax to benefit the poor and needy
4. sawm: fasting during the month of Ramadan
5. hajj: pilgrimage to and through Th Holy Land
6. taharah: purification
7. jihad: striving

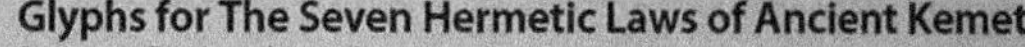

Glyphs for The Seven Hermetic Laws of Ancient Kemet

By Apuat En Heru / Jonathan Woods 8-7-2009
Inspired by Wayne B. Chandler's book Ancient Future.
Layout by Suji Lee

⬭
MENTALISM

The Principle of Mentalism
The All is mind; The Universe is Mental.

=
CORRESPONDENCE

The Principle of Correspondence
As above, so below; as below, so above.

≈
VIBRATION

The Principle of Vibration
Nothing rests; everything moves; everything vibrates.

+ / -
POLARITY

The Principle of Polarity
Everything is dual; everything has poles; everything has it's pair of opposites; like & unlike are the same; opposites are identical in nature, but different in degree; extremes meet; all truths are but half-truths; all paradoxes may be reconciled.

GENDER

The Principle of Gender
Gender is in everything; everything has it's Masculine & Feminine Principles; Gender manifests on all planes.

●•••
RHYTHM

The Principle of Rhythm
Everything flows out & in; everything has its tides; all things rise & fall; the pendulum swing manifests in everything; the measure of the swing to the right is the measure of the swing to the left; rhythm compensates.

>>
CAUSE & EFFECT

The Principle of Cause & Effect
Every cause has its Effect; every Effect has its cause;
everything happens according to Law;
Chance is but a name for Law not recognized;
there are many planes of causation but nothing escapes the Law.

VI. As Above so below: 8

The Noble 8-fold path:

1. right view (unimpaired vision)
2. right intention
3. right speech (juris=right + diction=words)
4. right action
5. right livelihood
6. right effort (moral effort is the key to life if you use it properly)
7. right mindfulness (foreknowledge)
8. right concentration

8 Moon Cycles:

the MOON

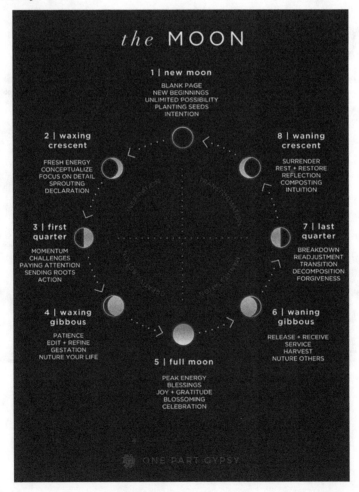

1 | new moon
BLANK PAGE
NEW BEGINNINGS
UNLIMITED POSSIBILITY
PLANTING SEEDS
INTENTION

2 | waxing crescent
FRESH ENERGY
CONCEPTUALIZE
FOCUS ON DETAIL
SPROUTING
DECLARATION

3 | first quarter
MOMENTUM
CHALLENGES
PAYING ATTENTION
SENDING ROOTS
ACTION

4 | waxing gibbous
PATIENCE
EDIT + REFINE
GESTATION
NUTURE YOUR LIFE

5 | full moon
PEAK ENERGY
BLESSINGS
JOY + GRATITUDE
BLOSSOMING
CELEBRATION

6 | waning gibbous
RELEASE + RECEIVE
SERVICE
HARVEST
NUTURE OTHERS

7 | last quarter
BREAKDOWN
READJUSTMENT
TRANSITION
DECOMPOSITION
FORGIVENESS

8 | waning crescent
SURRENDER
REST + RESTORE
REFLECTION
COMPOSTING
INTUITION

ONE PART GYPSY

VII. The order of 9: Completion

9 inseparable parts of the soul:

1. Ka: abstract personality, to whom it belongs, possessing the form and attributes of a human with power of movement, omnipresence, and ability to receive nourishment. Equivalent to what we call the shadow image.
2. Khat: the mortal concrete personality, the physical body.
3. Ba: the heart-soul, which lives in the ka and sometimes beside it, to supply Th Ka with food and air. Capable of metamorphosis
4. Ab: the heart, the physical life in humans, spiritual, rational and ethical. Associated with Th Ba (heart-soul). In the Kemetic judgment drama, it undergoes examination in the presence of Th God Ausar, Th Great Creator and judge of the dead.
5. Kaibit: the shadow. Also associated with the Ba, from which it receives its nourishments. Has the power of movement and omnipresence.
6. Khu: spiritual soul that lives forever. A heavenly being, closely associated with Th Ba.
7. Sahu: the spiritual body in which the khu or spiritual soul dwells. The moral nature of mental and spiritual qualities is united to form new powers that man has the choice to use for good or evil.
8. Sekhem: the power or spirit of the vital force in humans. Lives in the heavens with the spirit khu.
9. Ren: the name of an individual, the essential attribute for preservation of a being. The ancients believed that in the absence of a name, an individual ceased to exist. The quality of a name, therefore, was very important.

9 Floors of retribution (hell):

East (upper):

1st Floor:

- Name: chamber of tongue ripping
- Function: those who stir up troubles by gossiping will find their tongues ripped out.

2nd Floor:

- Name: chamber of scissors
- Function: those who break up the marriage of others will have their fingers cut off.

3rd Floor:

- Name: chamber of iron trees
- Function: those who cause discord among family members of other people will find their body being pierced by hooks and hung upside down on iron trees.

4th Floor:

- Name: chamber of mirror
- Function: those who escape the earthly punishment will find their true shape being displayed in the mirror, and old karmic debt will be paid with high interest.

5th Floor:

- Name: chamber of steamer
- Function: instigators and hypocrites will find themselves being steamed in a steamer.

6th Floor:

- Name: forest of copper column
- Function: arsonists will get themselves stuck to scorching hot copper columns

7th Floor:

- Name; mountain of knives
- Function: those who kill sentient beings with knife will find themselves climbing a hill of knives.

8th Floor:

- Name: hill of ice
- Function: cold-blooded schemers and ungrateful suckers, including those who ill-treat their partners and elders, will find themselves naked in this freezing cold environment.

9th Floor:

- Name: cauldron of boiling oil
- Function: sex offenders such as rapists, lechers and adulterers will find themselves being fried in boiling oil.

West (lower):

10th Floor:

- Name: chamber of ox
- Function: those who abuse animals will find themselves being bullied by animals.

11th Floor:

- Name: chamber of rock
- Function: those who abandon or kill newborns will find themselves being crushed under a rock and soaked in filthy water.

12th Floor:

- Name: chamber of pounding
- Function: those who willfully waste food will find themselves being pounded like crops

13th Floor:

- Name: pool of blood
- Function: those who do not respect others will find themselves soaked in blood. It is said that those who die of bleeding are actually given a preview of their afterlife.

14th Floor:

- Name: town of quitters
- Function: those who commit suicide will find themselves wandering in this town of misery where the wind of sorrow and rain of grief blasting day and night. They are the ones slipping off the normal incarnation paths and will live in the gaps of the worlds for a very long time.

15th Floor:

- Name: chamber of dismemberment
- Function: those who disturb the deceased by digging tombs will find their body being torn into pieces.

16th Floor:

- Name: mountain of flames
- Function: those who steal, bribe and rob will find themselves surrounded by inferno

17th Floor:

- Name: yard of stone mill
- Function: those who oppress the people will find themselves being ground into powder.

18th Floor:

- Name: chamber of saw
- Function: those who exploit the loopholes in the law to cheat and engage in malpractice in business will find themselves being sawed in half.

From the Buddhist point of view, being a sufferer in hell is just one of six ways of living, and once a hell mate paid off its karmic debt, it will become light enough to rise up and be reincarnated into other forms of existence. Hell, though terrifying, is as solid as this human world. Since it is a universally shared perception, like the Sun and the Moon and indeed the Universe itself, it won't burst into nothingness just because you do not believe in it, just as the Moon won't disappear because you do not see it–unless, of course, it is a moon or hell in your dreamland and being sustained by your solo consciousness.

VIII. The order of 10: Intercourse

The Tree of Life:

Mother:

1. Ra: Fire (triune: order, intellect and power)
2. Shu: air/ether (power of breath/ jurisdiction)
3. Tefnut: water/life force
4. Geb: earth (magnetism and vibration)
5. Nut: heaven (expansion)
6. Ausar: eternal soul
7. Auset: wisdom (intuition)
8. Set: ego (assurance)
9. Nebthet: mortality (humbleness and death of materialistic lust)
10. Heru-Ur: victory (duality: aspiration and challenge)

Son:

1. Kether: crown
2. Chochmah: wisdom
3. Binah: innerstanding
4. Chesed: grace/mercy
5. Gevurah: miraculous power
6. Tiphareth: beauty
7. Netzach: victory
8. Hod: honor
9. Yesod: foundatio
10. Malkuth: sovereignty

IX. The 11 Laws of God:

1. You were created in the likeness of peace which cannot be disturbed. Regain your original state of peace to attain to your reason for coming into existence. (Amun)

2. Your nature is an unconquerable peace. Therefore, nothing and no one can be against you. All experiences come to you to promote your reclamation of peace that you may in turn acquire wisdom and power. (Ausar)

3. When your thoughts, feelings and actions reflect the word of Th Creator Th power of Th Supreme Force and a peace that nothing can challenge will flow through your being. (Dwty)

4. When the emotions of man manifest in response to the word of Th Most High they have the power to influence any and all events in the world. (Sekher)

5. Th Great Spirit needs you in order to come into this world. Fulfilling Th Creator's commands is the highest act of love in existence for the protection of existence. (Maat)

6. Know that Th Spirits neither punish nor reward nor protects. You will have the comfort of controlling these for yourself. (Herukhut)

7. You have the power but not the right to ignore Th Creator's Law. Choose to follow Th Universal Law with joy and love that comes from innerstanding and the wisdom and power of Th Supreme Reality will flow through your being. (Heru)

8. It is not what you imagine but who is imagining. Are you a human or a divine being? (Het-Heru)

9. It's not what you think or affirm, it's who's thinking or affirming. Are you a human or a divine being? (Sebek)

10. Prepare to sacrifice everything to become the vessel of Th Creator on earth and you will, in turn, receive everything. (Auset)

11. Know that from heaven you came and to heaven you will return; seek not enduring works on earth. (Geb)

X. The 12 keys to Spiritual Activism

1. All actions must be based on compassion
2. Compassion must be fluid not mechanical
3. Compassion must be applied with wisdom
4. Apply synergy and teamwork to accomplish goals
5. Be selfless, non-prejudicial and fair-minded
6. Be dignified, honest and always within the realm of integrity
7. Do not hate your haters
8. Raising another up is also raising yourself up
9. Learn to listen with your heart and not your mind; master the management of both
10. Search out viable and sustainable solutions
11. Do not judge your success by immediate results or even tangible ones; seeds blossom in different seasons
12. Let loving-kindness be the motivation for your actions

XI. The Order of 13: Manifestation

13 Universal Laws

1. Law of Divine Oneness: everything is connected to everything else. What we think, say, do and our intentions have a corresponding effect on others and the universe.
2. Law of Vibration: everything in the universe moves, vibrates and travels in circular patterns. The principle of vibration in the physical world apply to our thoughts, feelings, wills and desires in the etheric world. Each sound, thing, and even thought has its own vibration frequency, unique unto itself.
3. Law of Action: must be employed in order for us to manifest things on earth. We must engage in actions that support our thoughts, dreams, emotions and words.
4. Law of Correspondence: this universal law states that any principles of laws of physics that explain the physical world; energy, light, vibration, and motion have their corresponding principles in the etheric world or universe, "As above so below, as within so without."
5. Law of Cause and Effect: nothing happens by chance or outside universal laws. Every action (including thought) has a reaction or consequence: "As you sow, so shall you reap."
6. Law of Compensation: this universal law is applied to blissings and abundance that are provided to and by us. The visible effects of our deeds are given to us/by us as gifts, money, inheritance, associates and divine talents/attributes unique to our being.

7. Law of Attraction: demonstrates how we create new things, events and people that come into our lives. Our thoughts, feelings, words and actions produce energies which, in turn attract like energies. Positive attracts the same and negative attracts negative as well.

8. Law of Perpetual transmutation of Energy: all persons have within them the power to change the conditions of their lives. Higher vibrations consume lower ones; each of us can change the energies in our lives by inner/overstanding divine principles and applying these formulas to our daily existence so as to bring about momentum and change that moves us further towards our aspirations.

9. Law of Relativity: each man will receive a series of problems for the purpose of strengthening the light within. Each test is to be a challenge and remain connected to our hearts when proceeding to solve problems. This law teaches us to analyze our lives in comparison to the problems of others and do so within the frame of proper perspective. Everybody goes through something and is going through something, so we overcome. "If you're going through hell the best thing to do is keep going."

10. Law of Polarity: everything is on a continuum and has an opposite. We can suppress and transform undesirable thoughts by concentrating on the opposite pole. It is the law of mental vibrations.

11. Law of Rhythm: everything vibrates and moves to certain rhythms. These rhythms establish seasons, cycles, stages of development and patterns. Each cycle reflects the regularity of Th Supreme Creator's universe. Masters know how to rise above negative vibrations by never getting to excited or allowing negative things to penetrate their consciousness.

12. Law of Gender: the law of gender manifests in all things as masculine and feminine. It is the law that governs what we know as creation. The law of gender manifest in the animal kingdom as sex. This law decrees that everything in nature must be male and female. Both are required for life to exist.

13. Law of Gestation: states that everything takes time to manifest. All things have a beginning and grow into form as energy is added to it. Thoughts are like seeds planted into our soil/soul, if we have properly nourished them, they bear good fruit in time. How to apply: stay focused and know that your goals will become reality when the time is right.

13 Attributes of Th Creator

1. Eheyeh: I Am
2. Adonai: I, Th Lord, am the compassionate source of all life and the ground of all being; I forgive the lower nature of yourselves; I, Th Lord, am compassionate to those who have strayed and have been corrected
3. El: I, Th Lord, am G-d Th almighty and omnipotent
4. Rachum: I, Th Lord, am merciful
5. Chanun: I, Th Lord, am gracious; I pour out favor to all of creation
6. Erekh Apayim: I, Th Lord, am slow to anger and patient
7. Rav Chesed: I, Th Lord, am abundant in love to both the righteous and the wicked
8. Rav Emet: I, Th Lord, am truthful and faithful in carrying out promises
9. Notzer Chesed La'alafim: I, Th Lord, retain love for thousands of generations, taking in account the merit of your worthy ancestors
10. Nosei Avon: I, Th Lord, forgive iniquity, defined in the tradition as wrongful deeds committed with perverse premeditation; I carry iniquity away for the penitent
11. Nosei Pesha: I, Th Lord, forgive transgression, defined as wrongful deeds committed in a rebellious spirit
12. Nosei Chata'ah: I, Th Lord, forgive sin, defined as those wrongful deeds inadvertently committed
13. Nakkeh: I, Th Lord, will not cancel punishment, but I will clear the guilt of those who genuinely return to me in repentance

13 Principles of Faith:

1. G-d esxists
2. G-d is one and unique
3. G-d is incorporeal
4. G-d is eternal
5. Palil (prayer) is directed to G-d and G-d alone
6. The words of the prophets are true
7. Musa (Moses) was a true prophet and a redeemer of mankind
8. The Torah (first 5 books of the bible) were given to Musa
9. There is but One Law
10. G-d knows the thoughts and deeds of man
11. G-d will reward the good and punish the wicked
12. The messiah will come
13. The Dead will be resurrected

N. Maat: Law and Order

I. 42 ideals of Maat (affirmations)

Maat is the Kemetic God-Principle that represents law, order and love. It is interesting that they put love and law together (See Romans 13:8, 10) in the same principle because in their philosophical view law was not about force and punishment. Instead it is the natural outcome of love which is the expression of our oneness with each other and Th Creator.

These ideals, from which the Mosaic law stems, are not a finite list of dos and don'ts, but are instead principles Th Creator set in motion and ingrained within our molecular make-up, so we could live a victorious life if we live by them.

Western culture has programmed us to go from pleasure to pain according to circumstances outside our control. We seek to maximize the circumstances that bring us pleasure and minimize the ones that bring us pain. Kemetic spirituality teaches us that many of the emotions we experience are programmed reactions to circumstances. Th Creator has given us the tools to deprogram and reprogram in a way that is conducive to our spiritual, emotional, mental and physical health. With this we go from pleasure to peace, pleasure to peace. Isn't faith enough to do all this? Don't be afraid to be honest. We know many people who believe very strongly that Th Creator has provided all their needs and yet they have no lasting joy or self-control because they are constantly waylaid by emotional ups and downs, so we must learn to rise above emotions.

Our Ancestors recognized the self as the true individual with the personality as the part of our make-up which houses our emotions and can be programmed. Society has already programmed us through the media to be "conformed to this world." Isn't it time for us to start programming ourselves to be "transformed by the renewing of our minds." (kemetpages.com)

42 IDEALS OF MA'AT

facebook.com/WakeUpAndRemember

1. I HONOUR VIRTUE
2. I BENEFIT WITHOUT VIOLENCE
3. I AM NON-VIOLENT
4. I RESPECT THE PROPERTY OF OTHERS
5. I AFFIRM THAT ALL LIFE IS SACRED
6. I GIVE OFFERINGS THAT ARE GENUINE AND GENEROUS
7. I LIVE IN TRUTH
8. I HOLD SACRED THOSE OBJECTS THAT ARE CONSECRATED TO THE DIVINE
9. I SPEAK THE TRUTH
10. I EAT ONLY MY FAIR SHARE
11. I SPEAK WORDS OF GOOD INTENT
12. I RELATE IN PEACE
13. I HONOUR ANIMALS AS SACRED
14. I CAN BE TRUSTED
15. I CARE FOR THE EARTH
16. I KEEP MY OWN COUNCIL
17. I SPEAK POSITIVELY OF OTHERS
18. I REMAIN IN BALANCE WITH MY EMOTIONS
19. I AM TRUSTFUL IN MY RELATIONSHIPS
20. I HOLD PURITY IN HIGH ESTEEM
21. I SPREAD JOY
22. I DO THE BEST I CAN
23. I COMMUNICATE WITH COMPASSION
24. I LISTEN TO OPPOSING OPINIONS
25. I CREATE HARMONY
26. I INVOKE LAUGHTER
27. I AM OPEN TO LOVE IN VARIOUS FORMS
28. I AM FORGIVING
29. I AM NON-ABUSIVE
30. I ACT RESPECTFULLY OF OTHERS
31. I AM NON-JUDGEMENTAL
32. I FOLLOW MY INNER GUIDANCE
33. I SPEAK WITHOUT DISTURBING OTHERS
34. I DO GOOD
35. I GIVE BLESSINGS
36. I KEEP THE WATERS PURE
37. I SPEAK WITH OPTIMISM
38. I PRAISE TRUTH
39. I AM HUMBLE
40. I ACHIEVE WITH INTEGRITY
41. I ADVANCE THROUGH MY OWN ABILITIES
42. I EMBRACE THE ALL

O. Universal Life equation

I. The Divine Paradox

"The half-wise, recognizing the comparative unreality of the Universe, imagine that they may defy its Laws–such are vain and presumptuous fools, and they are broken against the rocks and torn asunder by the elements by reason of their folly. The truly wise, knowing the nature of the Universe, use Law against laws; the higher against the lower; and by the Art of Alchemy transmute that which is undesirable into that which is worthy, and thus triumph. Mastery consists not in abnormal dreams, visions and fantastic imaginings or living, but in using the higher forces against the lower–escaping the pains of the lower planes by vibrating on the higher. Transmutation, not presumptuous denial, is the weapon of the Master." –The Kybalion.

This is the Paradox of the Universe, resulting from the Principle of Polarity which manifests when THE ALL begins to Create–hearken to it for it points the difference between half-wisdom and wisdom. While to THE INFINITE ALL, the Universe, its Laws, its Powers, its Life, its Phenomena, are as things witnessed in the state of Meditation or Dream; yet to all that is Finite, the Universe must be treated as Real, and life, and action, and thought, must be based thereupon, accordingly, although with an ever understanding of the Higher Truth. Each according to its own Plane and Laws. Were THE ALL to imagine that the Universe were indeed Reality, then woe to the Universe, for there would be then no escape from lower to higher, divine ward–then would the Universe become a fixity and progress would become impossible. And if Man, owing to half-wisdom, acts and lives and thinks of the Universe as merely a dream (akin to his own finite dreams) then indeed does it so become for him, and like a sleep-walker he stumbles ever around and around in a circle, making no progress, and being forced into an awakening at last by his falling bruised and bleeding over the Natural Laws which he ignored. Keep your mind ever on the Star, but let your eyes watch over your footsteps, lest you fall into the mire by reason of your upward gaze. Remember the Divine Paradox, that while the Universe IS NOT, still IT IS. Remember ever the Two Poles of Truth–the Absolute and the Relative. Beware of Half-Truths.

We do not live in a world of dreams, but in a Universe which, while relative, is real so far as our lives and actions are concerned. Our business in the Universe is not to deny its existence, but to LIVE, using the Laws to rise from lower to higher–living on, doing the best that we can under the circumstances arising each day, and living, so far as is possible, to our highest ideas and ideals. The true Meaning of Life is not known to men on this plane–if, indeed, to any–but the highest authorities, and our own intuitions, teach us that we will make no mistake in living up to the best that is in us, so far as is possible, and realizing the Universal tendency in the same direction in spite of apparent evidences to the contrary. We are all on The Path–and the road leads upward ever, with frequent resting places. Read the Message of The Kybalion–and follow the example of "the wise"– avoiding the mistake of "the half–wise" who perish by reason of their folly.

OUTRO:

"*The possession of Knowledge, unless accompanied by a manifestation and expression in Action, is like the hoarding of precious metals–a vain and foolish thing. Knowledge, like Wealth, is intended for Use. The Law of Use is Universal, and he who violates it suffers by reason of his conflict with natural forces.*" –The Kybalion.

"*We must stop confusing religion, and spirituality. Religion is a set of rules, regulations, and rituals created by humans which were supposed to help people spiritually. Due to human imperfection religion has become corrupt, political, divisive, and a tool for power struggle. Spirituality is not the theology or ideology. It is simply a way of life, pure and original as given by Th Most High. Spirituality is a network linking us to Th Most High, Th universe, and each other.*" -Haile Salassie

"*Men and women are to become God–like through a life of virtue and the cultivation of spirit through scientific knowledge, practice and bodily discipline.*" -Kemetic Proverb

"Knowledge is far different from sense. For sense is brought about by that which hath mastery o'er us, while knowledge is the end of science, and science is God's gift. All science is incorporeal, the instrument it uses being Th Mind, just as the mind employs the body." – Kemetic Proverb

Part 4: Trust Thyself

"*Man must learn by signs and symbols.*"-El Sharif Abdul Ali

Intro: The greatest tool/gift we possess is the one of intuition. This is that proverbial gut feeling that tells us whether we are moving in the right or wrong direction, essentially it is the voice of Th Most High conveyed in a way that we can innerstand. Also, to coincide with this innate compass is that of nature itself which is housed with many different messages that our ancestors use to communicate and advise us. The final aspect of navigation is that of the evidence of life i.e. the various modes of human communication and interaction; body language, vibe/energy, intent and sign language. All of these things must be combined in order to draw the perfect map of our lives and which roads we are to travel. I think most could agree that the majority of the problems we've faced as individuals and as a collective were do to us ignoring our own common sense and intuition which means we ignored and disregarded our ancestors, nature and Th Most High in turn leading to misery and pain. However, such is necessary for man for we are hard headed but through trial and error we reach our goals and we do so in humility and graciousness assuming we've learned from our past transgressions and have a view of life within the framework and mindset of proper perspective.

Chapter 1: Symbolism

A. Numerology

(The Symbolist: A simplified Guide to tarot symbols and terms by Corrine Kenner; sacredsribesangelnumbers.com)

I. Tarot: The 22 Numbers

Numerology is the study of the occult (hidden) meaning of numbers. Derived from Latin numerus-number + logy < Greek logia < logos-a discourse; one treating of < legein-speak (of), recount.

Now I must let it be known that I do not advocate paying finance to those who offer these kinds of services, unless the practioner is well respected and thus duly proven in their craft but I must admit that this is an actual science and that there are those who have the gift of divine interpretation. I ask that you tread wisely, and I am providing these study tools so as to spark a level of independence in you the reader in terms of mastering the sciences of the universe. Also, I must let it be known that I am by no means an expert in this science but like most of you who are reading this I am a novice, but this is what I've gathered through study and research.

These are the basic fundamentals in terms of numerology in terms of the tarot:

- 0: The Fool: a wanderer, representative of each of us-naïve travelers through life, off on a grand adventure, out to learn from what ever experiences that life gives us. Is the enhancer of all other numbers and takes on the attributes of the number 9; gateway to infinity and immortality.
- 1: The Magician: represents an individual in control of life's tools and techniques, like those on the table in front of him. Om, the first breath of Th Universe. I Am, Th name of G-d. Births all other numbers. Symbolizes that of the initiating force, the monad; the keynote uniting man and mankind with each other, spirit guides, Th Gods and other realms. Encourages you to take up challenges with total faith and trust in yourself and the universal energies.
- 2: The High Priestess: secretive and guarded, the high priestess knows the secrets that life holds-but shares them only with the wise. The divine feminine. Our

sacred mother. These are yin energies. Symbolizes the union of peace between different entities. It seeks to end separateness and unite all for Th Greater Good whether it be music, food or humanity. Encourages you to be diplomatic, co-operative and loving when relating to others.

- 3: The Empress: the archetypical mother, the empress nurtures and protects all of nature, including man and mankind. The synthesis, the offspring of 1 and 2, calls on man to remember we carry divinity within. Foundation of the superhuman. As the 3rd it symbolizes the exuberance of life; the spiritual being having a human experience. Encourages you to be communicative and social with others to live your life with joy, optimism and spontaneity.
- 4: The Emperor: the archetypical father, the authoritative emperor brings order out of chaos so that civilization can prosper. With 4 sides of the same size, a square has no weak points. It is organized, solid and enduring; built-to-last number. Symbolizes that equality on all sides creates security and stability. In the Bible the earth was created on the 4th day. Encourages you to put proper preparation into your plans and set things in motion with system and order so that you can achieve your goals and aspirations.
- 5: The Hierophant: a symbol of traditional authority and influence, the high priest is a spiritual link to humanity's higher powers. The inner and outer world intricately intertwined. Symbolizes the number of humanity. Turns the mystical into the norm. Is the energy of experience. Is a message to do with your health and wellbeing. Is telling you that only you know your true heart's desires, and only you can fulfill your own destiny in your own unique way.
- 6: The Lovers: while an appearance by this couple could encourage any hopeless romantic, the lovers also signify a choice to be made between two equally strong desires. Gaia, the ultimate nurturer, the giver of unconditional love. She, in all her many splendors, is the foundation. For the meaning of 6 symbolizes that of home and health, loving relationships of every kind and deep compassion bordering on empathy. Teaches true compassion and empathy. Energy of the mother Gaia. Encourages you to be loving, caring and nurturing of yourself and others.
- 7: The Chariot: the young character is in command of his physical and emotional drives, symbolized by the two opposing forces that pull the chariot. The dreamer of dreams. The ex- patriot of people. The mind who moves through the macrocosm at will; foundation of the psychic. Symbolizes the mind and its infinite possibilities. Reminds us that the answers to all the questions are in our DNA. It is the energy of the seeker. Spiritual awakening and awareness,

enlightenment, acceptance and development, inner-wisdom and psychic abilities.

- 8: Strength: a woman gently holds the jaws of a powerful lion, patiently controlling a force that could otherwise eat her alive. Karma, reaping what is sown, assumption of power, financial success; foundation of the enduring and eternal. Symbolizes mind over matter. Shows us that strength of will overcomes the material world and lives in perpetuity as our 'will' is synonymous with the soul. Reminds us the soul has a mind of its own and lives on, no matter what. Its energy is eternal life. Tells you to step into your personal power and have faith and trust in your own abilities, skills and talents, and to use them to their highest potential.
- 9: The Hermit: far removed from the hustle and bustle of everyday life. The hermit reflects on spiritual concerns. He carries his light of wisdom as a beacon for others to follow. Embraces the utmost in universal, selfless love. By the end of this incarnation, these old souls will have been through the lessons of the first 8 and find themselves in a space of wisdom, insight, kindness and vision. Filled with challenges, all of which act on the aura to increase the vibration service to all humankind. Keynote being "the greater good." Reminds us that by allowing our own divine light to shine, we can change the world. Its energy is that of the greater good. Encourages you to be compassionate, thoughtful, philanthropic and of service to others and humanity as whole and lead others by positive example.
- 10: The Wheel of Fortune: because nothing is certain but change itself, the wheel of fortune reminds us all that what goes up must also come down. Symbolizes love and light. It creates all that is imagined and contains the code, image and ordain. Is a number of 'rise and fall' according to the actions chosen. Represents the point of conversion when people see themselves as upright beings; power and protection. Encourages you to move forward in life with faith and trust that you are on the right path in all ways. Brings a message to step forward in new directions and look to new beginnings with an optimistic and positive attitude as they will prove to be auspicious and beneficial to you in many ways, now and in the future.
- 11: Justice: is blind to superficial concerns. She holds a two- edged sword-a reminder that fairness cuts both ways. Knowing of universal truths and living them. Reminds us that our inner voice can always guide us to a higher vibration. Its energy is that of spiritual enlightenment. Encourages you to assist and inspire the human race via your natural abilities, relying upon your inner wisdom and

intuition to guide you. Encourages you to be an inspirational guiding light to bring illumination to others and help raise spiritual awareness. Trust that Th Angels support you in your humanitarian work.

- 12: The Hanged Man: he sacrifices his comfort and passions for a time, knowing that better things will occur as a result. The completed cycle of experience. Warns of the necessity to be alert to every situation, to be suspicious of those who offer a high position, and to be aware of false flattery and those who use it to gain their own ends. Represents the educational process on all levels, the submission of will required and the sacrifice necessary to achieve higher knowledge and wisdom on both spiritual and intellectual levels. When the intellect is sacrificed to the feelings, the mind will be illuminated with the answers it seeks. Attention paid to the requirements of education will end suffering and bring success. Is a message from your angels to ensure that what you put out to the universe is of a positive nature. You are asked to stay on a positive path and to use your natural skills, talents and abilities to their utmost for the benefit of others as well as yourself; don't be hindered by old habits that need to be changed. Surround yourself with love and gaiety.
- 13: Death: foretells the completion of one stage of life and the exciting beginning of a new phase. Associated with genius, the transmutation of vices to virtues. 'Right judgment', spiritual growth through pain rather than pleasure. Upheaval so that new ground can be broken; adapting to change gracefully and decreasing any potential for negative. Is a message from your angels that some upheavals might take place in your life. This is for karmic reasons and will break new ground for you that will bring about new opportunities for you to grow spiritually. The angels ask that you adapt to changes gracefully; "blissing in disguise". Is a message that you are being guided and assisted with your soul mission. Trust that Th Angels and Ascended Masters are by your side as you go through transitions that will bring into perfect alignment your divine life purpose. If you are unsure of your next steps, ask your angels for guidance and assistance.
- 14: Temperance: with dexterity and grace, temperance demonstrates how balance can serve as a bridge to wholeness. Independence, self-initiator, unity and justice. Is a message from Th angels asking you to keep your focus, positive affirmations and intentions on manifesting your true desires. Can be sign from your angels that they are there to assist you with manifesting your true desires. Is a message that if you act with caution and wisdom you will be successful in business, money matters, and life in general. Begin worthwhile projects

that will bring long term benefits and future success. Encourages progressive change, renewal and growth, and tells you to share your knowledge and wisdom with others. It also tells you that what you put your efforts towards will reap rewards in the future. The message for this number could also mean, "be careful what you wish for."

- 15: Devil: shows us that a selfish devotion to material possessions and ill-conceived passions ties us down and keeps us from true happiness. Symbolizes or represents the purpose of spreading love and teaching others. Is a message from your angels that your ideas and thoughts are prompting you to make some much-needed changes in your life. Is a message to keep your thoughts and actions focused upon your goals and aspirations in order to manifest your highest ideals. Use positive affirmations and visualization in order to keep your outlook bright and receptive. Is also a message to use your initiative and personal tenacity when making choices concerning your wellbeing and life path as only you know your true heart's desires. You have the inner-wisdom, talents and abilities to achieve all that you strive to.
- 16: The Tower: should we build ourselves up too high, a bolt from the blue could shake us to our very foundations. Symbolizes the need to cultivate willpower, independence and initiative action so as to overcome obstacles that come into our life experiences; keeping of the feet on the path of higher learning. Is a reminder from your angels that your thoughts create your reality, therefore ensure that you hold only positive expectations about your life, lifestyle and material issues. Trust that all of your needs will be met as you live your life mission. Is a message that your angels want you to ask for their guidance and help in regard to the material aspects of life. Listen to the messages from your intuition and inner-wisdom as the angels are currently letting you know which choices to make and which steps to take that will ensure that you and your loved ones will have all that is required to maintain and sustain daily needs. Encourages you to maintain a positive attitude whilst the angels work with you to fulfill all your needs.
- 17: The Star: faith and hope, the star is a shining light in the darkness. Insight, responsibility, self-discipline, strength, compassion, spiritual consciousness, wisdom, a desire for peace and love for all of humanity. Highly spiritual number and has been expressed by the Chaldeans as the 8-pointed star of Venus. It is the star of love and peace and promises of spiritual ascension validated and empowered by the trials and difficulties of earlier life; relates to 'immortality'-a legacy that lives on after you have left this plane of existence and is the ability

to see beyond to find the hidden truth. It is universal healing, truth and inner/ overstanding. Indicates that you are on the 'right path' on your life journey. Is a message encouraging you to listen to your intuition and higher-self and take appropriate action as only you can serve your soul purpose and fulfill your destiny. The angels encourage you to maintain a positive attitude and use positive affirmations in order to manifest your highest ideals and aspirations. Can also suggest it is time to begin (or expand) a spiritually based practice, career and/or profession or heart-based service. Th universe and angels will ensure that all that you require will be provided for you, and you are to trust your inner-wisdom, skills and abilities. Use your talents to serve humanity and bring illumination to those who seek it.

- 18: The Moon: deeply rooted in the unconscious, the dreamlike moon symbolizes secrets and mysteries that may not be innerstood-or even recognized. The vibration of abundance, stepping into personal inner strength, leadership and karma. Is a message of encouragement and support from your angels. They ask you to think only positive thoughts to do with abundance . When you have high expectations and maintain a positive attitude the angles and universal energies help you to manifest your highest ideals and achieve success in all that you put your intentions and efforts towards. Th angels want you to know that positive things are manifesting around you at a rapid rate. Suggests that you are nearing the end of a phase or cycle in life, and the angles want you to realize that new opportunities will appear in due course. Your angles ask that you do not stress about present circumstances, as 'better' is on its way into your life. Do not fear lack or loss as the end of a cycle or situation denotes the beginning of another. Th angles ask you to have faith and trust in them, and in yourself Listen to the guidance from the angels as to the next steps to take.
- 19: The Sun: nothing can hide in the bright light of day, and even the most dour individuals come out to celebrate. The ancients called this the 'number of surrender' as your life needs to link up with the universal life. An endurance vibration. It brings everything into focus, winds up old accounts and starts off anew; beginnings and endings. Is a message from Th angels that your goal has almost come to completion, or that a place or situation in your life is coming to an end. Th angels want you to know that the one door is closing as another is opening. Your angels ask that you remain positive throughout these transitions and look forward to wonderful new beginnings and auspicious opportunities. Reminds you that self-help is often the best remedy, and your angels love and support you in your quest to help yourself (and others) lead happier and healthier lives. Your angels ask that you have a positive and optimistic attitude

about your life purpose and soul mission. Know that your destiny is yours to fulfill and the angels give you guidance and support along the way. You are encouraged to shed love and light on humanity. If you have an urge to begin a career that serves humanity this number encourages you to do so. Trust that all you need in your quest will be provided by the angels and universal energies in divine right time, and often in the most miraculous ways.

- 20: Judgment: all is revealed and reminds us to forgive and be forgiven. Symbolizes knowledge of good and evil and the consciousness to make choices that attain balance in all situations; self-awareness. Is a message of love, encouragement and support from the angels and universal energies. Know that you are well-blissed in your life. Th angels give you guidance and energy that enables you to live your life in harmony, compassion and balance in order to serve your life purpose and soul mission with enthusiasm and optimism. Is a message from your angels that things are happening behind the scenes that will be of great benefit to you in the near future. Even though you may not be experiencing these opportunities just yet believe that they are coming to you right now. Have faith and trust in Th Divine. Is a message from Th angels to have faith and trust that due to your positive affirmations and optimistic attitude towards your soul mission and life desires are manifesting in your life.
- 21: The World: completion and success; last stop on fool's journey. Symbolizes duality, communication, and society, versatility, energetic, easy going, charismatic and expressive. Suggests that there may be some new opportunities or directions for you to take that will lead you in a new and exciting direction. Trust that your angels are by your side throughout these transitions and are guiding your every step. They encourage you to remain calm, balanced and happy and you will find that all will work out for your highest good. Is a message from your angels for you to be aware of your thoughts as they are manifesting your ideas and beliefs into reality. Encourages you to be optimistic and maintain a positive attitude regarding current changes and/or circumstances in your life, as this will help to manifest your desired results. Asks that you maintain your faith and positive expectations about all aspects of your new life. Use positive affirmations to bolster your resolve and to keep you connected to Th Angelic realm.

Summaries:

- 0-new beginnings; happy wanderer; leap of faith; adventure
- 1-as above so below; self-mastery
- 2-intuition; keeper of spiritual secrets; the gateway
- 3-mother nature; fertility; creativity; growth
- 4-civilization; order; control
- 5-spiritual teacher; religious/ cultural hierarchy; tradition
- 6-choices; partnerships; duality; balance
- 7-travel; movement; independence; mastery of drives
- 8-courage; self-control; mastery of one's "ID" or primitive nature
- 9-solitude; acquired wisdom; a light for others
- 10-luck; circle of the year; inevitable cycles of life
- 11-fairness; blind justice; the double-edged sword that cuts both ways
- 12-time out; self-sacrifice; new perspectives
- 13-transition; new beginnings; make way for a fresh start
- 14-balance; moderation in all things; steel tempered by fire
- 15-materialism; blind choices; tongue in cheek "evil"; human nature
- 16-a bolt from the blue; sudden change; disaster; chaos; liberation
- 17-make a wish; guiding light; inspiration
- 18-reflection; wax and wane; ebb and flow; monthly cycles; secrets
- 19-bright light of day; full consciousness; ego; annual events
- 20-karma; destiny; responsibility; forgiveness
- 21-conclusions; full circle; completion; a new cycle begins

Th Universe is mathematics, so it always adds up. It is the universal language that transcends all barriers of human error.

II. Spectrums:

- Black: midnight; death; alchemical prime matter; absorption
- Blue: heaven; clarity; thought; spirituality
- Brown: earth; stability; groundedness
- Green: vegetation; growth; fertility; good fortune;
- Gray: depression; neutrality; indifference; refinement
- Orange: fire; nurturing; adventurous
- Pink: sensuality; emotions; love
- Red: blood; wine; passion; will; ambition; anger ("seeing red")
- Silver: the moon; passive lunar energy; intuition
- Violet: spirituality; royalty; power
- White: purity; reflection; healing
- Yellow: the sun; active solar energy; majesty; willpower

III. Nature: Trees

- Almond: early bloomer; sweetness; delicacy
- Apple: the world; totality; earthly desires
- Ash: mystic world
- Aspen: autumnal equinox; old age; shield makers
- Cypress: ceremonies; death and resurrection
- Fig: fertility
- Hazel: water dousing and rainmaking
- Holly: symbolic of mid-December and winter solstice; illusions
- Juniper: protection against evil spirits, witches and thieves
- Oak: strength and long life
- Olive: peace and prosperity
- Palm: fertility, fruitfulness, victory and birth; the nesting place of the phoenix
- Pine: immortality
- Poplar: symbolizes the tree of life; moon and sun; water and fire; positive and negative
- Sandalwood: love; self-defense; divination
- Yew: death

IV. Crystals, Gems, and Stones

- Agate: a stone of strength and protection
- Amber: symbolizes cycles and longevity
- Amethyst: enhances wisdom, tranquility, sobriety
- Aquamarine: offers protection and calm
- Bloodstone: improves circulation
- Blue Lace Agate: improves self-expression
- Citrine: relieves emotional and physical congestion
- Crazy Lace Agate: enhances self esteem and courage
- Diamond: hardest of all elements, symbolizes permanence and incorruptibility
- Emerald: strengthens memory, increases intelligence, preserves relationships
- Garnet: stimulates creativity and love
- Geodes: encourages freedom of spirit and independence
- Green Moss Agate: a gardener's talisman
- Hematite: grounds and connects with the earth; helps vent suppressed anger
- Jade: assures long, healthy life and peaceful death; strengthens relationships
- Jasper: promotes clear thinking, restrains dangerous desires and whims
- Lapis Lazuli: a symbol of wisdom, power, and royalty, as well as the journey into darkness in search of the Higher Self
- Malachite: absorbs energy; focuses inner vision
- Marble: protects the home; attracts money
- Moonstone: symbolizes the lunar cycle and femininity
- Obsidian: useful during grief and growth
- Onyx: transforms negativity; strengthens the will; helps separate from unhealthy relationships
- Opal: contains all the colors of the chakras; aids expression and purifies the spirit
- Pearl: symbolizes the hidden wealth of the soul
- Peridot: can teach self-parenting; stimulates physical healing; calms
- Petrified Wood: represents longevity and evolution; aids past-life recall; helps deflect negativity
- Pyrite: brings money and luck; aids in grounding
- Quartz Crystal: conducts and amplifies energy and thoughts

- Rose Quartz: comforts and heals wounded hearts
- Ruby: symbolizes strength, compassion, and life force; aids immunity; arouses passion
- Sapphire: a stone of prophecy and wisdom
- Shell: represents watery qualities of fluidity, movement, and a change
- Smokey Quartz: grounds and purifies the base chakra
- Tiger's Eye: represents integrity and personal power; promotes confidence, courage, and perception
- Topaz: brings strength and energy to the body
- Turquoise: a guardian of the soul; a connection

V. God Allah Supreme Alphabet

1. A: awareness/know-the-ledge so as not to fall off the edge
2. B: being; birth; self-realization
3. C: clarity; see things clear not as they appear; 1st eye
4. D: Divine DNA; I.S.L.A.M. our culture (way of life) freedom (free=release/transformation + Dom[e]= Th Mind)
5. E: Empirical; power refinement
6. F: fairness (to deal with your people equally)
7. G: G.O.D (Gem of divinity [Female/Mother]; Guardian of Divinity [Male/Son]); a vehicle that transports information from one place to another
8. H; heaven or hell; him or her; build or destroy; heal or hurt; holy or horrendous
9. I: Infinity; continuance; rebirth
10. J: Justice (penalty or reward depending on man's thoughts, words, actions, and deeds)
11. K: King (Sovereign; one who rules) + Dom (your consciousness [lost estate])
12. L: Love (highest form of evolution); perfection, completion
13. M: Mastery; manifestation; Matriarch
14. N: Now is the time; resurrection
15. O: cipher; intangible; spiritual knowledge
16. P: power (truth) which shall set you free
17. Q: queen; the foundation of all civilization; quintessential
18. R: Ra; fire; ether; serpent risen; ruler
19. S: self-saving
20. T: Truth is in the square
21. Universe (U & I versus Evil); all for/from one and one for/from all
22. V: Victory (the inheritance/destiny of Th faithful and active)

23. W: wisdom (the flow of knowledge that leads to an endless sea of inner/overstanding)
24. X: marks the spot; galactic cross; center of energy and incubation; combination of opposites; the teacher
25. Y: the key to salvation (You)
26. Z: Zenith; holy triune and hierarchy of humanity (Mother, Father and Sun/Child)

B. Sign Language: Masonic emblems, grips, postures and secret words

**Disclaimer: I am not now, nor have I ever been affiliated with any so- called Masonic order of any kind nor do I profess to be a scholar on so-called freemasonry and its rituals and grips. However, as a free Son of Ma I am obligated to share the knowledge , wisdom and understanding that has made itself available to me through the grace, benevolence and mercy of The Most High Creator and the ancestors who act as emissaries of such pristine force.*

I. Postures and conduct

- Always work with the right when speaking; when they speak with their left you respond and make them talk with their right.
- Open the door for a female for the door symbolizes a vagina thus the act is a spiritual representation of who came first in terms of physical manifestation. It also is us to symbolize the weaker species in terms of who goes through first which gives physical representation to the saying "the first shall be last and the last shall be first.
- Keep feet squared (at 900 angle); symbolizes master's degree and masculinity; uprightness. A male standing with feet at 450 or widespread is a sign of a servant and one who is drawing off feminine energy.
- Always keep back straight and head up. A slumped head is a sign of shame; slouched frame is sign of a peasant/wayward man.
- When walking on street the male should always be on the outside of the female so as to shield their consort/mother/seastar etc., from any and all danger.
- Whenever in a public place always sit with back facing the door and/or any other entries and exits so as to be alert to potential threats and escape routes.
- Always have thumbs out; symbolizes master; protection; symbolizes pineal gland (1st/3rd eye)

- Right hand is the giving hand (positive), the left is that of concealment (negative); so whenever you see someone with their left over their right it signifies something concealed; the right is that of revelation and giving; negative side is innerstanding, strength/miraculous power, judgment, order, and glory, also represents feminine energy; positive side is wisdom, grace, victory/conquering, and mercy; they come together in knowledge, beauty/ justice, foundation/stability and sovereignty which stems from Th All Seeing Eye.
- Winking and grinning symbolizes evil thought and intent; some trickery afoot; both hands behind back means their hiding something; one hand behind back is to symbolize cloak and dagger i.e. "I have sword"
- A lot of hand gestures when someone is talking is a universal sign of truth telling.
- Raised eyebrows is a sign of respect as is a tipped cap
- Traditionally, the right-handed glove is removed before a superior
- Whenever someone is directing negative energy in whatever manner and form your way cross your arms; this is the "X" a symbol as to block that unwanted currency.
- Biting lip symbolizes frustration of ignorance and is also a sign of protection; also, a symbol of passion as well
- Rubbing hands together symbolizes heat; friction; something's getting good; build-up
- If mature male's handshake is weak it is a sign of domesticity and submission; one who is feminine; a male's handshake that is too hard symbolizes a show-off and arrogant person; an aggressor. Should be firm yet subtle.
- Sitting on edge of seat symbolizes the interest in the conversation and/or the wanting to tall a story or that the story being told is truth.
- Whoever enters a place first is considered the weaker species; the wisest go last.
- Points of fellowship: (1) mouth to ear, (2) hand to back, (3) knee to knee, (4) breast to breast, (5) foot to foot
- To genuflect (kneel) is to submit to the will of another
- 3 steps (degrees): 1st step is right foot at 450 (apprentice; believer [neophyte], 2nd step is left foot at 450 (fellow craft; faith [scholar]), and 3rd step is both feet at 900 (master mason; fruition)

- The Sun stands on the right (light is knowledge; truth revealed); position of the scholar, and the warrior stands on the left as this is where the heart (courage; conviction) is.
- Never run from policy enforcers and always stand your ground and hold your square; running is a sign of wrongdoing and cowardice.
- Hitching up pants is a sign that says that the person spiritually wants you dead
- Pulling at collar is to say, "I want your head"
- Standing with left foot out is to stomp out evil; right foot is to symbolize searching for justice; traveler
- Standing on tip toes is to say that you are higher and superior
- Right hand gripping left forearm forming a 7 symbolizes that "I am the Sun of G-d; I am a godly man"; backwards/opposite is to say that I draw off negative energy
- To turn one's back is to cut off aid and assistance; to disassociate oneself from another.
- Legs crossed is a symbol of passiveness; leg straight on top of other forming a 7 is to say I am ready for battle; cross is X which is feminine, and 7 is a Y which is masculine.

II. Secret words

- "School" is a password for social engineering i.e. programming for mind control/unconscious voluntary servitude. < The ibri word shul which means both hell and synagogues. The current "school" system was set up in 1902 by John D. Rockefeller and Frederick T. Gates after during the period of reconstruction. *The Country School of Tomorrow: Occasional Papers No. 1* (General Education Board: New York, 1913) written by Frederick T. Gates contained a section entitled "A Vision of the Remedy" in which he wrote the following: "Is there aught of remedy for this neglect of rural life? Let us, at least, yield ourselves to the gratifications of a beautiful dream that there is. In our dream, we have limitless resources, and the people yield themselves with perfect docility to our molding hand. The present educational conventions fade from our minds; and, unhampered by tradition, we work our own good will upon a grateful and responsive rural folk. We shall not try to make these people or any of their children into philosophers or men of learning or of science. We are not to raise up from among them authors, orators, poets, or men of letters. We shall not search for embryo great artists, painters, musicians. Nor will we cherish even the humbler ambition to raise up from among them lawyers, doctors, preachers, politicians, statesmen, of whom we now have ample supply."

- To be called a gentleman is not a compliment; it refers to the gentiles; the proper term is nobleman; a gentile is one of no royal bloodlines.
- A lady is a female of low rank and is not a compliment.
- "Politicians" is password for thugs/freemasonic servants;
- "Pastors/Reverends/Imams/PhDs etc." are passwords for agents of Rome; lackeys for the popes of Rome and the beasts of England
- "John" is the password for Yochanan;
- "Jesus" is the password for Yahoshuah; also, a code word for justice and symbolizes the sun in the sky as none can hide from its light so it is that none can hide from the light of justice.
- "Moses" is the password for Musa;
- "Abraham" is the password for Th Holy Triune (Ab=Mother + Ra=Sun + Ham=Father);
- "12 Tribes" is the password for the Zodiacal Wheel; also refers to the 12 cranial nerves who are the "disciples" of Yahoshua ("Jesus")
- "Owl" is the password for the illumined (fruition), "Creeping thing" is the password for those who know some of the truth (faith), and "Fish" is the password for those who are ignorant (believer) i.e. initiates.
- "Hermes" is the password for Tehuti/Thoth/Dwty, "Isis is the password for Auset, "Osiris" is the password for Ausar, "Horace" is the password for Heru, "Seth" is the password for Set, "Egypt" is the password for Kemet/Kamat, "Jew" is a corruption of Yahudi from Dwty the Kamatan principle of intellect and Wisdom;
- "Christian" is the password for Krishna which is symbolic to the lighting of the pineal gland and the activation of the higher consciousness which is the merging of the five external senses thus enhancing the 2 internal senses of intuition and clairvoyance, creating the circle 7 which is the depiction of all saints whereas they have a halo or nimbus of light as their crowns marking them as ascended masters and transcendent beings;
- "Black, colored, negroes, niggers, African-Americans, et." are passwords denoting Roman Christian Property.

- "White" password for sovereign of the land and does not mean complexion but is a legal status denoting nationals though it has been usurped.
- "American" is a password for the primitive peoples of the land and is the copper-colored natives of the land, who were here thousands of years before Albion even existed let alone came over seeking safe haven and riches.
- "Race" is a password for the human family but is used as a social engineering tool to keep people divided particularly in this continent.
- "Indian" is a password for "GIs" (government issues) i.e. those amalgamated Moors who have been corralled into reservations, who are results of the raping of Moorish Moabite Women and who are also property of Romans. Indian people are from India and this is obviously not India so therefore anybody that accepts that brand name is agreeing to be a servant to Rome.
- "Light" is the password for knowledge of truth.
- "Estate" is the password for primordial consciousness which connects man to Th Land i.e. their inheritance hence the "lost estate" is man's disconnect from the planet from which he was formed and to which he must and will return either in harmony or destruction.
- "Tree of life or Garden of Eden" are passwords for Th mind of man. Falling from the garden/grace means we fell from divine consciousness into carnal/ lower nature and savagery thus we were cut off from the supernatural abilities we once used effortlessly.
- "Cross" is a password for man's body so to pick up thy cross is to elevate the vibration and frequency of self resulting in higher receptabiltiy to the higher cosmological forces of Th universe. So when they say Yashuah (Jesus) died on the cross it is code for man's Christ consciousness being stunted and halted thus we were thrown into the dark ages of ignorance and the persecuting or hanging of Christ on the cross is symbolic to the dark priesthood a.k.a. the M.I.B (men in black) who went to and fro suppressing the knowledge of higher science and hiding it amongst themselves via clubs and clandestine order while at the same time dealing with other entities from other worlds/ dimensions and opening up portals for demonic forces to come upon the planet which was the deal they made with the demi-gods in return for other worldly technology and ruler ship.
- "Church, temple, mosque, synagogue, et." are passwords for spy centers and mediums of social engineering and mind control in modern times. In the not so distant past they were universities where all manner of life's sciences were

taught; even more ancient is the fact that all these titles actually represent the human body itself where the deepest wisdom and intelligence lies.

- “Pharaoh” is the password for N’Gu which is what Th Ancestors called chiefs and royal heads pre-the dynastic invasion and amalgamation by and of the Hicksaw;
- “Peter is the password for Ptah which is Th “opener” and symbolizes the beginning of transformation and the forward progress of evolution; “Adam” is the code word for atom which are the building blocks of life, and “Eve” is the password for evolution hence why women are regarded as the problem in dogma because in actuality she is which in turn makes her Th Solution, she is what advances all life in all galaxies, that divine feminine energy of incubation and Creation.
- “Moor” is a password for Th mound builders (ants), Yisrolites, Moslems, Phoenicians, Kushites, Tamerians, Americans, Kemau, Guardians of Th Galaxy, mothers and fathers of civilization, Th White Man, Illuminated and enlightened ones (Illuminati), The Serpent People, Yahudi, Ibri, Asiatic, etc.” All of these and then some are under the umbrella of The Moorish Divine and National Movement as we the heirs of the world’s largest estate, also called Muurs/Moors, are the children of those who crafted and created and were gifted with the high science of mathematics which they used to build, establish and sustain the world. To be a Moor is to draw from and be a student of all manner of right spiritual expressions which govern the breath of man. Builders of the pyramids, masters of life force and conquerors of Th gates of immortality; Th Most High’s best and brightest. Moor spelled backward is “room” which symbolically represents the fact that acknowledging your bloodline as an Asiatic Original Man gives you space to grow and expand yourself. Also, a room must be filled, and knowledge of self opens gateways/portals that allow you to access the greater essence of yourself. It is a “way out” of the wicked indoctrination of this false paradigm but only for the pure of heart. Beware and be wise.
- “God” is the password for will and intent, the invocation of certain cosmological forces of nature via man’s thoughts, words, actions and intent; one of the triunes of existence; it is a verb transitive and is the judge of man i.e. man is judged by his actions; court is not just confined to a building as law is nature therefore the whole world is a courtroom, therefore God (action) is the judge, nature (sentient beings and their essence) is the jury and Th Creator (Ultimate Reality and Supreme Force) is the executioner, rewarding man for what he has

rewarded others and to himself; the parable of Daniel in the bible speaks to the triune of divine Law; Dan in Ibri (Hebrew) means judge, I in Ibri means my and El means G-d and the ancient way of reading was from right to left as opposed to today's modern way of left to right. So, it would be read as, "G-d (is) my judge", which is where that saying, "Only god can judge me", came from. In the parable of the lion's den Daniel goes through the 5 doors of refinement and advances to the 3rd degree. First, he is afraid of the lions, then he has a moment of grief, then he accepts his fate and shows his trust in Th Creator, then he is shown compassion by the lions because he transformed their hearts by the will of divine love within his own. First, he believed that he would be saved, then he knew, and then he was unafraid thus he was risen out of the lion's den for he defeated man's only real enemy, fear. Also, God stands as an acronym, Gomar, Oz, and Dubar which stands for the three grand pillars which are wisdom, strength and beauty.

- "Devil" is the password for "scapegoat" hence why it is always depicted with horns for it is the excuse by which man can place blame on something outside of himself.
- "Hello" is a code word for devil and is synonymous with hollo. It was conditioned into our lexicon and psychology due to the fact that it is a chant that opens a portal for demons to possess our aura. Also means hallow as in one who's aura is clearly seen.
- "Angel" is password for angle as in angles of light which are the universal cosmological forces of nature governed by Th Supreme Reality and utilized by man's aspirations and empirical nature to either create good or spread evil; there are many different angles of light, some of a lower vibration and others of a higher vibration.
- "Heaven" is the password for the perfect man when they have come to full fruition of divine consciousness which can only be achieved once they go through the 5 doors of refinement and transformation: true fear, true grief, true courage, true compassion and true love.
- "Hell" is the password for mental and spiritual stagnation, confinement and lack of imagination as well as physical restraints as well.
- "Law" is the password for nature and all it encompasses and reflects.
- "Wisdom" is the password for common sense; the highest science known and possessed by man.

III. Grips

- Thumb on top knuckle symbolizes the 3rd degree (master mason); middle knuckle is 2nd degree (fellow craft); lowest knuckle is 1st degree (apprentice); always shake in 3rd degree
- When those who shake hands put their hands-on top of each other it symbolizes the hiding of truths; collusion and subterfuge
- Hand to forearm middle finger rested straightly on arm is the lion's paw; symbolizes the lifting up of your brother out of darkness (ignorance)
- A proper shake for Asiatics is to press between the thumb and point finger without shaking. This divine symbol is representing the uniting of Asia and is also a form of initiation speaking to the fact of the continual process of renewal and aid.

IV. Emblems (signs)

- Brushing hair with hand: "I'm aware and conscious; I have knowledge."
- Pull right point finger across your nose, then mouth, then back across chin: to close someone's mouth with sword
- Thumb and all fingers on temple and head: "I have a problem."
- Hand on neck: "I acknowledge"
- Right hand touching ear: "I hear"
- Left hand touching ear: "I don't hear"
- Right finger touching nose: "I know"
- Left hand touching nose: "I don't know"
- Right finger touching eye: "I see; I know you"
- Left finger touching eye: "I don't see"
- Thumb on chin: "I Self Law Am Master"; always shoot especially when in the presence of aliens/Romans; the thinker
- Point finger on temple: "I have a sword of truth to behead; I am knowledgeable
- Leaning with right hand open on a wall: "I lean on the temple of Allah"
- Hand rested on top of eyebrows as if shading from the sun: "Looking for light"
- Rubbing hands over face: "He's lying"
- Hand stroking beard from right to left 3x: "I have wisdom and knowledge"

- All fingers rested together: "All around master"
- Hand rested on heart: sign of fidelity; "I have a good heart"
- Point finger and thumb acting both eyebrows together: "We are friends"
- Right thumb under chin, using first two fingers, tracing clockwise of your beard: "I am the father of civilization"
- Right hand rested on breast, point finger and thumb forming 900 angle, drawn vertically: "Mother of civilization"
- Brushing hair backwards: "I'm over your head"
- Thumb, point and second finger pulling face gently: "I have compassion"
- Point finger and pinky extended: symbol of bathphomet(Saturn/Satan) (fertility); also denotes those who took an oath to a lodge, "I rode the goat"
- Flipping pen: flipping man illustration; used to symbolize a trickster is in the midst; fuckery is afoot
- Washing hands: "It's no longer in my hands"
- Shaking hand as if shaking something: "my hands are free of crime; shaking off the past"
- Arms folded, 4 fingers showing on right, 3 fingers on the left: "Perfect man"
- Arms folded, thumb showing: "Conscious man"
- Arms folded, no hands showing: "house is closed"; not shooting signs
- Point finger and thumb scratching solar plexus: "I love all my brothers"
- Point and thumb rested together with last 3 fingers showing: "3 grand pillars (wisdom, strength and beauty)"
- Hand in pocket with last 3 fingers showing: "I'm in control"
- Both hands in pocket with last 3 fingers showing on each hand: "I'm in control of my flock"; (counter) hands on waist, 4 fingers showing on right, 3 on left and flap your wings forward and down comes the eagle.
- Arms folded, hand cupping elbow: "I extend aid and I ask"
- Patting someone on the back 3x: "I am the master"
- Hand resting behind ear: "I ask for justice"
- Right hand raised all fingers showing, point and second finger showing on left, with right thumb pointed upward toward sky: "I can make the sun stand still"; sign of high degree
- Arms folded, both thumbs showing: excellent supreme master; "I innestand both worlds"

- Forming steeple with both point fingers facing upward: "spiritual man"; drawing off the spiritual
- Points and thumbs rested together, rested on chest: physical master; "I am physically the master of this earth"
- Both point fingers rested together forming steeple facing down: physical; "drawing off the physical"
- Point fingers and thumbs rested together with thumbs rested on chin: spiritual master
- Point fingers and thumbs forming L's: "I am the aboriginal man"
- Thumb turned sideways and drawn up and down face: to make submit
- Hands interlocked on top of head, thumbs facing the ceiling: "I am the master"; for when there is a raid
- Right hand and elbow height of eyes, two first fingers extended like a fork, thumb and other fingers clinched then draw and dart hand back horizontally: penalty of S.E. master's sign; eyes gouged out
- When in the presence of a group of people shooting negativity (lefts over rights): clap once, stomp twice (right foot then left), and brush off your right leg with right hand
- When touched by a Christian vandal: brush yourself off
- Both hands rested on waist: "oh no you don't bitch"; blockade
- Single cough: cave person
- Hand drawn across throat: "shut the fuck up"
- Place hands over eyes, and quickly jerk arms downwards, as though tearing out your eyes and throwing them down on the ground: third select master sign; refers to penalty of obligation
- Sniffing: in the presence of or speaking of the unclean
- Hand touching tie: "I have a little light"
- 4 monkeys: hands over eyes ("see no evil"), hands covering ears ("hear no evil), hands covering mouth ("speak no evil), and hands covering groin ("do no evil")
- Point finger rested on chin: "I wonder when these people will wake up"
- Hand rested on top of head: "king in the building"
- Point finger and second finger rested together: kemetic sign of peace and oneness; "I speak in one tongue"

- Point finger and second finger showing apart: deuces; "I speak in two tongues"; forked tongue; also represents the Roman numeral 5 which stands for power
- Point finger rested between eyebrows: "I can't get that song out of my head"; symbol of déjà vu
- Right hand stacked on top of left gripping left thumb: "I have innerstanding and overstanding"
- Thumb and pinky extended: "stranger in the land"
- Flexing both arms: "man of bronze"; symbolizes strength and endurance
- Beating chest with fist: "I'm solid"
- Hand cupping other hand: "I'm bringing truth"; master, hand over fist
- Point finger touching under nose: "to blow one away"
- Point finger to lips: "I have a secret"
- Point finger rested on lips: "I stand mute"; to control one's tongue when someone is speaking
- Hand to back of thigh: "I'm breaking my oath"
- Pinky and four finger extended forming a K: Klu Klux Klan; symbolizes a deputy knight of Columbus
- Feet together with heel in arch: "I'm sharp and on point"
- Right hand rested on chest with left hand rested on top of eyebrows as if shading from the sun: hailing sign
- Raising left hand to right shoulder, hand open and draw diagonally down across body to hip: the hammer; "I am going to war with you"
- Palm to forehead: sympathy sign
- Hands locked together with thumbs rolling forward: "future"
- Hands locked together with thumbs rolling backwards: "past"
- Hands rested together forming pyramid: infinity; symbol of civilization: facing down is yin (feminine/negative energy) and facing down is yang (masculine/positive energy)
- Right hand held to edge against forehead then draw across to the right: rotal arch sign; penal sign of the 1st degree; skull smote off
- Right thumb under chin, fingers closed: eminent commander
- Pointing pinky finger at someone: "I am superior; you are a little man compared to me"

- Left pant leg rolled up: apprentice; first degree; due guard of an apprentice: right palm over left palm, positioned at navel; Penal sign of apprentice: draw right hand across throat; the grip of the apprentice: (Boaz) right thumb rested between 1st knuckle
- Right sleeve rolled up: fellow craft; second degree; due guard: right palm facing down and level with navel, with left hand raised palm flat and level with shoulder; penal sign: right hand drawn across chest; grip of fellow craftsmen: (jachin) right thumb rested on second knuckle
- Shirt off with left pant leg rolled up: master mason; 3rd degree; due guard of master mason: both hands inserted in pants at the front with both thumbs rested together; penal sign of master mason: right hand drawn across navel; the grip of the master mason: (machaben) thumb rested on third knuckle
- Left arm bent at elbow facing up: perseverance
- Kneeling on one knee with all fingers rested together: penitential sign
- Hood on head "hiding light"; taken off "revealing light"
- Hand on abdomen "man of wisdom"
- Tongue out 'ancient sign of protection"; sign of salivation "hungry beast"
- Hand over one eye "cyclops" i.e. half blind
- Point finger touching both temples "open observatory" "high mathematics flowing" "full storehouse"
- Both hands at side of head "divine mind"

Outro:

"*When someone shows you who they are, believe them the first time.*"-Maya Angelou

"*If you have no confidence in self, you are twice defeated in the race of life.*"-Marcus Garvey

Part 5: Will Thyself

"Watch your thoughts; they become words. Watch your words; they become actions. Watch your actions; they become habits. Watch your habits; they become character. Watch your character; it becomes your destiny."

-Lao Tzu

Intro: It is not the skill of a man but the will of a man that determines their destiny. The future is 50/50. One half is fixed what we would call destiny. The other half is fluid based upon the decisions we make and the lessons we've learned. Prophecy like all of the universe is predicated on the science of mathematics which in its purest form is repetition and ,we being creatures of habit, whatever we do regularly we eventually become and embody these daily practices of thought, words and actions. No great being became so without work, even those who were unique from the start still had to refine their glow so as not blind those they sought to share it with. One must deserve what they desire and as the saying goes Th Most High helps those who help themselves, and the lowest feeds on those who neglect themselves and their duty to existence.

Chapter 1: The Battlefield In The Garden

A. Conscious Perspective

I. The Battle within

"We battle not against flesh and blood, but against principalities, against powers, against the rulers of the blackness of this world, against spiritual wickedness in high places".-Ephesians 6:12.

The battle of Heru (higher self) and Set (lower self) is within you. One must become Heru-Ur (all seeing) to conquer the lower demons of self. One then becomes Heru-Set and using our lower nature to support our higher self, our divine self. Many are unaware of the forces of nature that dwell within which serves as reflections of the forces without.

"If man would find his savior he must look within; and when the demon itself has been dethroned the savior, love, will be exalted to the throne of power...But man will regain his lost estate, his heritage; but he must do it in a conflict that cannot be told in words...Without a foe a soldier never knows his strength, and thought must be developed by the exercise of strength...When man has conquered every foe upon the plane of soul the seed will have opened full out, will have unfolded in the holy breath. The garb of soul then have served its purpose well, and it will pass and be no more and man will then attain unto the blissedness of perfectness and be one with Allah."-El Sharif Abdul Ali Holy Circle 7 Koran Chapter 1: The Creation and Fall of Man

II. Hypnosis:

The induction of a state of consciousness in which a person apparently loses the power of voluntary action and is highly responsive to suggestion or direction. Late 19th century: from Greek hupnos 'sleep' + -osis 'process or condition'.

Its been said that we modern remnants of old use only about 5-10% of our brain power, consciously. The other 90-95% is unused or rather unconscious, the aspect that acts as our auto-pilot and is the hidden underline theme that motivates and dictates our perceptions and the way we interface with this so-called reality. We go in and out of hypnosis hundreds of times a day as we are bombarded with outside suggestions, whether it be from advertisements, radio, internet, television, personal associations, etc. These suggestions are implanted in us daily that have both adverse and beneficial.

Your personality determines the level of hypnosis you are susceptible to. People who ed with their hearts or are 'feelers', people who flow through life on their intuition and instincts are more susceptible to outside influence i.e. third-party interference, however, they usually have the most fun and are more at ease with life. Thinkers are harder to be influenced by others, but they function under a state of self- hypnosis. This in turn leads to a greater originality or freedom but also leads to rigidity and stagnation. It is my opinion that auto-suggestion is a major key in having a fulfilled life and is the hallmark of a mature being, one who can isolate their shortcomings and self-correct themselves.

Though we all may lean toward either of these classifications we are all essentially the sum of all parts meaning we function through both channels s we navigate this third density.

There are five hypnotic points on the body that if unconscious can be used to enhance the affect of suggestions and they are:

- Wrist
- Forearm
- Forehead
- Shoulder
- Back of the head

These are markers to look for when interacting with people. Also, be mindful that the left side is receptive being that it is controlled by the right hemisphere which is the feminine or intuitive aspect of the self. So, when interfacing with people and they are touching or attempting to touch any of these points, especially on the left side know that they are trying to influence you. Women being especially sensitive are more susceptible to this type of hypnosis in terms of touch. Men are more visual and thus can be enticed by an image i.e. beautiful women, clothes, etc.

Always remember the rule of five. If you can get someone to do or agree to 5 things then they are prime for whatever suggestion you may have for them and vice versa. It goes without saying, but I advise you to use your knowledge wisely and not be lead astray by carnal thoughts.

*7 Precepts for a Moorish Scientist: Wisdom of a Moorish Sage

Never accept the opinions of someone until you have verified them and are satisfied with their accuracy.

Remember that free advice no matter when received will bear the closest of examination until it is acted upon as safe and generally speaking this sort of advice is worth exactly what it cost.

Alert yourself immediately when you hear anyone speaking of others in discourteous or slanderous spirit because this very fact should put you on notice that what you are hearing is biased, to say the very least and may be an out-and-out misstatement.

In asking others for information do not disclose to them what you want the information to be, because most people have the bad habit of wanting to please under such circumstances. Well measured tactical questions can be of great benefit to you in thinking accurately.

Remember that anything which exist anywhere throughout the universe is capable of proof and where no such proof is available it is safe to assume that no such proof exist.

One of the greatest unexplainable miracles consist in the fact that truth and falsehood, no matter by what means they may be expressed, carry with them a silent invisible means that identify themselves as such. Therefore, remember this truth and begin cultivating the necessary initiative faculty to enable you to sense what is false and what is true.

Follow the habit of asking "how do you know", when anyone makes a statement that identify as true. Follow this habit faithfully and you will begin to see the person squirm and turn red in the face when you insist on a direct reply. The most accurate thinkers are The Moorish Scientists, because they investigate with open minds and never or should never allow their wishes (emotions) to become the fathers of facts but deal with such fact , not as they would like it to be, but what it is. Listen carefully and you may discover that your own emotions are your greatest handicap in the business of accurate thinking. It is easy to believe what you wish and unfortunately that is precisely what most people do, and it is a method that opens wide a sealed envelope which contains the list of penalties that most pay for, neglecting to take possession of their minds and the use of them for a constructive end to be beneficial toward themselves.

B. R.I.C.H (realizing I create happiness)

I. 30 habits of happiness

- be kind
- eat well
- exercise
- meditate
- be honest
- dream big
- be patient
- judge less
- smile often
- love yourself
- forgive easily
- show gratitude
- think positively
- drink lots of water
- believe in yourself
- keep an open mind
- put your needs first
- don't make excuses
- speak well of others
- listen to gain inner/ overstanding
- choose faith over fear
- make the most of now
- exercise self discipline
- look on the bright side
- avoid social comparison
- see failure as opportunity
- don't take opinions to heart
- pick associates that lift you up
- let go of what can't be changed
- have a healthy rest schedule

II. Zen things

1. do one thing at a time
2. do it slowly and deliberately
3. do it completely
4. do less
5. put space in between things
6. develop rituals
7. designate time for certain things
8. devote time to sitting
9. smile and serve others
10. make cleaning and cooking meditation
11. think about what is necessary
12. live simply

III. Karma Cleanse

1. be grateful
2. act with love
3. check your motives
4. watch your attitude
5. forgive

IV. Daily supplements of thought

- take time to heal; don't rush and hurt yourself even more in the process
- there are billions of people on this planet thus there are a billion different expressions of the same truth; we are all uniquely the same
- embrace quiet; listen and hear self
- embrace your individuality; the only true perfection is imperfection; everything you are not is what makes you everything you are; appreciate your uniqueness
- drop multiple and unreasonable expectations; focus on your truest heart's desire, that which is most essential to you
- we are our own best teachers; truth resonates because it is a reflection of you as we are the truth, so to know the intentions of another is know the intentions of self; the foundation of falsehood is truth, but it will eventually fall leaving only from which it came

V. 12 things to remember:

1. the past cannot be changed
2. opinions don't define your reality
3. everyone's journey is different
4. things get better with time
5. positive thoughts create positive things
6. you fail only when you quit
7. over thinking leads to depression and anxiety
8. kindness is free
9. smiles are contagious
10. what goes around comes around
11. judgments are a confession of character
12. happiness is found within

VI. Weightlifting: Realization

- You are not obligated to be there for someone 24/7.
- You are not obligated to deal with anyone who emotionally drains you.
- You are not obligated to maintain negative relationships because you've been close or known someone for so long.
- You are not obligated to be someone's counselor or help them with their problems if it's bad for your mental health.
- You are not obligated to do anything that makes you unhappy or puts your health at risk!

VII. Stop taking things so personally

- Realize that other people's rudeness is not about you; when someone is rude it's likely to be a reflection of their own inner turmoil.
- Ask yourself what else the comment or behavior might mean. For example, if someone doesn't smile or say hi, they might be shy.
- Take comments or criticism in a constructive way. Ask yourself if there's any truth to it, and what can you learn.
- Take a different perspective. Ask yourself how an unbiased outsider would see the situation.
- Realize that you can't please everyone.
- Know that you are not defined by your mistakes or criticism.
- Realize that your self-worth depends on you. It does not depend on what others say about or even think about you.

Chapter 2: Victory

A. Master

I. 4 precepts of self-actualization: Perfection

2. Discipline (practice of right habits)
3. Intuition (trusting instincts)
4. Courage (boldness and conviction)
5. Compassion (empathy)

II. 13 things mentally tough people don't do

- They don't give up after the first failure
- They don't wade in self pity
- They don't worry about pleasing everyone
- They don't resent other people's success
- They don't feel the world owes them something
- They don't expect immediate results
- They don't make the same mistakes twice
- They don't give away their power
- They don't fear taking calculated risks
- They don't waste their energy on things they can't control
- They don't shy away from change
- They don't dwell on the past
- They don't fear alone time

III. Keys to right innerstanding and clarity

- Faith: in the teachings, that it is something worth pursuing.
- Knowledge: of the teachings and their compatibility to logic and science.
- Experience: of the teaching through meditation techniques.
- Wisdom: through enlightenment experiences.

YOUR VOICE COMMANDS YOUR MIND, BODY & SPIRIT

Learn the true meaning of each word, the root and the original intention. Find the cousins to each word, say it, feel it, which one will move you forward in your own life?

ENERGY + VIBRATION = MATTER

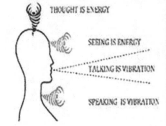

THOUGHT IS ENERGY

SEEING IS ENERGY

TALKING IS VIBRATION

SPEAKING IS VIBRATION

THOUGHTS + VOICE = REALITY

Help the self by Walking the Absolute Truth of your own life, Meditate & Pray...Keep thoughts, actions & words positive...Be self empowered and use the tools presented in a good way

WWW.INFINITEWATERS.NET

I can't I won't It's hard I Don't Believe I'm a skeptic I don't like it	=	• Will literally stop growth • Will literally put a block in your way • Can not is a command to self • Will literally stop you from achieving anything in your life • Is a taught behavior that is a conditional to hold a person back • Stops a person from learning • Stops a person from gaining intellect (IQ)
Try Trying I can try I'm trying I will try I will attempt	=	• Try and you will do it over and over and over never get to the end • Puts a block in your way • Try is a command to self • Try and trying is a taught behavior that is a condition to hold a person back • It has very little or no results • It is like running a race with no end • It is never ending • It is repetitious
I can I am I believe It is done I can do it I can do anything	=	• Literally promotes growth • Can is a command to self • Allows your wants, needs and desire to come true • Is a behavior of using good words • It is unconditional and moves a person forward in life • When you know inside you can do it your body needs to hear it • Your body reacts to key words

---

OUTRO:

"*I hated every minute of training, but I said, 'don't quit. Suffer now and live the rest of your life as a champion.*" -Muhammad Ali

"*It is better to conquer yourself than to win a thousand battles. Then the victory is yours. It cannot be taken from you, not by the angels or by the demons, heaven or hell.*" -Buddha

"*If you want to awaken all of humanity then awaken all of yourself. If you want to eliminate all the suffering in the world, then eliminate all that is dark and negative in yourself. Truly, the greatest gift you have to give is that of your own transformation.*" -Lao Tzu

KNOW THY SELF
Ma'at: I have never fouled the water.
A person who knows not
And knows not that they know not
Is foolish-disregard them
A person who knows not
And knows that they know not
Is simple-teach them
A person who knows not
And believes that they know
Is dangerous-avoid them
A person who knows
And knows not that they know
Is asleep-awake them
A person who knows
And knows that they know
Is wise-follow them
All of these persons reside in you
Know Thy Self
And Ma'at be true
FB:/THEANKHLIFE
THE ANKH LIFE
Seeking To Preserve and Restore Our Ancestral Legacy
IG-THEANKHLIFE

Afterword:

Salaam to all those who have read these pages. It is my sincere hope to not only educate but to elevate your consciousness to that which will help you to battle and defeat the demons within. We all struggle with the lower forces of creation, but we exist not singular but plural so as to assist each other to bring about healing and restoration for all which will set the foundation for those who shall come after. We build not for ourselves but for our babies so that they will not have to suffer as we have suffered and so that they will be able to live up to their highest ideals and principles. They walk in the footprints we leave behind as we have walked in our ancestor's light, guiding us to truth unequivocal. A lot of these things I did not personally author but rather I just put them together so as to show that there is but one truth and that it is our honorable duty to shine the light of truth on all the expressions of divine love as we are one and the same with truth, good, bad and ugly. I end this book with an ancient homily:

> *"Love is always stronger than death, and unto that love you have now returned. I order you, o sleeper, to awake! I did not create you to be held prisoner in hell. Rise from the dead, for I am the life of the dead. Rise up, work of my hands; you were created in my image. Rise: let us leave this place, for you are in me and I am in you. Together we form only one person and we cannot be separated."*

As Salaamu Alaikum

Once again, I appreciate you indulging this literature and I ask that you use this energy wisely and to the best of your ability for your education and edification. It is my opinion that the value of a book depends on what it instills in the reader. If you learned nothing new then I simply and sincerely apologize for any waste of energy caused and I ask that you pass it along to one which you feel might benefit from this combination of knowledge. Shalom, hotep, and shanti to you, yours and ours; one. Also, here is a list of honorable and respectable businesses that provide quality services:

1. CalifaMedia.com (literature and publishing)
2. RVBeyPublications.com (literature)
3. Dr.AlimElBey.com (herbs, crystals, literature and More)
4. MoorsandMasonry.org (etymology, history, jurisprudence and more)
5. MoreignaHeir.com (Moorish American Apparel)
6. WillofAllah.com (music)
7. Rise of the moors.com
8. 13krystalign.com (detoxes and cleanses)
9. UprisingTea.com
10. MoorishGold.com
11. Kemajikgems.com
12. KnovaArts.com
13. MoorsinFullLife.com
14. Matrix-five.com

SUPPORT YOUR OWN!!!

Suggested Reading:

- *Othello's Children In the New World* – Jose Pimenta Bey
- *Moors and Masonry* – Abdullah Talib El Mosi Bey
- *Illuminati and The Illumination of The Mind* – Abdullah El Talib Mosi Bey
- *How Her Moon and Venus Rule* – Abdullah El Talib Mosi Bey
- *The Masonic Compass & Square and Their Connection to Measurement and Timekeeping* – Abdullah El Talib Mosi Bey
- *Journal Of The Moorish Paradigm* – Hakim Bey
- *Darkskull 418* – Aseer The Duke Of Tiers
- *Exhuming Of A Nation* – Elihu Pleasant Bey
- *The First World Order* – Dr. Alim El Bey
- *Mer To Moor: Kemet Until Now* – Cozmo El
- *Black A Moor: Bridging The historical Gap between Black and Moor* – Cozmo El

- *Black A Moor Edition Ii: With Article Collection and Commentary by Aljimere Bey* – Cozmo El
- *Ancient Kemetic Islam and the Preservation of Ma'at: The Missing Link Between Kemetic and Moorish Civilization* – Cozmo El
- *Nationality The Order Of the Day* – G.S. Kudjo Adwo El
- *Who Stole The Fez, Moors or Shriners?* – G.S. Kudjo Adwo El
- *Noble Drew Ali Plenipotentiaries and the Negro, Black, Colored Addiction* – G.S. Kudjo Adwo El
- *You Are Not Negro, Black, Coloured, Morisco Nor An African Slave!* – G.S. Kudjo Adwo El
- *77 Amazing facts about the Moors with Complete Proof* – G.S. Kudjo Adwo El, Rami Salaam El
- *Moorish Jewels: Emerald Edition* – Rami Salaam El
- *Los Sin Dios a Native American Manual* – Ricardo Ignacio
- *Nature Knows No Color Line* – J.A. Rogers
- *100 Amazing Facts about the Negro with Complete Proof* – J.A. Rogers
- *We Are All Moors* – Anour Majid
- *The Miseducation of the Negro* – Carter G. Woodson
- *The Story of The Moors in Spain* – Stanley Lane Poole
- *107 Amazing Facts About the Indigenous Moorish-Americans of the Western Hemisphere*
- *5 G Wellness* – Ras Ben
- *Isonomi The Great Masonic Secret: Maser Keys* – Mishaal Talib Mahfuz El Bey
- *When Rocks Cry Out* – Horace Butler
- *Stolen Legacy* – George G.M. James
- *The Secret Science* – John Baines
- *The Kybalion* – The Three Initiates
- *Ancient Future* – Wayne Chandler
- *The Biology of Belief* – Bruce Lipton
- *The 7 Day Theory* – Wali Bey
- *Sacred Drift* – Peter Lamborn Wilson

- *Kemetic Tree of Life* - Muata Ashby
- *The Art Of Peace* - Morihei Ueshiba
- *Clock Of Destiny 1 & 2* - C.M. Bey
- *Holy Koran of the Moorish Science Temple of America, Circle 7* - Noble Drew Ali
- *How To Study* - Taj Tarik Bey
- *Mysteries of the Silent Brotherhood Of The East (Red Book)* - Sheik Shariff Abdul Ali
- *Are You In Denial Of Your Ancestry?* - Mizraim Aleph El
- *Who are Moors/Asiatics/Americans?* - Mizraim Aleph El
- *7 Principles of Love* - Rasmariah V. Bey
- *Metaphysical Bible Dictionary* - Charles Filmore
- *12 Powers of Man* - Charles Filmore
- *Outwitting The Devil* - Napoleon Hill
- *Holistic Philosophy 101* - Mishaal Talib Mahfuz El Bey
- *The Gospel and The Zodiac* - Bill Darlson
- *The Moor, The Mason, The Alien* - Richard Smith

Acknowledgments

First and foremost, I want to thank and give honors to Th Creator, Th Most High for thy mercy and grace. I extend my gratitude to all Th true divine manifestations and emulations of Th Grand Cosmic Mother such as all the great prophets and prophetesses that came before, that walk beside me now and those who shall come after. Peace and blissings be upon Sheik Sharif Abdul Ali who by the benevolence of Allah gave us everything it takes to save a nation. Full honors to Rvbeypublications for their due diligence in helping to uplift fallen humanity. A lot of the information within this manuscript is directly from that site. Honors to all the Great Seal Moors both official and unofficial such as Rasmariah V. Bey, Anaidah El, C.M. Bey (Clock of Destiny 1&2; Circle of Life), Hakim Bey (author of the Journal of The Moorish Paradigm), Taj Tarik Bey, Abdullah El Talib Mosi Bey, Yaffa Bey, Mario El Bey, Dr. Alim El Bey, Dolo King of The Moors, Aseer The Duke of Tiers and Th mighty Moors of Canaanland. I will all those who live right: peace, heath and prosperity both now and forever.

INDEX

Chapter 3: Fall of Th Nobles—168

Chapter 4: The Adversary—235

Chapter 2: Dis-Ease—360

Chapter 3: Nature's Remedies—369

Part 3: Build Thyself—396

Chapter 1: G.O.D—397

Part 4: Trust Thyself—452

Chapter 1: Symbolism—453

Part 5: Will Thyself—476

Chapter 1: The Battlefield In The Garden—477

Chapter 2: Victory—483

NOTES

Other Titles from Califa Media Publishing

The Holy Koran of the Moorish Holy Temple of Science - 1928 Reprint

The Holy Koran of the Moorish Science Temple of America

Mysteries of the Silent Brotherhood the East

77 Amazing Facts About the Moors with Complete Proof

Moors in America: A Compilation

Noble Drew Ali Plenipotentiaries

Official Proclamation of Real Moorish American Nationality

Moslem Girls Training Guide: Divinely Prepared for the Sisters' Auxiliary of the Moorish Science Temple of America

Moorish Children's Guide to History & Culture

"Watch My Prophesies."

Isonomi: The Great Masonic Secret: Master Keys

Holistic Philosophy 101

The Torch: A Guide to Self

Well, Come to Klanada: Colour of Law & Authority on Usurped, Annexed, Moorish Land

SpitFire: The Makings of a Revolutionary

You Are NOT Negro, Black, Coloured, Morisco, Nor an African Slave

Who Stole the Fez, Moors or Shriners

"I'm Going to Repeat Myself": A Collection of Artifacts Authored by the Prophet Nobel Drew Ali & the M.S.T. of A.

Nationality: The Order of the Day: Divine Message and Warning, All Garveyites, Rastafarians, Black Nationalists & Pan-Africans

Hold Me Up: Noble Drew Ali's Lessons on Law and Spirituality

Printed in the USA
CPSIA information can be obtained
at www.ICGtesting.com
CBHW061105101223
2545CB00009B/637

9 781952 828041